Praise for Beverley Milton-Edwards and St

'Hamas continues to polarise global debate and even more so since its bloody attacks of 7 October 2023 shattered the choreographed status quo of resistance, deterrence, and limited governance vis-à-vis Israel. But we need to go beyond these polarised debates if we are to fully contextualise the essence of Hamas and why its ideas, if not its military power, will continue to resonate. In this carefully calibrated analysis, Milton-Edwards and Farrell have again produced *the* go-to guide to a movement whose very essence cuts to the core of the Palestine-Israel conflict.'

Clive Jones, Durham University

'Balanced and hard-hitting, drawing on decades of engagement with Hamas activists and their adversaries to reveal the aims and appeal of the Islamic Resistance Movement. Essential reading for understanding the past, present and future of the Palestinian-Israeli conflict.'

Eugene Rogan, University of Oxford

'Hamas remains one of the main Islamist organizations of the Arab world whose status, voice and influence far exceed its current base in the Gaza Strip. As Milton-Edwards and Farrell expertly show in their outstanding analysis of Hamas, the rest of the world ignores it at its peril.'

Anoush Ehteshami, Durham University

Hamas

This book is dedicated to Reem Makhoul – an extra-ordinary wedding gift to you, Reem, from the authors.

HAMAS

The Quest for Power

Beverley Milton-Edwards
and
Stephen Farrell

polity

First published in 2024 by Polity Press

2

Polity Press
65 Bridge Street
Cambridge CB2 1UR, UK

Polity Press
111 River Street
Hoboken, NJ 07030, USA

ISBN-13: 978-1-5095-6492-7
ISBN-13: 978-1-5095-6493-4 (pb)

A catalogue record for this book is available from the British Library.

Library of Congress Control Number: 2024933946

Typeset in 11 on 13 Adobe Garamond
by Fakenham Prepress Solutions, Fakenham, Norfolk NR21 8NL
Printed and bound in Great Britain by CPI Group (UK) Ltd, Croydon

The publisher has used its best endeavours to ensure that the URLs for external websites referred to in this book are correct and active at the time of going to press. However, the publisher has no responsibility for the websites and can make no guarantee that a site will remain live or that the content is or will remain appropriate.

Every effort has been made to trace all copyright holders, but if any have been overlooked the publisher will be pleased to include any necessary credits in any subsequent reprint or edition.

For further information on Polity, visit our website:
politybooks.com

Contents

Illustrations

Photographs

Maps

Preface and Acknowledgements

There is no middle ground with Hamas. In the decades since the Islamist organization emerged from the crucible of the Palestinian–Israeli conflict, it has polarized opinion and will continue to do so.

Hamas's credo can be defined simply as 'Islam is the solution.' It offers an Islamic plan to Palestinians living under an Israeli military occupation, wrapping itself in the twin banners of religion and nationalism. Hamas's enemies define it as a terrorist organization that has killed and maimed Israelis for decades, and perpetrating by far its deadliest attack on 7 October 2023. They argue that it is little more than the proxy of a regional Middle East power – Iran – and shares with its patron an all-consuming desire to bring about the destruction of the state of Israel. Hamas's supporters see it through another prism entirely: for them, it is an uncompromising, yet clear-sighted organization founded by a leadership which spent decades in the political wilderness telling the unpopular truth that the political orthodoxies of their time were misguided and that, in Israel, the Palestinian people faced an enemy that had to be resisted, not accommodated. Hamas argues that it alone is prepared to stand up to win statehood and independence for the Palestinians.

But it ill behoves either enemy or friend to make simplistic generalizations about an organization that, whatever its true nature, in 2006 became the first Islamist movement to ascend to power in the Middle East by democratic means and two decades later demonstrated that it had the strategic capacity to deliver a humiliating body blow to a military machine that claims to be the best in the Middle East. It is neither ISIS, al-Qaeda, nor the Taliban. It owes something to Hezbollah and much to the Muslim Brotherhood. It is Islamist, but nationalist; Sunni, yet supported by a Shi'a power; has participated in democratic elections, yet remains opaque; and populist, yet cruel. Many see Hamas as a significant obstacle to peace with Israel and wider hopes for stability in the Middle East. Others, particularly in the Global South, believe that, until it is recognized as a legitimate political force and included in the accommodation of power, there can never be peace in the region.

To study is not to support. For enemies and friends – and in both camps passions often cloud reasoned debate – Hamas, the Islamic Resistance Movement, is a phenomenon worthy of analysis. Part political, part social, part military, it has proved adaptable and resilient in the face of opposition from regional and world superpowers. It has won parliamentary, municipal, student and professional elections, and it has emerged as a genuine threat to much longer-established Palestinian political movements.

The purpose of this book, through hundreds of interviews conducted over four decades, is to present first-hand accounts of Hamas's founders, leaders, fighters, social activists, victims, political supporters and opponents, and in so doing to give insights into how Hamas was born, grew and thrived in the Gaza Strip, the West Bank and East Jerusalem – the Palestinian Territories occupied and controlled through Israel's all-pervasive military, settlement and civil apparatus since the 1967 Six Day War. Many of the interviews with the founders and senior leadership of Hamas can never be repeated. Such leaders are dead, mostly assassinated in Israel's attempts, over the decades, to degrade and destroy the senior leadership of the organization. Other interviews are with leaders who rarely speak in public.

Hamas cannot be understood in isolation from other Islamist actors who preceded it. Context, no matter how controversial, does matter. There has been a history of Muslim opposition to foreign rule and occupation since the British were awarded political control of Palestine after the First World War and the Zionists sought to make their homeland there. Its roots lie in the radicalism of little-known Islamist sheikhs in the 1930s who called for 'jihad' to liberate Palestine long before the word entered the Western lexicon. A generation later, refugees of the first Arab–Israeli war of 1948–9 came to believe that, through a pious adherence to Islam, they could achieve political freedom and create a state ruled according to their Islamic principles. After the 1967 war, some of these early Islamists were tolerated, encouraged even, by Israel. Under the age-old principle of 'divide and rule', Israel saw in the fledgling Islamists an opportunity to undermine its then principal Palestinian enemy, Yasser Arafat, head of Fatah and chief of the Palestine Liberation Organization (PLO).

Out of these antecedents the modern Hamas movement emerged in 1987 from the tumult of the First Palestinian Intifada (uprising) against Israel's then twenty-year-old military occupation regime. Hamas claimed the Intifada in its name and embarked on a competition to wrest Palestinian hearts and minds from the PLO. It became a formidable foe, waging a murderous armed campaign of suicide bombings against Israel and, later, missile bombardment of Israeli towns.

But Hamas has won support from Palestinians, not just because of what they see as a legitimate campaign of violent resistance against Israeli military occupation, but also because Hamas is – at one and the same time – a movement with a powerful, highly motivated and well-organized social welfare network, which it used to support people during years of deprivation and enforced statelessness, earning their gratitude and trust. In this book we detail the ways in which Hamas forged these links with the Palestinian people, slowly ousting the PLO from its hitherto unchallenged position of pre-eminence.

Hamas has developed a powerful military wing and instilled in many Palestinians the belief that only through violent armed struggle and the reward of martyrdom will they achieve their political goals of freedom and independence. In the 1990s and early 2000s, Hamas suicide bombing campaigns encouraged hundreds of willing volunteers to sacrifice themselves, in a self-declared holy war, in attacks on Israeli targets. Hamas leaders defended their actions, coldly warning that, if Palestinian civilians continued to die at the hands of Israeli tank commanders, F16 pilots and snipers, then Israel's civilians would suffer the same fate.

In January 2006, Hamas won the Palestinian parliamentary elections, demonstrating that it could marshal its supporters – including thousands of women who turned out for rallies under the green banner of the movement. It also attracted the votes of many other Palestinians who were disillusioned by corruption in the Fatah-controlled Palestinian Authority (PA) and lack of progress in peace talks with Israel. The Western world refused to accept Hamas's victory at the ballot box, and Hamas refused to bow to the international community's demands that it should recognize Israel and renounce violence. The outcome was a double deadlock – internal and external – which saw a higher death toll and even more despair among Israelis and Palestinians about any prospect of a peace settlement.

Internally, Islamist Hamas and secular Fatah consistently refused to share power. Nor was this likely, given that each had forms of dependence on patrons with conflicting agendas – Iran and the United States. Two armed forces sharing a tiny slice of land, each ambitious for total control, was a dynamic that could not be contained. In 2007 – just eighteen months after it won the election – Hamas's armed forces routed Fatah in Gaza and seized full military control of the Gaza Strip. When the dust settled, there was a two-headed Palestinian Authority – Hamas in Gaza and Fatah in the West Bank. Externally, there was also a stand-off between Hamas and Israel, with the West supporting Israel.

Israel sought to isolate Hamas with an economic and military blockade imposed on the whole population of the Gaza Strip. Hamas hit back with rockets into Israel. The nearest either side came to any form of agreement was a six-month ceasefire, which ended in December 2008. Hamas immediately began firing hundreds of rockets into Israeli towns and villages, and Israel hit back with a three-week military offensive which left more than 1,300 Palestinians and thirteen Israelis dead. Gaza was shattered, but Hamas remained in power and as defiant as ever. This cycle of attack and counter-attack between the two sides continued in 2012, 2014, 2018, 2021 and, of course, from 7 October 2023 into 2024.

Hamas can be excoriated, but it should not be underestimated. As we demonstrate throughout this book, it rose from a Muslim Brotherhood seed planted in mandate Palestine to become one of the most important Islamic and nationalist organizations in the Middle East. Its credentials mean that it is admired by Islamic and other liberation groups active not just in the Middle East but in the wider Global South and beyond.

For them, Hamas's brand of religious nationalism echoes their own political aspirations more than the worldwide jihad of ISIS or al-Qaeda. But it also highlights the consequences for the West of refusing to acknowledge the role that such movements play in shaping and governing their societies and influencing their relationship with the regional and global order.

Militarily, Hamas has fatally exposed the weakness of a hitherto far more powerful enemy – Israel. Israel has suffered huge losses at the hands of Hamas, and this legacy of harm and humiliation will endure to reshape the future of relations between Israelis and Palestinians. While it is true that Hamas cannot conquer Israel, questions still linger over whether Israel can achieve its aim of eradicating Hamas. Past attempts to degrade and destruct killed neither the movement nor the idea behind it.

***

We want to thank the many people who helped us in the realization and writing of both the first and second editions of this book. Particular thanks to Nabil Feidy of Jerusalem, for inspiring the collaboration and friendship that has developed during the course of this project. Nabil's emporium was a unique meeting place of calm and companionship in a tense and uneasy world. We also want to thank many colleagues and friends who have been so generous in supporting us and sharing their own work and insights, giving us advice, views and resources which it has taken many decades in the field to amass.

They include, among nameless others, Hein Knegt, Franz Makkan, Tor Wennesland, Colin Smith, Jonathan McIvor, Colonel Michael Pearson, Colonel Barry Southern, Khadr Musleh, Bob and Mary Mitchell, Rema Hammami, Alex Pollock, Ray Dolphin, Aileen and Scott Martin, Mouin Rabbani, Jeff Aronson, Ilan and Galia Katsir, Don Macintyre, Rory McCarthy, James Hider, Jason Burke, Yonit Farago, Ilan Mizrahi, Ronen Zvulun, Quique Kierszenbaum, Sarah El Deeb, Diaa Hadid, Alan Johnston, Tarik Yousef, Hend Amry, Freddie Alpert, Bu Abdallah, Bu Chairman Mao, Dana, Vladimir Pran and colleagues on *The Times* (London), the *New York Times* and *Reuters*.

We have been enormously lucky to benefit from the help of a unique crew of people in Gaza who have put themselves at risk in their attempt to bring us to some of the most illuminating and important voices in this battered and brutalized conflict zone. For years, Azmi Keshawi has been a fantastic help in squirrelling out a range of usually reticent and publicity-shy Islamist sources to tell us their stories and share their experiences in Gaza, often at great risk to himself and his wonderfully phlegmatic driver, Abu Hanafi. In Gaza, Hassan Jabr and Fares Akram have also played an extremely important role in facilitating our research. Our thanks also to driver/bodyguard extraordinaire Ashraf al-Masri, who accompanied us on our many visits to the Gaza Strip and made sure we didn't get kidnapped, even during the most lawless times. Without Azmi, Ashraf, Fares, Hassan, Abu Hanafi and their unflagging sense of determination and bravery – and others whom we keep anonymous to protect them, this book would not have been possible. Since 2008 and to the present day our Gazan friends have endured huge losses resulting from the wars with Israel in Gaza. They have had family members, close relatives killed in Israeli attacks on them, their homes, and livelihoods destroyed – gone forever. They, like their fellow Gazans, have suffered displacement in war, injury, hunger, communications blackout and, increasingly, a loss of hope.

In the West Bank, Nuha Awadallah also cuts a unique figure and has been a dear friend in helping us to realize this project. Her many changes of fashion and headgear make her instantly recognizable, along with her deep passion for bringing the light of truth out of the darkness. She has gone to extraordinary lengths to introduce us to the great cast of actors that all have a place on the stage in this particular account of Hamas.

Most of the people we have cited in the text have been identified, but there were some instances when, for security reasons, interviewees requested anonymity. To those interviewees – Palestinian, Israeli, Qatari, Egyptian, European, Canadian, American – and to others who gave their time to listen to our questions and talk to us, we offer our profound thanks.

All the photographs in the book were taken by Stephen Farrell, apart from photo 6.2, for which we extend our thanks to Ronen Zvulun. At Polity we would very much like to extend our deep gratitude to Louise Knight, especially for helping us to produce this new and very thoroughly revised edition. Our sincere gratitude also to Caroline Richmond for her copyediting and Neil de Cort, once again, for his dedication to the printing of this book.

We would also like to give our thanks to Cara Milton-Edwards and Joshua Milton-Edwards for keeping the authors grounded in the real world of throwaway culture, sushi, chocolate, MIKA music, hi-energy drinks, more chocolate, mini-clips, ice cream, children's DVDs, mp3 players, more chocolate, and the everyday challenges of learning homework, taking school exams, playing rugby and acting, refining the fine arts of debating and film-making. And to Sheherazade and Nairouz Farrell for taking up the mantle when Cara and Josh grew up, as children should.

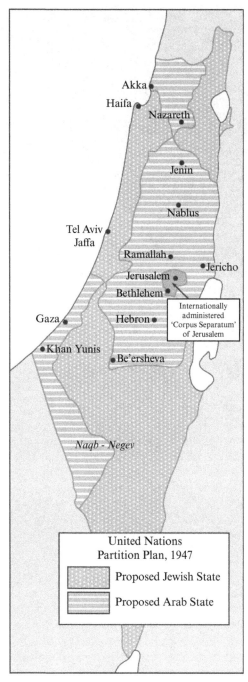

Map 1 1947 UN Partition Plan

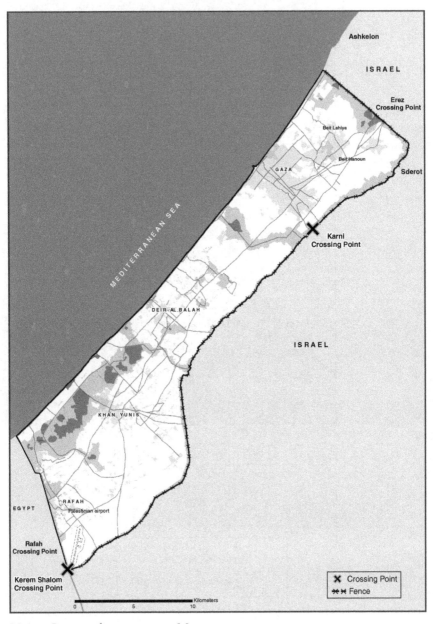

Map 2 Gaza pre-disengagement, May 2005

Map 3 Gaza post-disengagement, November 2005

What is Hamas?

We will come to you, God willing, in a roaring flood. We will come to you
with endless rockets, we will come to you in a limitless flood of soldiers.

Yahya Sinwar[1]

Shortly after dawn in southern Israel and music from an all-night festival
lingers in the air. Suddenly the peace of a holiday sabbath is broken by
sirens – harbingers of incoming rockets from nearby Gaza. Soon there's a
buzzing in the sky, but this time it isn't surveillance drones monitoring the
2.3 million Palestinians trapped behind Israel's fortified border that seals off
the Gaza Strip from the outside world. Instead, it's the unimaginable sight of
motorized paragliders soaring over the gates of Gaza bearing armed militants
belonging to the Palestinian group *Harakat al-Muqawama al-Islamiyya,*
better known to the world as Hamas.

A fusillade of gunfire soon alerts residents of border kibbutzim that the
rockets were cover for a concerted sea, air and ground attack orchestrated
by Hamas, unprecedented in its scale. In full view of the Israeli watchtowers
and automated gun turrets, coordinated groups of Hamas militants blow
holes in the Israeli fortifications and attack the military bases and checkpoints along Israel's 37-mile land border with Gaza.

As scores of gunmen overwhelm Israel's defences, around 3,000 Hamas,
Islamic Jihad and other raiders pour through breaches of the fence in pickup
trucks, on tractors and on motorbikes. Armed with automatic weapons and
rocket-propelled grenade launchers, some set up bandit checkpoints on
roads to seal off the area. Emptying their magazines into passing cars, they
drag survivors out and finish them off in the street. Some use body cameras
to record the carnage and later stream it worldwide, making real life and real
death look like a First-Person Shooter video game.

With the roads sealed, raiding parties storm into Israeli border villages
such as Netiv HaAsara, Kfar Aza, Nirim, Be'eri, Nahal Oz and Re'im.
Using guns, knives, machetes, grenades and even garden tools, they hunt
down and kill, including pensioners, women, children, migrant workers,
security forces and paramedics. Even – especially – Israeli military bases were

attacked: the army's Gaza divisional headquarters near Re'im, the Nahal Oz surveillance post and the huge Erez checkpoint in the north. Larger border towns such as Sderot also fall prey to the assault, Israelis locking themselves inside their homes as armed groups drive around the streets, taking over the police station and killing dozens inside.

'On Black Saturday, I was in my home in Nirim when terrorists infiltrated the kibbutz and homes. While they set fires, killed, kidnapped, looted, and vandalized, we hid in the safe room,' recalled Israeli survivor Avi Dabush. 'The only weapon we had against the terrorists – who gathered under our window for long minutes and hours, attempting to break into our house – was my sweaty hand on the door of the safe room. It is a horror that is hard to put into words and it lasted for eight hours.'[2]

As the scale of the assault emerges, the Israeli military escalates the level of its alerts, first telling people to stay near protected areas, then to 'remain in their homes' before, at 8.23 am on 7 October 2023, declaring a 'state of alert for war'. All on the Jewish high holiday of Simchat Torah.[3]

By the time the sun rose again the following day, a new reality was also dawning. Hamas had carried out the deadliest-ever attack on Israel in a single day. They killed more than 1,200 people, including thirty-six children. Families were hunted down in their homes. More than 300 youngsters attending the Nova music festival were killed as gunmen emptied magazines into tents and toilet cubicles and hunted others down as they fled. One victim was beheaded on film, others were mutilated. At least 240 were kidnapped and taken into Gaza as hostages, humiliated on camera as they were led into captivity. Police opened investigations to assess the sexual violence reported.

'Massacring civilians is a war crime and there can be no justification for these reprehensible attacks,' declared Agnès Callamard, the Secretary General of Amnesty International:

armed men shooting at civilians and dragging people away as hostages … armed men parading a woman through central Gaza, like a scene from a nightmare. All civilians who were abducted, including children, must be released immediately. These crimes must be investigated as part of the International Criminal Court's ongoing investigation into [the] crimes committed.[4]

Israelis were left feeling humiliated, vengeful and enraged at being made to feel fearful in one of the strongest military nations in the Middle East. Not only at the shock of what Hamas had done, but disbelief at the magnitude of the failure by the political, military and intelligence leadership of Israel, a world leader in surveillance technology that was supposed to be able to detect threats in advance. 'This is Israel's 9/11 and Israel will do everything to bring our sons and daughters back home,' said Gilad Erdan, the country's ambassador to the United Nations, outside a Security Council meeting on 8 October. 'We will not let the world forget the atrocities our country suffered.'[5]

Hamas, so it appeared, hadn't forgotten either, basing their justification for what they called 'Operation Al Aqsa Flood' on both historic and legitimate grievances. Usama Hamdan, a member of Hamas's Political Bureau, told one of the authors, 'It doesn't matter what Israel's military capacity or power is, the Palestinian people will achieve their liberation.' Pressed on why Hamas attacked Israeli civilians that day, Hamdan restated the long-standing Hamas position that all of historic Palestine belonged to the Palestinians:

> The whole world knows and recognizes that our land has been occupied since 1948. Israel occupied our whole complete land from the River to the Sea. Israel has built settlements on these Palestinian Territories. Those are settlements on our occupied land. Hamas considers these all to be settlements that deny the Palestinians their rights. These are settlements that Israel has built on stolen land, homes, and futures of our people.[6]

Gaza

Forced to put aside for the moment the domestic political fallout that would inevitably come for those in charge during such a security debacle, Israeli Prime Minister Binyamin Netanyahu's government launched a devastating air, sea and land bombardment of the Gaza Strip, calling it 'Operation Swords of Iron'. The barrage turned into a full-scale ground invasion that redrew the map of Gaza and hit the reset button on Israeli–Palestinian relations, probably forever. Through the winter of 2023 and into 2024, more than 35,000 Palestinians were killed, most of them children and women. By November 2023, as the United Nations Security Council debated the situation in Gaza, briefers fed through situation reports from the ground. Catherine Russell, the executive director of the United Nations Children's Fund (UNICEF), called for an urgent humanitarian ceasefire. Drawing attention to the plight of children, she stated, 'No place is safe in the Gaza Strip,' then went on to describe it as the world's most dangerous place for a child to be. She ended by noting that an unprecedented 40 per cent of killings in Gaza were of children.[7] Tens of thousands more Palestinian civilians were injured, with little by way of functioning hospitals and the risk of being hit by missile attacks even inside the ones that still worked. As Israel razed apartment blocks, refugee camps and neighbourhoods, reducing much of Gaza to rubble, more than 2 million Palestinians were displaced from their homes.

Israel's Defense Minister, Yoav Gallant ordered a total closure of Gaza while the bombardment continued. 'I have ordered a complete siege on the Gaza Strip. There will be no electricity, no food, no fuel, everything is closed,' he said.[8] He was as good as his word, leaving humanitarian organizations struggling to deliver enough food and medical supplies through the one lifeline that Gaza still had to the outside world – to Egypt. Many Palestinians were forced into huge tent camps that sprang up in the south of the Gaza Strip as they fled near incessant bombing in the north.

According to the International Rescue Committee six weeks after Israel's bombardment began: 'Civilians are bearing the brunt. Hamas has reportedly mixed military personnel and facilities with civilians and is holding over 200 hostages. Israel continues to use weapons with wide area effects in densely populated areas, is attacking hospitals, schools, and refugee camps and has cut the supply of water, fuel, and electricity to over 2 million people.'[9]

For older Palestinians, the scenes were a painful reminder of the tented refugee camps that they first lived in when they arrived in Gaza seventy-five years earlier as refugees from the 1948–9 war that accompanied the birth of the modern state of Israel. That mass dispossession saw around 750,000 Palestinians flee or forced from their homes in pre-1948 Palestine in a communal trauma known as the *Nakbah* (Catastrophe), which became the defining experience of Palestinian identity. Future generations vowed never to repeat it, but with their apartment blocks, refugee camps and neighbourhoods reduced to rubble they now found themselves bombed back into tents, and talk of a 'second *Nakbah*' became commonplace.

Palestinians in the occupied West Bank also bore the brunt. United Nations human rights monitors said 300 were killed from 7 October to late December 2023, amid airstrikes and Israeli military raids on refugee camps and Palestinian cities. A report also found there had been a 'sharp rise in settler attacks with an average of six incidents per day, such as shootings, burning of homes and vehicles, and uprooting of trees.'[10]

Israel said the goal of its Gaza operation was to destroy Hamas's tunnel, rocket-firing and military infrastructure. Specifically, to kill the Hamas leaders who planned the 7 October attack: military-wing leader Mohammed Deif and Hamas's Gaza chief, Yahya Sinwar.

Ten months before the cross-border attack, Sinwar had publicly trailed hints of what was to come. But he veiled them in the kind of bellicose rhetoric that Hamas leaders had delivered from the rally lectern for decades, ensuring that it was a warning only fully appreciated in the aftermath. 'We will come to you, God willing, in a roaring flood. We will come to you with endless rockets, we will come to you in a limitless flood of soldiers, we will come to you with millions of our people, like the repeating tide,' he declaimed at a Gaza rally in December 2022.[11]

Particularly galling for Israel was that Sinwar, an implacable Hamas hardliner, had spent nearly a quarter of a century in Israeli jails until he was freed in a prisoner exchange in 2011. The day after his release Sinwar told one of the authors that he had 'learned a lot' about Israelis during his time in their custody, learning Hebrew and studying history. 'We turned the prison into sanctuaries of worship and to academies for study,' he said, with his customary sense of certainty and self-assurance. 'You can say I am a specialist in the Jewish people's history, more than many of them.'[12]

While Israel held the entire Hamas leadership responsible, Sinwar was singled out for special vilification. 'This heinous attack was orchestrated by Yahya Sinwar, the leader of Hamas in the Gaza Strip. And so he, and the entire system underneath him, are dead men. We will target them, break them, and dismantle their system,' said Israel's chief of the general staff, Lieutenant General Herzi Halevi, in an address to the nation a few days after the attack. 'Gaza will not look the same. We will achieve a situation where those who led Gaza will suffer greatly, and we will dismantle it. And whoever remains there will understand that such a thing is not to be done to the State of Israel.'[13] His meaning was clear. For Israel, 7 October meant that there would be no return to the way things were before.

Why?

Shattering the status quo was also what Hamas sought, although for very different reasons. Just as Israel's messaging sought to project strength with biblical resonances, so Hamas's name for its cross-border attack – 'Operation Al Aqsa Flood' – was a declaration to the Muslim world that it was setting itself up as the principal defender of the Muslim holy sites in Jerusalem.

Al Aqsa Mosque, in Jerusalem's walled Old City, is the third holiest site in Islam after Mecca and Medina. But, unlike them, it is no longer under Muslim control since Israel captured East Jerusalem with the rest of the West Bank in the 1967 Six Day War. That loss is still felt keenly by Muslims worldwide, and it is one that Hamas has sought to tap into.

On 7 October, Hamas's leader, Ismail Haniyeh, gave a lengthy televised speech suffused with religious and nationalistic rhetoric outlining Hamas's public rationale for the attack. In an address of a length and complexity that suggested advance preparation, he praised Sinwar and Deif as architects of the attack and excoriated Netanyahu's government, accusing it of having let Israeli 'settlers and usurpers loose to sow corruption in the holy Al Aqsa Mosque' and of intensifying a 'colonization' of the West Bank by expanding Jewish settlements there.[14]

Haniyeh, himself a refugee, also said Hamas was punishing Israel for its 'unjust' blockade on the Gaza Strip. 'How many times have we warned them of the existence of a Palestinian people who, for 75 years, have been living in the diaspora in tents and refugee camps? You don't recognise our people, and you don't recognise our rights.' And he made it clear that one of Hamas's goals was to highlight Israel's weaknesses and to demonstrate – to its own supporters and to Israelis – Hamas's willingness and ability to scare them. 'God came to them from where they did not expect, and cast terror into their hearts,' he said, referencing a verse from the Koran.

But it was significant that the first people Haniyeh singled out for criticism were the Arab regimes who, since 2020, had signed 'normalization' deals with Israel. These US-brokered agreements were viewed with alarm by Palestinians, who feared Gulf Arab states such as the UAE and Bahrain were increasingly becoming concerned more with the economic and diplomatic benefits of doing business with Israel than in the Palestinian cause.

Even more worrying to Hamas were reports that Saudi Arabia was in talks with US President Joe Biden's administration to follow suit, a move that would further realign the Middle East to bring Israel, Sunni Arab regimes and Washington together in an axis of shared interests against Shia Iran, a sponsor of Hamas. Haniyeh pointedly contrasted the 'defeatists' of normalizing regimes with Hamas militants fighting on the ground: 'This entity which is incapable of protecting itself from our fighters is incapable of providing you with security or protection,' he told the viewing audience. 'All the normalisation and recognition processes, all the agreements that have been signed can never put an end to this battle.'[15]

Israeli officials brushed aside Hamas's rationales, accusing its leadership of being motivated by hatred and of dragging their own people down with them. Defending Israel against mounting international criticism for the scale of its attack on Gaza, Netanyahu's senior adviser, Mark Regev, said of Hamas:

> It said no to any peace with Israel, no to negotiations, an extremist, militant, totally inflexible approach that says my country must be destroyed and every Israeli is a legitimate target for murder.

But, more than that, what have they done for the people of Gaza? They've been in power for sixteen years, they've been running the Gaza Strip, they've brought pain. They've brought suffering, and they've brought impoverishment to the people of Gaza. When this is over and we've defeated Hamas, and we will, it will be better for the people of southern Israel of course who won't have to live next to this terror enclave, next to Hamas and its violence and its brutality. But, ultimately, it will also be better for the people of Gaza, who deserve better than this terrible terrorist regime.[16]

However, as the war dragged on, many questioned whether Israel's humiliated political leadership had fallen into a Hamas trap by being sucked into a protracted war on Hamas's home turf in Gaza, where a vast network of tunnels awaited them, allowing militants to emerge from tunnels and rubble to attack Israeli tanks and troops and then disappear again.

'There is no military solution to this,' predicted Bilal Y. Saab, with London's Chatham House policy institute. 'The issue here is the day after. Let's just say you do massively degrade Hamas. What happens the day after? Israel is not going to own Gaza; they are not going to occupy Gaza. This is not the Third Reich; this is not Imperial Japan. We're not going to turn Gaza into a democracy. And so Hamas 2.0 is very much a possibility, as long as Iran supplies weapons to Palestinians who are willing to take arms and do battle with the Israelis.'[17]

'Hamas is an idea. You cannot bomb an idea out of existence,' said Ayman Safadi, Jordan's deputy prime minister. 'If you are not happy with what Hamas is doing, convince the Palestinian people that they have a future and that Hamas is standing between them and that future. Thus far, that argument has not been made. Reality has not shown that. Palestinian people have been left with nothing left to lose on the West Bank and in Gaza. Are we not going to learn?'[18]

The Everywhere War

What the attack also did was to put the name of Hamas front and centre of any discussion about Israel and the Palestinians.

By filming its trail of destruction on 7 October and posting footage of its operatives carrying out attacks on Israeli troops – sometimes with martial music and taunting on-screen messages in Arabic, English and Hebrew – Hamas ensured that the scenes would be seen by hundreds of millions of people worldwide on television and social media, both supporters and opponents.

In similar vein, Israel's sophisticated and multilingual *hasbara* (advocacy) messaging operation moved into high gear, pushing out its dispatches through embassies, television, newspapers and social media, including the hashtag #standwithisrael. Supporters were mobilized on both sides, and opinions polarized amid acrimonious debate. The conflict triggered global debates about blame, international law, anti-Semitism, Islamophobia, censorship, freedom of expression, the global rules-based order and the limits of protest and academic freedom. And the aftershocks reverberated from the shell-scarred hills of south Lebanon to Red Sea shipping corridors and to university campuses, and all the way up to the international criminal and justice system at The Hague.

In one of the United Nations Security Council's first debates after the attack, UN Secretary-General António Guterres condemned what he called 'the horrifying and unprecedented 7 October acts of terror by Hamas' in Israel: 'Nothing can justify the deliberate killing, injuring and kidnapping of civilians – or the launching of rockets against civilian targets,' he said. But he added:

> It is important to also recognize the attacks by Hamas did not happen in a vacuum. The Palestinian people have been subjected to 56 years of suffocating occupation. They have seen their land steadily devoured by settlements and plagued by violence; their economy stifled; their people displaced, and their homes demolished. Their hopes for a political solution to their plight have been vanishing. But the grievances of the Palestinian people cannot justify the appalling attacks by Hamas. And those appalling attacks cannot justify the collective punishment of the Palestinian people.[19]

Israel was furious at Guterres's attempt to give historical context – its UN ambassador accused the Secretary-General of showing 'an understanding for terrorism and murder' and called on him to resign immediately.[20]

But around the world the questions kept coming. Governments, policy-makers and military analysts wanted information to strategize against Hamas or to prepare for possible regional escalation of the conflict. Others sought evidence to support arguments in favour of one side or the other. Some wanted to bring about a shift in their country's policy or a new alignment in the global order. But the core questions remained: What is Hamas? Where did it come from? And how did a relatively small Palestinian movement overwhelm the defences of the strongest military power in the Middle East?

Birth. Bomb. Ballot. Border.

Hamas has sprung several major surprises on the world since it was created in 1987, the 2023 attack being by far the largest, but certainly not the first. It was not a complex plan. In fact, it was a somewhat counterintuitive one – a militant group with an estimated 20,000 to 30,000 fighters overwhelming the defences of a superpower-backed state with a standing army, navy and warplanes. But its execution bore hallmarks of a long-established Hamas methodology: plan carefully, prepare thoroughly and in secret, lull enemies foreign and domestic into a false sense of security, and then use the benefit of surprise to maximize its advantage in any given situation.

At its simplest, Hamas executed on the ground what it had been testing for years in the air. Faced with Israel's advanced Iron Dome missile defence system that intercepted rockets fired from Gaza, during major hostilities it would fire so many that some would get through.

A variant of that tactic is what happened on 7 October. Cross-border attacks would scarcely get past the first border fence if Israel was expecting them. But such a plan could work – once – if the border was rushed with surprise and in overwhelming numbers.

Birth

The first surprise Hamas sprang on the world was its sudden creation in Gaza in the opening days of the First Palestinian Intifada in December 1987. It was set up as a Palestinian wing of the Muslim Brotherhood, the Sunni Islamic revival movement founded in Egypt in 1928 by Hassan al-Banna. The key Brotherhood figure in Gaza was Sheikh Ahmed Yassin, an inspirational preacher and organizational genius who spent the 1970s and 1980s setting up a grassroots network of mosques and institutions in the Gaza refugee camps where he had grown up. These were seeds planted early with a long-term view of later harvesting hearts, minds, and souls.

Yassin made the strategic calculation that he needed time to Islamize Palestinian society from the grassroots up, so he decided not to jeopardize his fledgling network by risking immediate conflict with Israel. But when the Intifada (uprising, or 'shaking off') broke out in Gaza and spread to the West Bank, Yassin saw an opportunity to capitalize on – and take control of – the spontaneous outburst of anger. So he accelerated the Islamization process and created *Harakat al-Muqawama al-Islamiyya* – 'The Islamic Resistance Movement'.

From the outset it was an Islamist alternative to the secular brand of nationalism represented by Yasser Arafat's Fatah and Palestine Liberation Organization, and it caught them off guard. Unlike Yassin, Arafat and the PLO leaders were not in Gaza. Instead, they had spent decades in Israeli-enforced exile in Jordan, Lebanon and Tunisia, and they did not grasp the daily humiliations of Palestinians chafing at two decades of Israeli military occupation, or the inexorable and quickening expansion of Jewish settlements that Israel was building across the territory that it had occupied in the 1967 Six Day War – the West Bank, Gaza and East Jerusalem.

And while the PLO leadership viewed Hamas as an irritant, it did not appreciate the scale of the threat posed by an organized Islamist newcomer with a long-term plan to undermine, supplant and eventually replace the PLO as leaders of the Palestinian people.

Key to Hamas's appeal to its support base of refugees, religious fundamentalists and stateless Palestinians was its refusal to recognize Israel or to accept any compromise that would settle for some of the territory of pre-1948 Palestine rather than all of it.

Hamas's founding Covenant spells out that it claims all the land:

The Islamic Resistance Movement believes that the land of Palestine is an Islamic Waqf [endowment] consecrated for future Moslem generations until Judgement Day. It, or any part of it, should not be squandered: it, or any part of it, should not be given up.[21]

In 2002, Dr Abdel Aziz Rantissi, then Hamas's deputy leader in Gaza, voiced its position even more explicitly during an interview with one of the authors:

In the name of Allah we will fight the Jews and liberate our land in the name of Islam. We will rid this land of the Jews and with Allah's strength our land will be returned to us and the Muslim peoples of the world. By God, we will not leave one Jew in Palestine. We will fight them with all the strength we have. This is our land, not the Jews' ... We have Allah on our side, and we have the sons of the Arab and Islamic nation on our side.[22]

Yassin's early strategic calculation to avoid taking on Israel worked in the Islamists' favour. For years his network of Islamic charities in Gaza was overlooked, or even tacitly encouraged, by Israel, which was seemingly content to see the emergence of an internal rival to Arafat, on the principle of divide and rule. 'When Hamas laid out its charter, it made it an alternative to the secular PLO charter,' said Ibrahim Ibrach, a Gaza political analyst. 'Right from the start it considered itself an alternative to the PLO, but it didn't declare it because both parties were busy with the first intifada, fighting the Israelis.'[23]

Bomb

But by the 1990s the situation had changed. Arafat's PLO had negotiated its way home, raising hopes for a negotiated solution that would deliver both an end to occupation and Israel and Palestine living side by side. This 'two-state solution' envisaged Israel in roughly its existing borders – 78 per cent of pre-1948 Palestine – and the Palestinians in 22 per cent – Gaza, East Jerusalem and the West Bank.

It was Arafat who led the PLO into the Madrid and Oslo peace negotiations with Israel, and it was he who stood on the White House lawn with US President Bill Clinton and Israeli Prime Minister Yitzhak Rabin to attend the signing of the Declaration of Principles in 1993, the undoubted high point of Israeli–Palestinian relations. The PLO promised peace dividends that would deliver Palestinians independence and a state to call their own, with East Jerusalem as its capital.

For Hamas such a compromise was anathema. But throughout that era it stood marginalized on the sidelines, with most Palestinians too optimistic to listen to its warnings that Israel could not be trusted, and that armed resistance, as they term it, was the only way to achieve the Palestinians' goals. Determined to carry the fight to Israel without the PLO, Yassin formed his own military wing, the soon to be infamous Qassam Brigades. During the 1990s its bombers ripped through the peace process. It was not the only Palestinian faction to do so, but the name Hamas soon became synonymous with suicide bombers, as it remained resolutely outside the Palestinian political mainstream, refusing to participate in any political process with its Zionist enemy.

And gradually through the 1990s the era of optimism came to an end; Israeli troop redeployments did not occur as planned, Palestinian elections were delayed, and Rabin was assassinated in 1995 by an Israeli gunman who, like many on the far right, bitterly opposed giving any land to Palestinians. And Israel's settlements continued to grow, in contravention of international law.

Israel, for its part, accused the Palestinians of failing to meet their obligations under security agreements by multiplying their armed forces and of failing to stop Hamas suicide bombings. Peace talks were deadlocked or produced little tangible for either side, and a Second Palestinian Intifada broke out in 2000. In such conditions, Hamas's implacable world view found more supporters than during the era of peace and optimism. 'Israel has already taken a decision never to resolve the Israeli–Palestinian conflict,' Sheikh Saleh al-Arouri, the founder of Hamas's military wing in the West Bank, told one of the authors in 2007.

> Fatah is saying 'One Palestinian state on the 1967 borders, resolve the issue of refugees and that is enough for them to recognise and justify the existence of the state of Israel.' Hamas's position is that the existence of the state of Israel is bigger than it seems because it involves the whole Arab world and the Islamic world. And what is apparent right now is that the Israelis are refusing Hamas's position, and Fatah's position also.[24]

Arouri, speaking just after he was released from jail, was later deported by Israel and rose through the ranks to become Hamas's deputy leader. He was killed by a drone strike in Beirut in January 2024.

Sometimes in the middle of fast-paced events such as the Second Intifada it is hard to pinpoint exactly the incident that shifted a momentum or hardened a transition into a new reality. But sometimes it is immediately clear. On 27 March 2002 Hamas carried out its deadliest attack on Israel up to that point, one which transformed the dynamic of the then eighteen-month-old Palestinian uprising.

On the day that the Arab League was gathering for a summit in Beirut at which it endorsed a Saudi proposal for Israel to have normalization of relations with the Arab world in exchange for its withdrawal from the occupied territories, Hamas upstaged them by sending a suicide bomber who killed thirty Jewish celebrants at a Passover dinner in the Israeli town of Netanya. As in 2023, the 2002 Passover bomb struck to the core of Israel's religious, cultural and national identity. In response, Israel's government launched a full-scale reinvasion of West Bank cities and soon afterwards began building a 500-mile razor wire and concrete military barrier around – and in many places deep into – the West Bank. There were to be no more Israelis and Palestinians at signing ceremonies on White House lawns, and Hamas's main domestic rival, Arafat, besieged by Israel in his Ramallah headquarters the Muqata, became increasingly isolated until his death, taking with him much of the energy of the Fatah movement he founded and had dominated for so long. Hamas had effectively turned its pessimism about the peace process into a self-fulfilling prophecy by shooting and bombing it out of existence, in parallel with rejectionists on the Israeli side whose opposition to allowing a Palestinian state to come into existence matched that of Hamas refusing to recognize the Israeli one that already did.

Ballot

Then, just as Hamas had spent years demonstrating its proficiency with the bomb and the bullet, it pivoted to embrace the ballot box. In the five years leading up to the 2006 Palestinian parliamentary elections, its militants, according to Israel, had killed more than 400 people and carried out more than fifty suicide bombings.[25] True, Fatah was handicapped by Arafat's death and a reputation for mismanagement, nepotism and corruption over its stewardship of the PLO, the Palestinian Authority (PA), the Palestinian Legislative Council (PLC), and the near-impenetrable alphabet soup of organizations through which Fatah had long exercised control over Palestinian affairs. But Fatah's leaders remained confident to the point of complacency about the election. And many in Hamas also expected Fatah to win.

So it did not come to pass. Once Hamas decided to follow the path of other armed groups – such as Lebanon's Hezbollah, the Provisional IRA and, indeed, some of Israel's own founding fathers – from bomb to ballot box, the rhetoric, planning and sophistication of the political newcomer proved far superior to that of its veteran secular rival.

It mobilized women supporters, told its followers to lie to opinion pollsters and positioned itself as a new broom standing under the banner 'Change and Reform'. And, amid the near universal perception among Palestinians that Arafat's cadres had siphoned off millions of dollars in foreign aid that should have gone to their people, it benefited from its image of being intolerant of corruption. But while Hamas could win, it could not change how it was seen. It was immediately treated as a pariah by Israel, the United States and much of the international community, which demanded that it lay down arms and recognize Israel before they would deal with it.

Nevertheless, it could not be ignored as a political force, and the wellspring of its support was summed up by two messages that delighted and inspired its supporters and enraged its foes. One was a populist slogan run in the final week of the election campaign: 'Israel and America say no to Hamas. What do you say?' The other was a statement of intent that played into Israel's fears of Hamas's long-term intent: 'Jerusalem and West Bank after Gaza.'

On election day, Ismail Haniyeh, a Yassin protégé who was about to become prime minister, made it clear that Hamas was not about to abandon the gun. 'We still have the questions of the Israeli occupation, refugees, Jerusalem, and our prisoners. It's premature for Hamas to drop its weapons,'[26] he said, while casting his vote near his home in Gaza's Shati refugee camp.

So it was that, in January 2006, Hamas, which means 'zeal' in Arabic, was victorious while Fatah, which means 'conquest', was defeated. It was a surprise victory but a comprehensive and democratic one, in elections widely regarded as the freest ever held in the Arab world.

Many, particularly in the West, could not understand how the Palestinians could elect an armed extremist faction that made no secret of one of its main goals – the end of a Zionist state in Palestine. Especially as in presidential elections just twelve months before they had voted for Arafat's successor, Mahmoud Abbas – a man openly critical of the path of the gun. The answer lies in the profoundly different perceptions of the Palestinian–Israeli conflict. Where Israel's supporters see a small, vulnerable Jewish state surrounded by Arab enemies, Palestinians see a nuclear regional superpower backed by the US which seeks to control, or even expel, them. In summary, where the world saw a vote for Hamas as a setback for the peace process, many Palestinians saw no evidence of a peace process, so voted for Hamas.

As Palestinians absorbed the shock of Hamas's victory in January 2006, the question being shouted down the phone to every diplomat and foreign correspondent in Jerusalem was: 'What does this mean for the peace

Photo 1.1 Hamas graffiti in Gaza, March 2008

process?' One of the most succinct analyses came from Michael Tarazi, a former legal adviser to the PLO who had watched the descent from Intifada in 2000 to war in 2002–3: 'Anyone who says this is going to destroy the peace process has not been paying attention to the fact that there isn't a peace process to destroy.'[27]

Breaking down Hamas's victory, Professor Ali Jarbawi, of Birzeit University in the West Bank, said its success lay in its appeal to many different voters: religious Palestinians naturally more inclined to vote for an Islamic party than a secular one; pessimists sceptical of the 'negotiate forever' policy of Fatah in dealing with Israel; protest voters angry at Fatah for enriching itself; and the thousands who benefited from Hamas's social and charitable services over the years. Where Hamas went wrong, he said, was in trying to be both a political party and a resistance movement after the election. 'They made mistakes because they got entangled with ruling. They couldn't understand that rule ruined Fatah, it ruined Abu Ammar [Arafat]. So why are they different?' he said. 'You cannot be an "in-between" about having a state, quasi-state or whatever, and being a liberation movement.'[28]

Border

The border between the Gaza Strip and Israel is a mere 37 miles long – running to the north and east of a sliver of territory that to the west is bounded by the Mediterranean Sea. At the southernmost tip of Gaza is a short 8-mile border with Egypt, which has just one small crossing, at Rafah. In such a confined space, the border with Israel exercises Hamas greatly – representing as it does the limits of Hamas's own control and the physical reminder of prolonged occupation, dispossession and lack of Palestinian sovereignty.

'The state of Israel is at the forefront of the world's fight against the terror threat,' Netanyahu said in 2009. 'Israel has the strength to defend itself, but we expect greater international determination in confronting the common danger we share.'[29] The keynotes of his message were unchanged in 2023. 'We will continue at full force, at full strength, until victory,' he said. 'Our war is also your war.'[30]

In response, Hamas and other Palestinian factions argue that they have a legitimate right of resistance against an occupying military force – a right, they claim, that is recognized by United Nations General Assembly resolutions, including 3236 and 3375, as well as Article 51 of the UN Charter and international humanitarian law. Israel, they maintain, has a far more powerful military arsenal, with which it defends its own state, enforces its occupation of millions of Palestinians, and has refused to let them have a state or to recognize the right of return of refugees from pre-1948 Palestine.

One key factor is Hamas's constant goal to establish itself as a driving force in challenging Israel's force at the border – 'a big number in the equation', as one of its officials, Mushir al-Masri, put it.[31] Certainly, after 7 October everybody was talking about the boundary, the line, the fence, and military posts that bordered the Palestinians in Gaza and Israel.

By testing Israel's heavily fortified and monitored border to Gaza on 7 October, Hamas had exposed real weaknesses in the self-proclaimed security architecture of Israel, and *ipso facto* its allies and supporters. Israel's previous approach to bordering technology, long held up by itself and its supporters as the 'best in the world', has formed part of huge export packages for Israel's contribution to the market for the tech border surveillance industrial complex. Israeli companies selling their surveillance control systems, command and control equipment, electro-optics and perimeter security solutions would claim that, unlike those of many of their competitors, their products were tried and tested in Gaza as well as other Palestinian territories. In modern-day border surveillance and warfare, unmanned aerial vehicles (UAVs) are considered to be a fundamental element of technology. Israel, alongside an increasingly competitive China, is one of the largest exporters of such technology. It was in Gaza that Israel felt that it had truly developed and deployed UAVs to maintain an asymmetric advantage over Hamas. That advantage was maintained until 7 October 2023.

In terms of grand strategy and the future for such practices of bordering and surveillance, as well as their export to vast markets such as those in the US, or Europe, the Hamas attack on that heavily militarized and technologically superior border line had a seismic impact.

US intelligence agencies voiced fears in the weeks after 7 October that, by launching such a high-profile strike, Hamas might inspire groups such as al-Qaeda in the Arabian Peninsula and the Islamic State of Iraq and Syria to escalate their activities not only within the borders of their own territories but beyond. Yemen-based Houthis had already begun, they pointed out. 'How AQAP, ISIS, or other regional groups may seek to capitalize on Hamas's 7 October attack to recruit and rebuild anti-West attack capabilities will be critical to assess as tensions and violence rise as the conflict continues,' Christine Abizaid, director of the National Counterterrorism Center, told a Senate Committee on Homeland Security and Government Affairs hearing on 31 October 2023.

It's absolutely been a feature of messaging and propaganda since the attacks. We've seen it from al Qaeda affiliates, almost every single one. We've also seen it from ISIS, which ideologically isn't aligned with a group like Hamas, but is still leveraging this current conflict to try and sow the kind of violence, bring adherents to its cause, in sort of an exploitative way.[32]

'We Are Not in a Hurry'

It is an article of faith in Israel that Hamas is dedicated to the end of a Jewish state. But this is to mistake a milestone for destination. For Hamas, the removal of the Zionist state is a necessary condition to achieve its ultimate goal – a Palestinian state governed in accordance with Islam – but not a sufficient one. Secular and leftist Palestinian movements are just as much of a threat to its mission. Whereas Israel is a military obstacle, these rival factions compete with Hamas for the hearts, minds and souls of Palestinians.

To achieve its ends, Hamas is unambiguous about its definitions, credo and methods. The Hamas crest depicts crossed swords and the Palestinian flag against the distinctive scimitar-shaped slice of land which includes all of Israel, the West Bank and Gaza. It also bears a picture of the Dome of the Rock, flanked by the Islamic exhortations 'There is no God but Allah' and 'Mohammed is the messenger of Allah.' Certainly, it is firmly rooted in Islam, but it has had repeated disagreements with worldwide jihadi organizations such as al-Qaeda, which castigated Hamas's decision to enter politics, arguing that holy war is the only path. Hamas leaders insist that, despite its proclamation of jihad, it is not engaged in a war against Jews or Christians as such. 'For us as Muslims it is not a religious war because we lived together here before 1948,' said Qassam Brigades commander Saleh Arouri.

> Christians have been living here since the start of the ages. If it were a religious war the Jews and Christians would not have lasted 1,400 years. Religious war means what happened in Europe in the Middle Ages where they didn't accept anyone who wasn't a Christian. In our area there was never a genocide based on religion. This is only a nationalistic issue and a nationalistic war because of occupation.[33]

Nevertheless, Hamas's 1988 founding covenant contained passages which left the movement with little answer to the charge that it formally advocated a strain of anti-Semitism. Article 20 stated: 'In their Nazi treatment, the Jews made no exception for women or children. Their policy of striking fear in the heart is meant for all ... They deal with people as if they were the worst war criminals.'[34] The rest of the covenant developed the theme, citing the anti-Semitic propaganda forgery *The Protocols of the Elders of Zion* and talking, in Article 22, of how the 'enemy' was behind 'the French Revolution, the Communist revolution and most of the revolutions we heard and hear about, here and there. With their money they formed secret societies, such as Freemasons, Rotary Clubs, the Lions and others in different parts of the world for the purpose of sabotaging societies and achieving Zionist interests.'[35]

One of the main disputes is the name of the land itself: Israel or Palestine. Israel has been a Member State of the United Nations since May 1949.[36] Palestine is not a Member State but became a Non-Member State to participate as an observer in the General Assembly in 2012.[37] Despite infinite permutations of what are, were, or should be the exact boundaries of the most disputed patch of ground on earth, in common usage both Israel and Palestine refer to some or all of the territory bounded by Lebanon and Syria to the north, Egypt to the south, the Mediterranean to the west and the Jordan River to the east, giving rise to the slogan 'From the River to the Sea'. Controversy has surrounded that phrase, which critics take to be a distillation of Hamas's demand for all the land and the destruction of Israel.

The phrase has also become a solidarity slogan for Palestinians living in different parts of the divided land: Gazans, West Bankers, Jerusalemites and Israel's 20 per cent Palestinian Arab minority. In protests and marches demonstrating support for a ceasefire call across the globe, the chant 'From the River to the Sea, Palestine will be Free' was constantly raised, and on social media platforms the hashtag #fromtherivertothesea started trending worldwide. In America, legislators in Congress tried to introduce a law designating the slogan as anti-Semitic.

A version of the very same slogan, however, was also used in the original party platform of Israeli Prime Minister Binyamin Netanyahu's Likud party in 1977: 'The right of the Jewish people to the land of Israel is eternal and indisputable and is linked with the right to security and peace; therefore, Judea and Samaria will not be handed to any foreign administration; between the Sea and the Jordan there will only be Israeli sovereignty.'[38] In January 2024, Netanyahu reinforced his long-held opposition to a two-state solution, telling a press conference that, in any future arrangement, Israel 'must have security control over the entire territory west of the Jordan River.' He added: 'That collides with the idea of sovereignty. What can we do? This truth I tell to our American friends, and I put the brakes on the attempt to coerce us to a reality that would endanger the state of Israel.'[39]

Semantics are of immeasurable importance. 'Terrorism' versus 'resistance' is only one of the significant linguistic disputes characteristic of the debate about Israel's occupation and the ensuing conflict, in which cities, regions and neighbourhoods have different names according to religious or political perspective: Jerusalem or Al-Quds; Hebron or Al-Khalil; Judea and Samaria or the West Bank; Temple Mount or Al-Haram al-Sharif. One person's Arab terrorist murdering Jewish innocents to conquer Israel's eternal capital Jerusalem is another's Palestinian freedom fighter avenging the blood of innocents murdered by Israel to liberate occupied al-Quds from Zionist military occupation and an apartheid regime founded on a racial injustice.

Hamas's blend of nationalism, religion and charitable support within a community of believers (*ummah*) explains its appeal beyond the immediate base of its natural supporters. A Gaza psychiatrist, the late Dr Eyad Sarraj, said that – unlike its secular rivals – Hamas gave its followers 'a new identity of victory and belonging to God. Hamas people are ideologues, and they have a project, to resurrect the Islamic *ummah*. They believe this is their mission and what they do on the way is to transform Muslims to be good Muslims.' Inevitably, he added, such an appeal draws on powerful cultural and historical sentiments. 'Of course we sympathize as Palestinians and Arabs and Muslims with this. We Arabs and Muslims have suffered from chronic failure for the last 1,000 years. Since we lost Andalusia we have been defeated. This has gone deep into the collective unconscious of the Arabs.'[40]

It is instructive that military reverses suffered by the Muslim rulers on the Iberian peninsula between the eleventh and the fifteenth century are still causes for lamentation. Because, fortified by religious certitude, and in a region where all sides share an acute sense of historical grievances and entitlement, Hamas is nothing if not patient.

Indeed sometimes its leaders draw on surprising historical models to illustrate the length of the time they are prepared to wait. 'In such matters we should look to how the Jews conduct their affairs,' said Dr Abdel Aziz Rantissi in 2002. 'King David had a state in this area 3,000 years ago. For 3,000 years until now did they ever once say that it wasn't their land, although they didn't have it. But through 3,000 years they lived by adapting and living with what was the reality there.'[41] The same message was put more bluntly by Abu Bakr Nofal, a Hamas negotiator in Gaza. 'The world is in a hurry. We are not in a hurry.'[42]

However, there is no shortage of resilience on the other side. Avi Dichter, Israel's former minister of public security and intelligence chief, spent many years of his professional life in Gaza and argues that Palestinian advocates of violence utterly fail to comprehend Israelis' durability.

My parents lost their whole family during the Holocaust, and they came to Israel. I don't have any intention to go anywhere and, believe me, it's not going to happen. It is a question of time. What will happen first? Are we going to get tired or are they going to get tired? I can assure you; we are not going to get tired.[43]

2

In the Path of al-Qassam

> If the Arabs despair of justice then every soul and family will become an Izz
> ad-Din al-Qassam.
>
> *Al-Jamia'a al-Islamiyya*, editorial[1]

Sheikh Izz ad-Din al-Qassam's name meant 'Might of the Faith', and he was
an early prototype of the Islamist radical leader and fugitive, nearly a century
before Yahya Sinwar. Bearded, white-robed and ascetic, Qassam relied on a
small band of armed followers to survive for years in the 1930s as an outlaw
among the valleys and jagged hilltop ridges of British colonial-governed
Palestine, using the inhospitable terrain to evade capture. Preaching Islamic
revivalism and resistance through jihad – the radical creed of faith and
firearms that would serve as a model for future generations of Islamists
– the Syrian-born preacher urged his fellow Arabs to rise up against their
'infidel' British overlords, against the plan to create a Jewish homeland in
Palestine, and against the successive waves of Jewish Zionist immigrants in
the 1920s and 1930s. The influx of these new arrivals was transforming the
political and social fabric of the land, leading to the dispossession of the
Palestinian peasantry from a way of life it had known for centuries.

When Qassam was finally hunted down and killed by British police in a
shoot-out in Ya'bad, near the northern town of Jenin, on 19 November 1935,
thousands attended his funeral to pay tribute to a cleric who was scorned
by his British pursuers as the 'Brigand Sheikh', a derogatory epithet that
was a colonial forerunner of the 'terrorist' label applied to Hamas in the
modern era.

After his death Qassam's armed followers, bands of self-styled Islamic
mujahidin (holy warriors), went on to instigate the 1936–9 Arab revolt
against British rule. But while Qassam was certainly an obstacle to
the British, he failed both to overthrow them and to stop mass Jewish
immigration. Indeed, the extent to which Qassam failed during his own
lifetime is epitomized by the fact that his grave now lies in Israel, the Jewish
homeland whose very creation he fought in vain to prevent. The grave is in
a dilapidated Muslim cemetery near Haifa. His headstone bears a Koranic

verse and the exhortation 'Together in the path of al-Qassam'. This message is the key to Qassam's enduring appeal for later generations of Islamists: not the destination he reached, but the path he laid down and the example of personal sacrifice – martyrdom – which he set in doing so.

Within the Middle East the impact of the 'Brigand Sheikh' has far outlasted the events of his lifetime. Indeed, the word Qassam has passed into the lexicon of the conflict. For years, Israeli motorists have unknowingly driven within a few yards of Qassam's grave beside the Haifa to Nazareth highway, tuning in to Hebrew-language radio bulletins to hear Israeli politicians denouncing the latest outrage of Hamas's military wing, the Izz ad-Din al-Qassam Brigades, or to be updated on the latest 'Qassam' rocket fired by Hamas from Gaza into Israeli towns.

It is no accident that Hamas chose Qassam's name. His story has endured in the imagination of Palestinians. 'He was known to be an Arab nationalist, one who fought for the Palestinian cause,' remembered one elderly Palestinian veteran of the Mandate era. 'Everybody knew of him – he was in all the Arab newspapers and was considered to be a hero and a nationalist.'[2]

For Hamas, the particular appeal of the 'Brigand Sheikh' was that he provided the template of how to build a populist grassroots movement founded on faith, social and political works and, eventually, arms. These are fundamental elements of Hamas's own agenda – as evident from the three pillars of its full name in Arabic: *Harakat* ('Movement'), *al-Muqawama* ('Resistance') and *al-Islamiyya* ('Islamic'). In its founding Covenant, Hamas pays direct tribute to Qassam, proclaiming that he is 'one of the links in the chain of the struggle' against Zionism, dating back 'to the emergence of the martyr Izz ad-Din al-Qassam and his brethren the fighters, members of Muslim Brotherhood'.[3]

Upheaval

Mohammed Izz ad-Din bin Abdul Qadir bin Mustafa al-Qassam was born in 1882 in the village of Jablah, near the Syrian coastal town of Latakia, into a family of prominent Muslim leaders and scholars. After he showed promise his parents sent him to study in Cairo, the seat of the Islamic world's most prestigious centre of learning: al-Azhar University. Its sanctified arcades had changed little over the centuries, but the young Syrian arrived at a time of political turmoil in Egypt as it entered the twentieth century. In 1882 the British had occupied Egypt and were busy remaking Cairo according to the European model. Tensions ran high as Egyptian nationalists agitated against the British and their puppet Ottoman ruler, the Khedive.

At al-Azhar a new generation of Muslim scholars such as Mohammed Abduh and Rashid Rida had been preaching that Muslims had strayed from the true practice of Islam. Calling for the faith to be cleansed of superstitions and rituals that had accrued in the 1,200 years since the time of the Prophet Mohammed, they argued that such purification would strengthen the Islamic world and ensure that it would no longer be subject to humiliations such as the subjugation of the once great Muslim nation of Egypt to European, and in particular British, colonial subjugation.

For some of these scholars, an integral part of their credo was anti-colonial hostility towards the foreigners who had conquered them. Qassam became an early adopter and sought to put these ideas into practice. In Syria, after he returned from his studies in Cairo and took up a post as a preacher, Qassam promoted the reform of Islam as a means of resistance.

During the First World War Arab armies had fought alongside Britain and the victorious Allied Powers and had helped bring about the final demise of the Ottoman Empire by driving the Turkish army out of Damascus. Throughout the war Arab leaders had made clear their plans for independence after living for four centuries under Turkish rule. But their plans proved short-lived.

In April 1920, the victorious Allies met at a peace conference in San Remo in Italy to divide up the former Ottoman territories. France was awarded the mandate for the area that is now Syria and Lebanon, and in July 1920 in Damascus the French promptly deposed newly crowned King Faisal, the Arab leader who, with Lawrence of Arabia at his side, had led the Arab revolt and captured the city from the Ottomans.

Now back in Syria experiencing first-hand his fellow Syrians' disillusionment and frustration, Qassam was already hard at work teaching and preaching. He tried to organize a local jihadist force and agitated against the French. In his home town he built a school and ran a campaign to encourage Muslim piety, urging his townspeople to return to the mosque and commit themselves to fasting for Ramadan. At the same time, he was directing his energies against the colonial power, organizing fund-raising drives and preparing small companies of fighters.

His hostility towards the French derived from his deeply held belief that all Muslims should strive to maintain the fundamental precepts of their faith, free from non-Muslim or foreign rule. This striving was articulated as a 'jihad' or holy war, directed both at making his community a better model of faith and at organizing armed struggle against foreign interlopers who, he believed, would threaten the practice of Islam.

He had every cause to fear France's potent secularism. In Algeria, which the French had occupied since 1830, their 'civilizing mission' and colonial occupation had led to the demise of Ottoman Islamic power. The Muslim majority was then subjugated to more than a hundred years of French domination and colonial rule. Qassam wanted to resist any prospect of this happening in Syria. But although his efforts gained widespread support, they also brought him to the attention of the French, who put him on trial in absentia and condemned him to death for leading an uprising.

Realizing he was unlikely to survive long, Qassam fled south to preach the message of jihad in Palestine. There the capture of Jerusalem and the surrounding territories by British forces during the First World War had put the Holy Land back in Christian hands for the first time since the Crusades. At San Remo the victorious powers had granted Britain the mandate for Palestine. At first the British appeared intent on being seen as benign administrators, in comparison with the often brutal Ottomans. But even before its forces captured Jerusalem in December 1917 the British government had already made separate agreements about Palestine's fate with the Arabs, the French and the Zionist movement that the Arabs, in particular, later considered duplicitous. Throughout 1915–16 the British entered into discussions – the Hussein–McMahon correspondence – with the Arab leadership and promised territorial independence (including, the Arabs would argue, Palestine) in return for their support against the Ottoman Turks on the desert battlefields of Arabia.

However, the British had also entered into a secret agreement with the French in 1916 (the Sykes–Picot agreement) in which they agreed to divide the Middle East into spheres of control and influence. Britain had also issued a declaration to Jewish Zionists that it would help bring about their dream of a homeland for the Jewish people. The British commitment to the Jews was enshrined in the Balfour Declaration of 2 November 1917, which read:

> His Majesty's Government view with favour the establishment in Palestine of a national home for the Jewish people, and will use their best endeavours to facilitate the achievement of this object, it being clearly understood that nothing shall be done which may prejudice the civil and religious rights of existing non-Jewish communities in Palestine, or the rights and political status enjoyed by Jews in any other country.[4]

When the British intentions became public, they immediately set Zionist ambitions on a collision course with Palestinian national interests and rights. It was into this atmosphere of social and political upheaval that Qassam arrived in Haifa in the early 1920s. He was to become the figurehead of a very different and highly politicized model of religious opposition to British rule, for he carried with him the scent of a rebel, the precepts of jihad and the lessons learned from his previous encounters with foreign occupiers in his native Syria.

Fertile Soil

Haifa was a city in flux. On the steeply sloped terraces around Mount Carmel, newly built villas and apartment blocks housed recently settled Jewish residents, while down in the Muslim quarter, and beside the docks and railway yards, unpaved roads and squat single-storey dwellings offered only the most basic of shelter to thousands of poor Palestinian labourers. It was here, around the docks area and the neighbourhood of Wadi Salib, that Qassam came to preach at the *Istiqlal* (Independence) mosque. A man who devoted his energies to the practical rather than the theoretical, his strength lay in harnessing the energies of the poorest among Palestinian society.

As a self-declared enemy of colonialism and Zionism, Qassam certainly found in Haifa and the surrounding villages of northern Palestine an audience receptive to his ideas about the need to reform Islam and organize armed resistance in defence of Palestine. Palestinian leaders were increasingly alarmed by the escalating rate of Jewish immigration and land settlement and by the bloodshed caused by the upheaval.

By the early to mid-1920s Jewish immigration to Palestine was causing an accelerated and unprecedented rate of land dispossession among the Palestinian peasant classes. Palestine, as a predominantly peasant society, was being forcibly altered by Zionist land settlement. As absentee Arab landowners sold out to Jewish immigrants, poor Palestinian Arab villagers were being displaced and were pouring into cities such as Haifa. There they joined the ranks of the urban under-privileged and swelled the audiences for Friday prayers at Qassam's mosque, where they heard a message of Muslim resurgence and identity. Believing that, through the framework of Islam, Palestinian opposition could be translated into direct action, Qassam began literacy programmes for the poor, taught the Koran, ran evening classes, and became heavily involved in the Muslim Young Men's Association (MYMA). He also established agricultural cooperatives for the rural poor. By 1929 he had assumed leadership of the MYMA and was getting audiences of thousands at the mosque. Crucially, he was also appointed marriage registrar by the Muslim court in Haifa. This position gave him the perfect cover to travel around the countryside on official business, allowing him to forge relationships with Palestinian leaders in villages and hamlets. Amid the celebrations Qassam would have the opportunity to meet with the most influential figures of the village and discuss his ideas. One of the most significant issues was the preaching of jihad against both the British and the Zionist settlers.

As one British police official observed, 'during his tours Qassam would bring together the more religiously minded of the villagers and preach to them the doctrines of Islam, cleverly interpolating such passages from the Koran as were calculated to stimulate a spirit of religious fanaticism.'[5] The British also believed that Qassam's interpretations of the Koran 'sanction the use of physical violence.'[6]

Qassam was different from establishment Muslim leaders because his lifestyle was similar to that of the people among whom he worked. This was quite different from the studied aloofness of Hajj Amin al-Husseini, the British-appointed mufti of Jerusalem and leader of the Supreme Muslim Council, who, as a leading member of a notable family and senior official in the British Mandate authority, had a status which dictated distance rather than familiarity. Qassam – although himself from a notable clerical family – was renowned for living plainly. He was far from aloof; he trod a common path. This was a path that his spiritual and political descendants in Hamas would also strive to follow. He was convinced that foreign occupation and settlement would not deliver Arabs their rights. This was the message he proclaimed in his sermons and public speeches, rapidly bringing him to the attention of the British governing authorities and his Zionist foes.

Black Hand Gang

By the late 1920s and early 1930s Qassam was spending more and more time with the stevedores, the urban poor of Haifa and peasants from surrounding villages. These workers lived, according to contemporary accounts, in hovels made out of old petrol tins, without a water supply. The high cost of living meant that, for thousands, life was subsistence, while Jewish workers were paid double by the British Mandate. Qassam began to identify select groups of followers to train as mujahidin. One of them was captured and put on trial by the British authorities:

> According to the statement of Assad el-Muflah, one of the accused, he had been a vendor of eggs in Haifa but his income was not sufficient to support

his wife and four children. After prayers at the mosque he would ask for charity and one day a man took him to see Sheikh Izz ad-Din Qassam. The accused joined the gang voluntarily, he told police, in order to escape from his miserable existence.[7]

It was easy for Qassam to highlight the growing disparities between the Arab workers' situation and that of the British authorities and the new Jewish immigrants. Yet this was no ordinary workers' struggle. For Qassam there was always an Islamic agenda, and his meetings took an increasingly strident political tone. At one meeting he asked his listeners whether they knew about Jewish plans to 'take the country by force', including the smuggling of arms into Palestine and military drills in Haifa. To this he added bitterly: 'Jews and Arabs are subject to the same laws … Jews do not have to take the country by force as the Arabs are selling it to them.'[8] Such statements were also a challenge to the Palestinian notables and national leaders, whom Qassam often attacked for their inability to mount an effective challenge to what he considered the calculated British policy to turn Palestine from a Muslim land into a Jewish state.

News reports, memoirs, memorandums and accounts from the period indicate that, at some point in 1930, Qassam decided to escalate to armed action. With a small group of supporters he took to the hills and villages of northern Palestine in readiness to launch armed attacks on their enemies. His secretive group became known as the Black Hand gang, and they engaged in fund-raising, military training, and preparations to launch jihad. The poorest peasants who joined him even donated part of the compensation for their forfeited lands for 'the purchase of arms'.[9]

For five years they carried out attacks on Jewish settlements, Jewish settlers and the British in northern Palestine. Among others, they were held responsible for the murder in November 1935 of a British Mandate policeman, Sergeant Moshe Rosenfeld, for an attack on Zionist pioneers, and for inspiring numerous conspiracies and murder plots. Certainly, those who remember that era recall the ruthlessness of Qassam and his followers. 'Everybody who dared to say anything bad about him used to be killed by his people. He had many supporters and they used to protect him. Even policemen were killed because they said bad things,' said one nonagenarian Palestinian ex-policeman in the Galilee.[10]

These attacks, which many claimed sparked the Arab revolt of 1936, were portrayed by Qassam as an act of jihad, so that his followers would see not just a national struggle but a religious war against the occupation of Muslim lands. As early as 1930 Qassam had secured a *fatwa* (religious edict) from a religious cleric in Damascus which declared that jihad against the British and the Zionist settlers was permissible.

Many young Palestinian preachers were also receptive to his call. Among their number were Sheikh Farhan Sa'adi, Sheikh Hussein Hamadi, Sheikh Attiyeh Ahmad and Sheikh Khalil Issa. Sheikh Sa'adi, a devoted follower of Qassam, would later become a 'notorious gang leader' during the Palestinian revolt. He was captured by the British in November 1937, sent to trial and executed by hanging in Haifa, all within the space of five days. His execution was the first by the British-instituted military court in Palestine.[11]

Qassam argued that the strategy of appeals to the British relied upon by the leaders of institutional Islam and the notable families was completely ineffective in dealing with the dual challenge of British colonial might and the Zionist drive to settle the land. Qassam had met with Hajj Amin al-Husseini, the mufti of Jerusalem, and asked him to support the jihad. The mufti declined, arguing that a political solution could still be found to give the Palestinians freedom – much as, nearly a century later, Qassam's rejectionist Islamist descendants Hamas and the pro-negotiation Palestinian establishment of Fatah would differ over the means to achieve their ends. The mufti believed that Qassam was not allowing enough time for a negotiated political solution to emerge. In time he changed his perspective, but only after Qassam was already dead and his disciples had triggered the Palestinian revolt.

Qassam's campaign came to an abrupt end in a fatal gunfight with British police in November 1935. As news of his death was reported, demonstrations and protests broke out across Palestine. The British complained of a 'tendency in the Arab press to regard these gangsters as "martyrs" to the cause' and noted bitterly that, 'as was to be expected, the Sheikh ... and [his] fellow conspirators are now being canonised.'[12] British news reports observed that the editor of one Arabic newspaper was 'insisting upon regarding the gangster as a hero.' One local newspaper editorial appearing in the wake of Qassam's death declared: 'Although we differ from the dead martyr as to the means, we are partners with him in the attainment of the ultimate objective. If the Arabs despair of justice then every soul and family will become an Izz ad-Din al-Qassam.'[13]

In true colonial style, it was difficult for the British to conceive of Palestinian demands as legitimate or to see beyond their own hostile stereotypes of the Arab 'other', demonized as they were so comprehensively in the Western imagination. There were, of course, a few exceptions – individual British officials and administrators who urged a more attenuated approach to the Arabs – but they did not occupy senior positions in Jerusalem or London.

At his funeral in Haifa, thousands of people mourned Qassam's loss and proclaimed him as a new leader and symbol of Palestinian resistance. As the printing presses rolled with hurriedly produced eulogies, poems and letters addressed to the 'martyr' sheikh, thousands of ordinary working people came to the mosque in Haifa where his funeral was to take place. Schoolchildren, scouts with flags and the members of the MYMA led the funeral cortege, amid the wails and cries of veiled women and anti-British slogan-shouting from the assembled crowd. Hours later the cortege arrived at Qassam's final resting place.[14]

Palestine's 'notables' and national leaders were initially unsure about how to respond to the sheikh's death. Rawiya Shawwa remembers her father, Rashad Shawwa, a prominent Palestinian figure, recounting the events of that day to her when she was a child. 'He told me that he was in Haifa to act as one of the bearers of the dead sheikh's body.'[15] Other notables steered clear of this and other public events. Their absence symbolized one aspect of the divide between the masses and their leaders. Qassam's death epitomized a form of self-sacrifice that many ordinary Palestinians suspected would never be found among the leaders of the establishment.

The strength of feeling among working-class protesters in the wake of Qassam's death, however, alerted some notables to the increasing sense of desperation pervading Palestinian society, and at a private meeting with British officials they expressed fear that their influence might be waning. The only remedy that the leaders could commend was 'a suggestion that the government should change its present policy.'[16] The British ignored such entreaties. But they were to discover that, in Palestine, as in Ireland and India, they were not to have it all their own way.

Fury and Retribution

In Zohar el-Kokhab, a café in Haifa's working-class district, 4,000 men from the MYMA met under a black-draped portrait of the slain sheikh to hear speeches lauding him as a 'hero', a 'martyr' and a champion of the Palestinian cause. At other meetings in the Arab workers' clubs, speeches were made declaring Qassam a 'great nationalist who fell for the cause'. Sensing the tide in favour of the slain sheikh, journalists, prominent nationalists and religious figures began to vie with each other in calling upon the masses to throw off their British yoke and demand freedom and independence.

At another meeting in Haifa at the MYMA, which was held at the end of the traditional forty-day mourning period, more than a thousand people lamented the late sheikh. Rejecting statements in the Hebrew press denouncing him as a 'brigand', they declared that Qassam should be commemorated as a hero. His death was described as an act of martyrdom in 'defence of his country against the British'. He was also declared a 'great nationalist who fell in the cause'.[17] In death, Qassam became a symbol of national resistance for all Palestinians – irrespective of their ideological hue.

In so doing he challenged the traditional leadership of Palestine, preaching resistance and steadfastness at a time when they were often squabbling. His legacy found almost instant expression in the outbreak of the Palestinian revolt in 1936. The revolt and general strike – which lasted for three years – paralysed the country and forced Britain to introduce harsh measures as it sought to restore law and order among the increasingly divided Palestinian Arab and Jewish communities.

In April 1936 a band of Qassam's armed followers ambushed and killed two Jews. In retaliation, the Jewish resistance attacked and killed two Palestinian Arabs. In the coastal city of Jaffa tensions rose as sporadic violence broke out between Palestinian Arabs and Jews. The British, struggling to maintain control, declared a state of emergency. Later that month Palestinian leaders called for a general strike, and all sectors of Arab society banded together to protest against what they saw as draconian British measures and Zionist encroachment. It appeared that the ordinary Palestinian Arabs had had enough. Their livelihoods, their society, their structures of power, their sense of place, space and dimension were all under threat, and a collective sense of despair now propelled people towards rebellion. The Qassamites and the resort to an armed resistance signalled a popular uprising that took Palestinian leaders as much by surprise as it did the British authorities.

The Qassamites targeted mandate officials and those accused of land sales, arms trading or collaboration with the Zionist cause. But they never succeeded in transforming the revolt into a full-scale jihad with the goal of establishing an Islamic state in Palestine. Ultimately their revolt was to fail. Within a decade the Zionists had their state and, amid the bloodshed which accompanied the end of the British Mandate, hundreds of thousands of Palestinians had fled to become refugees, stateless, homeless and dispossessed in foreign lands and refugee camps in Gaza and the West Bank. But it was in these very camps, among the children and grandchildren of the refugees, that later generations of Islamists would emerge to pick up from where Qassam left off and begin rallying the poor, the angry and the dispossessed to the call of Islam. For them Qassam had shown the path.

Sowing

None of the political organizations paid it any attention. It was apolitical and was not perceived as a threat.

Dr Haider Abdel Shafi[1]

The British eventually succeeded in putting down the 1936–9 revolt that was inspired in large part by Sheikh Izz ad-Din al-Qassam. The spirit of Islam as a political force appeared to be spent, along with much of the energy that had propelled the Islamists' nationalist counterparts.

The British Mandate authorities punished the Palestinian leadership: they were deported, exiled, put in prison camps and executed, and their followers were subjected to severe measures. The religious leadership, personified by the mufti, Hajj Amin al-Husseini, embarked on a collision course with the same British authorities that had installed him at the head of the Muslim institutions of Palestine. Increasingly, however, the *ulama* (religious elite) of this vast institutionalized network of mosques, courts and schools had become too tainted by its association with the British to enjoy widespread support among those who were agitating against colonial rule. Forced to assert himself, al-Husseini tried to direct the Palestinian general strike and 1936 revolt. The British decided that the mufti should be dismissed. When he gained advance intelligence of their plans he fled into exile.

During the Second World War, al-Husseini based himself in Berlin, where he cooperated with Hitler's propaganda machine in the vain hope that the Germans, once victorious, would drive the British out of Palestine. This was a blunder of historic proportions, not only because he picked the losing side, but because his readiness to further his people's national interests – even to the extent of allying with a Nazi regime which dragged the world into war and perpetrated the Holocaust – has ever since been held up by some Israelis as evidence of the Palestinian leadership's anti-Semitism.

Unprepared

The movement of political Islam, which made such an impact on Palestinian destiny during the British Mandate, simply failed to rise to the subsequent challenge of losing Palestine in 1948. It had certainly tried. In the late 1940s the Muslim Brotherhood opened new branches in Palestine: more than 1,000 people attended the opening of its Jerusalem branch in the Old City in May 1946.

West of Jerusalem in the coastal region of Gaza, long a neglected backwater of the British Mandate, some heads of the notable Palestinian families had been imprisoned or deported during the 1936–9 revolt. But afterwards many were allowed to return because the British no longer considered them a threat. Islam had its place in Gaza, through the formal offices held by these families during the Ottoman era. But revivalist Islam was also becoming a factor with the steady arrival of Muslim Brotherhood representatives from Egypt. Throughout the 1940s the Muslim Brotherhood's branches in the Gaza area grew in importance. So much so that in 1947 the Brotherhood's founder and supreme leader, Hassan al-Banna, visited them.

But even as the Brotherhood was laying its roots, the region was shaken by the announcement in 1947 that Britain would terminate its mandate the following year, and that the United Nations planned to partition Palestine into separate Jewish and Palestinian Arab states.

Worse, the Palestinians and neighbouring Arab countries were outraged that the UN partition resolution proposed to award about 56 per cent of the land between the Mediterranean and Jordan River to the Jews, who represented 32 per cent of the population, leaving 44 per cent for the majority Palestinians. The majority of the Jewish leadership accepted the United Nations partition plan. The Arab sides refused but lost the vote at the UN. In the ensuing months, as Zionist armed groups readied for statehood, Arab leaders simply reassured the Palestinians that they would protect them and that they should not panic or flee their homes. The Muslim Brotherhood, however, began to organize for jihad. In the early months of 1948, mujahidin from Egypt began to arrive in Gaza to 'fight with the Palestinians in the war as a serious attempt to support the Palestinian issue'.[2]

By the end of the British Mandate, Israeli historians later documented, armed Jewish paramilitary groups such as the Irgun and Stern Gang conducted raids, assaults and massacres, such as at Deir Yassin in April 1948, against the Palestinians. Historians have evidenced the killings of Palestinian men, women and children, as well as plans in the making to ethnically cleanse the area.[3] Experts pointed to official policy documents that outlined

Israel's plans to maintain forms of demographic superiority. Some Israeli officials have openly condoned such policies. In March 2023, a senior Israeli minister called for the Palestinian town of Huwara to be wiped out.[4] There are many instances of Israeli politicians, including former prime ministers, who have underscored a desire to demographically engineer the Palestinian territories.[5] And as an Amnesty International report noted:

> [S]tatements by leading Israeli politicians over the years confirm that the intention to maintain a Jewish demographic majority and to oppress and dominate Palestinians has guided Israel's policies since the state's creation ... successive Israeli politicians – regardless of their political affiliations – have publicly stated their intention to minimize Palestinians' access to and control of land across all territories under Israel's effective control.[6]

During the Arab–Israeli war of 1948–9, however, the mujahidin and all the other Arab armies lost. They lost territory to the new Israeli state, and by the end of 1949 around 750,000 Palestinians had fled or been driven out of their homes and lands, each of them turned into a refugee. This was a mass dispossession that was soon seared into the Palestinian consciousness as the *Nakbah*.[7]

After the war it was clear that the small number of Islamists could do little to support the huge new refugee population that had flooded into Gaza, the West Bank and beyond. 'There were no big mosques, just small buildings which we call mosques. We were penniless and we didn't have the means to build our movement,' recalls one Brotherhood activist.[8] Among the arrivals in Gaza was Ahmed Yassin, a young refugee from the village of al-Jura, near what is now the Israeli port city of Ashkelon. 'Our lands and homes were taken from us and we had to fight. From this early age I dreamt of martyrdom if it would bring freedom,'[9] recalled the man who would later go on to become the founder and spiritual leader of Hamas.

The dispossession convinced some God-fearing Muslims that only through faith, patience and arms would they ever return to the homes and villages they had been forced to abandon. 'I always thought about my village of al-Jura, and when I became involved with the Brotherhood I knew we would be in a war to restore Palestine and return to my village,' recalled one Muslim Brotherhood veteran of that era.[10]

Ferment

Such hopes were, however, to go into abeyance. The Islamic trend was soon to be overwhelmed by the dominant ideology of Arab nationalism that had taken hold across the region. The years following the war of 1948 would prove crucial in establishing a collective sense among Palestinians of being a nation denied a state, of forging a national consciousness, and of pursuing the struggle for liberation and self-determination. Growing consciousness of an identity shaped through turmoil, statelessness and the experience of becoming refugees bound the people together through nationalism, not religion.

The political message of Islam – liberation through jihad – was lost in the drumbeat of Arab nationalism and the promises of radical new Arab leaders that Palestine would be recovered by their armies. These forces were not armed, as Izz ad-Din al-Qassam's mujahidin had been, merely with a few rifles and bullets, but with the kind of heavy weaponry that had the whole region believing that the new state of Israel would soon be defeated and the lost lands of Palestine would be regained.

By the late 1950s and early 1960s the Palestinian refugees became politically restive in places such as the Egyptian-controlled Gaza Strip. The Egyptian regime there placed Gaza under military administration and implemented the same crackdowns on Islamists there as inside Egypt itself. Gaza's shanty-tented refugee camps had been a fertile recruiting ground for the Islamists, and the Brotherhood's adherents were rounded up and sent to prison, forcing the movement underground. It responded by establishing military cells with grandiose names such as the Young Men of Vengeance (*Shabab al-Tha'r*) and the Battalion of Justice. New recruits gained only the most rudimentary training in paramilitary activities, along with assurances by their instructors that Islam would provide the solution to their miserable existence as refugees. Abu Mohammed, a young recruit to the *Shabab al-Tha'r*: 'I was not afraid to go to war because I was now armed with God's power and faith in him. I understood that if I died I would go to paradise and therefore alive or dead it didn't matter.'[11]

Some of the leading lights of the Muslim Brotherhood's military cells at this time were young men such as Salah Khalaf (Abu Iyad) and Khalil al-Wazir (Abu Jihad), who later left to play a central role in the Palestine Liberation Organization (PLO). The Brotherhood's members were bound together as refugees and potential mujahidin who believed that only Islam could deliver them from their daily ordeals. But after the 1952 Free Officers' coup deposed the monarchy in Egypt, the Islamists were confronted with a powerful new rival: Arab nationalism.

The Egyptian figurehead of that movement, Gamal Abdel Nasser, had a fractious relationship with the Brotherhood. It had played a part in the coup that brought his Revolutionary Command Council to power, but only two years later, in 1954, a gunman tried to assassinate Nasser at a mass meeting in Alexandria, and later confessed that he did so at the behest of the Muslim Brotherhood. Thousands of Egyptian and Palestinian members of the Brotherhood were arrested, branch offices were closed down and activists were executed. Even today the memory of those times is seared into the collective consciousness of the Islamists, and there is an enduring mistrust of Egyptian motives. 'We felt it was bad enough to be dispossessed by the Jews, but then to have no control over our lives in Gaza because our Arab brothers were ruling us ... it was too much,' declared Sheikh Yassin in 2002.[12]

In the late 1950s there was 'no affection for the *Ikhwan*', noted Abu Zaki. 'Most of the *Ikhwan* changed their political orientation or went to the Gulf countries, and thus they vanished completely from Gaza and the minds of the people.'[13] The members of the Brotherhood who settled in Gulf countries such as Saudi Arabia and Kuwait would later serve as an important ideological and financial conduit for a revived Islamic movement in Gaza and the West Bank. But for the moment Nasser's brand of Arab nationalism was the dominant ideology. 'At the time I fully supported Nasser's system – just as everyone else did. He taught us how to dismiss Israel and work towards the creation of one Arab state ... we were amazed by the personality of Abdel Nasser,'[14] recalls Mahmoud Zahar, a senior Hamas leader who studied medicine in Egypt during this era, and who began his political life as a nationalist. Yet, for Zahar and other young conservative Gazan refugees, the heady populism of the 1960s, decadence and further victories by the Israelis in wars against the Arabs would prove to be a turning point in the revival of Islam as a political force for change among certain sections of Palestinian society.

Between 1948 and 1967 new Palestinian political organizations began to emerge, and often they were patronized by the Egyptian authorities. But increasingly the Muslim Brotherhood was greeted with mistrust and suspicion by the Egyptians, and support eroded in favour of the new Palestinian nationalists arising in their midst.

Gaza too began to change. Under Egypt's influence it became more urban, less conservative and traditional. Popular pastimes of cafés, beach picnics, parties and cinema-going occupied people. Dreams of liberation centred on a new generation of charismatic young personalities such as Yasser Arafat. In this popularity contest, the traditional stalwarts of the Muslim Brotherhood seemed to represent a defunct and bygone age.

Swinging Sixties: The Wilderness Years

As Gaza began to turn to Nasser's way of seeing the world, Palestinians enjoyed some political benefits under the new dispensation. More young people turned to the ideas of liberation associated with the Arab Ba'ath, Nasserist, nationalist and leftist movements. The social conservatism of Gaza's traditional families and structures was challenged by a new generation. Young men swapped the tarbush of an earlier generation for Elvis-like quiffs, sunglasses and skinny-Mod ties. Their traditional galabaya were replaced with shirts and trousers. Women wore mini-skirts and sported beehive hairstyles. 'To us during this time ... living well in Gaza was as normal in the 1960s as Beirut or Cairo. It was a decent society,'[15] recalled Rawiya Shawwa, a member of a wealthy and influential Gaza family. Gaza City developed and became a leisure destination for Egyptians seeking tax-free shopping, beach-side restaurants, and cinemas showing the latest Egyptian movies.

Egyptian universities were opened up to hundreds of Gazan students, and the experience of studying in Cairo and exposure to the wider currents of Arab political thought proved to be a seminal factor in the development of Palestinian political movements, for Islamists and nationalists alike. Dr Mariam Abu Dagga, a teenage radical and member of the Guevara faction of the Popular Front for the Liberation of Palestine (PFLP) in the 1960s, also remembers the changed atmosphere: 'Gaza then was totally different from now ... I found all the women now have put on scarf and shari'a hijab, but in the past even my mother didn't wear such things.'[16] Mariam, like so many others, came to believe in the Arab socialist solution to the refugees' predicament. Gaza fell under the Nasserist spell.

In the West Bank, the Islamic movement endured a different experience under Jordanian Hashemite rule. Most West Bank branches of the Muslim Brotherhood were closed directly after the 1948 war. The movement judiciously sought a more harmonious relationship with the conservative monarchy in Amman. As a result, the Brotherhood not only survived the Jordanian political crackdown of the 1950s, which banned other political movements, but by the 1960s it was the only significant political opposition in the country. Nevertheless, although identified as pro-Hashemite and conservative, the Brotherhood knew that it was under constant scrutiny by the ubiquitous Jordanian secret services – the *mukhabarat*. In the West Bank, the Brotherhood maintained close ties with preachers and acted as a religious institution rather than a political party.

The enforced geographical separation of the Gaza Strip and the West Bank – with Israel between them – meant that the path of Palestinian Islamism had a dual character. It was Gaza which emerged as the heart of a particularly Palestinian interpretation of political Islam. In Gaza, progressive politics and radicalism would eventually inspire Islamists to react to the changes around them and formulate their own vision of liberation. In the West Bank, Islamism remained conservative and traditional, tied to elite power structures associated with preserving the power of the Hashemite monarchy as well as traditional family and clan structures.

The 1967 War and Israeli Occupation

The Six Day War of June 1967, in which Israel comprehensively defeated the combined Arab armies of Egypt, Jordan and Syria, led to another period of profound upheaval for the region, especially the Palestinian people. The war led to the Israeli occupation of the Palestinian Territories of East Jerusalem, the West Bank and the Gaza Strip. And Israel not only defeated the Arab armies of the largest countries in the region but captured and occupied East Jerusalem, which it subsequently annexed.

Forty years after the war, the veteran Iraqi diplomat and politician Adnan Pachachi, Iraq's foreign minister in 1967, told one of the authors that he regarded the Six Day War as the single most seismic event in the Middle East during his political lifetime. 'I think, sadly, the defeat that was inflicted on the Arabs – the Arab states – the whole concept of Arab nationalism which was represented by President Nasser was greatly weakened,' said Pachachi, sitting in his home in Baghdad after the US-led invasion of Iraq.

> Just a few years before the 1967 war there was really a very credible effort, a determined effort, to form a federal union between Iraq, Egypt and Syria. That was 1963. Because the idea of Arab unity was so strong. Then the defeat of 1967 no doubt really retarded that whole idea. It weakened it. I think it has survived but I don't think it was able to regain its momentum and its strength.[17]

It quickly became clear that Arab nationalism had failed in its promises. For Palestinians, thousands became refugees for a second time, and, shattered by yet another defeat, it took years for the nationalists to regroup. But they did so, this time under the leadership of Yasser Arafat, Nayef Hawatmeh, George Habash, Khalil Wazir (Abu Jihad) and Salah Khalaf (Abu Iyad), through the umbrella group of the PLO. As Arafat and his *fedayeen* fighters grew in stature across the region, the socially conservative and anti-nationalist Muslim Brotherhood was, yet again, perceived as badly out of step with the ethos of the time.

The Brotherhood initially put its jihad on hold, arguing that it was not ready for such a step. Instead it became convinced that it should first launch a social jihad to Islamize its own society. A leading Islamist figure, Abdullah Azzam, who went on to become a mentor to al-Qaeda leader Usama bin Laden, later admitted that this was a mistake that 'allowed revolutionary organizations to outstrip [us], organizations which the Brotherhood berates for their leftist leanings, their deviation, their bungling and for brainwashing the youth.'[18]

For all their fervour, Arafat's *fedayeen* forces were waging a losing battle. By 1971, Israel had deported as many as 15,000 guerrillas and activists to prison camps in the Sinai desert, and in 1973 Israel once again inflicted further humiliation on its Arab enemies, repulsing the Egyptian and Syrian armies who attacked on the Jewish holy day of Yom Kippur.

Some Islamists had long regretted the Brotherhood's early decision to lie low and cede the initiative to the nationalists. These Muslim opposition forces sought to capitalize on the return to Islam which Dr Mahmoud Zahar and other prominent Islamists believed they had begun to notice in the mid- to late 1970s. 'The people', Zahar claimed, 'returned to their religion [and] started to study Islam thoroughly and began to live Islam as a system governing their way of life.'[19]

The 1970s: Yassin and the Rise of the Islamists

In the 1970s, the predecessors of Hamas set about remaking Palestinian society in the image of Islam, prepared if necessary to impose their vision by force. The chief architect of this revival project was the educator and preacher Sheikh Ahmed Yassin. Yassin was a young child when he and his widowed mother became refugees in Gaza in 1948. Attracted to the ideas of the Muslim Brotherhood, Yassin served as a teacher, community worker and preacher at a mosque and became a prominent figure in the refugee neighbourhood of al-Sabra in Gaza City where he lived. But his Muslim Brotherhood affiliation was well known, which led to his brief imprisonment in 1966 by the Egyptians during one of their regular anti-Brotherhood purges.

Increasingly Yassin came to believe that his role as an activist in Gaza's Muslim community was to bring Islam to the secularized youth, to get them to commit to the fundamental tenets of the faith: to pray five times a day,

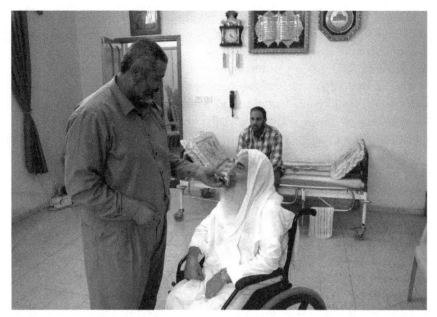

Photo 3.1 Hamas's founder Sheikh Ahmed Yassin in his Gaza City home before his assassination in 2004; with him is the future Hamas leader Ismail Haniyeh.

to fast during Ramadan – in essence, to be pious and exemplary Muslims in all aspects of life. Yassin devoted himself to promoting Islamic revivalism through preaching and education. As he himself later asserted, 'our faith is tied to the future of this society and the command to make Islam flourish again.'[20]

Yassin proved to be an inspirational educator among his natural constituency: stateless refugees like himself. 'His experience was a shared experience,' said his biographer Dr Atef Adwan. 'This is part of his appeal to so many in Gaza.'[21] Yassin's vision advocated individual change as the instrument to bring about the overhaul of society. In 1973 he and a group of followers established *al-Mujamma' al-Islami* (The Islamic Centre), an organization whose prominent figures would later win international notoriety as the leaders of Hamas: Dr Mahmoud Zahar, Dr Abdel Aziz Rantissi, Ibrahim Yazouri, Abd al-Fattah Dukhan, Issa al-Najjar and Salah Shehadeh.

Yassin's role was pivotal. He engendered formidable loyalty and devotion in his followers. Yassin, who had been paralysed in a childhood accident, was also physically dependent on these acolytes. Seated in front of the television mounted high up on the wall, he would follow the screen with his eyes until he saw something which prompted him to whisper instructions to lieutenants in his distinctive thin, high voice. He had to be lifted in and out of cars and at mealtimes would have to be spoon-fed, with a napkin around his neck. His only means of communication with the outside world – beyond the pulpit – was when aides held up a telephone handset to his ear. Despite his physical frailty, there was strength of spirit apparent in any encounter with Yassin. He would make firm, well-articulated pronouncements on the serious questions of the day.

Those with whom Yassin surrounded himself seemed to absorb from him a confidence not only to make their mark on society but to take on their enemies, apparently without fear. 'No one can deny that the resurgence of Islam depends on such people … he was the creator of the new Islamic movement in Gaza,'[22] was the later assessment of Mahmoud Zahar. Yassin and his followers were concerned, first and foremost, to return society and politics to the true path of Islam. Therefore, their first targets were their fellow Palestinians, specifically the secular nationalists and leftists of the PLO. Only later would they turn their attention to Israel. 'We have to be patient because Islam will spread sooner or later and will have control over the world. Patience will shorten the journey of Islam,' Yassin declared.[23] They directed their energies at every aspect of society and demanded that their rivals relinquish political control. They objected to the new world view promoted by the secular nationalists. On university campuses they shouted down lecturers teaching Darwin's theory of evolution, spreading conspiracy theories that Darwin's thinking was inspired by Jews.[24]

The Islamists organized demonstrations to protest against leftist or secular institutions and targeted professional associations. However, the Israeli authorities did not, at that time, appear to believe that the Islamists' agitation against their fellow Palestinians was something to worry about. 'The Israelis turned a blind eye to all the harmful activities that the Mujamma undertook against the people … ambushes against individuals on the streets, raids on houses of leaders of nationalist groups,' said Dr Riad al-Agha, a former president of the Islamic University of Gaza.[25]

Other Palestinian analysts believe that Israel was merely opportunistic about the Mujamma's growth. 'I don't go as far as to say that Israel created Hamas or the Islamic movement, but Israel of course used all the existing Palestinian mosaic to its advantage,' said Professor Ali Jarbawi. 'They were not as harsh on Hamas or the Islamic movement as on the nationalist factions, because of what they were standing for. If you were not for resisting the occupation, then why should Israel at that time crack down on them?'[26]

In these early days there was little indication to suggest that this group of activists would become one of the most formidable groups in the Middle East.

While Israeli officials deny that Israel went so far as to arm or actively encourage the Islamists, some concede that governments at the time regarded them as a useful tool to use against secular nationalists in the PLO. 'At the beginning I think some elements within the Israeli government – not the government, some elements within the Israeli government – were thinking that, by strengthening Mujamma, they could put some more pressure on Fatah in the Gaza Strip, back in the mid-80s,' said Brigadier General Yossi Kuperwasser, a former director of intelligence analysis for the Israeli military. 'I think it was a mistake, yes.'[27]

Brigadier General Itshak Segev served as the Israeli military governor of Gaza from 1979 to 1981, just after he returned from a posting to Iran. Having just seen the 1979 Iranian Revolution and the opening weeks of Ayatollah Ruhollah Khomeini's regime up close, he had no illusions about the dangers posed by Islamist fundamentalists. But during his time in charge, he said, Sheikh Yassin's people presented him with 'zero, zero, zero' problems. Segev remarked that he even arranged for Yassin to be taken to hospital in Tel Aviv to see if the best surgeons in Israel could operate on his spine, but they pronounced the damage too severe to be corrected by surgery.

Nevertheless, although the Mujamma was ostensibly religious and social in its intent, Segev warned his superiors in 1980 that they faced a 'catastrophe' if they stayed in Gaza, because its population was growing so fast and was likely to be affected by the wave of Islamic fundamentalism apparent across the region, not just in the Palestinian Territories. 'There was a demographic atom bomb that was going on,' he said. 'I didn't think about Yassin or Islamic Jihad, but I saw this society was going in the direction of fundamentalism, and this phenomenon was all over – Algeria, Egypt, Iran. This phenomenon had come about because of the failure of the regimes in these countries to satisfy their people.' Even then, according to Segev, it was apparent that the Islamists in Gaza were exploiting the failings of the PLO.

The people in the refugee camps were very poor. If money went to Arafat's people they took it and put it in their pockets, but when Yassin got money he gave it to the people. If he took money from Saudi Arabia he built a mosque, he gave education to children, or started ping pong for them. He did a lot of things, really, to help the people.[28]

Indeed, Sheikh Yassin founded a small sports club and youth association on some waste ground at the back of his humble home in the al-Sabra neighbourhood of Gaza City. His ambitions, however, could not be enclosed by the dusty football pitch, dilapidated chairs and decrepit hut.

The first obstacles in their way were secular Palestinian nationalists and the PLO. Sheikh Yassin and his associates were appalled at what they considered to be pernicious leftist and infidel tendencies among Gaza's youth. There was a sense that the PLO, while reviled as a terrorist organization in Israel, had captured the imagination of the wider world. Even as Yassin was an unknown teacher labouring among Gaza's refugee community to set up an Islamic framework, Yasser Arafat was becoming one of the most famous and instantly recognizable figures in the world. In an era of revolutionary politics, international socialism, liberation movements and anti-colonial movements rising in Africa, Latin America and the Middle East, the PLO and its guerrillas were regarded as populist icons. Arafat headed a movement which could count on hundreds of thousands of supporters spread across the Middle East. By the mid-1970s the PLO had grown in stature and was identified as a state within a state, first in Jordan and then in Lebanon.

Confrontation

The message of Sheikh Yassin's Mujamma inevitably led to Palestinian on Palestinian confrontation. Although many denied that they had political ambitions, it was clear from their rivalry with the nationalist-secularists that power was on the minds of Yassin and co. 'They emphasized that the only path to liberation was through the realization of an Islamic state. Even at this stage they were voicing political ideas – they belittled fighting the occupation,' declared Dr Haider Abdel Shafi, a Gaza notable and nationalist leader.[29]

The Mujamma received a boost in 1978, when it was granted official status by the Israeli occupation authorities ruling Gaza. This was a game-changer. Officials in the office of the Israeli prime minister, Menachem Begin, gave approval to the registration. Many Palestinians believe, and some former Israeli officials concede, that this happened against the background of an Israeli strategy to produce a counterbalance to the PLO and to divide and rule in Gaza: 'The [Israeli] authorities kept their eyes closed to the realities of what they were allowing to be created ... because at that time the PLO factions had power ... and the Israelis wanted an adversary to fight them.'[30]

By the early 1980s the Mujamma had acquired a confrontational reputation – not against Israel but against their fellow Palestinians. Local health-care institutions, universities and professional associations which traditionally bore allegiance to the PLO were targeted by the Mujamma, and such places quickly became battlegrounds. The Israeli authorities and their soldiers allegedly stood by as blood was spilt on Gaza's streets. Mujamma supporters attacked their own – denouncing people as 'atheists' and 'communists' in sermons, leaflets and speeches.

After Friday prayers, burning torches were held aloft as Mujamma thugs set fire to libraries, newspaper offices, billiard halls and bars. They burned cinemas and cafés, closed liquor stores, and ran intimidation campaigns in the community and on the university campus. The apparent indifference of the Israeli authorities to such violence was noted. 'Israel turned a blind eye to distribution of Mujamma leaflets, and it appears that the authorities also ignored its stockpiling of crude weapons,'[31] said Dr Haider Abdel Shafi.

Danny Rubinstein, a left-wing Israeli journalist, also perceived an extension of Israeli support for the Islamists in the West Bank:

> As a young journalist in the early 1970s, I joined Israel's deputy prime minister, Yigal Allon, at the dedication ceremony of the Islamic Academy in Hebron, which the Israeli military authorities even funded for more than seven years. Many graduates of this very institution became the most vicious enemies of the State of Israel. Ever since, many have accused Israel of providing the raison d'être for the Islamic religious movement – a phenomenon identical to American support for the Mujahedin in Afghanistan during the Soviet occupation.[32]

Seizing Control

Dr Eyad Sarraj, who was one of Gaza's most prominent figures, remembered the day in January 1980 when the Mujamma attacked the offices of the Palestine Red Crescent Society (PRCS), a humanitarian health-care service that is the Muslim equivalent of the Red Cross. The leaders of the Mujamma had failed to get control of the PRCS through recently contested elections to its administrative council and were incensed by rumours that the nationalists were also planning to found their own university:

> I heard shouting in the street, so I went out into the road, and it was a big Islamist demonstration, [thousands of] people with beards shouting their slogans. At the end of the demonstration was an Israeli military jeep which did not interfere. That day the Mujamma went to the Red Crescent, shouting slogans 'Liberation of Afghanistan'. I confronted one of them one day and said, 'Why the liberation of Afghanistan when Jerusalem is closer? We should liberate Jerusalem.' He said, 'No, no, you don't understand. Our problem

is not with the people of the Book. Jews are the people of the Book. Our problem is with the infidels – people who don't believe in God. These are the real enemy.

Sarraj said he later saw Brigadier General Segev, the Israeli governor, and told him: 'You are playing with fire. This could really come back to you in a violent way.' Sarraj claimed the Israeli governor reassured him: 'He said: "Don't worry, we know how to handle things. Our enemy today is the PLO."'[33]

The Mujamma mob proceeded that day to the offices of the PRCS, attacking cafés and video stores along the way. When they arrived they set fire to the building, including its library and offices. Palestinians were left shocked at the fury behind the attack and the destruction in its wake. Social control was an important dimension of the Islamists' agenda, and they came close, on occasion, to consolidating control through coercion.

At the secular-oriented al-Azhar college, Fatah fought successfully to keep the institution affiliated to the PLO through its students and faculty. But it was relatively easy for the Mujamma to establish a monopoly of power at the neighbouring Islamic University of Gaza (IUG). The ways in which the university would become Islamic were soon apparent; segregation between men and women was enforced throughout the university, in its classrooms, cafés, and library and campus areas. Strict Islamic dress codes were introduced for men and women. Opponents of the Mujamma accused it of suppressing political diversity through a climate of fear. Nationalist students and lecturers were regularly targeted for humiliation by their fellow students, the university administration and even the university's doormen and guards, who were bearded Mujamma members with a reputation for meting out violent beatings to dissenters. Activist supporters of the PLO were singled out for attack and denunciation and were publicly condemned as atheists and infidels, accused of elevating the PLO leader Yasser Arafat above Islam.

It also became common knowledge that the Mujamma had a cache of crude weapons at the university that it used in its attacks against the secularists and nationalists. For women in particular, Islamic dress implied a stricture to wear the hijab (headscarf), as well as a long *thobe* (coat). The Islamic movement established wings in the university, first for its male adherents and then later for women. Money for such dress was often made available to poor students, the cost met by pledges from overseas donors.

By 1981 the Mujamma and its supporters had succeeded in having seven out of the thirteen members of the university senate ejected or forced to tender their resignations when called to a meeting at the headquarters of the Israeli civil administration in Gaza. Many questioned why such a meeting was being held under Israeli auspices at all. One critic who alleged that the Israelis were tacitly backing the Islamists, and denounced the latter as 'collaborators and a danger to us all', was attacked and severely beaten.[34]

From the highest to the lowest employee in the university, the Mujamma's influence was increasingly apparent. Gazan journalists wrote that faith appeared to matter more than qualifications to those appointing university lecturers, and one caustic observer accused the university authorities of filling the staff 'with sheikhs rather than PhDs'. Students were often singled out for denunciation campaigns and attacks, culminating in ostracism on campus and at home. 'It reached a point where friends would stay at my house to protect me and certain members of my family would not even speak to me because they believed what Mujamma were saying about me,'[35] one student recalls. Men and women students were severely beaten or had acid thrown at them for speaking out against the Mujamma.[36]

The Islamists forced compliance by demanding that 'bad Muslims' and 'PLO agitators' return to the mosque and submit to their faith in front of the congregation. Mujamma slogans proclaimed 'An uncovered woman and Beatle-haired men will never liberate our holy places.' Every year thousands of IUG students graduated with degrees born out of a pedagogic mindset that was strictly Islamic in character. These graduates would go on to form the backbone of the Mujamma and, later, Hamas.

Mujamma activists had also joined, and attempted to dominate, many of the professional associations that substituted for formal political parties in the Gaza Strip during an era when Israel's occupation authorities denied Palestinians the right to form their own political parties. Free assembly was also strictly prohibited, unless the Mujamma was taking to the streets.

Growth

As with any other Islamic organization, it was difficult for the Mujamma to pretend that it maintained a strict separation between politics and religion. From his own home and the nearby mosque, Sheikh Yassin developed the political base to undermine the PLO-dominated power structures of Gaza.

In the years before the outbreak of the First Intifada in 1987, thousands of people had started returning to the mosque, and the Mujamma built more than a hundred new mosques to accommodate the new Muslim generation. It created an infrastructure that not only rivalled the PLO, with its reputation for building 'states within states', but often surpassed it.

Still, many in the PLO did not take the Mujamma seriously. Even Yasser Arafat's most senior lieutenants, Khalil Wazir (Abu Jihad) and Salah Khalaf (Abu Iyad), both former members of the Brotherhood, did not consider it a major threat. They and others overlooked the fact that, by 1987, the Mujamma had gained a reputation for clean and honest leadership, even if – thus far – it had held back from confronting Israel.

But by the late 1980s the Israelis themselves were beginning to realize the danger posed by the new Islamic force, fearing that the Islamists might turn their sights on Israeli targets. In 1984 they issued orders to arrest Sheikh Yassin and some of his associates. Yassin was accused of founding a military cell calling for an end to Israel's occupation. The Israeli charge sheet alleged that he had amassed weapons and explosives. Yassin was sentenced to thirteen years in prison but was released a year later as part of a prisoner exchange deal that also secured the release of PFLP–General Command detainees held by Israel.

Yassin was not allowed to return to his position as the chairman of the Mujamma. But this did not mean that he would desist from his activities. In 1986 he set up a group called *al-Majd* (Glory) to threaten and expose drug-dealers. Military wings were being grafted onto the social, and an embryonic Hamas was taking shape. But, as the proto-Hamas activists prepared their lengthy campaign to Islamize Palestinian society, little did they know that their long-term planning was about to be overtaken by events in the form of a spontaneous civil rebellion.

The First Intifada

We defend ourselves with nothing but stones while Israel rains bullets and missiles on us … and still the West calls our resistance unjustified violence.

Sheikh Ahmed Yassin[1]

In December 1987, the rains fell and a sense of gloom pervaded Palestinian towns and cities across the Israeli-occupied West Bank and Gaza Strip. Every day, thousands of Palestinian workers congregated long before daybreak to begin a commute in battered and overcrowded vans and cars to their menial jobs in Israel. Thousands of men with nothing more than a packet of cigarettes and a black plastic bag with pitta bread and olives would travel to service Israel's booming economy, while at home their wives and mothers would try and make meagre earnings stretch through yet another week of unrelenting poverty, hardship and occupation.

On 8 December, some of these workers from Gaza's Jabalia and Maghazi refugee camp were killed when the driver of an Israeli vehicle struck their cars as they returned home from a day's work. The deaths triggered the uprising the next day. When their bodies were returned to Gaza, rumours and angry rhetoric swirled around their funerals, with many convinced that the accident had in fact been deliberate because an Israeli had just been killed in Gaza, and protests broke out in the refugee camps.

'Kill us all!' taunted the young Palestinians throwing rocks at the Israeli soldiers. 'Come and kill us all or get out!' The band of several hundred at Shifa hospital in a squalid refugee district was at the center of the fiercest confrontation on the worst of seven straight days of clashes in the Israeli-occupied territories. A mosque's minaret across the street blared encouragement. 'O, you young people, go at them, don't back off!' an amplified voice cried as the youths, in a day of scattered fighting, fell back behind the walls of the hospital's courtyard.[2]

This was the birth of the Intifada, the Arabic word for 'shaking off' or 'uprising' which was soon to enter the international lexicon. The marches, protests, demonstrations, petrol bombs and stones were all directed at one target: the Israeli occupation. Preachers, many of them Mujamma loyalists, joined the fray, insisting that it was a religious duty to avenge the men's deaths. From funeral to funeral, the prayers of mourners and imams contained calls for revenge on Israeli soldiers.

Within days of the accident, thousands of Palestinians had taken to the streets from refugee camps, cities, towns and the smallest hamlets to hurl rocks and stones at Israeli soldiers and border guards. Tyres were set on fire, their black acrid smoke creating a pall in the sky. The crowds used anything to build barricades – rubbish skips, old bicycles, boulders and oil drums – to stop Israeli soldiers breaking up demonstrations.

It appeared as if one mighty force was uniting the Palestinians, their desire to bring the Israeli occupation to an end through an unprecedented campaign of mass rebellion and civil disobedience. Thousands took to the streets, closed their shops, stayed away from work and scrawled graffiti condemning the 'Zionists' and urging the people to join in the Intifada.

Initially taken by surprise, the PLO leadership hundreds of miles away in Tunis quickly moved to harness that anger. Arafat and his lieutenants supported the creation of the PLO-led United National Leadership of the Uprising (UNLU). The Islamists also reorganized – by creating Hamas. The founders included Sheikh Yassin, Dr Abdel Aziz Rantissi, Dr Mahmoud Zahar, Musa Abu Marzouq, Ismail Abu Shanab, Salah Shehadeh, Ibrahim al-Yazuri, Issa al-Nashar and Abdel Fattah al-Dukhan.

By 23 December, twenty-one Palestinians had been killed and 158 wounded, while, according to Israeli officials, thirty-one Israeli soldiers and border guards had been wounded.[3] The Israelis admitted that they were taken by surprise. 'I think the situation has come as an unexpected flood. I don't think someone organized it, and predicted it, and wrote – as they say – a scenario: You'll do this, and I'll do that. I think that most of the difficulties encountered were due to the uncontrolled and unexpected nature of this event,'[4] said Shimon Peres, the vice premier and foreign minister in Yitzhak Shamir's government.

Israel's defense minister, Yitzhak Rabin, was visiting the United States and returned to deal with the crisis. He provoked international controversy with what became known as his 'iron fist'[5] policy, saying in the opening weeks of the uprising that 'the first priority is to use force, might, beatings' to restore order.[6] 'The PLO terrorist organizations and activists in the territories seized on this wave of events and did everything they could, both inside and outside the territories, in order to heighten and intensify the events,' he told members of the Israeli parliament – the Knesset.[7]

The Israeli cabinet moved to counter the worldwide criticism, which provoked domestic and international headlines such as 'The week of the sticks', 'Israel's new violent tactic takes toll on both sides' and 'Israelis worry about their image.'[8] Rabin defended the conduct of Israeli soldiers, saying that Israel had to protect its 'military rule' in Gaza and the West Bank 'with all the means at our disposal within the framework of the law', including curfews, closures, 'deportation and administrative detention against the inciters and the organizers', tear gas and rubber bullets.

Soldiers were permitted 'to fire with the intention of wounding those leading the riots and throwing petrol bombs, initially at their legs, as far as[9] this is possible, and this only after shots in the air have also failed to disperse the rioters.' Some of the legislation relied on defence emergency regulations left over from the British Mandate.

Avner Cohen, then an adviser to the Israeli military authorities on Palestinian religious affairs, recalls the urgency of the mood: 'He gathered everyone together for a meeting and said: "This Intifada, what tanks and warplanes couldn't do to us, women demonstrating and stones did, because the world cannot tolerate seeing these demonstrations."'[10]

It was the opening move in a power struggle that was to continue and escalate over decades. But, at the time, Hamas was preoccupied not with long-term issues but with challenging the PLO for control of the Intifada. It made it clear almost from the outset that it saw itself as the embodiment of the Muslim Brotherhood in Palestinian form and, first and foremost, as an Islamic organization. Communiqué number 3 issued by Hamas stated the objectives of the new group:

> Here is the voice of Islam, the voice of the Palestinian people in the West Bank, Gaza Strip and the rest of the Palestinian land. Here is the voice of an erupting volcano … Objectives (short-term) – liberate the prisoners, reject colonialism, political exile and administrative detention, the barbaric practices against our civilian population and prisoners, the political ban on travel and harassment, the disgraceful expansionism, the corruption, subordination … end to all the taxes to the abominable occupation and all their supporters.
>
> Objectives (long-term) – reject negotiated solutions, break with the deviations of Camp David, reject proposals for autonomy, reject the idea of an international conference, open the way for a permanent end to the occupation and liberate the homeland and the places of our holy saints which have been sullied and subject to profanity … To achieve these efforts the people must redouble their activity.[11]

49

This linkage alarmed many in the nationalist camp, who saw such a move as undermining the Palestinian cause by provoking fissures. Many in the newly created UNLU saw Hamas's rival activities as placing an untenable burden on a society engaged in a mass rebellion against a well-armed state.

Hamas quickly established an organizational framework of activists that made it difficult for the UNLU to challenge it. Drawing on the grassroots network it had prepared over years, it established a credible profile for itself in the early months of the Intifada. But it was also careful to insist that it regarded the Intifada as a Muslim rebellion against the occupiers: 'The Islamic Resistance Movement is the Palestinian national resistance movement, and we fight for Palestinian rights … our resistance is against the occupation of our country,' said one of its early prominent figures, Musa Abu Marzouq.[12] One of its early communiqués declared:

> At this time the Islamic uprising has been intensified in the occupied terri-tories. In all the villages, all the refugee camps our martyrs have fallen … But they have died in the name of Allah and their cries are those of victory … In the name of Allah, Allah is Great … Death to the occupation.[13]

Hamas was relatively free from Israeli interference in the early days of the Intifada. Its leaders and members were largely untroubled by Israeli prohibi-tions, arrest campaigns, deportation or imprisonment without trial. Israeli soldiers did not at first raid its secret printing presses or committee offices or break up its political, military and intelligence cells, so Hamas continued to grow and to define its Islamic message to the Palestinian people. In an age before electronic and social media, Mahmoud Musleh was one of the organizers of the Hamas communiqués in the West Bank. 'I used to write the communiqué and then, through an underground network of people throughout the West Bank, we would print and distribute it once a month.' He claims that poor Israeli intelligence meant that they avoided arrest and detention: 'It was difficult for the Israelis to find us, and it was only through later security breaches that they then made arrests.'[14]

By the summer of 1988 Hamas had issued its covenant – a charter to rival that of the PLO – and in leaflets distributed clandestinely on the streets claimed the Intifada as an Islamic possession: 'We are with every person who truly works for the liberation of Palestine, the whole of Palestine. We will continue to have faith in Allah and his power.'[15]

Secular national activists regarded Hamas and its agenda with suspicion, despite some close personal friendships. Bashir Barghouti, a West Bank Intifada organizer, argued that the Islamist leaders 'were strong characters, charismatic and good orators,' but he dismissed them as having 'no history of addressing Palestinian issues'.[16]

By August 1988 there were disputes between Hamas and the secular nationalists. Israel's policy of mass arrests to quell the Intifada resulted in tens of thousands of Palestinians ending up in prisons or in hastily erected 'prison camps', as the Israelis swept through the occupied territories, hoping that by detaining enough Palestinians they could end the Intifada. Once inside jail, the Palestinians organized themselves into the same structures as on the outside. Tensions erupted over Hamas leaflets, which called for separate strike days. Matters worsened when Hamas published its covenant in August 1988. 'In it we read statements against the PLO ... The nationalist factions decided to take a unilateral action against Hamas in the [prison] camp and stop all coordination with them,' recalls one ex-prisoner.[17] As more Hamas prisoners began to arrive in the 1990s, fights often broke out between the different factions.

For a disempowered people, the withdrawal of labour and the closure of shops, offices, factories, schools and universities were acts of mass defiance that symbolized Palestinian unity. Strikes were a defining feature of the First Intifada; they regulated the uprising, punctuating the months and years of protest with 'days of rage', 'days of mourning', 'solidarity with the prisoners', and the commemoration of key events in Palestinian history, such as the *Nakbah*, the founding of the PLO, May Day, Women's Day and later dates commemorating the death of key Palestinian figures killed in the Intifada.

Although they often hurt Palestinians more than the Israelis against whom they were directed, the strikes assumed a potent symbolism in the Intifada. They were non-violent protests and involved everyone: schoolchildren, farmers, merchants, shopkeepers, public and private sector employees, and students.

Hamas understood that leadership of the Intifada lay in organizing and enforcing strikes, and by the late summer of 1988 it was calling its own stoppages. Hamas supporters enforced them by attacking shops that remained open, beating up drivers who broke the traffic embargo and throwing Molotov cocktails at political rivals, leading to clashes in PLO strongholds such as Ramallah.[18]

Nationalists appealed to Hamas leaders to avoid an escalation of internal conflict and urged it to 'place national interest above their factional concerns. However, Hamas had other ideas, spelled out in its covenant. This criticized the PLO for accepting UN resolutions 181, 242 and 338, which in effect accepted a two-state solution to the conflict with Israel and, in so doing, abandoned the goal still proposed by Hamas: liberating all of Palestine.

Friend or Foe?

As the Intifada wore on through 1988 and 1989, Hamas's popular support base grew in both the Gaza Strip and the West Bank. Its penetration in the latter was unprecedented and disturbing for many nationalists. One key factor was Israel. Initially the Hamas–Israel connection was a legacy of the relationship that had developed between the Israeli authorities and the Mujamma in the late 1970s and the 1980s. Even pro-Islamic newspapers complained about Hamas's links to Israel. 'For all the anti-Israeli rhetoric', opined one editorial, 'its [Hamas] efforts were dissipated in infighting rather than against the common enemy.' As one source asserted: 'The Israelis essentially followed the same policy towards Hamas as they followed against the Mujamma earlier: not suppressing it in the hope that it would distract young Palestinians from supporting more dangerous groups.'[19]

Hamas's leaders publicly identified Israel and its occupation of the West Bank and Gaza as a primary cause of Palestinian woes. Yet they were also finding it difficult to break their ties with the Israeli authorities which had, at a minimum, benignly supported them during the Islamists' early revivalist campaigns in Gaza. Early on, Israel also extended legitimacy and, therefore, a form of recognition to Hamas by meeting with its leadership, including founding members such as Dr Mahmoud Zahar. Hamas leaders reciprocated by remaining in communication with the Israeli political leadership – in turn extending a form of recognition to the Jewish state at a time when their secular nationalist rivals were refusing to recognize it.

During this initial period, from 1987 to the early 1990s, Hamas held back from launching attacks on targets in Israel proper, limiting itself largely to military targets or Jewish settlers in the occupied territories.

However, in its public rhetoric it continued to complain bitterly about the 'Zionist' entity and called on its supporters to wage jihad for Palestinian freedom. By the second year of the Intifada, Hamas's leadership recognized that its links to Israel were becoming a hindrance to the movement. By this point, however, the relationship was at its strongest.

Israel regarded Hamas as a convenient foil to the PLO, and Hamas exploited this. The large amounts of money that were flowing into Hamas's coffers from Muslim supporters abroad were ignored by the Israeli authorities, while those same authorities did everything they could to stem the dollars heading to the PLO. Israeli officials involved in the administration of the West Bank and Gaza Strip still maintained contacts with the Islamic activists of the Mujamma who were now heading Hamas. In the Gaza Strip,

Hamas leaders were able to keep Palestinian schools open when the Israeli authorities were closing them in the West Bank.

In March 1988, three months into the uprising, Dr Mahmoud Zahar was meeting with Israel's political establishment and speaking the language of negotiations. As he said in an interview two years later:

When I met with Shimon Peres on 23 March 1988 we put our proposal to him. It consisted of the following: a call for Israeli withdrawal from the 1967 territories, put the occupied territories under a neutral side, choose our representatives by our own methods, elected by us. Everything should be on the agenda, and we should even discuss Israel's existence and the right of return.

Zahar insisted that Hamas had nothing against Jews as such, but saw for them only a politically subservient role in Palestine. 'We are not anti-Jewish ... we accept Jews under the Islamic umbrella. But never a secular state. We want an Islamic state.'[20]

The same year that Zahar met Peres, he was also widely reported to have met Rabin to discuss a solution to the conflict. Sheikh Yassin also indicated at this stage that Hamas was not averse to entering into dialogue with Israel so long as Israel was prepared to recognize Hamas and its demand for Palestinian rights.

Rabin confirmed that both he and Shamir had met with Palestinians from 'the territories'. He defended the contacts, saying they provided a promising alternative 'address' for future negotiations, giving Israel other options from the neighbouring Arab countries, which had long sought to control Palestinian affairs, and the exiled Arafat-led PLO leadership, which was still – at that point – anathema to Israel. Rabin told Israeli television in 1989:

I have met with figures spanning the entire conceptual spectrum existing in the territories, from Islamic fundamentalists to very moderate individuals, all shades of the spectrum were present at the talks, including those who had been detained for many months. I still believe that it is indeed possible to realize the peace initiative directed at one address: the Palestinian residents in the territories. For the first time since 15 May 1948 the Palestinians in the territories are the ones leading the struggle for the fate and future of the territories and the Palestinians.[21]

Israel and Hamas both calculated that their enemy's enemy was their friend. Raanan Gissin, a former media adviser to Ariel Sharon, was frank about the Israeli political establishment's pursuit of what he termed a 'divide and conquer' strategy during this era:

> The broad consensus was that here is a religious movement that has great sway among the public and could actually, because of its animosity to Fatah, because of its policy of opposing the corruption of Fatah and all those manifestations of Fatah people taking money for their pocket, could serve a useful purpose in weakening the strength of Fatah on the street. That would benefit Israel in its struggle against Fatah. We are talking about before Oslo. The major leading terrorist group was Fatah. Statistically speaking, or in any way you look at it, they were responsible for the major terrorist attacks; they had the most sophisticated and largest terrorist organization. [Hamas] at that time was not involved in terrorist activity, didn't even have a military arm ... Later, when they started developing their military arm, I think the Shabak [Shin Bet] was the first one to point out the change in their policy, or the fact that they were actually now becoming a terrorist organization.[22]

The difference in emphasis is significant. While Yitzhak Rabin, a future architect of the Oslo Accords, talked of political progress by encouraging those who 'desire to transfer the solution from the conflict in the street to the negotiations table', the Israeli right viewed it in security terms, stressing the need to neutralize Arafat. However, there were warning voices cautioning that Israel could one day suffer from its tacit – at best – encouragement of the Islamists. This was a phenomenon that the Americans were to term 'blowback' when, later, the CIA channelled money and weapons to Usama bin Laden and other mujahidin fighting the Soviet Union in Afghanistan, only to see their former proxies turn against them.

Avner Cohen, the former Israeli adviser on Palestinian religious affairs in the 1980s and early 1990s, said that in June 1984 – a full three years before the Mujamma metastasized into Hamas – he was already becoming concerned about reports that Yassin's Islamists were using mosques to store weapons, train fighters and incite against Jews. Cohen says he sent a letter to the then head of the Israeli civil administration and security forces headlined 'A survey of mosques in the Gaza Strip area'. One copy, which he kept at his home in a small Israeli *moshav* within Hamas missile-firing range of Gaza, reads: 'If we keep covering our eyes or continue with our forgiving attitude to *al-Mujamma' al-Islami* it might go against us in the future, therefore I recommend that we focus our efforts on looking for ways to break up this golem before reality blows up in our faces.'

Cohen said that he was made even more nervous ahead of the Intifada by a meeting with prominent Palestinians in Gaza, including one former director of the Islamic University of Gaza who, he recalls,

> earned huge applause from the Palestinian audience when he stood up and told the meeting: 'The Jewish ruler who is living among us, he is the last to know what is happening in his own kingdom. He is behaving like a deaf man at a wedding.' We were so innocent: most of the Mujamma were refugees and we thought that we could create an alternative leadership to the PLO. They warned us, the hard days are coming, and this was before the Intifada. A week later I received a telephone call from Ahmed Yassin's gang. They told me, 'If you don't stop causing trouble for Sheikh Yassin, you will be killing yourself.'[23]

However, other veteran Israeli officials have different perceptions and analyses of events. Brigadier General Shalom Harari, a former senior adviser on Palestinian affairs for Israel's Defense Ministry, insisted in 2007 that Israel 'never backed' Hamas. 'The only thing that you can accuse it of is that it started to treat it too late,' said Harari, who long warned that the Islamists' underlying popular support was greater than showed up in opinion polls and political studies. 'The rise of the Muslim Brotherhood here and there, in Syria and Jordan, is an overall Middle East process,' he said.

> I am not saying that Israel hasn't influenced it here and there in the margins. But generally this is an overall rise, after the fall of Arab Nasserism and other dreams that the Arab world had. And every country around us fights the Muslim Brotherhood in their own way. Jordan in its own way, hot and cold. Egypt in its own way, hot and cold. Israel in its own way.[24]

The Israelis' relationship with Hamas changed abruptly when in 1989 Hamas murdered two Israeli soldiers, Avi Sasportas and Ilan Saadon. Sasportas was kidnapped in February 1989 and his body lay undiscovered for several months. Saadon was kidnapped and murdered in May 1989 by the same Hamas cell, and his remains were not recovered until seven years later, when the Israelis received information from Yasser Arafat's security officials in the newly created Palestinian Authority.

The killings were a turning point for Israel. It rounded up more than 300 Hamas supporters, Sheikh Yassin and Zahar among them, and declared that the Israeli authorities which administered the West Bank and Gaza would cease all contacts with the organization. By the end of the year Israel had declared membership of Hamas a punishable offence.

In January 1990 Sheikh Yassin was put on trial in Israel charged with fifteen offences, including 'the organization of attacks on civilians and causing the deaths of two soldiers'. In court Yassin denied the charge, while the mother of Saadon, whose remains were then still missing, cursed him, saying, 'God will pay him back ... He knows where my boy is. I don't even have a grave to weep at.'[25]

The arrest, imprisonment and deportation of the Hamas leadership was designed to have a deterrent effect, to demoralize Hamas's supporters and to weaken its chain of command. But while Sheikh Yassin remained in prison awaiting trial, other senior cadres in the movement were released by the Israelis, allowing them to play a part in organizing against their rivals in the PLO. As support for the movement increased, Hamas strengthened its activities on university campuses among the students, in professional associations, among the educated middle classes and in its charitable activities. Still the secular nationalists remained disparaging and failed to take the Hamas threat seriously. Another prominent figure in Gaza offered the following perspective: 'I don't feel threatened by these fanatics [Hamas]. They are like a small cloud passing through a summer sky.'[26]

Hamas, well aware of the hostility, countered by stepping up its campaign against Fatah and by seeking alliances with its old enemies on the Palestinian left. By contrast, the tension between Hamas and Fatah was far more deep-seated. Newspaper headlines carried daily reports of Fatah activists being attacked and wounded by 'masked fundamentalists ... motivated by political and personal grudges'.

The relationship went from bad to worse over the following years, as Hamas and secular nationalist leaders clashed over the direction of the Intifada, its organization, the demands being placed on the Palestinian people and whether there should be negotiations with Israel. In private, Hamas leaders regaled listeners with tales of PLO excesses, their disgust palpable despite the public rhetoric of being 'brothers' in the national struggle. The PLO, for its part, saw Hamas as lackeys of Israel or as a passing phenomenon.

In 1990, Saddam Hussein's invasion and occupation of the oil-rich state of Kuwait had far-reaching consequences for the Palestinians. Yasser Arafat supported the Iraqi dictator, while Hamas condemned the invasion. It quickly became evident that the PLO leader had made a major strategic blunder, delighting the Palestinian street at the cost of alienating much of the Gulf, where the PLO had enjoyed the generosity of wealthy Arab rulers sympathetic to the Palestinian cause.

Hamas was far more attuned to the mood of its Gulf donors, who funded many of its social and welfare projects, and who were greatly alarmed by Saddam's expansionism. The reverberations of the Gulf War also had a significant impact on the Intifada. After the war, the US president, George H. W. Bush, announced a new peace initiative for the Middle East, which brought Israel and the Arabs to the negotiating table in October 1990 in the Spanish capital of Madrid. The talks were the first in which Israel negotiated with Syria, Jordan and a delegation of Palestinian representatives, who were the PLO in all but name.

The PLO, having chosen the wrong side during the war, was also losing its superpower patron with the collapse of the Soviet Union, so it had little choice but to go with the emerging international consensus on the need for a peace process. The Bush administration, in its strategic rethink and vision for a New World Order, considered the resolution of the Arab–Israeli conflict key to the stability of the Middle East.

Hamas was not as constrained as the PLO. It denounced the Madrid process. When the rounds of talks hit the inevitable obstacles, Hamas railed from the sidelines, launched attacks on Israeli targets and employed other strategies to derail the peace process.

Some secular nationalists believed that a policy of co-opting Hamas into Palestinian national political institutions might dissuade them from attacking the Madrid process, and in August 1991 Hamas's leadership was offered the chance to be integrated into the Palestine National Council, the 'legislative' body that elects members to the PLO's all-powerful central committee. Hamas consented, but then imposed conditions which it knew the PLO could not accept. 'We told them that the price for entry would be at least 40 per cent of the seats of the PNC and that recognition of Israel would not occur,' stated Dr Mahmoud Zahar, reversing the position he had taken four years earlier when he told Shimon Peres that Israel's right to exist was on the table. Unable to neutralize Hamas by absorbing it into the political mainstream, Palestinian secular nationalists felt they were left with no choice but to continue confronting it on the street.

This caused no little satisfaction to Hamas. 'There have been years of success for us ... we came as kittens and now we have emerged as lions,' said Zahar. 'We are bringing the message of jihad to the people here and winning the war against our enemies in Israel too.'[27] The lion's 'roar' came from the newly created armed wing of Hamas – the Qassam Brigades.

Kidnap and Deportation

Late in 1992, Hamas tried to seize the initiative with Israel. In December that year it kidnapped a border officer from an Israeli town across the Green Line that divides Israel from the Palestinian Territories it occupied in 1967. A ransom note demanded the release of Sheikh Yassin from prison. Israel refused, and when the body of the kidnapped officer was discovered a few days later there was widespread outrage across Israel.

Many Israelis, particularly those on the right wing and within the settler movement, demanded definitive action against Hamas. Retribution was swift. Israeli troops stormed Hamas and Islamic Jihad offices, homes and institutions throughout the West Bank and Gaza Strip and rounded up some 400 men. The detainees were unceremoniously deported and dumped on a snowy hillside in south Lebanon, which was then under Israeli occupation. Human rights organizations condemned the act as a mass deportation and a major violation of international law. One of those deportees recounted the events:

> It was very late at night. They took us on a bus and then another, but we were blindfolded and had no idea of our journey's end. Of course our hands and feet were in plastic cuffs and there was no possibility of escape. After some hours they told us that our fate would soon be decided on the order of the Israeli court. There was more than one bus and we realized that there were many hundreds of us. It felt like a *Nakbah* all over again.
>
> The soldiers were jeering and shouting at us and then when we crossed the border they put us on open trucks and through the Lebanese checkpoint at Marj al-Zahour ['Meadow of Flowers']. It was very cold, and then we had to walk, and they started firing their guns to make us go faster. When we arrived it was like the destination of nothing and no return. It was snowing and there were just some tents with water coming in from many holes in them. We lived like natives, walking to find wood for our fires and only getting food from people in the villages nearby.[28]

Amid international censure over the illegal deportations, Yitzhak Rabin, by then elevated to prime minister, remained defiant. 'This government will fight any manifestation of violence and terror, and will not permit, and will not allow either Hamas or Islamic Jihad to harm citizens of the State of Israel, and it will take all … steps at its disposal to battle murderous terrorist organizations,' he said. The statement was tantamount to a declaration of war on Hamas: 'to battle to the end against terror … to temporarily remove from the occupied territories Hamas ... who nourish the flames of terror.'[29] Israel by now knew what it was dealing with.

But Hamas was unrepentant. In the wake of the deportations it enjoyed unprecedented popularity and recognition among Palestinians and across the Middle East, and it became the new cause célèbre of the international Islamist movement. The PLO was forced, as the official representatives of all Palestinians, to halt peace talks with Israel in protest and to champion the cause of the Hamas leaders on the hilltop. Thousands of Palestinians protested at the deportations, while Hamas leaders held television audiences in thrall as they declared their unbending dedication to jihad against Israel.

Dr Abdel Aziz Rantissi, one of the movement's co-founders, acted as the deportees' spokesman. As they were filmed huddled around the campfires outside their tents, he declared that Hamas had only been strengthened. 'The movement has achieved great benefits after the deportation. It emerged from being a local and regional movement into an international movement ... Therefore we now find that public opinion in Palestine is in full harmony with the stand of Hamas,' he proclaimed.[30]

The practice of deportation has long been a practice by state powers to neutralize the threat of terrorism. This was not the first time, nor would it be the last, that Israel would rely on this counterinsurgency measure. The deportations, however, did not stop Hamas's attacks or eradicate the movement. By the spring of 1993, Israel was in the midst of a wave of Hamas violence. Settlers, soldiers and civilians alike were all targeted in lethal attacks. The Israeli approach had backfired; there was no deterrence, and no end in sight to what now appeared to be the inexorable rise of Hamas.

Peace and Politics

However, the area in which Hamas appeared to be out of step with the very Palestinians that it claimed to represent was the issue of peace negotiations and settlement of the conflict with Israel. Although they were not initially a declared goal of the Intifada, the logic of the Palestinian demands for statehood and an end to occupation was negotiations. The PLO leadership had quickly determined that the Intifada created a unique opportunity to press for the realization of Palestinian demands for freedom – the international community was increasingly sympathetic and the resolution of the conflict through an unarmed uprising appeared to be the way to achieve their ends. This meant that the PLO's historic pledge to liberate Palestine through armed struggle would have to be abandoned in favour of negotiation.

Yasser Arafat had always kept his options open when faced with a choice between armed struggle and peace. In 1974 he famously addressed the United Nations General Assembly while wearing an empty gun holster and telling them: 'Today I have come bearing an olive branch and a freedom fighter's gun. Do not let the olive branch fall from my hand.'[31]

The PLO – now bereft of its wealthy Gulf patrons – was nearing financial collapse, Hamas was gaining a foothold among Palestinians in the West Bank and Gaza Strip, and pressure was building for some kind of tangible reward for the huge sacrifices they were making in the daily confrontations, campaigns of civil disobedience and demonstrations against Israel. Palestinian public opinion, and many on the Israeli side, favoured peace negotiations that could be based upon the formula of a two-state solution.

When the PLO bowed to the inevitable and entered peace talks with Israel, Hamas reacted with fury. It condemned the PLO as traitors to the cause, opening up a public rift. Hamas issued countless leaflets denouncing the 1991 Madrid talks and the subsequent rounds of negotiations. It urged instead an escalation of the Intifada and continuation of the armed struggle against Israel.

As pro-peace rallies in the Palestinian city of Ramallah featured Palestinians and Israelis standing beneath banners reading 'TWO PEOPLES SPEAK PEACE', a few miles down the road in Nablus Hamas organized an even bigger rally against Madrid. In leaflets, speeches and Friday sermons, Hamas leaders assailed the talks as 'a heresy that will lead to the surrender of Muslim lands to Jews'. When Palestinian negotiators returned to address public meetings and rallies, Hamas activists pelted them with stones and bottles and broke up the meetings.

Among the most prominent in the Madrid talks process was Dr Mahmoud Zahar. A thyroid surgeon by profession – and Sheikh Yassin's personal physician – the pugnacious Zahar would often use medical metaphors to make political points: Israel referred to as a 'cancer'; the 'illness' of Palestinian society can only be treated by 'inoculation' according to Islamic 'prescription'; and 'radical surgery' is often the prescribed Zahar remedy for political problems.

Gazan-born and Egyptian-educated, Zahar is one of the most formidable leaders of the Palestinian Islamic movement. He has survived Israeli assassination attempts which killed and wounded members of his immediate family. A co-founder of Hamas, he was vehemently opposed to peace negotiations with Israel but has never been confounded by the high art of pragmatic politics. He is also a veteran of the clashes between the Islamists and secular nationalists. In 1995 he complained that, while the attention of the world was focused on the peace talks, the PLO was taking the opportunity to launch attacks and 'make provocations' in Hamas strongholds such as Rafah to weaken the movement at a time when it, like everyone else, faced increased curfews, arrests and other collective punishments. 'But we'll defend ourselves against Israel and the PLO,' Zahar declared. 'We will stand strong and not weak.'[32]

Frustrated and increasingly marginalized by the peace process, Hamas set about trying to derail it.

Oslo and Collapse

The problem is that we have reduced the issue from one of sacred liberation to merely a dream of independence, a dream that a Palestinian policeman will organize traffic.

Musa Abu Marzouq[1]

'The peace of the brave', proclaimed newspaper headlines across the world, as two old enemies stood on the White House lawn shaking hands. The Oslo Accords were hailed as the curtain-raiser for a final peace agreement between Israel and the Palestinians.

While Israel's prime minister, Yitzhak Rabin, and the PLO leader, Yasser Arafat, stood before cheering crowds in Washington on 13 September 1993, their host, President Bill Clinton, told the assembled dignitaries: 'A peace of the brave is within our reach. Throughout the Middle East there is a great yearning for the quiet miracle of a normal life. We know a difficult road lies ahead. Every peace has its enemies, those who still prefer the easy habits of hatred to the hard labors of reconciliation.'[2]

In a move that completely outflanked Hamas, the PLO promised to recognize Israel and renounce violence. In return, Israel would grant Palestinian autonomy in parts of the West Bank and Gaza Strip. The most difficult issues, including Jewish settlements in the West Bank and Gaza Strip, borders, Jerusalem, and the internationally recognized right of return for Palestinian refugees, would be left for final status negotiations. With the signing of the Oslo Accords it appeared that peace-making would deliver real dividends: freedom, prosperity and eventual statehood for the Palestinians; recognition, security and prosperity for Israel.

The horizons were further expanded when King Hussein of Jordan signed a peace treaty with Israel in 1994. Even *Sesame Street* was illuminated in the glow of improving Israeli–Palestinian relations, with special episodes of the children's programme featuring Big Bird and other multicoloured puppet characters promoting peace, education and fun. Hundreds of young people from both sides of the conflict were invited to encounter groups and to attend joint theatre productions of *Romeo and Juliet* by Israeli and Palestinian actors.

Despite the difficulties, such events revealed a sizeable pro-peace constituency. Within a year of the Oslo agreement, Arafat and his PLO staged a 'triumphant' return to Gaza to begin laying the foundations of what they thought would become a Palestinian state. But the overcrowded coastal strip was a cold dose of reality for the optimists. Just 139 square miles in area, it was dominated by nearly a million 1948 refugees and their descendants, who for decades had dreamt not of building a state there but of returning to their homes in Jaffa, Al-Majdal (Ashkelon) and Beersheba – all of which now lay within the modern state of Israel.

One of Arafat's greatest challenges would be to unite his own movement and deal with critics who were already condemning the deal before the ink was dry. Furthermore, there were aspects of the new agreement with the Israelis which, upon closer scrutiny, caused concerns not just among the usual rejectionists. On the Palestinian side, respected national figures such as the writer and academic Edward Said publicly complained that Arafat had capitulated by signing up to the Palestinian equivalent of the 1919 Treaty of Versailles, a surrender that a defeated party had no choice but to accept. Other critics argued that the agreement would store up dangerous levels of resentment for the future, as Versailles had with the defeated Germans. Yet perhaps the most vocal of Palestinian detractors – the 'enemies' referred to by President Clinton – was Hamas. 'Proceeding from our awareness of our enemy's nature and in accordance with the teachings of our great Islam, we have declared a relentless war,' said a Hamas statement released after the agreement.[3]

Hamas insisted that its opposition was not based on its desire to be declared a 'partner for peace', or because it wanted to enjoy American support and Israeli recognition, but because it believed the deal was a poor one for Palestinians living under occupation, denied statehood and living as refugees across the globe. 'We need a peace process, not a security arrangement,' complained Dr Mahmoud Zahar in 1995. Pointing to a map of the Gaza Strip, he fulminated: 'They are still controlling the crossings, preventing pilgrimage. Every day they harass people who search for work ... This is not a peace process ... this is still occupation.'

Hamas leaders such as Zahar believed that the PLO had sold out the Palestinians, particularly those who had made huge sacrifices during the Intifada. 'We suffered under occupation,' opined Zahar. 'We lost hundreds of our youth ... and financially the Gaza Strip is still suffering from the occupation. We do not enjoy this occupation and so we are still looking to eliminate it.'[4]

Aside from its publicly enunciated reasons, the Hamas leadership was angered at being excluded from the Oslo process, seeing that Arafat had immeasurably strengthened its domestic position. The PLO was now the official 'partner for peace'; it enjoyed American support and recognition and was at the helm of a project that would attract hundreds of millions of dollars in foreign aid. Yasser Arafat acquired the status of an international leader on the global stage. In 1994, along with Shimon Peres and Yitzhak Rabin, he was awarded the Nobel Peace Prize.

Nevertheless, Hamas leaders complained that Oslo was a chimera. A Hamas communiqué declared: 'This agreement is just a different face of the occupation.'[5] The split over Oslo clarified the internal Palestinian battle lines, pitting Hamas and Fatah against each other again with two very different visions of the future. 'We and the Tunis group [PLO]', announced one Hamas leader, 'are now competing for the hearts and minds of the average Palestinian.'[6]

But, for once, Hamas was badly out of kilter with popular sentiment, which favoured a peace settlement. The Palestinian street was growing weary of the daily struggle of life under unrelenting illegal occupation. The Oslo Accords, with the promise of initial autonomy and negotiations for a final peace settlement, was what the majority of Palestinians had hoped their struggle would deliver.

Acting as spoiler, Hamas launched coordinated attacks against Israeli targets on the eve of the White House signing ceremony. It also called on all Palestinians in the West Bank and Gaza Strip to participate in a comprehensive strike to 'protest the signing of the accord of humiliation and disgrace'.[7] It continued to maintain that only through armed struggle, resistance and jihad could the goal of liberating all of historic Palestine be achieved.

Rejecting Oslo

Hamas also rejected Oslo because it appeared to set the parameters of any future Palestinian state. 'The problem is that we have reduced the issue from one of sacred liberation to merely a dream of independence, a dream that a Palestinian policeman will organize traffic,' said Musa Abu Marzouq, then head of Hamas's Political Bureau. 'We have diminished the Palestinian cause to a very simple thing.'[8]

Musa Abu Marzouq's opinion counts in Hamas. Born in Rafah refugee camp in southern Gaza in 1951, he was a follower of the Muslim Brotherhood. He studied engineering in Egypt, where he was actively involved in student politics, and completed his studies in the US, where he lived for more than a decade until the early 1990s. Urbane, cosmopolitan and a fluent English speaker, he played a pivotal role in the movement almost from its inception and was a lynchpin in the development of Hamas outside the Palestinian Territories, believing that its leadership needed both an internal and an external dimension. Veteran Hamas leaders say it was Abu Marzouq who travelled to Gaza in 1989 to oversee the reorganization of Hamas when Sheikh Yassin and hundreds of other members were jailed. He headed the Political Bureau for much of the 1990s, promoting Hamas abroad.

Abu Marzouq was arrested in New York in 1995 when he tried to return to the US and spent nearly two years in jail. The US courts accused him of helping to finance and organize Hamas attacks in Israel. Israel requested extradition. Abu Marzouq admitted heading Hamas's politburo but denied claims that he raised money for Hamas weapons. Israel dropped the extradition request in 1997, apparently fearing it would disrupt the peace process. The US expelled Abu Marzouq to Jordan, and he later moved to Syria, where he served as deputy to Khaled Meshaal, who had by then already taken over as leader. In 2004 a US court finally indicted him in absentia on allegations of conspiracy to finance terrorist attacks against Israel.

A year later Abu Marzouq was a key interlocutor with former CIA chiefs at a secret meeting in Lebanon to discuss Hamas and the political process. At this meeting, held in Beirut's luxurious Albergo Hotel, he was described by one former CIA senior official as the 'face of Hamas that wants to talk with Israel and progress to statehood through negotiation.'[9] He has never forgotten his roots. Moving among a group of former Western diplomats and intelligence agents in the hotel, he suddenly broke off to ask one guest to stop by his family home in Rafah and call on his sister for him.

Two years later Abu Marzouq underscored his call for negotiations with Israel in an article he wrote for *The Guardian*, emphasizing Hamas's breadth as a movement. 'Talking to Hamas is a prerequisite for any sustainable solution,' he wrote. 'It is not sufficient for Israel or its allies to continue to dismiss Hamas as "extremist", as we are made up of every part of Palestinian society.'[10]

Hamas's mistrust of Western intervention stems from its interpretation of centuries of Palestinian history. The litany of wrongs cited by its leaders stretches from the Crusaders to the Balfour Declaration of 1917 and beyond to twenty-first-century positions of UK governments and prime ministers. Tony Blair was frequently excoriated by such leaders. For Hamas, only unity beneath the banner of Islam would liberate Palestine from foreign rule, whether Crusader, British or Zionist.

Hamas also questioned the sincerity of Fatah's motives for choosing the path of Oslo. It denounced every aspect of the negotiated process with Israel and the role of the international community: the meeting place, the date of the first meeting, the choice of Palestinian representatives, the hotels and the nature of negotiations. Hamas discerned the hand of externally imposed humiliation in every aspect. From its perspective, Oslo was not a peace agreement: it failed to guarantee the legitimate and internationally recognized rights of the Palestinian people. Hamas pointed out that the Oslo Accords contained no agreement on the continuing presence and expansion of Israeli settlements in the West Bank, Gaza and East Jerusalem, in contravention of international law; they offered no right of return for Palestinian refugees and did not establish Jerusalem as a capital city for the Palestinians. Hamas complained that there was no land exchange and that Israeli redeployments were delayed.

Marginalized from mainstream Palestinian opinion, Hamas joined with secular Marxists within the Damascus-based Palestinian Alliance Force to promote themselves as the alternative to Oslo: 'We must mobilize all our efforts to confront the occupation,' read one contemporary Hamas communiqué. 'There must be a withdrawal from all negotiations and an end to the rejection of our rights, cause and future of our homeland.'[11]

By and large the call was ignored, as Palestinians attempted to enjoy the fruits of the Oslo peace and celebrated the return of their deported leaders, the release of their prisoners from Israeli jails, the reunification of families, and the return of the national leadership of the PLO, including the iconic Yasser Arafat's triumphal homecoming to Gaza in 1994. Palestinians were also encouraged by the sense of protection afforded by the newly established Palestinian security forces and Palestinian Authority (PA), which was created to administer Palestinian affairs in parts of the West Bank and Gaza. In the absence of a Palestinian state, it was the closest thing they had ever had to a government and security.

After years of death, suffering, sacrifice and occupation, the simple pleasures of life were a relief: children returned to the streets to play football and fly kites, and families flocked to parks, municipal gardens and the beach. These brief escapes from the reality of their squalid lives were seen as a respite delivered by Fatah, not Hamas. As one young resident from a refugee camp in the West Bank put it, 'Fatah are here to help us share the peace and the good time. When we need Islam is that point when our suffering returns to us from Israel's hands and to our hearts and heads.'[12]

Turning Points

Yasser Arafat never hid his attachment to Islam. 'There is one thing bigger than the Palestinian people,' he said shortly before his death – 'one thing that also unites us all and reminds us of our attachment to this land, and that is Islam.'[13] But Arafat, unlike many of his contemporaries in Fatah, had never been a member of the Muslim Brotherhood. He had tried to bring Hamas under the PLO umbrella in 1993, when he met with its leaders in the Sudanese capital, Khartoum.

The PA also acknowledged the reality that it would simply be impossible to eject Hamas from the mosques. Nevertheless, in August 1994 its police, security forces and intelligence agencies began a crackdown, calling upon members of Hamas's Qassam Brigades to surrender and hand over their weapons. Hamas activists were arrested by the Palestinian police and told that they must sign a pledge promising not to engage in any more clashes with the PA. Throughout 1994 and 1995 tensions grew and clashes erupted regularly.

Confronted by the PA, Hamas's leadership settled for other strategies, following the cautious approach advocated by Sheikh Yassin. Even hardliners such as Dr Abdel Aziz Rantissi understood the benefits of playing the long game at this critical stage in the movement's development. Faced with mass support of the PLO's peace overtures, Hamas crafted a critique of the newly created Palestinian Authority's institutions based on religion. 'You can't compare the institutions of the PLO and Islam,' asserted Dr Mahmoud Zahar, shortly before PA forces arrested him in 1995. 'In one there is corruption, bad management, violation of human rights, destruction of integrity and a failure to meet promises made to the people. In one there are representatives debauching themselves, drinking, singing, carrying on like they did in Jordan, Lebanon and Tunis. But what they forget is that this is Gaza.'[14]

Weapons were a major issue between the two sides. Until 1993, both Hamas and Fatah had controlled their own armed wings: Hamas's Qassam Brigades and the PLO's Fatah Hawks, Black Panthers and Red Eagles. But, under the Oslo Accords, Arafat formally disbanded the Fatah militias and rewarded many of their members with jobs in the newly formed official PA security services that were now at his disposal. Additionally, Arafat was allowed to bring in 7,000 members of the Palestine Liberation Army (PLA) from their bases in Jordan, Yemen and Sudan. Each was armed, and by the summer of 1995 the Palestinian Authority had tens of thousands of security forces in its areas of control.

Hamas found itself outnumbered and outgunned. Many were publicly critical of a recruitment process which, they believed, was based on 'jobs for the boys' and discriminated against Hamas in what was supposed to be a national authority. The same patronage extended to other Palestinian

Authority ministries, which scarcely bothered to hide their pro-Fatah and PLO affiliations. With hindsight, some senior PLO officials from that era now concede that it made a grave error from the outset by allowing Fatah to become so identified with the Palestinian Authority that it effectively became the executive and legislative branches of the party. 'Before 1994 the PLO in exile had a certain glow to its image, lustre. But they weren't made to build institutions. They were *fedayeen*, not statesmen,' conceded Ambassador Dr Abdelrahman Bsaiso:

> Fatah let its membership slip; people in the party felt left behind. They were disenfranchised. It neglected its basic institutions and concentrated on government. Fatah's big problem was that, when it came time to retaliate, the people wanted to punish Fatah the party, but it was interchangeable with the government. The people couldn't distinguish between Fatah the party and Fatah the government.[15]

Hamas criticized Fatah for its partisan approach to recruitment, convinced that the latter's intent was to exclude Hamas and others from the funds that were now flowing into PLO coffers from the international community – the 'peace dividend'. It told its supporters to be patient and to return to the mosque. As one senior leader, Ismail Abu Shanab, remarked, 'Our youth spent too long during the years of the Intifada throwing stones, making demonstrations and missing school. Now the Intifada in Gaza is over and it's time for the youth to return to the mosque, be educated and prepared for their role in society – there must be social reform along Islamic lines.'[16] Abu Shanab represented what became known as the 'pragmatic' wing of the Hamas leadership, moderating the influence of 'hardliners' such as Rantissi. The pragmatists always tried to signal that the organization was the repository of differing political perspectives and approaches.

Abu Shanab was a refugee, born in a village near Ashkelon in 1940, and had been one of the founders of Hamas. Like Abu Marzouq, he had studied in the US, qualifying in civil engineering. A 'bridge builder' politically, he promoted dialogue with Arafat's deputy and future successor Mahmoud Abbas (Abu Mazen) and spearheaded various rounds of intra-Palestinian dialogue. He was the first Hamas leader to promote internal debate on the possibility of a ceasefire, holding secret meetings at his home with Western interlocutors. Quietly spoken, he would engage in debate while his children played around the legs of the important visitors to his home. He was assassinated by Israel on 21 August 2003.

Fatah was more circumspect in its public criticisms of Hamas. It ensured that the official face of Islam within the Palestinian Authority was represented by senior Sunni clerics from Jerusalem's Al Aqsa Mosque and the religious courts. It also ensured that religious affairs, including *waqf* (endowments) and courts, as well as the salaries of official clergy, were removed from Jordanian hands and placed in the new Ministry of Religious Affairs. This was the official Islamic establishment of the PA.

In the contest for the political support of the Palestinian people, both Hamas and the PLO used Islam and nationalism. Both sides also sought to promote their ideology of liberation – nationalist or Islamist.

As the PA consolidated its security forces, Hamas began building up its own arsenal by smuggling weapons into Gaza through tunnels and other means. This was to facilitate its twin-pronged strategy of carrying out armed attacks against Israel and building up parallel structures of authority in Gaza to rival the PA. Hamas also began infiltrating the myriad PA security forces. Abu Islam, a leader of the Qassam Brigades, said: 'We are everywhere, but not in public, only in the shadows. And we are even inside the *sulta*'s [PA's] security.'[17] Years later these infiltrators would apply their knowledge to help break Fatah in Gaza and to create a Hamas police force and other paramilitary units.

Wreckers

The presence of Palestinian security forces did not deter Hamas from attacking Israeli targets, even after Israel carried out the first stage of withdrawing its troops – from Gaza's major Palestinian towns and from Jericho in the West Bank. The Brigades and Hamas's internal intelligence apparatus also continued punishment attacks against Palestinians accused of collaborating with Israel. The PA proved unable to stop the killings, and bodies of Palestinians began to turn up bearing the marks of summary execution. Hamas also became increasingly convinced that its weapons would prove just as useful protecting itself from the PA as from Israel.

Then suddenly the whole post-Oslo situation changed because of the actions of one Jewish settler: Baruch Goldstein. On 25 February 1994, Brooklyn-born Goldstein walked into the Ibrahimi Mosque in the West Bank town of Hebron wearing an Israeli soldier's uniform and opened fire on Palestinian worshippers as they knelt in prayer during the holy month of Ramadan, killing twenty-nine people. The mosque stood on the Tomb of the Patriarchs, reputed to be the burial site of the Old Testament Prophet Abraham, and is a site revered by Jews and Muslims alike.

In the furore that ensued, Israeli soldiers killed more Palestinians and imposed curfews. Palestinian Muslims, and Hamas in particular, questioned how such a 'massacre' – as the attack was universally described across the West Bank and Gaza – could be perpetrated by an Israeli settler while Israeli guards and soldiers were protecting the area. Yitzhak Rabin, the Israeli prime minister, launched a crackdown on extremist Jewish groups and gave a powerful speech to the Israeli parliament three days later condemning the massacre. 'I am shamed over the disgrace imposed upon us by a degenerate murderer,' he told the Knesset. 'This murderer came out of a small and marginal political context. He grew in a swamp whose murderous sources are found here, and across the sea; they are foreign to Judaism ... To him and to those like him we say: You are not part of the community of Israel.'[18]

In direct contrast to Rabin, Goldstein was an inspiration to some on Israel's far right. A young Itamar Ben Gvir, Israel's future minister for national security, was filmed calling Goldstein 'a hero' and 'righteous' and saying Arabs – as the Israeli far right invariably refers to Palestinians – should all be expelled.[19]

Less than two years later, Rabin himself was assassinated by a right-wing Israeli fanatic as he attended a peace rally in Tel Aviv. Although he was replaced by Shimon Peres, another principal architect of the Oslo peace process, the Hebron massacre and Hamas's reaction to it were landmark events in the unravelling of that process over the next decade. Hamas vowed revenge. In a communiqué entitled 'The settlers will pay for the massacre with the blood of their hearts', it said that, if Israel was indiscriminate in distinguishing between 'fighters and unarmed civilians', then Hamas would be 'forced ... to treat the Zionists in the same manner. Treating like with like is a universal principle.'[20]

After the traditional forty days of Muslim mourning, Hamas struck – but not at settlers. The target was Afula, an Israeli town a few miles north of the West Bank. On 6 April 1994, a nineteen-year-old Palestinian, Raed Zakarneh, carried out a suicide bombing there, killing eight Israelis and wounding thirty-four. At a stroke, Hamas forever altered the Israeli–Palestinian conflict. Hamas's bombing outraged Israelis. But the PLO, and Yasser Arafat personally, were also vilified by Israelis for a PLO statement that expressed 'its regrets for the incident'. Shimon Shetreet, Israel's economics minister, urged a suspension of peace talks until Arafat condemned the bombing more forcefully, and some right-wingers called for negotiations to be called off altogether. The very next day Hamas shot dead an Israeli hitch-hiking near Ashdod, and a week later – in the midst of Israel's Memorial Day and Independence Day holidays – another Hamas suicide bomber killed five Israelis on a bus in Hadera.

Although right-wing Israelis gathered at the bus station chanting 'Death to the Arabs', Prime Minister Rabin insisted that he would not let Hamas derail the seven-month-old peace deal. 'There are those who say the peace talks have to be stopped,' he said. 'What this will lead to is more elements joining in the terror. Even on Memorial Day, Jewish lives are being sacrificed in the quest for peace, a quest which we shall not abandon no matter what.'[21]

The change in strategy signalled by the suicide attacks was an ominous sign of things to come. Nothing would ever be the same again. Exploding suicide bombs inside Israel and against Israeli civilians, on a scale designed to kill as many as possible, was a deliberate assault by Hamas on the Israeli psyche. From this point onwards the wider dynamic of Israeli occupation against Palestinians would be irrevocably altered. 'We were against targeting civilians', said Musa Abu Marzouq several years later, 'but no one asked about Palestinian civilian deaths ... no one cared ... After the Hebron massacre we determined that it was time to kill Israel's civilians ... we offered to stop if Israel would, but they rejected that offer.'[22]

Many of Hamas's leaders sought to justify suicide bombings in religious terms, as 'an eye for an eye'. Dr Rantissi argued that, 'if the other side has done this, we find ourselves obligated to do the same. We are mandated by Islam – in a war situation – to do unto others as they have done unto us.'[23] Other Hamas leaders offered as justification not religion, but tactical necessity and reciprocation. 'We have done our best to target the military, not civilians,' argued Usama Hamdan in Beirut, 'But the talk of suicide bombers in Israel misses the major point – which is the occupation. All other channels have been closed to us, so we use violence.'[24]

Rabin ordered a major crackdown on Hamas and the closure of the crossing points into Israel. His government arrested more than 1,600 Islamists in the West Bank and Gaza Strip to halt the suicide attacks, and he demanded that Arafat use his new security forces to tackle Hamas. Arafat's forces duly rounded up thousands of suspects and threw them into prison, prompting Hamas to react to the dual crackdown with defiance: 'The latest insane arrests will not affect Hamas strength one bit. Rabin must understand that only when he is able to make the sun rise in the West will he be able to affect the strength of Hamas,' said one communiqué.[25]

In the eight months after the Ibrahimi Mosque attack, Hamas organized five suicide bombing missions, killing nearly forty Israelis and injuring hundreds. It both demonstrated that it had the technical and operational ability to pull off such attacks and discovered that there was no shortage of Palestinian 'martyrs' offering themselves for such missions. Palestinians had grown used to the idea of their young people being willing to die in the name of the struggle for freedom and liberation, but the notion that they would strap explosives to their bodies and throw themselves at Israeli civilians was a new development. Israel's security services also grew frustrated, as they were, at least initially, unable to infiltrate the secret cells which were organizing the bombings.

Although many were imprisoned, the attacks continued. Israeli soldiers were shot at and ambushed. In October 1994, Hamas kidnapped an Israeli soldier near Gaza, demanding the release of imprisoned Hamas leaders in return, and in October 1994 a Hamas suicide bomber killed twenty-two people aboard a busy commuter bus in Tel Aviv. The bomber, Salah Abdel Rahim Sawi, appeared in a posthumous video, declaring, 'We will continue our brave martyrdom operations. There are many young men who long to die for the sake of God.'[26]

The Israelis responded by arresting hundreds of Hamas people in raids on homes, institutions and mosques throughout the West Bank. Once again the Israelis applied intense pressure on Yasser Arafat to bring his own house to order. Israel reminded him of his obligations under the Oslo Accords to preserve Israel's security from Palestinian threats, and from Hamas and Islamic Jihad in particular. Hamas thus found itself as much at war with Arafat and his forces as with its Zionist enemy.

Gaza's PA security chief, Mohammed Dahlan, had hundreds of Hamas leaders and members arrested and interrogated. At one point Hamas leaders such as Dr Mahmoud Zahar had their beards forcibly shaved off. Speaking from his headquarters in Gaza's Saraya security compound – its name a legacy from the Turkish Ottoman era – another of Arafat's security chiefs, Nasr Yusuf, declared, 'This is not a popularity contest. The people of Hamas have to understand that they can't end the peace process with their bombs and we won't let them.'[27]

The security chiefs, however, also complained of Israeli foot-dragging over the implementation of Oslo, particularly on issues such as settlements, security coordination and troop redeployment. Jibril Rajoub, head of the PA's intelligence services in the West Bank, argued that, while the PA could contain the threat from Hamas within its jurisdiction, Israel was making it difficult to 'build a bridge of trust over a river of blood'.[28]

Dual Purpose

Hamas claimed that it carried out bombings in revenge for Israeli attacks, but it was also motivated by a determination to undermine negotiations between Israel and the PA. For this it was made to pay a heavy price by Arafat's forces.

Firstly the PA demanded that it disarm. Hamas's spokesman replied in July 1994 that 'We will not hand over our fighters' weapons and jihad will continue.'[29] When it was announced that only PA security forces would be legally permitted to carry arms, Hamas's Ibrahim Ghosheh retorted: 'As far as we are concerned, we tell the self-rule authority to go to hell. We are keeping the arms to carry out the jihad.'[30]

The situation deteriorated further after Yitzhak Rabin was assassinated in November 1995. In the subsequent elections, Peres faced a resurgent right wing led by one of the principal opponents to the Oslo process, the young and telegenic hardline Likud party leader Binyamin Netanyahu.

On both sides of the conflict there was growing disillusionment about Oslo. Palestinians saw Jewish settlements continuing to grow every year in Israeli-occupied Gaza, the West Bank and East Jerusalem, hemming in their villages and confiscating their farmland. Within their own society they also saw disturbing evidence that corrupt Palestinian Authority officials were siphoning off money. Israelis saw Palestinian bombers and gunmen on their high streets, many wondering what was the point of Oslo if it gave autonomy to a Palestinian Authority with tens of thousands of security officials who either would not, or could not, deliver safety for Israelis.

With the Israeli elections set for May, Hamas mounted a bombing campaign in early 1996. The deadliest was a suicide bombing on a bus in Jerusalem in which twenty-six people were killed. Three more bombings by Hamas and other factions brought the death toll to more than sixty, fast eroding support for Mr Peres's fragile government. Hamas claimed the attacks were revenge for Israel's assassination in January 1996 of Hamas's most notorious bomb-maker, known as Yahya 'the Engineer' Ayyash.

But two months later Palestinian television ran an interview with a jailed Hamas suspect, Mohammed Abu Warda, who said the leaders of Hamas's military wing told him that they wanted an escalation in bombings to ensure the defeat of Mr Peres's Labour Party at the hands of Mr Netanyahu's right-wing Likud. 'They thought that the military operations would work to the benefit of the Likud and against the left,' he told the watching Palestinian public. 'They wanted to destroy the political process, and they thought that, if the right succeeded, the political process would stop.'[31]

The broadcast was clearly designed to show Hamas intent on wrecking the peace process. The Israeli right was furious, accusing Arafat of stage-managing the 'confession' to boost Peres. Hamas leader Musa Abu Marzouq claimed Abu Warda's statement had been coerced. He repeated Hamas's consistent line that its military and political leaderships were 'completely separate'.[32] Netanyahu went on to win the elections, narrowly, and became Israel's new prime minister. His premiership was marked only by the most limited steps on the road to peace, and these came largely as a result of intense US pressure.

First Palestinian Elections

As the Palestinians' own January 1996 presidential and legislative elections neared – with Yasser Arafat the overwhelming favourite for president – Hamas leaders viewed Fatah's promotion of the ballot with suspicion. Some, such as Ismail Haniyeh and Ghazi Hamad, were in favour of participating, but others, including West Bank-based Bassam Jarrar, were opposed, arguing that 'participation in self-rule gives legitimacy to the peace process.'[33]

Believing that Arafat's every move had more to do with Fatah's compliance with Israeli demands than a genuine desire to bring democracy to Palestinian society, many in Hamas dismissed the elections as tainted by association with Israel. Countering this, Fatah supporters sneered that if Hamas had contested the elections it would have discovered the true measure of its support: 'They knew that even Sheikh Yassin would never be voted by the Palestinian people as the president, and they knew that they would never form a majority in the parliament, so they prefer to sit on the side and moan while we get on with the really difficult stuff,' said one Fatah supporter.[34]

Although in prison, Sheikh Yassin remained a hugely influential figure within the movement. In a series of 'letters from the cell', he urged his supporters to consider participating in elections to the PA to create an 'opposition from within' the Oslo institutions they hated so much. He also addressed the issue of peace with Israel. Yassin claimed there was a precedent for Hamas's participation in Palestinian self-rule but also made it clear that Hamas was only offering a fixed-term *hudna* (truce), during which it could participate in elections.

Haniyeh and his supporters decided to stand but were quickly persuaded by hardliners to withdraw. Public opinion polls from this period also illustrated how little popular support there was for Hamas. Only 3.2 per cent trusted Sheikh Yassin in 1996, compared with 41 per cent for Yasser Arafat.

Palestinians ignored Hamas's pleas for a boycott and turned out in unprecedented numbers. The elections were held on 20 January under Article III of the Oslo Accords, with the Palestinian Territories divided into sixteen electoral districts – eleven in the West Bank and five in the Gaza

Strip. Of 1,028,280 registered voters, turnout was 736,825, or 71.66 per cent. The presidential race was a foregone conclusion: Arafat won 88.2 per cent of the vote and was opposed by only one other candidate, Ms Samha Khalil. In the elections to the parliament – the Palestinian Legislative Council – Fatah won or controlled sixty-eight of the eighty-eight seats, giving it an insurmountable majority. Within the assembly, thirty-seven seats were from Gaza and fifty-one from the West Bank. Only five women were elected, representing 5.7 per cent of the members.

Hamas had signally failed to win the argument at a political level and prepared for several years in the wilderness, to push – for events to turn against the Oslo peace process.

Symbol and Threat

As they waited, Hamas's supporters continued to rely on its leadership to guide the movement politically and strategically. One of the most influential was Yassin, who had been imprisoned, yet again, by Israel in 1991. The circumstances of his release in October 1997 were so bizarre that they could have been taken from a bad movie script.

The chain of events began with a bungled operation by Israel's Institute for Intelligence and Special Operations, better known as Mossad, to assassinate the exiled Hamas leader Khaled Meshaal by poisoning him. Born in a village near Ramallah, Meshaal has been in exile ever since 1967 when his family left for Kuwait. He rose through the ranks of the movement, first as a student leader in Kuwait and then later through the political echelons. Astute, and famed for his calm demeanour, he was a leading light among the younger generation of Hamas leaders.

In 1997, two Mossad agents with false Canadian passports were sent to Amman in Jordan on the orders of the newly elected Netanyahu with instructions to kill Meshaal. Although they succeeded in getting close enough to spray poison on him, they were caught and taken into custody. Meshaal was rushed, critically ill, to hospital in Amman. King Hussein intervened personally, telling Netanyahu that he would get Israel's agents back only if he provided the antidote and if Yassin were freed. Humiliated, the Israelis agreed, releasing Yassin among other Palestinian and Jordanian prisoners. King Hussein was reportedly infuriated that Israel had been prepared to jeopardize their relationship in pursuit of Hamas.

When Yassin arrived at hospital in Amman he was feted by both King Hussein and Arafat. A few days later he returned by helicopter to a tumultuous welcome in Gaza, greeted by banners welcoming back the 'Sheikh of the Intifada' and pictures of him alongside the assassinated bomb-making hero Yahya Ayyash.

The drama surrounding the assassination attempt and the release of Yassin temporarily strengthened popular support for Hamas. At a press conference, Yassin declared: 'There will be no halt to armed operations until the end of the occupation ... I would address the whole world and say that we are peace-seekers. We love peace. And we call on them [the Israelis] to maintain peace with us and to help us in order to restore our rights by means of peace.' But he added: 'If these means are not available, we will never accept the occupation to remain on our shoulders.'[35]

The Second Intifada

The first intifada was the stone-throwing intifada. Now, who now believes in stones?

Jamila al-Shanti, Hamas MP[1]

For years a mosaic stood in the centre of Gaza City of a Palestinian boy confronting an Israeli soldier. The youth is armed only with a catapult. The soldier is aiming an M16 automatic rifle straight at the boy's heart. The chiselled stone fragments proclaim: 'We will not bow.' In icon and slogan there is no better insight into how the Palestinians see themselves. The stonework inverts the biblical legend of David and Goliath. For Jewish boy-king David and his sling, read Palestinian and catapult. For Goliath and his javelin of bronze, read Israeli soldier and M16. Much to Israel's frustration, this was the defining worldwide image of the First Intifada in the late 1980s: overmatched Palestinian youths hurling rocks at Israeli tanks and heavily armed soldiers. The abiding image of the Second Intifada was altogether different. Seared into the world's consciousness was the near daily sight of bloodstained Israeli buses and restaurants blown apart by Palestinian suicide bombers.

In fact the Palestinian death toll was far higher in both uprisings. What accounted for the shift in perceptions was the different nature of the Palestinians' weapons: a difference summarized by Hamas's most prominent woman politician, Jamila al-Shanti: 'The First Intifada was the stone-throwing intifada. Now, who now believes in stones?'

The immediate events which led to the outbreak of the Second Intifada – or Al Aqsa Intifada, as it also came to be known – are not in question.

On 28 September 2000, two months after US President Bill Clinton failed to broker a peace agreement between Israel and the Palestinians at Camp David, Israel's right-wing opposition leader, Ariel Sharon, went for a highly publicized walkabout in Jerusalem's Old City. He visited the site revered by Jews as Har Ha-Bayit (Temple Mount) and by Muslims as Al Aqsa or Al-Haram al-Sharif (the Noble Sanctuary).

Sharon, nicknamed 'the Bulldozer', was a hate figure like no other in his era across the Arab world. A former general and veteran of successive

Photo 6.1 Mosaic outside the Palestinian parliament building in Gaza City of a Palestinian boy with a catapult confronting an Israeli soldier

Israeli–Arab wars, he was also a long-time champion of Jewish settlers. He acquired notoriety when, as Israel's defense minister in 1982, he master-minded the invasion of Lebanon, only for Israel's Christian Phalangist allies to massacre Palestinian refugees in Beirut's Sabra and Shatila refugee camps.

The site of Sharon's walkabout was once home to the Jewish Temples of antiquity, and according to the New Testament it was where Jesus drove away the moneylenders. Its hilltop plateau is today adorned by two huge shrines built by the early Muslim conquerors of Jerusalem: Al Aqsa Mosque and the golden Dome of the Rock. The site's recapture from the Crusaders by the Muslim commander Salah ad-Din in 1187 is an epochal event in Islamic history, signifying Muslim victory. Directly beneath these is the Western Wall, a sacred place of prayer for Jews. The plateau's capture by Israeli troops during the Six Day War is equally a defining moment in Zionist history, immortalized by the battlefield radio transmission on 7 June 1967 by the Israeli paratroop commander Colonel Motta Gur: 'The Temple Mount is in our hands.'

Ariel Sharon's appearance was a deliberate political provocation over a site of contested sovereignty. Demonstrations soon broke out and Israeli responses led to an escalating death toll. Soon the deaths were on both sides and a spiral of new violence seemed to be in motion. As the casualties rose, any prospect of a peace settlement faded. The government of the Israeli prime minister Ehud Barak collapsed, and barely four months after his provocative walkabout Sharon was prime minister.

Israeli intelligence officials argue that the Intifada was not spontaneous, claiming that the Palestinian leadership began planning for violence months earlier and that they detected an increase in Palestinian attacks around the time of Israel's unilateral pull-out from Lebanon in May 2000. 'We as an intelligence service failed a little bit to recognize the time and the day when the Palestinian Authority, which was supposed to be backing counter-terrorism, started to carry out terror activities,' said one of Israel's most senior intelligence officials.[2]

Looking back from an era in which Hamas has become Israel's *idée fixe*, it is remarkable to note how little focus Israel placed on Hamas during this period, only five years before they became the elected Palestinian government. Instead the Israeli political and military establishment's public rhetoric was devoted almost entirely to Yasser Arafat and the Fatah-dominated Palestinian Authority. In speech after speech, Israeli officials from the very top down hammered home their main talking point in the Second Intifada – that, while Hamas posed a danger, the main threat to Israel's security was the Fatah-led apparatus of the PA, which Israel had allowed to be created under the Oslo Accords, but which it now regarded as a terrorist quasi-state. Before long, Israeli leaders would be equating Yasser Arafat with al-Qaeda's Usama bin Laden, just as in a later era they would do with Hamas and ISIS/Daesh.

Methods

For the first month of the Second Intifada, the vast majority of the fatal attacks on Israelis were from gunshots, through ambushes, sniper fire or drive-by killings. The first car bomb came on 2 November 2000, an Islamic Jihad blast which killed two Israelis near Jerusalem's Mahane Yehuda market. Hamas then perpetrated a series of suicide bombings which greatly escalated the toll. One of the deadliest was on 1 June 2001, when a suicide bomber killed twenty-one youths outside a disco in Tel Aviv.

Two months later, on 9 August 2001, a similarly deadly Hamas blast killed fifteen at the Sbarro Pizzeria in Jerusalem's city centre. Hamas said the restaurant bombing was in revenge for the assassination of Hamas leaders. But more Palestinians were dying from Israeli missile attacks, tank incursions and bombing raids. Twelve months into the Second Intifada, 564 Palestinians and 181 Israelis had been killed. The death tolls on both sides were far higher than in the first year of the 1987–8 Intifada, which saw around 300 Palestinians and fifteen Israelis killed.

Whatever Hamas's rationale for its suicide bombings, the international context changed utterly on 11 September 2001, when al-Qaeda carried out its attacks on America. Israeli leaders made the parallels to their American allies. Two days after 9/11, Prime Minister Ariel Sharon told the US secretary of state, Colin Powell: 'Arafat is our bin Laden.'[3] Sharon's was by no means the only attempt to link Palestinians and al-Qaeda. Yet the initial concern of the Bush administration, as it sought a response that would meet the demands of a devastated people, was to ensure that the crisis between Israel and the Palestinians did not undermine US efforts to keep Arab states such as Saudi Arabia on board as it prepared to launch its Global War on Terror. But would Hamas halt the suicide attacks on Israel?

As 2001 drew to a close, the death rate accelerated. On 23 November, Israel assassinated Mahmoud Abu Hanoud, a senior Hamas military leader in the West Bank, and Hamas struck back by killing thirty-seven Israelis. International opprobrium was forcing Arafat to act. President Bush's envoy, General Anthony Zinni, said: 'Chairman Arafat and the PA must move immediately to arrest those responsible … coexistence with these organizations or acquiescence in their activities is simply not acceptable.'[4]

Arafat ordered the closure of all Hamas and Islamic Jihad offices. Israel demanded more. They accused Arafat's security forces of either refusing or failing to rein in the violence.

During a lengthy interview with one of the authors in 2002, Sharon barely mentioned Hamas except as an afterthought, reserving his venom for his old enemy Arafat, whom he had tried and failed to kill in Beirut twenty years earlier. Pointing out that 646 Israelis had been killed during the violence of the previous two years, he said that Arafat's security chiefs must close down Hamas and the others. 'They have to arrest terrorists, their leaders, interrogate them and sue them ... they have to dismantle terrorist organizations like the Hamas.' Significantly, he also cited the country that was to feature increasingly large in Israel's list of enemies over the next decade: Iran.

Already identified by President George W. Bush as a member, alongside Iraq and North Korea, of the 'Axis of Evil', the Iranian regime was referred to by Sharon as 'a danger to the Middle East, to Israel and a danger to Europe', and he called upon the Americans to target it 'the day after' they finished in Iraq.[5] Sharon gave a detailed list of accusations against the Iranians, citing their alleged efforts to acquire weapons of mass destruction and ballistic missiles, providing Hezbollah with up to 10,000 short-range missiles along Israel's northern border with Lebanon, and their efforts to smuggle weapons to the PA.

The specifics of Iran's alleged links to Hamas were dealt with by one of Sharon's most senior intelligence chiefs. Armed with colour flip charts and flow diagrams, the senior official claimed that 'something changed' with Hamas in the twelve months following 9/11. It had initially 'kept its independence since being established in 1987, but during the last year we could see how it has been changed, and Hamas became more dependent on Iran. The leadership of Hamas sits in Damascus, and they travel every three or four weeks to Tehran.'[6]

Palestinian security officials protested that Sharon's demands were impossible. 'They want us to do the job that their own "most sophisticated" army in the Middle East has been unable to do themselves,' said one senior Palestinian intelligence officer.[7] Another, as he picked among the rubble of his buildings recently bombed by Israel, said: 'They tie our hands behind our backs, take our weapons, uniforms, communications, equipment, destroy our HQs and prisons, allow the prisoners and [those] wanted to go free, shoot at us if we move from one area to the next, and then say we have to destroy the terrorists among us ... but how?'[8]

Arafat found himself trapped between Hamas and Israel. When Arafat did try to satisfy Israel's demands by putting Yassin and Rantissi under

Photo 6.2 A bus 'graveyard' in Kiryat Ata, where the Israeli public carrier Egged stored the remains of buses blown up by Hamas and other factions during the Second Intifada. Photo: Ronen Zvulun, August 2002

arrest and shutting their offices in Gaza, their supporters rioted. Zahar was angered by the suggestion that Hamas ought to heed Arafat's call to desist from suicide bombings and allow the PLO to continue with peace talks:

> For how long is Mr Arafat going to negotiate? What is the alternative? Even when there are talks, Israel still kills us. Give me one wise man in this world that can convince us that Israel really is ready to leave our soil and enter negotiation. No one believes negotiation is possible. Everyone is calling for continuation of the Intifada. And sooner rather than later Israel will realize the price of their existence here ... We need our liberty and sovereignty.[9]

Polarization

By 2002, continuing violence was also eroding Ariel Sharon's authority, with his rival Netanyahu waiting in the wings. Sharon's problem was that, for more than half a century as general and politician, his role as a 'Warrior' – the title of his autobiography – was to make Israelis feel safe. But he was failing at that primary task. Matters disintegrated still further on 14 January 2002, when Israel – during a ceasefire – assassinated Raed al-Karmi, a prominent Al Aqsa Martyrs' Brigades leader from Tulkarem. Karmi's death took an extraordinary posthumous hold on the collective imagination of Palestinians, no matter what faction.

From the northernmost olive farmer in the West Bank to the southernmost tunnel-digger in the Gaza Strip, it became an unshakeable article of faith that Karmi's assassination during a ceasefire proved that Israelis could not be trusted. Israeli officials rebutted the allegation. One senior Israeli military officer later claimed that they had intelligence that Karmi was about to carry out attacks on Israelis: 'We thought that maybe it was the right thing to do to try and stop him.'[10]

Amid Palestinian shootings and bombings and Israeli airstrikes and tank incursions, Sharon's popularity continued to plummet. From 57 per cent public support in mid-January, his rating went into freefall, rates of dissatisfaction reaching nearly 80 per cent. And the political weathervanes were being watched carefully by Hamas, always on the lookout for signs of political weakness in its enemy. 'He [Sharon] has been scared by the recent polls that show he's losing his control. It's an indication of his failures,' sneered Hussein Abu Kweik, a member of Hamas's political wing in Ramallah.[11]

Poised, although they did not know it, on the brink of a major escalation in the violence, Israelis found themselves divided between those on the right, such as Mr Sharon, who argued for no concessions to Palestinian 'terror', and those who raised yet again the criticism which had dogged Sharon throughout his career – that, while he was a master short-term tactician, he lacked the strategic vision to look beyond his 'security-first' stance and find a political solution. Hamas only felt encouraged. In February 2002 Rantissi told a Hamas crowd: 'I say it clearly, that Hamas will continue the martyrdom operations. Let's not care if they say that we are terrorist organizations ... Your choice is your gun.'[12]

Squeezed

Rantissi was talking from Gaza, Hamas's stronghold. But Gaza was mostly sealed off from Israel by a high fence that limited their reach. The real wellspring of attacks against Israel came from the much larger West Bank, where Fatah was dominant. Their coexistence was uneasy, but differences would often be put aside for personal friendships or solidarity over deaths. In March 2002, an Israeli tank fired into the West Bank capital of Ramallah, killing five Palestinian children and two women on their morning school run. The Israeli army expressed regret over the death of 'innocent Palestinian civilians' and claimed to have hit the wrong car.

But Palestinians were sceptical, as the dead included the wife and three children of the Hamas leader Hussein Abu Kweik. Hamas left little doubt that there would be retaliation. 'Don't we have the right to defend ourselves? The military wing will take the decision, but the Israeli occupation is pushing us toward responding,' said Sheikh Hassan Yousef at the crowded condolence ceremony in al-Bireh. Yousef was careful to use the formula always employed by Hamas when its leaders were attacked. To stop cults of personality, they emphasize that leaders are not important in themselves, only because their suffering reflects that of all Palestinians. 'They are targeting the entire Palestinian people,' he said, surrounded by Hamas supporters.[13]

As the Hamas leader spoke, a short, stout figure sat beside him nodding, glad-handing and exchanging greetings with friends. His face was already known to everyone in the West Bank and Gaza. This was Marwan Barghouti, officially Fatah's secretary-general in the West Bank, but a figure of far greater importance in the movement than that middle-ranking position suggested. A Fatah member of parliament and skilful orator, Barghouti had been an organizer during the First Intifada. By the time of the Second, he was the face of Fatah's younger generation. Despite their religious and political differences, Barghouti chatted amiably with his Hamas rival Yousef at the condolence ceremony.

It was a rare sighting. Barghouti had drastically curtailed his public appearances since the escalation of the Israeli military operations in the West Bank, fearing arrest by Israeli snatch squads. Israelis – and his internal enemies within Fatah – claimed that it was Barghouti who had persuaded Arafat that the only way to counter Hamas's inexorable rise in popularity was to match its tactics by carrying out attacks inside Israel itself, not to confine themselves to targeting Israeli settlers and soldiers in the occupied West Bank. Barghouti vehemently rejected the accusations, insisting that he was a political leader committed to a two-state solution. But he voiced satisfaction that Fatah's violence had strengthened the movement, giving it a stronger bargaining hand with Israel and relegating its internal foes back to the sidelines.

A senior Israeli military official alleged that Fatah's escalation was part of an internal struggle to succeed Arafat. A new militant organization associated with Fatah had sprung up during the Second Intifada – the Al Aqsa Martyrs' Brigades. Barghouti's internal aim, the Israelis said, was to use the newly created group to bring Fatah back under the control of the political party machinery and bypass the official PA forces of Mohammed Dahlan and Jibril Rajoub. The other goal, the Israelis said, was to neutralize Hamas's growing reputation on the Palestinian street as champions of the armed struggle. One Israeli official said those advocating violence argued to Arafat that, 'since his organization contained many more potential activists than Hamas or Islamic Jihad, he should give them full freedom to act ... Arafat was persuaded.'[14] Although evidently self-serving, the Israelis' analysis was useful, if only to give an insight into how they were tailoring their narrative. Once again their message centred on Fatah – and Arafat personally – not on Hamas.

The Israelis caught up with Marwan Barghouti on 15 April 2002. He was arrested near his home in Ramallah and convicted in a Tel Aviv court of murder, despite his protestations that he was innocent and that he had immunity as an elected Palestinian MP. He has remained in prison ever since, but the cross-factional relationships that he went on to forge during his years in jail were to make him an influential figure among prisoners – an important decision-making constituency in Palestinian society – and he has figured prominently in opinion polls identifying popular choices for president in future elections.

As the Intifada ground on, the rhetoric of some of Fatah's armed groups became increasingly indistinguishable from that of Hamas, scornful of Israel's right to exist, and calling on Israelis to 'go back' to their homes in Russia and Eastern Europe. But there was also growing internal discontent at Fatah's leadership.

Speaking in a nondescript office block in Ramallah in March 2002, the head of the city's Al Aqsa Martyrs' Brigades berated his party's senior leaders for corruption and inefficiency: 'When Israel started the assassinations we could not be silent. That is why we went out and took revenge. The other factions were quiet. At other times we cooperated with the military wing of Islamic Jihad and Hamas,' he said. By this stage, like Hamas, he appeared to have little time for the distinction between Israelis living inside pre-1967 Israel and Israeli soldiers and settlers in the occupied territories. 'I don't know what is civilian in the matter of Israel because I believe they are a militarized people.'[15]

Fatah appeared to be going through an identity crisis, attempting to out-hawk Hamas while protesting that it remained a dove at heart. Hussein ash-Sheikh – then one of Barghouti's mid-level Fatah rivals – later rose through the ranks to become a serious contender to succeed the aging Mahmoud Abbas. Two months after Barghouti's arrest he was moving carefully around the streets of the West Bank capital to avoid the risk of arrest by the many Israeli units patrolling the area. After slipping into the back room of a café and sitting where he could not be seen from the street, he bridled at the suggestion that bombings meant there was now no difference between Hamas, Fatah and Islamic Jihad:

> Fatah is strategically not interested in having operations inside Israel. The big difference between Fatah and Hamas is that our political vision is totally different and the background of these attacks is different. The main reason is that the Al Aqsa Brigades are nationalist and political, not religious. What the Al Aqsa Brigades did was not a result of hatred of Israel and Jews. This was not the reason. The reason was a reaction to Israeli aggression.[16]

Fatah was trapped: rejected by Israel and losing relevance on the Palestinian street because it was trying to be what Hamas already was. Unsurprisingly, less than a year after 9/11, its tortuous rationalizations cut little ice with the Israelis or the Americans. On 22 March 2002 the US State Department declared the Al Aqsa Martyrs' Brigades a 'foreign terrorist organization', alongside Hamas, Islamic Jihad and al-Qaeda. By this time Israel was confidently asserting that Fatah was the main problem because Hamas was much smaller. 'We are in conflict with some dozens of very dangerous Hamas activists, but hundreds of Tanzim [Fatah] activists,' said one senior Israeli military official. He also assessed that Hamas's military capabilities had been 'reduced dramatically' by raids against its weapons-making facilities. 'It doesn't mean that they can't carry out suicide attempts, but 70 per cent fail simply due to the fact that the military capability was affected by a series of operations – for example, against four of their experts in Nablus a month ago.'[17]

The strikes and counter-strikes were by then coming nearly hourly. It was not uncommon to have two or three Palestinian suicide bombings a day, and journalists became uncertain whether to cover the afternoon funeral for that morning's suicide bombing or wait for the inevitable afternoon rush-hour explosion. Television screens were filled with a montage of bloody stretchers and hospital emergency rooms, and so quickly did they segue into each other that viewers on both sides were left straining to glimpse a Jewish Star of David or an Islamic Red Crescent on speeding ambulances to tell whether those attacked were from Palestinian suicide bombs or Israeli airstrikes.

8 March 2002 saw the bloodiest day of the Intifada thus far, with forty Palestinians killed in Gaza during Israeli tank and airstrikes. The very next day Hamas penetrated to within a few yards of the Israeli prime minister's office in Jerusalem, when a suicide bomber with dyed blonde hair and wearing a heavy coat walked into the fashionable Moment café in Aza Street and killed eleven Israelis. Aza is the Hebrew name for Gaza. Surveying the wreckage of the café, one Israeli onlooker named Efrat said bitterly: 'Here is a big feeling that we are helpless because we can't stay in the middle. Either you have a big war, or you give them what they want. You can't stay in the middle.'[18]

The big war was coming.

Passover Bomb

From its birth as the military wing of the Muslim Brotherhood in 1987, Hamas has operated on a working assumption: when Palestine burns, its support grows. That calculation was tested as never before by its deadliest-ever attack against Israel on 7 October 2023. But the 2023 attack was not the first in which it sought to ensure that an Arab peace initiative anathema to the Hamas credo would be delivered stillborn.

The diplomatic backdrop was that, in 2002, Saudi Arabia's crown prince Abdullah bin Abdul Aziz al-Saud had proposed a peace initiative that offered Arab normalization of relations with Israel in return for Israeli withdrawal from the occupied Gaza Strip, West Bank and Golan Heights. Many welcomed the Saudi proposal, seeing it as an imaginative move that offered a long-term solution to the intractable Middle East problem.

Not Hamas: on 27 March 2002, the very day that the Arab League was gathering for a high-level summit in Beirut at which it endorsed the Saudi proposal, Hamas upstaged the proposal by killing thirty Jewish celebrants at a Passover dinner in the seaside town of Netanya.

Those targeted were assembled for the most important Jewish family gathering of the year, the Passover seder, with its biblical resonances of suffering, exile, deliverance from slavery and escape from the Angel of Death. Further compounding the evil in Israeli eyes was that most of the dead were pensioners in their seventies, eighties or older, from the Holocaust generation.

Hamas's claim of responsibility showed that the message from Netanya was also directed 120 miles north of Netanya to the Arab rulers gathered in Beirut. 'This operation comes as a response to the crimes of the Zionist enemy, the assassination of innocents and as a message to the summit convening in Lebanon that our Palestinian people's option is resistance and resistance only,' Hamas declared in a communiqué.[19]

At a stroke, the bombing erased whatever remaining interest Israelis had in troubling themselves with distinctions between various Palestinian factions. It was immediately apparent that Ariel Sharon had carte blanche to launch massive retaliation. As she stood among the incinerated ruins of her hotel's ballroom, Paulette Cohen, the Park Hotel manager who lost her son-in-law, said:

> I never hated the Arabs. I used to bring Arab workers here, and one of my former staff called me from Jenin after the bomb and cried and said he was sorry for what happened ... I don't want to destroy, I don't want to kill. But if they come and destroy people who are sitting down at a party and they come on this holy holiday, they have crossed the line.[20]

Arye Mekel, an Israeli government spokesman, put it more succinctly. 'Every Jew in this country saw this as a personal attack on his Passover seder, and I don't think that the people of Israel can accept this.'[21]

Soon the details emerged – the Hamas bomber was from the West Bank town of Tulkarem, just 10 miles from Netanya, had worked in the Israeli resort and used his knowledge to penetrate the hotel. The day after the Netanya bombing a Hamas gunman killed three Jewish settlers, and on 31 March Hamas unleashed another suicide bomber in Haifa, killing fifteen in a restaurant.

The Haifa bomb appeared deliberately chosen by Hamas to strike at the city most often cited as a model of Jews and Arabs coexisting peacefully. 'This is a mixed city and, as you can see, we also suffer together,' said Amram Mitzna, Haifa's mayor.[22] Still, Sharon did not allow the Hamas affiliations of the Netanya and Haifa bombers to nudge him off message. Israeli officials remained focused laser-like on laying the blame at the door of Arafat. Meir Sheetrit, an Israeli cabinet minister, listed Arafat's past sins, including rejection of the Camp David agreement, and claimed that Fatah's gunmen and bombers had since 2000 carried out 'five times the number of attacks committed by the Hamas and Islamic Jihad. Arafat is thus committing five out of every six attacks that kill Israelis.'[23]

Israel declared many Palestinian areas of the West Bank a closed military zone. As thunder and lightning rolled across the skies on Good Friday – or Sad Friday, as it is known to Palestinian Christians – Israel's tanks rolled into the West Bank to carry out its largest military operation in years – what Israeli officials termed 'Operation Defensive Shield' but what Palestinians experienced as a full-scale reinvasion of West Bank cities.

The Israelis' first target was Yasser Arafat's hilltop Muqata compound in Ramallah. They cut off water, telephone and electricity to the neighbourhood. Then, smashing into the front wall of the Muqata, they trapped Arafat inside one wing. There he would remain, behind the rubble and sandbags, until shortly before his death in a Paris hospital two years later.

The Israeli forces besieged cities, smashed PA ministries and security headquarters, and detained thousands. As a deterrent to suicide attacks, they also demolished the homes of bombers. Some were deterred. Others were not. After the departure of yet another Israeli raiding party from Nablus's Balata refugee camp, one gunman, who gave his name only as Mustafa, shrugged unconcernedly, saying he didn't care how much Israel damaged it because it was never his home anyway. 'This camp is not my country. We left our home in 1948, in Deir Tarif, near Ludda [Lod],' he said. 'Where else shall I go? If we die, we die here.'[24]

Over the following weeks, masked Palestinian fighters from different factions fought running gun battles with Israeli troops on the streets. But there remained very real differences between the leaderships.

There was widespread outrage on the street when Fatah's West Bank security chief Jibril Rajoub surrendered half a dozen Hamas activists to Israeli troops which had surrounded his Preventive Security compound in Beitunya. Hamas's military wing issued a communiqué saying: 'Rajoub sticks to treachery, hands six Hamas activists to IDF.'

Hamas was in its element. For years marginalized during the era of negotiations, it now saw an angry younger generation increasingly in despair at the 24-hour Israeli curfews, tank raids and dismantling of the Palestinian Authority. And while Hamas competed with Fatah for control of the street, there was growing support for Hamas to capitalize on its popularity by challenging Fatah in parliament.

But the paradox at the heart of Hamas's entry to politics was that its embrace of the ballot was intended not to end the violence but to ensure its continuance. Hamas feared that Arafat would sooner or later do a deal with Israel and the Americans and crush Hamas's much smaller forces. 'The international community's plan was, "If we get Hamas involved in politics, they will become more involved, and then it will become harder for them to do resistance,"' said Jamila al-Shanti. 'But it was clear from day one that we came with the purpose of protecting the resistance.'[25]

The other factor working in Hamas's favour was that, as Israel destroyed the PA's ministries, the collapse of its social and welfare institutions created more of a need. Hamas organized food runs, donations, medical supplies and support across the West Bank, providing compensation for destroyed homes and support for the families of prisoners.

Walled Off

Jenin, the northernmost city in the West Bank, proved by far the deadliest single battle for Israel throughout Operation Defensive Shield. More than twenty soldiers were killed, including thirteen in a single ambush in the refugee camp on 9 April. Around fifty Palestinians were also killed, most of them fighters. Although Nablus was deadlier, Jenin drew more attention because Palestinian leaders grossly exaggerated the death toll, accusing Israeli soldiers of killing hundreds during the fierce battle for control of its refugee camp.

In a pattern that was to become familiar over the following decades, the accusations flew on both sides – Israel saying their soldiers encountered 'dozens of heavily armed terrorists shielding themselves behind Palestinian civilians'[26] and the Palestinians accusing Israel of collective punishment because it razed part of the refugee camp where some of the fiercest fighting happened.

Capitalizing on the furore, Hamas drew attention to the battle in Jenin by sending a suicide bomber from Jenin itself to blow up a bus in Haifa, killing eight Israelis. Although it was unclear when the bomber slipped out of the camp, it was a deliberate attempt to goad the Israelis. Hamas wasted no time trumpeting its self-proclaimed coup, crowing: 'To Sharon and his ministers and generals, we have shown that there is no Defensive Shield.'

In fact, just such a shield was coming. Sharon the arch-Zionist had long resisted a physical barrier to separate Israelis from Palestinians because he feared that it could one day become a de facto border, forcing Israel to cede some of the occupied West Bank. But he reluctantly embraced it as a security and political inevitability. Gaza had been fenced off from Israel since the mid-1990s, but West Bank Palestinians had only to walk across a road or unguarded field to enter Israel. The result was Israel's West Bank barrier – a 500-mile stretch of razor wire and concrete that snaked around the Jewish settlements and cut off parts of the West Bank and East Jerusalem that Israel wanted to keep.

Palestinians protested that it was a land grab, pointing out that in places it pushed up to 13 miles deep into the West Bank. The UN condemned it as illegal under international law. Israel insisted it was a security fence, necessary to cut off the terrorists. At a stroke it made it far harder for Hamas and other factions to penetrate Israel. The level of suicide bombings and shootings declined sharply.[27]

Redirection

The Second Intifada continued after 2002, although increasingly casualties were on the Palestinian side. From 2003 to 2004 there was an estimated 45 per cent drop in the Israeli death toll, from 214 to 117,[28] whereas Palestinian deaths rose by approximately 35 per cent, from 637 to 866.[29] Throughout the five years after the outbreak of the uprising in September 2000 to December 2005, the Israelis lost 1,080[30] and the Palestinians 3,570.[31]

Hamas began a process of reorientation. When, in late 2001, European Union envoys made overtures about a ceasefire, it proved receptive, a signal that it wanted to be treated differently, not to be regarded as part of a global jihad and consistently equated with al-Qaeda.

Ismail Abu Shanab, the main architect of the ceasefire, devoted all his energies to the process, believing it could bring Hamas in from the sidelines and eliminate civilian casualties from both sides. In the summer of 2002 as he sat in the salon of his home – after waiting to speak while one of his young daughters came into the room to ask when he would be finished with his visitors – the Hamas leader insisted that the movement's followers 'support resisting the occupation, developing better Palestinian life and reform and developing a Palestinian state and struggling towards the return of the refugees.' But then he paused and added: 'The ceasefire should be tried, because no one should have to bury their children in the heat of this war.'[32]

The second factor, and the one that Hamas leaders will never admit in public, is that Israel's unrelenting attacks on the Hamas leadership from 2002 on did have an impact. Within two years almost the entire senior tier of Hamas leadership in Gaza had been assassinated, in what Israel's former defense minister Shaul Mofaz called a plan to 'liquidate the terrorists'.[33]

In July 2002, the head of Hamas's military wing, Salah Shehadeh, was killed. Israel assassinated two other senior military leaders – Ibrahim al-Maqadmeh in March 2003 and Ismail Abu Shanab in August of that year. One Israeli attack severely wounded Shehadeh's replacement as leader of the military wing, Mohammed Deif, the future mastermind of the 2023 cross-border attack. In March and April 2004, Israel finally assassinated Hamas's founder, Sheikh Ahmed Yassin, and his hardline deputy and successor, Dr Abdel Aziz Rantissi.

Israel appeared to believe that Hamas, like the PLO, was led through the will of one or two individuals. But this was not Hamas's style.

The death of Yassin had long been expected by the movement he created. Yassin himself had stated that he was ready for paradise. It was the manner of his assassination that elevated him into a symbol of martyrdom – killed by Israeli missiles as he was pushed down the street in his wheelchair after attending dawn prayers at his local mosque. For every leader lost, Hamas declared that there were hundreds of others lining up. Hamas's diffuse process of decentralized decision-making also made it harder for Israel to destroy its core.

On a strategic level, however, Israeli security chiefs believed that they could weaken their enemy by targeting its leadership. The first hints of Hamas having a change of direction had come from statements made by Yassin before his death and in the movement's offer in June 2003 of a formal unilateral ceasefire with Israel. That announcement was greeted with approval from the Palestinian street that had paid the price in Israeli reprisals for Hamas suicide attacks. Popular support was evidence enough to convince sceptics in Hamas that their appeal would not decline if the campaign of 'resistance' was suspended. But there were many doubters. Neither Israel nor the US believed that Hamas was sincere, and Israel continued to target the Palestinians with arrests, airstrikes and assassinations that soon rendered the ceasefire untenable to Hamas hardliners.

Nevertheless Yassin had indicated that Hamas would allow a *tahdiyah* (period of calm). He had also, five years earlier, proposed a lengthy truce (*hudna*) in return for a Palestinian state in the occupied West Bank and Gaza. But it was an offer that Israel always scorned, protesting that it could never trust an enemy whose founding covenant devoted itself to Israel's destruction. Hamas's apparent intention was to fine-tune its campaign of 'resistance' in a way that would win it back regional and international support. This also gave it leverage in discussions with the Palestinian Authority. But, once again, external events were to work in Hamas's favour.

In what was to be his last major act on the political stage, Ariel Sharon announced that he planned to withdraw Israel's troops and thousands of Jewish settlers from Gaza unilaterally. The 2005 withdrawal would dramatically shift the power balance in Gaza, then home to 1.5 million Palestinians and Hamas's power base. It was hugely controversial within Israel. Many on the left believed that Gaza was no longer worth the price in blood and treasure to defend a few thousand Jewish settlers.

The settlers and their supporters argued that to pull out would be an unconscionable sign of weakness and serve only to encourage Palestinian 'terror'. Sharon pushed it through against considerable opposition – those inclined to take the withdrawal at face value accepting the argument that it was an act necessary to ensure Israel's demographic survival, while sceptics suspected Sharon of sacrificing Gaza in order to secure its hold on the West Bank.

Sheikh Yassin indicated that Hamas was prepared to participate in power-sharing in any post-withdrawal government. Details of this had been hammered out over the following months during rounds of inter-Palestinian dialogue and were formalized in the Cairo declaration of March 2005. The new orientation, however, would lead to the greatest changes of all, not just for Hamas, but for its secular rivals and the government of Israel.

Qassam Brigades

They can destroy all of Gaza. We can only harm them. We are just sending a message to tell them: we can act against you.

Abu Mohammed[1]

Hamas's military wing has a striking logo. It depicts a gunman standing in front of the golden Dome of the Rock in Jerusalem's Al Aqsa compound. He is brandishing a semi-automatic rifle in his right hand and a Koran in his left. He wears a green headband saying 'We are at your service, oh Al Aqsa'. Alongside him a banner proclaims, 'There is No God but Allah' and the Koranic verse 'Therefore you did not slay them, but Allah slew them.'

The Islamic shrine at the centre of the emblem firmly roots Hamas in geographic, religious and political symbolism. The centrality of Jerusalem's holy shrines to Hamas was demonstrated on 7 October 2023, when the public codename 'Al Aqsa Flood' was given by the military chief who masterminded it, Mohammed Deif.

The Qassam Brigades had grabbed worldwide headlines decades earlier – during countless bus bombings and shootings, and other missions including suicide bomb attacks in Israel. But the assault of 7 October 2023 was in order of magnitude larger than anything the Qassam Brigades had carried out before and catapulted it to a level of global attention and notoriety that it had never had. Now the name Qassam was in thousands of news headlines, social media posts and newspapers.

The military wing is at the same time both ultra-secretive and publicity hungry. On an individual level, families of its members killed in attacks will often express bewilderment that their late relative had been recruited. But on an organizational level it has photographers, video production units, social media teams, messaging apps and, in Gaza, its own uniformed spokesman, Abu Obaida. Despite having met him in person on more than one occasion in Gaza, it was difficult to know if it was always the same person or sometimes a body double. In earlier rounds of hostilities, he would sometimes appear in the open, usually in narrow alleyways or in a copse, to be sheltered by buildings or tree branches from aerial surveillance above. He would deliver the military wing's statements wearing combat fatigues beneath a khaki jacket with the Qassam Brigades logo and 'Information Office' stencilled on the rear. By 2023, when he could not appear in public, he was the face of the Qassam Brigades' social media, pumping out thousands of posts to subscribers on its Telegram channel. Each notification carried statements or footage of its attacks on Israel and defence of Gaza – almost in real-time – and Abu Obaida's voice became a familiar one across the Arab world.

The audacity of the 7 October attack was magnified by the unprecedented Israeli death toll that surpassed even the era-defining Palestinian attacks of the 1960s and 1970s – the PFLP hijackings of international airliners and 'Black September' murders of the Israeli team at the 1972 Munich Olympics. Certainly, Israel itself viewed it in these terms. President Isaac Herzog delivered a televised speech to the international community calling for support and framing the attack in existential and generational terms. He declared:

> To my mind, not since the Holocaust have so many Jews been killed on one day. And not since the Holocaust have we witnessed scenes of Jewish women and children, grandparents – even Holocaust survivors – being herded into trucks and taken into captivity. Hamas has imported, adopted, and replicated the savagery of ISIS. Entering civilian homes on a holy day, and murdering in cold blood, whole families. Young and old. Violating and burning bodies. Beating and torturing their innocent victims – Jews and Muslims and other faiths. The brutality. The inhumanity. The barbarity of monsters – not humans – monsters.[2]

Ever since its creation, Hamas has claimed that the Qassam Brigades serve to organize armed resistance – jihad in its terms – and self-defence on behalf of Palestinians living under Israeli occupation. Israel has always called it terrorism. Both sides claim that each uses force and violence for strategic and ideological goals. And although the attack of 7 October 2023 and Israel's retaliatory bombardment of Gaza over the following months brought a level of attention to the Israeli–Palestinian conflict not seen in recent decades, they followed a grim and consistent pattern familiar to historians of Israel's decades as occupiers of Palestinian territory, and of Palestinian resistance to it, including armed violence.

One thing Hamas seemed always guaranteed to do – at least in the short term – was to receive an upswing in support when the Qassam Brigades hit Israel. 'Here is the equation,' said one Gaza refugee camp dweller during a round of hostilities in 2006. 'The [Israeli] army comes and besieges us from one house to the next. They call for our surrender, but if we give it we still have occupation. So we say let us confront rather than surrender for life. We have no choice.'[3] In the long-term aftermath of 2023, it remained to be seen only if Hamas's strategic calculus of loss and gain would still hold up amid the unparalleled levels of death and destruction on both sides.

Origins

The roots of the Qassam Brigades go back to the 1980s when Sheikh Yassin founded the embryonic military group *al-Mujahidoun al-Filistinioun* (the Palestinian Fighters). As a fledgling group it had few weapons. Abu Khalil, a veteran military activist of that era, said it was 'personally supervised' by Yassin and his close aides Salah Shehadeh and Ibrahim al-Maqadmeh, and its first recruits made clumsy efforts to obtain guns through the Israeli black market. 'They managed to collect some weapons. But because the eyes of Shin Bet were so open to our activities at this time the Israeli authorities arrested everybody involved.'[4] A colleague, Mohammed, recalled in the early days paying middlemen for weapons that either did not work or had been sabotaged by the Israelis. 'We only had one bazooka and we bought it for $24,000 from a Bedouin officer in the border police,' he said. 'We didn't know how to use it or even how to inspect it, and it was broken.'[5] These early attempts led to Sheikh Yassin's arrest. In April 1984, Yassin was sentenced to thirteen years in prison. Qassam Brigades veterans concede that his arrest was a 'severe blow' to the movement,[6] but he was released just eleven months later in a prisoner exchange deal and went straight back to work.

In 1985 Yassin set up a new armed organization called *al-Majd* (Glory) – an acronym for *Munazamat al-Jihad wa al-Da'wa* (the Organization of Holy War and Preaching). This was headed by Rawhi Mushtaha and Yahya Sinwar – a future architect of the 2023 attacks. Sinwar's family were refugees from the village of Al-Majdal Asqalan, which lay a few miles north of Gaza and is now part of the Israeli city of Ashkelon. His refugee mother gave birth to him in a refugee camp in Gaza in 1962. He went to school in Gaza, studied at the Islamic University there and then, as an acolyte of Yassin, co-founded *al-Majd* and became a feared enforcer, gathering intelligence and punishing collaborators. But he was arrested by Israel in 1988 and was sentenced to four consecutive life terms for planning the abduction and murder of two Israeli soldiers and the murder of four Palestinians suspected of collaborating.

Although Hamas had been in existence for two years when the first Palestinian Intifada broke out in December 1987, it did not initially strike against Israeli military targets. It would be fourteen months before it acted, kidnapping and then killing 21-year-old Israeli paratrooper Sergeant Avi Sasportas while he was hitch-hiking near Gaza. After long experience dealing with cross-border *fedayeen* attacks from the Gaza Strip in previous decades, Israel quickly followed the trail back to Sheikh Yassin, and he was arrested along with hundreds of other Hamas members. Yassin was found guilty and sentenced to two life terms in prison. In his absence, pressure grew within the newly formed Hamas movement to hasten jihad against Israel. The outcome was the formation of a new military wing, which was to become the Izz ad-Din al-Qassam Brigades.

Qassam Brigades

In classic insurgency fashion, the new organization was created out of the need for compartmentalization – to avoid any risk of the new group being compromised by information emerging from confessions or interrogations of their colleagues who were now in jail alongside Sheikh Yassin. 'For security reasons we changed the name so people would not connect us with the old cases,' said Qassam commander Abu Khalil. The first cell was set up in 1990 in Rafah, the city at the southernmost edge of the Gaza Strip. 'After Sheikh Yassin was arrested we started to form groups, all in the Gaza Strip, but we lacked weapons. The Rafah group was the only one which managed to get their hands on guns because they were closer to the Egyptian border. They mainly targeted collaborators,' said Abu Khalil. The other cells were devoted to intelligence and arms-gathering, he said, 'collecting information about collaborators and Israeli intelligence and getting ready in case we managed to obtain weapons. But we didn't.'[7]

In 1991 the military structure was overhauled and formally given its new name. Its new leader was Salah Shehadeh, from Beit Hanoun in northern Gaza, whose family were refugees from Jaffa. In his late thirties, Shehadeh was no stranger to Israeli prisons. Detained with Sheikh Yassin in 1984, he had been released with the cleric in a 1985 prisoner swap before being rearrested again in a crackdown in 1988. Israeli intelligence claimed that in 1989 Shehadeh had 'admitted during questioning ... to the establishment of a terrorist element within Hamas.'[8]

Naming the Brigades after the Syrian sheikh of the 1930s is thought to have been the idea of one of Shehadeh's senior lieutenants from southern Gaza, a refugee named Mohammed al-Masri, who was later to change his name to the *nom de guerre* under which he would go on to achieve international notoriety: Mohammed Deif. Other significant early figures included Yahya Ayyash from the West Bank. Ayyash held a degree in electrical engineering, and his bomb-making skill earned him the sobriquet 'The Engineer'. He was credited with assembling the first bombs that Hamas used on its suicide attacks against Israel between 1994 and 1996. Ayyash's success in eluding capture by Israel turned him into a hero for many young Palestinians. Perhaps inevitably, Ayyash was himself assassinated by an Israeli bomb, in January 1996 in northern Gaza. Adnan al-Ghoul, Deif's right-hand man, was referred to within the Brigades as the 'father of the Qassamite missiles' and is considered to have played a pioneering role in the military expansion and capacity-building of the organization. Israel killed Al Ghoul and Imad Abbas in a targeted assassination in Gaza in October 2004. Al Ghoul and Abbas had both joined the Qassam Brigades in the early 1990s, rising through the ranks to positions of senior leadership.

A Spreading Web

Once the military wing became established in Gaza, its members began travelling to the West Bank to activate new cells. There a key figure was Sheikh Saleh al-Arouri. An inscrutable man with an expressionless face, Arouri's every phrase betrayed the precise vocabulary and cadences of a committed ideologue.

During a March 2007 interview with one of the authors of this book, Arouri served fizzy orange Fanta in his home in the remote West Bank village of Aroura. Neither the home nor Arouri still exist. The house was destroyed by the Israeli military shortly after the October 2023 attack. And on 2 January 2024 Arouri was killed in a drone strike in Lebanon, where he was living after being deported by Israel in 2010. Israel did not claim responsibility for the killing, but it was widely taken to be an assassination of a hardliner who was deeply involved with Hamas's military wing during his earliest days in the movement; in his later years in the movement's senior leadership, he had served as a key liaison figure with Iran and its Lebanon-based ally Hezbollah.

Israeli officials and other Hamas military wing members confirmed that Arouri was the original founder of the Qassam Brigades in the West Bank – effectively Sinwar's counterpart there. Even many years after the events in question, he was still instinctively reticent about his exact early role in the movement. But over two days of interviews he was forthcoming about the early dynamics of the Hamas movement as it expanded out of Gaza. 'The military wing in Gaza was initially set up as a security/intelligence apparatus, but when the Qassam Brigades were formed in the West Bank, automatically the apparatus in Gaza was shifted to a military apparatus because the Gazans who had been needed here in the West Bank went back to Gaza,' he said.

Arouri said the early Qassam Brigades network in the West Bank expanded and became an important 'link in the chain' of the wider Hamas movement. 'It is a natural progression for people under occupation to take up to a method of resisting as civil resistance, and then gradually move into operational resistance,' he opined, sitting beneath portraits of Sheikh Yassin and Rantissi.

Captured by Israel in October 1992, Arouri was convicted of heading the military wing and jailed for fifteen years. Even a decade and a half later, he maintained that the Israeli authorities were unable to 'prove anything' and that he was accused of being the military head only after other Hamas detainees identified him during interrogation. 'While I was in administrative detention there were arrests of certain Hamas military cells, and some of those who were arrested confessed that they had some relationship with me,' he said.[9] Among the Israeli torture methods that he and others were subjected to, he alleged, were beatings, sleep deprivation, starvation and being chained to a wall and left out in the snow in mid-winter. A report from the well-respected human rights group Amnesty International published in 2008 seemed to verify some of Arouri's allegations.[10]

Did he know who informed on him? 'Naturally I know, they were my friends,' he said, quietly, and with a touch of scorn. 'The pressure upon me was the same as others, but no more. There were many who did not break.' Arouri confirmed that Qassam activists in prison remained involved with the movement outside through smuggled mobile phones and regular visits with family and lawyers. 'The prisoners, whoever they belong to, are respected and highly regarded, even idolized by their own communities because of the respect that they have gained.'[11] That respect across political divisions was on full display in his own front room, in the shape of a red and yellow bouquet of plastic flowers congratulating him on his release, in the name of President Mahmoud Abbas's Palestinian Authority.

Arouri was not one to sink into retirement. After his deportation he moved around the region, rising to become deputy chairman of Hamas's political bureau and located in Lebanon. His links with prisoners still in jail were also put to use when he played a key role during the 2010–11 negotiations that saw 1,027 Palestinian prisoners freed in exchange for Gilad Schalit.

The Americans also had Arouri in their target sights. In 2014 he praised the kidnap and killing of three Israeli teenagers in the West Bank and said it was carried out by the Qassam Brigades. One of the teenagers had dual American nationality.[12]

A year later the US government declared Arouri a Specially Designated Global Terrorist, and in 2018 the State Department announced a $5 million reward for him under the Rewards for Justice programme, saying that he 'funded and directed Hamas military operations in the West Bank and has been linked to several terrorist attacks, hijackings.'[13]

Suicide Bombs

As the Qassam Brigades grew in size and sophistication, they acquired cult-like status among their supporters. Hamas activists glorified them as the defenders of the Palestinian people. Throughout the late 1980s and early 1990s, however, the organization did not carry out suicide attacks. As a military tactic, they had been ruled out. The turning point came in 1994 when an extremist Israeli settler – Baruch Goldstein – massacred twenty-nine Muslim worshippers at prayer in the Ibrahimi Mosque in the West Bank city of Hebron, one of the most sacred sites in the Holy Land. Goldstein's attack led to a new calculus in the political leadership of Hamas. It approved and ordered the Qassam Brigades to respond with suicide bomb attacks, which they carried out in Afula, then Tel Aviv, and beyond.

Hamas had discovered that with a suicide bomber they could strike at Israel 'throughout the length and breadth of Occupied Palestine'[14] – once again making clear the Hamas claim that Israel was occupying all the Palestinians' historic lands from the 'river to the sea'. The impact on Israel was seismic. Hamas bombers now had the potential to be in every street, café and shopping mall, and the sight of bomb-shattered Israeli buses and restaurants became a defining image of the Second Palestinian Intifada of 2000 to 2005, just as stone-throwing Palestinian youths with slings and keffiyehs had been in the first. From Hamas's perspective, its new tactic had succeeded in creating what Mushir al-Masri, a Hamas leader in Gaza, later called a 'strategic balance of terror'.[15] Other Hamas activists were less grandiose. 'Not a balance of terror', demurred one veteran. 'We are trying to achieve some kind of balance, but they can destroy all of Gaza. We can only harm them. We are just sending a message to tell them: we can act against you. We can harm your children as you are doing ours. When our children can't go to school, your children will not go to school.'[16]

'Mowing the Grass'

The suicide bombers compelled Israel to rethink its political, military, intelligence and economic strategy towards the Palestinians, and Hamas in particular. Defence planners at Israel's military headquarters in Tel Aviv hoped that a combination of tactics would help degrade the Qassam Brigades' operational capacity and make it harder to work in the environment in which they operated. Israel's campaigns against Hamas in Gaza were frequently referred to by the military euphemism 'mowing the grass' – periodically attempting to neutralize the threat from Hamas to the point that it would be forced to seek a temporary ceasefire with Israel.

Qassam Brigades command and control centres, armouries, weapons 'factories' and training grounds would be targeted, all with the aim of allowing Israel to secure a period of calm on its southern borders once more. Israel also sought to decapitate Hamas's leadership echelon through a policy of assassinations – using its aerial advantage with drones and other unmanned surveillance to identify Hamas targets. One of the most high-profile of those killings was on 22 July 2002, when an Israeli jet dropped a 1 ton bomb on a house in a crowded area of Gaza City, killing Qassam Brigades leader and co-founder Salah Shehadeh. Also beneath the rubble lay more than a dozen other dead Palestinians, including women and children.

The killing of so many civilians unwittingly caught up in an airstrike on a Hamas military target drew widespread domestic and international criticism and raised the same issues of collateral damage and disproportionality that were to surface time and again in the conflict over the coming years, especially during Israel's prolonged bombardment of Gaza after October 2023.

Following the 2008–9 war in Gaza, a United Nations fact-finding mission delivered a 575-page report which found evidence of war crimes by both Israel and Hamas. About the scale of Israel's response, it said:

> The tactics used by Israeli military armed forces in the Gaza offensive are consistent with previous practices, most recently during the Lebanon war in 2006. A concept known as the Dahiya doctrine emerged then, involving the application of disproportionate force and the causing of great damage and destruction to civilian property and infrastructure, and suffering to civilian populations. The Mission concludes from a review of the facts on the ground that it witnessed for itself that what was prescribed as the best strategy appears to have been precisely what was put into practice.[17]

Israel vehemently denied such charges.

Among the first on the scene at the Shehadeh bombing was Knel Deeb, a Dubliner who was visiting his Palestinian cousins in a nearby building. He ran to the scene, where he saw

> pieces of flesh everywhere, one man running away holding a lump of flesh on a metal tray and another pulling out a baby boy with half his face blown away, obviously dead. Everyone was screaming, shouting, crying and shouting 'Revenge to the Israel child-killers'. The situation was extraordinary. I have never seen anything like it. I just kept thinking: if the British army wanted to take out Gerry Adams, would they use a bomb that size in a residential area like this?[18]

Shehadeh was a well-known hawk opposed to any deals with Israel and blamed by Israeli security officials for dozens of suicide bombings. Yet the timing of the Israeli strike dismayed Palestinian leaders and European intelligence officials, who believed they were on the verge of getting Hamas to halt the violence. Just a few hours before the bomb, Mohammed Dahlan, Arafat's former security chief, was in Gaza holding discussions with Hamas, and indicated that he had secured their acceptance of the principles of a ceasefire announcement.

Some suspected Israel of trying to spike any rapprochement with Hamas. However, Gideon Meir, an Israeli Foreign Ministry spokesman, insisted the strike was dictated by intelligence reports on Shehadeh's whereabouts at that precise time. 'The timing is nothing to do with politics. The decision to target this man was taken six months ago.' He also dismissed talk of Hamas signing a deal. 'Hamas is dedicated to the elimination of the state of Israel. There is no ceasefire, there was no ceasefire.'[19]

Israel set up an investigatory commission which concluded that Shehadeh 'was the driving force behind the Hamas, its ideology and its operations.' After nine years the internal Israeli investigation concluded that the strike was a 'legitimate targeted killing', although the panel conceded that the 'difficult collateral consequences of the strike against Shehadeh, in which uninvolved civilians, mostly women and children, were killed', were, in hindsight, 'disproportionate'. But while the commission found 'incorrect assessments and mistaken judgment due to an intelligence failure', its 2011 report delivered only systemic recommendations about how to carry out such killings in future. It cleared all Israeli officials of criminal wrongdoing, saying that it 'does not recommend that personal measures be taken against any of those involved in the operation.'[20]

Shehadeh was gone, but the idea of a ceasefire (temporary or even permanent) had been planted in the minds of both Hamas and Israeli tacticians. The Qassam Brigades had the discipline required to make their fighters' guns and rockets go quiet – but only on the orders of the political leadership. And, as was proved in the years to come, a ceasefire from Hamas came with demands on Israel. These included, variously, halting violence from both sides, freeing Israeli hostages in return for Palestinian prisoners, easing Israel's blockade of Gaza, and halting Israeli police raids on Jerusalem holy sites such as Al Aqsa.

There were sceptics in Hamas, especially within the Qassam Brigades. They believed that Israel only understood the language of violence, that force was justified, and that concessions from Israel only came after a certain level of Israeli pain. Such hardliners believed that, if it compromised its principles of self-defence, jihad and resistance, Hamas would lose. 'Israel wages war on us, they want us gone [from this land], and we will fight them till the end,' said Hamas co-founder Abdel Aziz Rantissi.[21]

Meet the New Boss

Shehadeh's replacement as head of the military wing was to provide no respite for Israel: it was Mohammed Deif, one of the future architects of the 2023 cross-border attacks. After spending thirteen years in Israeli jails, from 1982 to 1995, Deif had been released in a prisoner exchange. By the 2000s he was a commander responsible for ordering some of the suicide attacks carried out by the Qassam Brigades. Israel tried, frequently, to assassinate him, so he never stayed long at one address, giving rise to his nickname Deif ('The Guest').

Israel's most wanted man for more than two decades, Deif has long been wary of having a public profile after seeing the fate of his contemporary Ayyash. He is rarely seen or interviewed by the media, and his few appearances were mostly with his face obscured by a red keffiyeh. And after taking over from Shehadeh, Deif came up with new measures designed to overcome Israel's defences, one that the Israeli military termed the 'Over and Under' strategy.[22] This involved building a network of tunnels both under Gaza and beneath the borders into Israel and Egypt. He and his planners also expedited Hamas's capacity to send more and more missiles over Israel's fences around Gaza. But Deif was badly wounded in one of Israel's assassination attempts and was smuggled to Egypt for medical treatment, leaving his then deputy, Ahmed Jaabari, to take over the Brigades on a day-to-day basis for several years.

Jaabari was widely considered to hold radical and extremist views. During one 2006 TV interview he appeared dismissive of those within Hamas who sought only political office, saying, 'I am a fighter for God. You will find me anywhere, any place, fighting the enemies of Islam ... We don't seek positions in the government or leadership; our aim is to fight the enemies of Islam.'[23]

Divisions within the military wing intensified after Hamas's military takeover of Gaza in June 2007, when it ousted Palestinian Authority forces loyal to President Mahmoud Abbas. A few months later, in November, Deif was smuggled back into Gaza through tunnels from Egypt to head off a challenge from Jaabari and his political patrons in the radical wing of Hamas, including Ali Jundiyeh and Sheikh Nizar Rayan, who was considered the strategic head of the Qassam Brigades. The inspiration behind the takeover, Rayan even regarded the secular-nationalist Palestinian Authority in Ramallah as *kufaar* (infidels) and to be regarded as legitimate targets. He viewed any form of recognition of Israel as dangerous to Hamas's Islamist credentials.

Rayan and Jaabari – by then in charge of an estimated 20,000 Qassam Brigade fighters in Gaza – represented a more radical wing in the Brigades compared with the more 'pragmatic' Deif. To outsiders such distinctions might be academic, but it had wider significance in terms of the developing direction of the military wing of Hamas, its relationship to the political leadership, and Hamas's wider position in the Middle East. In private, Deif reportedly bemoaned the radicalization, warning that such tendencies could lead to links with al-Qaeda and complaining to friends that he no longer wielded any real influence in the Qassam Brigades and that 'the *salafis* had taken over'.

Suicide Bombs to Rockets

The flow of suicide bombers into Israel during the Second Intifada led Israel in 2002 to begin the construction of a wall and fortified fence around and through the occupied West Bank. Israel's tactic – a security measure rather than a political solution – proved to be no more than a temporary salve. The move also drew the censure of the International Court of Justice, which delivered an advisory opinion ruling it as 'contrary to international law'.[24] As would-be suicide bombers and gunmen found it increasingly hard to reach Israeli towns from the West Bank, Hamas and other factions increasingly turned to other means to attack. While its military wing continued to mount surprise 'spectacular' strikes, its principal weapon increasingly

Photo 7.1 Hamas military wing members in Gaza, July 2005

became the crude but potentially deadly Qassam rocket, which it manufactured in secret workshops across the Gaza Strip.

Although Israeli security hawks argue that the pull-out from Gaza led to its becoming a base for rocket attacks into Israel, in fact all Palestinian militant factions had used rockets before the withdrawal. Indeed, Israel's pre-2005 settlements in Gaza were regular targets for mortar and rocket attacks. But it became far easier for the militants to launch rockets after the Israelis withdrew.

Though their attacks were rarely fatal, the sheer numbers of Qassam rockets and mortars turned survival into a lottery in Israeli border towns such as Sderot – soon nicknamed Sderoket. The launches were also unpredictable, setting off early warning sirens at all hours of the day and proving a deliberate reminder to Israeli residents of their occupied and blockaded neighbours next door.

Hamas had also learned lessons from Israel's 2006 war with Hezbollah in Lebanon, when the Iran-backed Shia group launched a cross-border attack into northern Israel, abducting Israeli soldiers under cover of rocket fire and then engaging in five weeks of hostilities with Israeli troops who crossed in pursuit into Lebanon. Chatham House analyst Bilal Y. Saab argued that:

> You've got to remember, Hezbollah is the author of what Hamas just did in terms of actual incursion deep inside Israeli territory, and kind of mounting a Blitzkrieg and sowing panic and chaos. They are the senior partner; they are the ones the Israelis worry about a whole lot more. And it's not like they don't have tunnels either. But they also have precision-guided missiles, they have all sorts of training that Hamas doesn't have. And so, the Israelis have a very healthy respect for Hezbollah's capabilities.[25]

Hamas certainly noted Israel's failure to stop Hezbollah's Katyusha rockets landing in northern Israel, terrifying the Israeli population living there and causing many of them to move south. 'This war has had a huge negative effect on the Israeli street, and it has sent a message that the occupation can never stand against the resistance if you have a really good resistance,' said Abu Bakr Nofal, a senior Hamas official in Gaza.[26]

Israel claimed to have 'clear intelligence' about how many weapons Hamas had begun smuggling into the Gaza Strip. However, in the mid-2000s, one senior Israeli intelligence official professed himself to be concerned more about the expertise Hamas was gleaning abroad than about the hardware it has smuggled. 'One of the bad fruits of the isolation of Hamas is the influence of Iran and its money,' said Yuval Diskin, the director of Shin Bet:

> What we see that is more dangerous than any weapons is the training that Iran has promised Hamas. We know that Hamas has started to dispatch people to Iran, tens with the promise of hundreds, for months and maybe

years of training. I see this as the strategic challenge more than any smuggled weapons. You need expertise to use weapons, and in the long run the Iranian training is what is dangerous.[27]

The threat became graver as the Qassam Brigades smuggled ever-longer range rockets into Gaza, including Grad missiles capable of reaching Ashkelon and Beersheba. 'Yes, the Grads were a leap up. We don't have a military arsenal. Ours is tiny compared to them. But what we possess, these simple weapons, are effective against the Israelis,'[28] boasted one Hamas rocketeer in northern Gaza, who gave the *nom de guerre* Abu Khaled.

This prompted Israel to mount a large-scale attack on Jabalia refugee camp in northern Gaza in March 2008, in which sixty-one Palestinians were killed in one day. 'Everybody needs to understand that Israeli citizens are being terrorized by rockets coming from Gaza Strip,' said Tzipi Livni, Israel's foreign minister. 'This is something that we cannot live with.'[29]

By the end of 2008, Israel claimed that 10,000 rockets had been fired from Gaza. But although it responded with attacks on missile sites, the rocket teams were usually long gone, and the widespread destruction inflicted by the thousands of Israeli artillery shells fired into the crowded Gaza Strip drew condemnation from the international community and more accusations about disproportionate use of force. Israel denied the accusations, however, and human rights groups also criticized Hamas for using weapons that indiscriminately targeted civilians. Indeed, in 2009, a UN-ordered report into Israel's military assault on Gaza also concluded that, in fact, the Hamas missiles launched indiscriminately at Israel constituted a war crime.

While the Hamas leadership is reticent about its exact ties with overseas suppliers, on the ground in Gaza its fighters make no effort to deny that it gets weapons and training from Iran. 'As Hezbollah in Lebanon, as Hamas in Gaza,' shrugged the rocketeer Abu Khaled. 'To achieve our goal we are allowed to ask for help to obtain power from wherever we can, from whoever provides it ... The only one that provides them is Tehran.'[30] Another Qassam Brigades leader said he commanded men who had been trained in Iran, Afghanistan, Syria, Jordan, Egypt and even – he claimed – by the FBI. 'It's not a question of special assistance from Iran. We'll use the experience of our men and training wherever they get it.'[31]

The escalation of rocket attacks brought a swift end to the *salafi* vs pragmatist divide in the military wing – in 2012 Deif's radical deputy Ahmed Jaabari was assassinated by Israel while driving his car through Gaza City. Israeli military spokeswoman Avital Leibovich confirmed that Jaabari was specifically targeted in an effort to halt the growing number of rocket attacks on southern Israel.[32]

Video Wars

In the decade that followed Jaabari's death, the Qassam Brigades kept the pressure up by regularly launching rockets and missiles across the Gaza border. Their defensive capacity also grew. This had a form of deterrent effect on Israel – although they were loath to admit it, there was a reluctance from decision-makers to have their forces constantly drawn into engagement – particularly on the ground in Gaza against Hamas's military wing. So the modus vivendi became more carefully and strategically calibrated.

With each military encounter – 2008–9, 2012, 2014, 2018 and 2021 – Hamas members became astute planners, understanding that knowing and adapting to their operating environment was crucial. While in theory its military doctrine could be summed up in one word – jihad – in practice it was clear that, as the years went by, Hamas was capable of security evolution. The figurative swords in its logo had evolved into rocket-propelled grenade launchers, remote rocket-firing mechanisms, bodycams and UAVs. Its military wing was better apprised of urban warfare tactics than Israel was; it honed forms of insurgence mixed with resistance and self-defence tactics to sow fear in Israel. Gaza was an operational milieu that the Qassam Brigades knew well, and in which they were effective.

Once they secured control of Gaza in 2007, the commanders of the Qassam Brigades could devote their time and resources to recruiting, training and deploying committed personnel. This was a frequently overlooked contrast to Israel's armed forces. Though far larger in size than Hamas's, a large part of Israel's military is made up of men and women aged eighteen to twenty-one undertaking compulsory service and, at the other end of the demographic scale, the more than 350,000 plus reservists (up to the age of fifty-one) who take time away from their full-time jobs to do their duty on an annual basis for their country. Typically, Israel's young soldiers were very different in disposition to the highly trained rank and file of the Qassam Brigades, hardened by long sessions at boot camps among the sand dunes or abandoned Israeli settlements in Gaza. They seemed effortlessly to combine dedication to cause and country – the liberation of Palestine.

Qassam commanders acknowledged that Israel enjoyed far superior firepower. Yet they came to be keenly aware of what made Israelis fearful and how to leverage that to meet their own aims and objectives.

The same was true of the concept of victory. Of course, Israel was always capable of denying Hamas ultimate victory – realists knew that Hamas's military forces could never overwhelm Israel's defences completely to end its subjugation of the Palestinian people. What Hamas did manage to do, and especially the Qassam Brigades and its communication wing, was to magnify even the smallest successes into a triumph. Every Israeli setback, every soldier killed, injured or kidnapped, every tank immobilized, destroyed or captured – then streamed on Hamas social media – served as a series of little victories that then fed into important narratives of resistance (*muqawwama*), steadfastness (*samud*), striving (*jihad*) and self-defence that gave succour and hope to the populations of Gaza, the West Bank and East Jerusalem.

Three weeks after the 7 October attack, an Israeli journalist, Anshel Pfeffer, spelled out with clarity the unavoidable link between modern warfare and modern communications. 'About 18 months ago, after returning from a reporting trip to Ukraine, an Israeli general asked me what I thought the main lessons were from that war. I answered that … if there was anything Israel should learn from it, it's the power of videos made on the battlefield to influence the international narrative of a war,' he wrote. Ukraine had learned that lesson, he explained.

> We knew of course that both sides were taking heavy casualties, but very few visuals came out. What did emerge were well-produced videos of Ukrainian missile teams ambushing and destroying Russian tanks. It doesn't matter that this was only a small part of what was happening: it was the image of those early stages of the war. In a future war in which Israel is involved, I warned the general, the tanks will be Israeli Merkavas and even if the enemy side manages to hit just a tiny handful of them, the videos will be online almost immediately, and Israelis back home will suddenly be seeing their sons dead and wounded besides the tanks.[33]

As it turned out, he was 'only half-right', he reflected. It was to be the bodycam videos from Hamas's military wing raiders inside Israel's border kibbutzim that would prove the most traumatizing to Israelis, not footage of reverses inflicted by the Qassam Brigades on the battlefield that Gaza had become.

Furthermore, as Palestinians had long abandoned the hope that any outside Arab or Muslim force would ride to their aid, Hamas's military wing represented an important indigenously constituted force. In many respects, by the early 2020s, Hamas's forces, including the Qassam Brigades, were the only group of any size in the Occupied Palestinian Territories providing the local population with anything like the kind of security force they wanted. The armed forces of the Palestinian Authority were widely perceived by most Palestinians in the Israeli-occupied West Bank to be little more than security sub-contractors for Israel. The decision by President Abbas to enter security coordination arrangements with Israel was widely seen as a strategic error. West Bankers openly criticized Abbas when his security forces carried out raids and arrests against populist Palestinian factions at – it was widely believed – Israel's behest. Such cooperation with Israel also spurred the growth in the West Bank of paramilitary armed factions operating autonomously of the Palestinian Authority in cities such as Nablus and Jenin.

Like any armed force, Hamas military strategists convened after any battle to assess the victories and failures and to address lessons learned. After the 2008–9 war on Gaza, the Qassam Brigades leadership did just this. One important outcome of their review was the decision to establish an elite (nukhba) military unit that only the best in the Qassam Brigades would be chosen to join.

Training was highly demanding, specializing in commando-style naval and ground-based operational scenarios. The Nukhba Force was given detailed training on how to target Israel's military infrastructure most effectively, close to the border fence, checkpoints and watchtowers that enclose Gaza. The newly created unit was also responsible for operating out of the vast tunnel network that Hamas had built beneath the Gaza Strip, which served as a covert insurgency facility from which Israel could be penetrated as part of a multi-pronged approach.

Over the ensuing decade the Nukhba Force became one of the most secretive and highly organized units of Hamas's military wing. It was involved in leading Hamas operations during the 2014 and 2021 conflicts. It managed to penetrate Israeli maritime and coastal border positions, including an attack in 2014 on an Israeli military base at Zikim beach just north of the Gaza Strip – after which Israel's prime minister publicly vowed that he would act against the Hamas 'terrorists' to ensure that such a breach would not be allowed to happen again. That 2014 attack on Zikim foreshadowed a much larger seaborne attack accompanied by intensive rocket fire that Hamas fighters launched against the facility in October 2023, which, again, failed to capture it.[34]

However, in 2020 there was significant speculation about whether the Nukhba Force had been seriously compromised, after Saudi news media reported that there had been a high-level defection of one of the Nukhba's top officers to Israel, and that following an internal investigation Hamas arrested sixteen more of the unit's members and accused them of spying for Israel. It was considered a major intelligence coup for Israel, but it would appear that the intelligence gleaned was not enough to prevent the cross-border attack on Israel three years later.[35]

By 2023 Hamas had an armoury that consisted of smuggled and locally manufactured missiles and rockets, automatic rifles, ammunition, grenades, RPGs, explosively formed penetrators (EFPs) and armed drones. Drone technology had become available to the Qassam Brigades in the mid-2000s: like other non-state armed groups, Hamas had learned from the techno-logical developments in insurgent territories such as Iraq and, later, Syria, Lebanon and Yemen. Operatives did not need to be in the same country to train together, develop and identify suitable technology or operationalize it. Virtual reality technology and good trainers were all that Qassam Brigades fighters needed to grasp what the new weapons were, how they could be operated and what their capacity was.

The Israeli military estimated that Hamas had an arsenal of at least 10,000 rockets before 2023, most with ranges of up to 12 miles, but many capable of reaching central Israel. Before October 2023 there were also estimates that the Qassam Brigades had 25,000 fighters, with others believing the number reached 35,000 to 40,000. The stage was set for 7 October 2023.[36]

Going Underground

Of all the groundwork laid down by the Qassam Brigades in preparation for its 2023 cross-border attack, it was the literal working of the ground that created its most entrenched defences and the biggest challenge to Israel's much larger and better-equipped invading force.

Palestinian militant factions had used smuggling for decades in a region that had no shortage of expertise in the illicit movement of goods, going back centuries to when Gaza lay on the ancient Via Maris trading route between Egypt and Damascus, connecting Asia and Africa.

The Palestinians' need to evade scrutiny became more acute in 1982 when Israel handed back the Sinai peninsula to Egypt after the 1979 peace treaty, creating a border that left half the coastal city of Rafah in Egypt and half in Israeli-occupied Gaza. To keep tighter control over what moved in and out of Gaza, Israel insisted on keeping a strategic 100-metre-wide 'buffer zone' along the Egyptian border. Known as the 'Philadelphi Corridor', this strip was regularly patrolled by Israeli military vehicles. But even while the Israeli buffer zone was there a tunnel industry sprang up; families with members on each side of the border set up tunnels to move illicit goods under the border fence.

In 1992 the Israeli military uncovered a cross-border tunnel in Rafah refugee camp and said it was used to smuggle weapons and wanted Palestinian militants. And in 1994 Egyptian soldiers found ten tunnels and destroyed them.[37] Although the tunnels were of necessity secret, Hamas is thought to have begun its digging operation around the mid-1990s, when Arafat's Palestinian Authority was established with some degree of self-rule in Gaza. Tunnelling activities were hampered, however, by the presence of Israel's Jewish settlements and the accompanying security apparatus of watchtowers, sniper positions, tanks and road closures.

Military tunnel-building in Gaza accelerated dramatically after two developments – when Israel pulled its soldiers and settlers out of Gaza in 2005 and when Hamas seized control of the 139 square miles of the Gaza Strip from Abbas's Palestinian Authority forces two years later. Once the buffer zone on the Egyptian border disappeared, Palestinian factions found it far easier to smuggle in weapons and rocket parts, and Hamas was also forced to bring in ordinary consumer goods, food, cement and fuel through the tunnels to evade the tight Israeli-led blockade imposed on Gaza after it came to power.

The once heavily guarded strip of land between Rafah and the border came to resemble a Klondike mining operation, with uniformed Hamas forces operating where Israeli patrols once drove, and hundreds of Palestinians working in full sight of the Egyptian border watchtowers at a long line of tunnel entrances covered by wooden planking, tarpaulins and corrugated iron lean-tos servicing a tunnel economy. Hamas took its cut through an unofficial tax on the tunnel operators and ran its own clandestine weapons tunnels that were not so visible to the public. The cross-border tunnelling was at its height during the years 2011 to 2014, especially during the chaotic 'Arab Spring' period between the fall of Egyptian President Hosni Mubarak, the rise and rapid fall of the Muslim Brotherhood in Cairo and the ascension of strongman former general Abdel Fattah al-Sisi. Al-Sisi saw Hamas as an Islamist ally of the Brotherhood, so he closed the border and attempted to destroy the tunnels by flooding them.

Israel was by then targeting the tunnels inside Gaza, and after a round of fighting in 2012 claimed to have destroyed 140 of them. But Hamas was quickly back at work building new ones and repairing the old. After another bout of hostilities in 2021, Hamas's leader in Gaza, Yahya Sinwar, claimed: 'We have 500 km of tunnels and Israel has destroyed only 100 km of them. We will be able to restore everything in a few days.'[38]

In an effort to stop any more underground cross-border raids such as the one in which Gilad Schalit was kidnapped by Hamas in 2006, Israel spent three years building an underground barrier equipped with sensors, radar and cameras, which, upon its completion in December 2021, it called an 'iron wall'.[39]

But this did little to stop the tunnel-building inside Gaza itself. Although the full extent of Hamas's tunnel network may never be known following Israel's extensive bombing of 2023–4, few challenged Sinwar's boast that the network extended hundreds of miles. Yocheved Lifshitz, an 85-year-old Israeli woman who was taken hostage by Hamas and kept in the tunnels, said after her release: 'It looked like a spider's web, many, many tunnels … We walked kilometres under the ground.'[40] Indeed, Lifshitz, a peace activist, said she met Sinwar himself in one of the tunnels and confronted him. 'Sinwar was with us three to four days after we arrived. I asked him how he is not ashamed to do such a thing to people who have supported peace all these years,' she said.[41]

When Israeli ground forces moved into Gaza with bulldozers and clearance equipment, they claimed to have found entrance shafts hidden among the Gaza Strip's devastated urban neighbourhoods, with others concealed in sand dunes in rural areas. Footage and photographs from the Israeli military, and journalists who accompanied them, showed concrete-lined tunnels hundreds of feet long, with metal doors, electrical cabling, ventilation and beds.[42]

But with Gaza sealed off, many of the areas in question too dangerous for Gaza-based journalists to visit, and Israel refusing access to international journalists other than those embedded with the Israeli military, claims by both sides were greeted with caution by many international news organizations.

Challenged about the scale of civilian casualties – including children – during one Israeli airstrike on Gaza's Jabalia refugee camp, Netanyahu's senior adviser Ambassador Mark Regev said Israel had attacked an underground bunker sheltering a Hamas commander involved in the 7 October cross-border attacks. 'We don't target civilians. We target Hamas's military machine, we target Hamas command and control,' Regev said. 'It's possible that when we hit the underground headquarters of Hamas, that because it's the underground tunnels, it caused other structures to fall. We don't want to see collateral damage. We do our best to avoid collateral damage.'[43]

Some countries cut off diplomatic ties with Israel in protest at the scale of the devastation its airstrikes were inflicting. As the war went on, even Israel's closest allies, including Canada, voiced concern that the soaring Palestinian death toll was eroding support for Israel internationally.[44]

It was a 'rewind and play again' of the same argument about the Shehadeh assassination two decades earlier – except the Palestinian deaths in 2023–4 were not confined to one Gaza City neighbourhood but were replicated across the Gaza Strip on a massive scale, far in excess of 1,000 times the fatalities in the 2002 Shehadeh bombing. Again, Israel focused on what it said was its intent and Palestinians on the outcome, rejecting Israel's claim that it was not targeting civilians. In the West Bank, then Prime Minister Mohammad Shtayyeh was at one point reduced to tears at the scenes broadcast from Gaza and called on the International Criminal Court to intervene. 'Israel has never stopped killing our children,' he said. 'Israel must be held accountable for its crimes.'[45]

In December 2023, the Israeli military released a video of Israel's defense minister accompanied by soldiers in a concrete-lined structure large enough for a person to walk through. It claimed – without providing evidence – that it was a Hamas tunnel leading to an entrance in sand dunes near the main Erez border crossing between Israel and Gaza.[46] Erez, a huge complex of body scanners, metal and explosives detectors, passport booths, interrogation rooms and surveillance cameras, was one of the Israeli bases attacked and overrun by Hamas fighters on 7 October. So high and seemingly impenetrable are its concrete blast walls, fortified turnstiles and wire cage walkways that the notion of its being overwhelmed was almost inconceivable before it happened.

In response, the Qassam Brigades 'military media' unit spliced the Israeli military footage with their own video clips from the bodycams of Qassam Brigades militants running towards Erez on 7 October and attacking it. The video appeared to taunt Israel, carrying a message in Arabic, Hebrew and English: 'You arrived late … Mission had already been completed.'[47]

8

Martyrs

There is no path except that of martyrdom – armed resistance and martyrdom operations. This is what will support Gaza. This is what will lift the oppression from you. We do not take up arms except in the face of the Zionist enemy.
Khaled Meshaal, Hamas leader, 2008[1]

It was 11 September 2001, and Jenin had only one hour left to revel in its status as the suicide attack capital of the globe. Nineteen hijackers who were at that very moment aboard airliners heading towards New York and Washington were about to change everything. But until then a small cluster of Hamas, Fatah and Islamic Jihad militants looking up nervously at the sky in a besieged Palestinian refugee camp were the most wanted suicide bombers in the world.

Since dawn, Jenin refugee camp – a deprived, permanently half-finished concoction of dust, potholes, breezeblock homes and corner shops – had found itself surrounded by Israeli tanks and helicopter gunships. Israel had a list of the men that it suspected of masterminding suicide bombings, and it wanted the Palestinian Authority to hand them over. The northernmost Palestinian town in the West Bank, just 6 miles from where Izz ad-Din al-Qassam was killed in a shoot-out with British forces sixty years earlier, Jenin had acquired a reputation as an outlying centre of resistance against Israeli military occupation, as Gaza was to become in later decades. It lay just on the other side of the Green Line which divided Israel proper from the West Bank.

Nearly a year into the Second Intifada, the Green Line, although invisible on the ground, had at least served as a reassuring psychological construct for Israelis because it mentally separated 'us' from 'them'. Israel believed that, through its checkpoints, walls, razor wire, settlements and military bases, the West Bank was a place that could be ringfenced off. But just two days before 9/11, Israelis had suffered an unexpected development: a suicide bomber not from 'over there' but from within their midst.

On 9 September 2001, an Israeli man blew himself up near the train station in the northern Israeli town of Nahariya, killing three of his fellow

Israelis. The bomber belonged to Hamas, which was not unusual. But he was also an Israeli citizen, which was. Muhammad Shaker Ihbeishi, aged forty-eight, was the first suicide bomber to come not from the West Bank or Gaza but from Israel's own Palestinian Arab minority. Although Israel is often described as a Jewish state, it is more accurately a Jewish-majority one. One-fifth of its population are Arabs, the descendants of the Palestinian residents of British Mandate Palestine who did not leave their Arab villages and cities when they suddenly found themselves part of the newly created state of Israel in 1948. Ihbeishi was born in Israel, raised in Israel and lived in Israel. His village of Abu Snaan was only 20 miles from Nazareth, the largest Arab city in Israel. In other words, he was both Israeli and Palestinian.

It was a frightening prospect for some Israelis – those who believed that the Palestinians living among them were a fifth column. In fact, Ihbeishi proved to be a rarity. But his attack had served its purpose for Hamas – to make Israelis worry about where the next bomb would come from. Hamas military planners said this was precisely their game plan, to create uncertainty among ordinary Israelis and avoid setting any pattern. 'To turn Arabs into a point of fear for Israelis, the most important thing was the variety of people who committed these suicide attacks,' explained Mohammed, a veteran Qassam Brigades commander in Gaza City in 2007.

> First we started with university graduates. The Israelis used to say suicide bombers were a bunch of poor people, despairing of life, so at the beginning we used educated young university students. Sometimes it was an old man who had a family or a stable life. Sometimes it was women, although that wasn't the policy of Hamas at that time to use women. They came later. This had a very negative impact on the Israelis. They couldn't draw a profile of suicide bombers. It was anybody, in every category. It was absolutely deliberate that there should be no pattern. It was just honest, decent people who had a huge will to sacrifice for their own people. That was the only thing they had in common.[2]

In Jenin, the besieged bomb-makers were delighted to see the Israeli consternation over the Nahariya bombing. But one Hamas fighter had a different perspective from his Gaza colleague. For him, suicide bombings were a tactic born of desperate necessity, not a tool of psychological warfare. 'You have to understand nobody wants to die; there is no other way to achieve our goal. Suicide bombs are our Apache helicopters. They are all we have,' he said.[3] One of his fellow wanted men, huddling close to a wall to avoid being spotted by Israeli spy drones, questioned what the Israelis had achieved by using F16s and Apaches. 'Now Israel cannot live in peace. There used to be immigration into Israel and now it is going the other way. Israeli factories are closing, they are suffering ... We can bear these kind of conditions ... Can they?'[4] It was a classic piece of bravado fusing three elements central to the Palestinian narrative: redefining military weakness as moral superiority and survival as victory, plus a widespread conviction that Israelis are weaker than them, especially without the help of advanced military technology. These fighters gloried in their self-proclaimed capacity not only to inflict suffering on the enemy but to be better at enduring it.

Zealots

Hamas prizes sacrifice around the concept of martyrdom. Article 8 of its founding constitution proclaims: 'Allah is its target, the Prophet is its model, the Koran its constitution: Jihad is its path and death for the sake of Allah is the loftiest of its wishes.'[5]

In June 2003, after Israel declared open season on the Hamas leadership, Hamas's founder Sheikh Ahmed Yassin scorned the threat of assassination, saying: 'If I saw the rocket coming I would jump and hug it' – a vow given added force because he was a quadriplegic who had to use a wheelchair all his adult life. He continued: 'If they kill Ahmed Yassin another 100 Ahmed Yassins will grow up ... Our desire is martyrdom: the day we become martyrs is a wedding day for us. We are not afraid of their threats, and when we get killed it is the happiest day of our lives.'[6]

So unfathomable is the rationale of suicide bombing to most onlookers that the bombers – who are by definition unavailable to provide further explanation – become a blank canvas upon which all parties tend to project their own rationalizations. For Hamas, they are useful vehicles for videotaped propaganda messages; for Israelis, they are the duped tools of evil despatchers who fill them with hatred for Jews before sending them to their deaths. In family mourning tents after explosions, relatives and friends of the 'martyr' usually serve up, with dried dates and a thimbleful of coffee, explanations attributing their son or daughter's final gesture to despair, revenge or an attempt to burst out of a lifetime of powerlessness. For Israeli casualties of the bomb attacks, there is despair and even greater enmity. All see through their own prism an act which none can truly comprehend.

Although the concept of martyrdom is by no means exclusive to Islamist movements, the fusion of religion and armed struggle within the ideology identifies them most closely with the phenomenon of suicide bombings. The late Dr Eyad Sarraj, a Gaza psychiatrist and director of the Gaza

Community Mental Health Programme, cited the prolonged effect of many decades of Israeli occupation on Palestinian society and the sway of religious movements such as Hamas. He argued that, for would-be bombers convinced that God is 'waiting for them on the other side', attacking Israel became a form of 'divine duty, the ultimate expression of faith ... the ultimate expression of heroism'. He also maintained that, after the humiliation of the Arab states in the wars against Israel of 1948, 1967 and 1973, the religious certainties imparted by groups such as Hamas – and Hezbollah in Lebanon – were welcomed by many Palestinians. Islamism, he said, gave them 'a new identity of victory and belonging to God compared to the identity of your father who was powerless and dying in defeat. This kind of new identity gives so much power.'[7]

The concepts of martyrdom (*shahaada*), resistance (*muqawama*) and occupation (*ehtilaal*) are now ingrained in the identity of peoples who have for centuries lived under a succession of foreign invaders, from the Romans to the Mongols (Tatars), Ottomans and British. That historic desire to throw off the yoke of alien oppressors is shrewdly invoked by the Hamas Covenant, which places its struggle with Israel within this tradition:

> The Islamic Resistance Movement views seriously the defeat of the Crusaders at the hands of Salah ed-Din al-Ayyubi and the rescuing of Palestine from their hands, as well as the defeat of the Tatars at Ein Galot, breaking their power at the hands of Qataz and Al-Dhaher Bivers and saving the Arab world from the Tatar onslaught which aimed at the destruction of every meaning of human civilization. The Movement draws lessons and examples from all this. The present Zionist onslaught has also been preceded by Crusading raids from the West and other Tatar raids from the East. Just as the Moslems faced those raids and planned fighting and defeating them, they should be able to confront the Zionist invasion and defeat it.[8]

Of course, Hamas has no monopoly on martyrdom, although it strives hard to make it appear so. But it has played on the powerful rhetoric and historical myths of the ancient Crusades made manifest in modern form in Israel's military occupation of their lands with support from its closest ally, America. As one scholar and Hamas supporter, Dr Atef Adwan, argued, 'We understand the echo of history on our own land and that the banner of Islam can only be raised again in the face of Crusader occupation through resistance.'[9]

In the 1960s and 1970s, long before Hamas existed, Yasser Arafat's PLO guerrillas were lionized by Palestinians as *fedayeen* – 'those who sacrifice'

– and the word *shaheed* (martyr) is used across the Arab and Muslim world to invest the death of those killed in conflict with the comfort of their faith. By no means all Palestinians support suicide attacks as a valid tactic, either morally or militarily. But for the vast majority of Palestinians, as for Arabs across the Middle East, they were called *a'maliyya istishhadiyya* (martyrdom operations) rather than *a'maliyya intihariiyye* (suicide operations). Hamas people are prone to admonish anyone who calls them suicide attacks in their presence. For many Palestinians, every victim of Israel's violence is a martyr whose death is commemorated as a symbol of national sacrifice towards freedom and an end to Israeli occupation. 'Resistance' and 'occupation' are concepts so imbued with significance – one positive, one overwhelmingly negative – that they are constantly invoked.

In 2023–4, as Israel waged war in Gaza following Hamas's cross-border attack, and the number of Palestinians killed in the bombardment and airstrikes rapidly mounted into the tens of thousands, each person killed was called a martyr, whether a baby, a child, a woman, a Hamas militant, or emergency workers such as doctors, ambulance drivers and UN humanitarian officials.

And 'martyr' is not a word used only by Muslim Palestinians in the context of the conflict. When the prominent Palestinian-American journalist Shireen Abu Akleh – a Christian – was killed by a bullet to the head on 11 May 2022 while reporting on an Israeli army raid on Jenin refugee camp, Palestinians blamed Israeli troops for her death. And the Israeli army concluded that, while it could not unequivocally determine the cause, there was a 'high possibility that Ms. Abu Akleh was accidentally hit by IDF gunfire.'[10] When a mural of the slain TV reporter in her press jacket was unveiled in the city where her father's family came from, the mayor of Bethlehem, Hanna Hanania, also a Christian, described her in his speech as 'a martyr of the truth' who conveyed the Palestinian cause to the world.[11]

Culture of Martyrdom

Hamas carried out a greater percentage of suicide bombings during the Second Intifada than any other militant faction – 39.9 per cent between 2000 and 2005 according to one 2007 study.[12] As the attacks multiplied and the television coverage and newspaper headlines they generated reached saturation level, the movement was accused of promoting a culture of martyrdom that damaged Palestinian society. The notion of encouraging people to sacrifice by offering themselves up to be suicide bombers was criticized: theatre performances, student groups, pop chants and rap songs, films, poems, art, impromptu memorials, websites, posters, flags, postcards, necklaces – even slush puppies dubbed 'suicide reds' – all encouraged the cult of sacrifice. Some websites allowed their users to access hundreds of Hamas martyr or *shaheed* video clips, which followed a popular format of showing a succession of photos of gun-toting males interspersed with romanticized images of Arab steeds, red roses and Israeli soldiers being defeated on the battlefield. Each video was accompanied by a song, the lyrics of which talked about the nation, Islam and martyrdom. By 2003–4 the images were ubiquitous. In Gaza City, Beit Hanoun, Jenin, Rafah and Hebron, martyrs' portraits hung from homes, shops, public buildings and traffic intersections, alongside advertisements for Nokia mobile phones and Samsung electronics. Martyrdom was everywhere, even in movies. 'If we can't live as equals, at least we'll die as equals,' lamented one would-be suicide bomber in the 2005 Golden Globe-winning Palestinian film 'Paradise Now'.[13]

By far the deadliest suicide bombing in Israel was the 27 March 2002 attack on the Park Hotel in Netanya, in which thirty Passover celebrants were killed by Abdel Basset Odeh, a 25-year-old member of Hamas's military wing. At Odeh's family home in the Palestinian town of Tulkarem, less than 10 miles from Netanya, his family kept his portraits on the wall, brandishing a semi-automatic rifle, in his Hamas bandana, with the Hamas military logo prominently displayed. They insisted they knew nothing of his intentions in advance, but attributed it to the 'accumulated' pressures of being a Palestinian, talking of how he was detained during the First Intifada as a child and suffered the impotence and frustration of a young man forced to submit to Israeli soldiers at checkpoints. 'There are many who say that they are fed up with this life, are frustrated and they don't want to live any more,' said his father, Mohammed, five years after the attack. 'People get so frustrated and so oppressed. Not only Abdel Basset but every Palestinian feels that he has suffered, and he has lived a bitter life.'

Although Odeh was engaged to a Palestinian from Iraq and had made all the arrangements for marriage, including obtaining a furnished apartment, his family said he found it increasingly difficult to travel to neighbouring Jordan to meet his fiancée's relatives. Finally, in the summer of 2001 – nine months before the bombing – the Israelis refused him passage through the border, denying him a chance to make a future and a family for himself. Soon afterwards Odeh disappeared, they said, just as the Israelis were beginning to ask awkward questions about him. Odeh's father professed his son's actions a 'good operation' which 'made people very happy. They hit the street in joy the minute they heard of the attack.'[14]

In its essentials, Odeh's tale was little different from hundreds of others in which anger, desperation or frustration did not escalate into a violent attack. Furthermore, suicide bombing is by no means the only form of martyrdom to which impressionable youngsters can succumb. As Israeli battle tanks fought Palestinian militants in Gaza's Jabalia district in 2006, Muhammad Zakout ordered his children to stay indoors. The 44-year-old labourer left his house briefly to check on his elderly mother, and when he arrived back home he found that his fourteen-year-old son Ala'a had sneaked out of the house to throw stones at Israeli soldiers and had been shot in the shoulder. 'He doesn't listen to me,' lamented Mr Zakout at his son's hospital bedside in Gaza City. 'It's very hard to keep him away. If he's older and he chooses to join the resistance I could understand. But not why they throw stones. It is because they don't have a real life. They are looking for excitement.'

Inside the hospital, Ala'a's grandmother and mother asked why he wanted to die: 'Is it to meet the martyrs? To see the next life? Has the cat got your tongue?' As they did so, Mr Zakout continued to expostulate. 'It is not easy to raise a child in this society,' he said.

> He becomes a young man and all of a sudden you lose him. He promises me he won't go to these things, and the next day he goes. I blame both the Israelis and the big Palestinian politicians. I have nothing against fighting the occupation. They are the terrorists and the ones with the upper hand. If you don't stop them at a certain point they will carry on and on. If you are occupied, it is your right to resist. But older people can make the choice. It is the duty of the mosques and the teachers to tell children that is not their role.

Eventually the wounded Ala'a, wincing from an injured shoulder, provided an answer to his family's questions about his apparent death wish. 'I'll tell you why,' he finally mumbled. 'We are just bored of this life and we want to die.'[15] Asked what they wanted to do when they grow up, the injured boy's teenage friends looked blank, seeing no possibilities in a Gaza Strip steadily being degraded by year after year of Israeli attacks and the Palestinian civil war that was then raging around them. Twenty years previously, Palestinian refugees dreamt of professions in medicine, engineering and education. But by then the young, who formed and still form the majority of Gaza's population, saw no hope, no peace, no prosperity, and no economic future. 'We have already grown up,' shrugged his friend Muhammad Abu al-Jidyan.

> We have no chance to do anything else. Probably when we grow up a little more we will just carry Kalashnikovs and fight. What else do we have to do?

The resistance don't ask us to throw stones, they kick our asses for it. But we do it anyway. At least it means the soldiers will not be able to put their heads out of the tank to shoot people, or to move into buildings. We want to become martyrs and we want to help the resistance, whether they like it or not.[16]

Husam Khader, a Fatah member of the Palestinian parliament and resident of Nablus, lamented that support for radical Islamist groups such as Hamas and Hezbollah had soared in a city where youths already wore portraits of dead 'martyrs' around their necks. His eleven-year-old daughter Amani had already become dangerously infatuated with the idea of suicide:

She says 'I recognize Fatah because of Yasser Arafat, but I am Hamas because they fight against Israel, because they are honest, they help the poor and they pray to God' … She said she wrote to her friend saying they wanted to make a military operation [suicide bombing]. I spent two or three hours a day saying, 'You should become a doctor, it will be better for your people, you are a child.'[17]

Not all Palestinians, however, supported the notion of sacrificing themselves or their children, for any cause. At the height of the suicide bombings in the Second Intifada there was growing concern and disquiet among sections of the Palestinian leadership that extremist factions were inculcating a death wish in their children. There were periodic calls for an end to the bombings from those arguing that, by glorifying martyrdom, they risked losing an entire generation to fanaticism. In June 2002, fifty-five prominent Palestinian officials, academics and community leaders, including Hanan Ashrawi and Sari Nusseibeh, took out a full-page advertisement in the most influential Palestinian daily newspaper urging a halt to such attacks. 'We appeal to those who stand behind the military operations to rethink and reconsider these actions, and to stop sending young men to carry out such attacks targeting civilians in Israel,' said the document. It called the attacks a counterproductive 'gift' to Israel's then prime minister, Ariel Sharon, by encouraging Israelis 'to continue their aggression and attacks against the Palestinian people'.[18] However, the signatories were criticized by fellow Palestinians for voicing public dissent, even on such pragmatic, rather than moral, grounds. The same month an opinion poll showed 68 per cent of Palestinians supported suicide bombings, only slightly down from 74 per cent six months earlier.[19]

Recruiters

To utilize the willing recruits, Hamas had a grassroots network of enlisters. They would monitor potential candidates carefully over months and even years to study their suitability, temperament and religious convictions before they were selected for an active role in the Qassam Brigades. Secrecy was paramount, it being a familiar refrain among family members that the first they learned of their son or daughter's involvement was a posthumous video proclaiming their martyrdom. Some Israelis asserted that impressionable young Palestinians were exploited by Hamas to further its own ends and sometimes by families with a baser motive than jihad or glory: money.

In October 2002 the Israeli government accused Saudi Arabia and Iraq of channelling millions of dollars to families of suicide bombers as a reward for attacking the Zionist enemy. A senior Israeli military official said that, while the Saudis donated 'much more' to individuals and organizations in total – $100 million as against $15 to $20 million from the Iraqis – Saddam Hussein's regime in Baghdad gained far more publicity by concentrating on suicide attackers. By prioritizing such missions – $25,000 per bomber compared with $5,000 from the Saudis – Iraq 'invested less money than the Saudis but they did it in a smart way.'

The Israelis' information came from documents and information said to have been gleaned from a captured middleman. After being arrested on 2 October 2002, this man allegedly told his Israeli interrogators that he had met regularly with Hamas and other organizations to speak with them 'about initiating terrorist activities against Israel', and that the Iraqi money was allegedly channelled from Baghdad through banks in Jordan and Ramallah. The Israelis said Iraqi donations came in three phases: up to August 2001, when Baghdad assigned $10,000 per attacker irrespective of the type of attack; from August 2001 to March 2002, when Saddam began prioritizing suicide bombers by raising the reward to $15,000; and from March 2002 on, when suicide bombers' families received $25,000 and others only $10,000. According to an Israeli official:

> The mechanism is based on the knowledge of the suicide bombers and suicide bombers' families that, after their son is martyred, they are going to get a lot of money from the Iraqis. They know that they would get most of the money if their son is a martyr, but if he is an ordinary terrorist who was killed they would get only $10,000. If crippled, less.

He said that the Israeli authorities found documents from one family asking the middleman, 'Why did we get only $10,000? Our son was a suicide bomber. Please give us the suicide bombers money. Please give us $25,000.' He maintained that, although would-be bombers did not get the money in advance, they knew that their families would be taken care of. 'When they are trying to recruit them, part of the argument is that first you will contribute to the Palestinian cause, but you know that the future of your family is much better,' he said. 'We know from the interrogation of suicide bombers who failed to kill themselves that the money was a consideration.'[20]

Hamas was contemptuous of Israeli assertions that its operations were motivated by financial reward. 'We struggle for freedom, not for money. Money won't buy a place in paradise for the martyr or his family,' said Abu Ashraf, a Hamas military leader. 'Do you see the families of the martyrs living in luxury in the wake of their son's death? Or do you see them sitting in the shattered ruins of their homes as Israel's punishment?'[21] Sheikh Yassin, in an interview in 2003, remarked on the Hamas motive: 'This is a society raised on war, and it wears the clothes of occupation. We have the right to retaliate if they kill our civilians and target them. And they have killed many more of our women and children than we have done.' He ended by declaring: 'A sacrifice in this way is for the nation and brings our people one step closer to liberation.'[22]

Most relatives of suicide bombers, at least in public, proclaimed full support for their dead 'martyr' and acceded to the intense pressure from family, neighbours and factions to bedeck their homes in the regalia of martyrdom and proclaim loyalty to the Palestinian cause. However, not all succumbed to such peer pressure. In January 2004 the family of a seventeen-year-old Islamic Jihad bomber, Iyad al-Masri, accused the Islamist faction of exploiting his feelings of grief and rage at a vulnerable time, just after the Israeli army had killed his brother and cousin. Iyad's father, Bilal, said he blamed both the Israelis and Islamic Jihad for his son's death. The teenager had left his home in Nablus, heading for Jerusalem, but blew himself up when he was tracked down by Israeli troops, injuring no one.

> This family is very angry. The Israelis recruited my son as a martyr because they killed his brother in front of him. Then they killed his cousin in front of him too. Mohammed's brains were thrown all over Iyad. If he hadn't seen his brother and cousin die, he would never have become a martyr. But those who sent him [as a suicide bomber] exploited his grief.[23]

So deeply ingrained were the Palestinian factions' conviction of the virtue of their cause that many failed to comprehend how their actions were seen in the wider world. On 11 September 2001, when the Palestinian Authority was quick to condemn al-Qaeda's attacks on the US, all the Palestinian factions appeared to realize the inadvisability of persisting with bombings in the immediate aftermath. Although they continued to kill Israelis with the gun, there was only one suicide attack in the next ten weeks. Khalil Shikaki, a Palestinian opinion pollster and political analyst, said: 'Hamas and Islamic Jihad have concluded separately that it would be suicide for them to continue suicide attacks. They don't want to be the focus of American attention, and they don't want to be on the wrong side of the war. They would like to keep their war against Israel in a completely different realm.'[24]

It did not last long. By early December 2001, Fatah, Islamic Jihad and Hamas had all resumed their suicide campaigns, echoing Rantissi's attempts to justify them by blaming Israeli provocations. But, from their rhetoric and actions, they appeared so wedded to a tactic that inflicted damage on their enemy that they were blinded to how they were becoming international pariahs to those who saw no distinction between burning buses in Jerusalem and burning aeroplanes in New York. For Hamas there was genuine, or at least professed, astonishment that the world could not distinguish between 'our' and 'their' suicide bombings. 'We condemned 9/11,' said Usama Hamdan, a senior Hamas leader in Beirut in 2005. 'We have condemned these acts in Iraq. But I will answer in one way: we don't have jets, we don't have tanks. So we made the decision. It is one of the ways we resist … there is nothing wrong with our way, because we are under occupation.'[25]

The unavoidable sense gained from scores of interviews with Hamas fighters and leaders, and with many ordinary Palestinians during this period at the peak of the suicide bombing phenomenon, is that many embraced suicide bombings because they inspired a feeling of strength and empowerment by inflicting hurt on an otherwise near-invincible enemy. One veteran member of Hamas's military wing said it was a way of Hamas asserting power. 'That way you send a message to the whole world: you should respect Hamas.'[26]

Opponents

Israel's military and psychological experts studied the suicide and martyrdom phenomenon, looking for a profile upon which to draw up a defensive strategy. Some believed that the bombers reflected the very fabric of Palestinian society. 'There was no psychopathology to speak of. These were normal guys, just a cross-section of society,' said Israeli expert Ariel Merari. 'I came to think that suicide terrorism is not a personal phenomenon – it is an organizational phenomenon, an organizational system.'[27]

For other experts there were alternative explanations. Some argued that, for young men growing up in a socially conservative Palestinian society where sex before marriage was prohibited, the lure of seventy-two dark-eyed virgins awaiting them in paradise was enough to motivate them. Still others spoke of putative bombers being compromised and blackmailed into bombing Israeli civilians, or a Palestinian psyche dominated by evil and hate. Few, if any, saw Israel's policies of prolonged military occupation controlling the lives of Palestinians as causal.

Determined to stamp out the threat from suicide bombers, Israel ordered tight closures on the West Bank, sealing off major cities such as Nablus and Ramallah, and enforcing curfews. Human rights groups have long condemned such measures as 'punitive home demolitions and sweeping movement restrictions against entire areas or communities' as collective punishment amounting to war crimes.[28]

But in October 2002, outside the sealed-off city of Nablus, the Israeli commander of the area – who would identify himself only as Colonel Noam – said that Israel's policy of closures and checkpoints would stay in place to stop the suicide attacks. 'My job is to stop bombers getting to Tel Aviv, and I am determined to do it,' he said. 'They will suffer until they understand. This is the price of terror.'[29] Inside the cordon around Nablus, the Palestinian mayor of the city, Ghassan Shakah, cautioned that such measures would only provoke more violence among the 200,000 inhabitants. 'When you put pressure on a seventeen-year-old, he will react with bitterness and anger. The reaction will be to make bombs and commit suicide, because young people are losing hope,' he warned.[30]

It was a cause-and-effect argument. Israel said it needed more checkpoints, raids and assassinations to stop the bombing. Palestinians argued that the occupation, checkpoints, raids and assassinations were what had caused the bombings in the first place.

Other Israeli tactics included targeted assassinations of Hamas leaders – which also killed many Palestinian civilians – and so-called preventive measures such as mass arrest campaigns, roadblocks, travel restrictions, and raids on suspects.

By 2003 Israel had embarked on its most radical counter-measure: physical separation by building walls and fences in and around the West Bank. The 500-mile barrier often cut through Palestinian villages and farmland within the territory Israel had occupied since the 1967 Six Day

War. Palestinians feared that the move was a prelude to annexation of the West Bank. The International Court of Justice issued an advisory opinion in 2004 which said: 'the Court concluded that the construction of the wall, along with measures taken previously, severely impeded the exercise by the Palestinian people of its right to self-determination and was thus a breach of Israel's obligation to respect that right.'[31]

Human Shields

One of the principal accusations levelled by Israel against Hamas and other Palestinian factions is that they make use of their own civilian population as human shields, with their fighters frequently too ready to sacrifice others.

The allegations were made repeatedly during Israel's months-long bombardment of Gaza after Hamas's cross-border attack in October 2023. There were daily briefings from Israeli military officials that Hamas was hiding behind Gaza's 2.3 million civilian population. Hospitals became a particular focus of Israel's messaging – its military issuing heavily annotated – and unverifiable – photographs, video clips and audio recordings claiming that Hamas hid command and control posts and entrances to its underground tunnel network in hospitals.

Hamas official Ezzat El-Reshiq rejected the Israeli accusation, saying there was 'no basis in truth to what was reported by the enemy army spokesman.'[32] But it is one that has surfaced many times in the Israeli–Palestinian conflict and is as old as the notion of guerrilla warfare – small groups hiding from a larger enemy in mountain passes, jungles, deserts or cities from where they can strike and then retreat back under cover.

The allegations surfaced during the battle for Jenin refugee camp in April 2002, in which twenty-three Israeli soldiers and more than fifty Palestinians were killed, most of them militants. Israel accused Palestinian fighters of waging war from behind their own civilian populace. 'Terrorists used groups of civilians, women and children to get close to our troops,' said Major Rafi Laderman, an Israeli reservist who fought in the battle.[33]

Hamas responds to the human shield accusations by saying that, with Gaza sealed off from the outside world – by Israel – it has little choice but to wage war in the deeply densely populated city centres and refugee camps where it lives. On the ground there has often been a considerable grey area about how much the so-called human shields are willing participants. In 2006, after Israel began using F16 strikes to destroy suspected militants' homes, Gazan civilians in Beit Hanoun began standing on rooftops to make the Israelis abort the raids. They often responded voluntarily to appeals broadcast over mosque loudspeakers and radios, rushing to the threatened building within minutes to stand on the roof, giving the Israeli pilots no option but to cancel the bombing mission or kill scores of civilians.

When Israeli tanks and fighter-bombers pounded Gaza during the three-week 2008–9 Israeli assault designed to curb Hamas's rocket fire, many Gazan civilians complained that Israeli troops were attacking them under the guise of targeting the armed fighters. 'The streets are totally empty,' said one resident. 'Those that dared to leave only went to buy food for their families … but we were targeted by Israel in our homes, on the street, in our schools, in ambulances and refuges run by the UN that were supposed to protect us,' said Umm Subhi from Gaza City. 'We spent all night reading the Koran and praying to God that the attacks would stop, and still they targeted us.'[34]

During that war in 2009, Israel frequently used the 'human shields' accusation against Hamas to explain the unprecedentedly high rate of civilian casualties among the more than 1,300 Palestinian dead. 'Once we go into Gaza, we're of course faced with a terrorist organization which operates from within civilian surroundings. For example, they fire rockets from the homes of people. And, actually, the families are accomplices,' said Isaac Herzog, Israel's then minister of welfare and social services.[35]

A decade and a half later, in 2023, having risen to become president of Israel, Herzog found himself deploying almost exactly the same arguments when faced with questions about the rules of engagement of Israeli troops while fighting Hamas in the densely populated Gaza Strip. He called it a 'nerve-wracking game' against a Hamas leader –Yahya Sinwar – who 'doesn't really give a damn about his people in Gaza, and all he wants is his mission to be a big Salah ad-Din-type leader in history. That's what we're dealing with.'[36]

After October 2023, human rights groups, international lawyers and diplomats also found themselves making the same pleas and the same arguments about civilian casualties, human shields and disproportionate use of force as they had been for decades. In 2009, Amnesty International warned both sides about using Palestinian human shields in contravention of the Fourth Geneva Convention. 'Our sources in Gaza report that Israeli soldiers have entered and taken up positions in a number of Palestinian homes, forcing families to stay in a ground floor room while they use the rest of their house as a military base and sniper position,' said Amnesty official Malcolm Smart. 'This clearly increases the risk to the Palestinian families concerned and means they are effectively being used as human shields.' But Palestinian militants were also endangering the lives of Gaza by firing from behind civilian buildings, he said. 'The use of these tactics at a time when armed confrontations are taking place in streets in the middle of densely populated residential areas underlines the failure of both sides to respect the protected status of civilians in armed conflict.'[37]

In October 2023, Amnesty was again critical of both sides, but with the stakes – and the death tolls – catastrophically higher. 'In their stated intent to use all means to destroy Hamas, Israeli forces have shown a shocking disregard for civilian lives,' said Agnès Callamard, Amnesty's secretary general. 'We are calling on Israeli forces to immediately end unlawful attacks in Gaza and ensure that they take all feasible precautions to minimize harm to civilians and damage to civilian objects.' After Amnesty accused Hamas and other Palestinian groups of having 'flagrantly violated international law' on 7 October,[38] Callamard urged them 'to urgently release all civilian hostages, and to immediately stop firing indiscriminate rockets. There can be no justification for the deliberate killing of civilians under any circumstances.'[39]

Harvesting

We build for you, and we also resist for you.

Mushir al-Masri, Hamas rally, 2006[1]

The football soared high above the schoolyard towards the makeshift goalmouth, positioned beneath green and white Hamas banners. It was a goal, and victory to the boys' team named after a 'martyred' Hamas local hero – except all the teams were named after dead Hamas heroes. As the young players took a breather on the sidelines, Hamas volunteers provided them with green bottles of Mecca Cola. Even the refreshment was political: the bottles were stamped 'The Taste of Freedom' and 'Made in Palestine'. When they saw the authors, a group of young boys rushed forward, shouting: 'We are Hamas. Are you Hamas or Fatah?' At the mention of Fatah and its West Bank stronghold Ramallah, the youngsters drew fingers across their throats, in a slitting motion.

This was a summer camp, Hamas-style, for thirteen- to fifteen-year-olds in July 2008, a year after Hamas's takeover of the Gaza Strip. The camp was just one of the movement's hundreds of community, education and social projects in Gaza. While other organizations also had such activities, Hamas ran the most. Asked how they selected recruits for the camps – which were a popular summer activity in the fun- and money-starved Gaza Strip – one of the organizers said it was open to all. 'The goals of the movement's summer camps are to continue the education of the children and to teach them about the movement, and religion, and how to be a good Muslim. It also goes with the general goals of Hamas to create a new generation which is able to face the problems and hard life we face.'[2]

The boys' next activity was marching drills. They practised flag-bearing and parade ground formations, wearing Hamas caps and motivational Hamas tee-shirts bearing a logo of Gaza wrapped in barbed wire and the slogan 'Despite the Siege, We Are Steadfast'. In the building behind them, more boys were packed into a classroom for a religious knowledge quiz in which instructors instilled knowledge of the Koran and Islamic history using the top-of-the-form quiz format. In rapid succession they fired off questions

Photo 9.1 A Hamas summer camp for boys in Gaza

to the competing teams from Fallah, Amin and Hidayah mosques: 'What was the name of the cave where the Prophet Mohammed received the message from God? ... What was the surname of his wife Aisha? ...'

Girls, of course, were nowhere to be seen. They were half a mile away in another school entirely, learning to be dutiful daughters and future mothers under the watchful eye of Hamas women instructors and trusted, bearded minders.

Across the high razor-wire fence and closed border crossings that separate Gaza from the Jewish state, Israeli officials have long excoriated Hamas for mixing indoctrination with youth activities. After October 2023, Israeli Prime Minister Benjamin Netanyahu singled out schooling among his demands that any future leadership of Gaza must be different from what came before:

> My goal is that the day after we destroy Hamas, any future civil adminis-
> tration in Gaza does not deny the massacre, does not educate its children to
> become terrorists, does not pay for terrorists and does not tell its children
> that their ultimate goal in life is to see the destruction and dissolution of the
> State of Israel. That's not acceptable and that is not the way to achieve peace.[3]

Hamas does not deny that the promotion of Islam is the prime purpose of such activities. Indeed, they proclaim it. 'The most important thing in our camp is to teach them the rules of our religion,' said Riham al-Wakil, one of the girls' instructors. 'We teach them all the ideas from the Koran, how to be mothers, how to treat their relatives and fathers, and how to respect them.'[4]

As for the anti-Israel ethos, Hamas makes no attempt to hide it. As he drank the Mecca Cola, a camp instructor sought to dispel notions that Hamas is a crudely anti-Jewish organization by drawing a distinction between Jews living outside Israel – with whom Hamas had no argument – and those inside it helping to implement the Zionist project, and therefore denying the Palestinians their land. 'The Jews raise their children to hate Palestinians, and especially Muslims,' he said.

> We teach the children how to respect others, to be open to other civiliza-
> tions and cultures, and to respect others' points of view. We teach them
> that the Christians and Jews pray to the same God. We must respect them
> and we must not attack them unless they attack, occupy or fight us. In that
> case we will fight them. For the Israelis, the Zionist country, there is special
> treatment. We teach the children here that Israel must be fought and must

be removed because it is illegitimate, and the Jews came from different places around the world to occupy a land which did not belong to them.[5]

The principle behind many of Hamas's youth, kindergarten and educational projects is an adaptation of one long familiar in the West: 'Give me a child until the age of seven, and I will show you the man.' Indeed the principle of inculcating Islamic values early is enshrined in Hamas's founding covenant. It is one of the ways that the organization's value system is transmitted. Hamas aims to shape the social values of Palestinian society according to its own prescriptions, with impacts that are apparent in religious law, marriage, segregation of the sexes, moral and family matters, religious law, dress codes, young people, women, sexuality, education, and attitudes towards alcohol, drugs and social recreation activities.

Welfare Weddings

In what seems like an image left over from a different millennium, a different universe, even, from the shattered Gaza of the post-2023 era, the four smartly tailored Gaza bridegrooms line up on stage for a photograph, as riders on horses and camels race up and down in front of the flower-bedecked stage. It was 2006, nine months after its victory in parliamentary elections, and Hamas was hosting a mass wedding ceremony in the football stadium in the southern Gaza border town of Rafah. In more ordinary times, Hamas's leaders seemed aware of the benefits of occasionally giving Gaza residents – and future voters – a break from the miserable circumstances in which they lived. The event was held the same week that the United Nations trade and development agency, UNCTAD, said a Western aid freeze and Israel's closures and confiscation of Palestinian tax revenues after Hamas's victory had left the Palestinian economy 'on the verge of collapse'.[6]

The strategy behind the mass weddings was to provide a memorable ceremony on one of the most important days of their lives for would-be couples who could not otherwise afford such celebrations. As a socially conservative religious movement, Hamas not only abhors the concept of sex outside marriage but has also promoted marriage as a form of resistance – a union of man and woman producing future generations to wage jihad against Israel.

During the First Intifada, Hamas in Gaza endorsed the marriage of girls as young as thirteen to Palestinian men as progenitors of jihad in a demographic war against Israel. In later years it organized such weddings to

Photo 9.2 Palestinian bridegrooms at a mass wedding in Rafah, Gaza, paid for by Hamas

secure husbands for the widows of their fighters killed in earlier battles and encounters with Israel.

At the September 2006 wedding the brides were not there – they had had a separate ceremony two days earlier. But relatives of the grooms were there – men and women sitting on different sides of the football pitch, drinking orange juice and eating roasted nuts and sunflower seeds. Among the eighty-four grooms present, Saher Jarbouah, a 24-year-old accountancy student, said that he was among the two-thirds who were not religious but professed his gratitude to the Islamists for saving him the thousands of dollars he could not afford and for laying on a ceremony in front of 10,000 people to mark the beginning of his married life. 'Of course this is useful for us,' he said. 'It would cost a lot of money if you have to organize a wedding celebration yourself, hiring the band, the chairs, the video, and so on. Most people can afford only a small celebration, but this way you have the chance to be part of a really big event.' Gazing around him, he declared, 'It saves people money, it brings joy and happiness and it brings people together. It unites the families of eighty-four people, so that rich and poor can celebrate, not just the wealthy.'[7]

Nasser Barhoum, the event organizer, said that Hamas had held similar events since 1996 – halting only for three years at the nadir of the post-2000

Second Intifada because of the regular Israeli raids. The $10,000 cost of the wedding was 'money well spent' for the movement, he assessed.

> In a poor town like Rafah there is a huge percentage of bachelors who cannot afford their own ceremonies. We recognize the importance of the institution of marriage and we are doing our best to make good Palestinian families. The Islamic Society's main job is to take care of poor families and their welfare, and Rafah is the poorest place.[8]

And, of course, the Hamas message ran through the wedding ceremony like marzipan through the cake.

Rivals emulated the idea in Gaza and the West Bank. In 2015, the former Fatah security chief Mohammed Dahlan had his local community organizations hold similar large-scale matrimonial events. He and his financial sponsors in the United Arab Emirates, where he lives in exile, showcased a mass wedding event of 200 couples as an 'appointment for joy'. Abbas and his most senior aides attended a similar event in the West Bank in 2018, again to cultivate support by helping out couples with little money.

The Hamas leadership had also reached the conclusion that, while destruction of the enemy had its place, construction in its heartlands was a tool that was just as important. And, by providing social welfare, reconstruction and other programmes for people, Hamas hoped to create new generations of supporters. 'We build for you, and we also resist for you,' Mushir al-Masri, a former Hamas spokesman, had shouted to a crowd of delighted supporters at one rally in Gaza City.[9]

Inside and Outside

Hamas's enemies do regularly accuse Haniyeh and the senior Hamas leadership of leading lavish lifestyles. Newspaper articles, blogs and social media posts – especially after 7 October – claimed Hamas leaders lived it up in Gulf countries while ordinary Palestinians languished in poverty and deprivation in Gaza. 'Hamas leaders live comfortable lives abroad,' an Israeli military *hasbara* (public diplomacy) release said in 2023. 'While Hamas is forcefully preventing Gazans from evacuating to southern Gaza for their safety, these leaders are not even present in Gaza.'[10]

Israel maintains that Haniyeh, Sinwar and the rest of the Hamas leadership have systematically diverted huge amounts of humanitarian and reconstruction aid to the Qassam Brigades to pay for its vast tunnel network under Gaza and for weapons, rocket-firing infrastructure and training facilities.

'Although a large amount of building materials enters Gaza from Israel (more than 3.5 million tons of construction material in 2016 alone), a significant portion does not reach construction companies, and is instead diverted to Hamas' tunnel building activities. With many building projects frozen as a result, housing prices have risen significantly, and unemployment has swelled,' the Israeli military said in 2018, without providing evidence. Of Hamas's total budget, it said, '55% goes to the military wing, a significant increase from 15% in 2014. Meanwhile, Hamas' civil affairs budget has decreased by nearly 50% in that same period. Hamas' financial reports further reveal that tens of millions of dollars designated for rebuilding Gaza were actually being invested in real estate projects in Saudi Arabia, Syria, and Dubai.'[11]

In 2021 Yahya Sinwar, one of the future architects of 7 October, rejected the Israeli accusation that aid was diverted to the Qassam Brigades when appealing for international aid to help rebuild Gaza after the latest round of fighting. 'We will ease and facilitate the task for everyone, and we will make sure that the process will be transparent and fair and we will make sure that no penny goes to Hamas or Qassam,' he said. 'We have satisfactory sources of money for Hamas and Qassam. A major part of it from Iran and part in donations from Arabs, Muslims and liberals of the world who are sympathetic to our people and their rights.'[12]

The attack on 7 October 2023 inevitably saw Israel's allies double down on tracking and blocking Hamas's sources of revenue. A year previously, the US Treasury's Office of Foreign Assets Control (OFAC) had moved against a so-called Hamas Investment Office, which, it said, held assets estimated to be worth more than $500 million in companies across the Middle East and North Africa. It said that, while Hamas's *shura* council had oversight of the group's international investments, the Investment Office it was targeting – and the officials who ran it – had day-to-day management of the portfolio and used it to 'conceal and launder funds'.[13] Less than two weeks after the 2023 attack, OFAC moved again and imposed sanctions on ten more Hamas operatives, once more targeting what it called 'financiers and facilitators':

> In addition to the funds Hamas receives from Iran, its global portfolio of investments generates vast sums of revenue through its assets, estimated to be worth hundreds of millions of dollars, with companies operating in Sudan, Algeria, Türkiye, the United Arab Emirates, and other countries. The companies in Hamas's portfolio have operated under the guise of legitimate

businesses and their representatives have attempted to conceal Hamas's control over their assets.[14]

It all pointed to an ever-tightening set of restrictions on Hamas's financial revenue streams. But in the early days of money freezes and sanctions, everything was much easier to intercept, through Israeli raids and seizures from individuals or money changers. Digital financing mechanisms changed the picture, with counter-terrorism financing watchdogs increasingly looking to the exponential rise in online financing, digital money-laundering, transfers and crypto-currency. The crypto-currency giant Binance hinted at the scale of Hamas money-laundering in 2019 when its then head of compliance admitted they were aware that their platform was being used to raise funds. Significantly, when subsequent news of the huge fines and the extent of Binance crypto-currency money-laundering became public, it was the Qassam Brigades that were first cited in the US Treasury readout.[15]

Among the other Hamas operatives targeted by the US Treasury's OFAC in 2023 was a 'longtime Hamas operative based in Qatar with close ties to Iranian elements' – a West Bank member of the political bureau said to have received tens of thousands of dollars from Beirut-based Hamas deputy chief Saleh Al-Arouri 'to purchase a variety of weapons' – and the Gaza-based owner of a money transfer and virtual currency exchange. 'Hamas often relies on small-dollar donations, including through the use of virtual currency,' OFAC said, as it appealed for information from members of the public about Hamas online fund-raising campaigns and virtual currency wallet addresses.[16]

The British government and the European Union also publish lists of targets for financial sanctions which include Hamas. Since 2001, Hamas's Qassam Brigades – and, since 2003, Hamas as a whole – have been on the UK Treasury's 'consolidated list of financial sanctions targets',[17] meaning that their assets are frozen, and they cannot receive financial support from anyone. Meshaal, Hamdan, Marzouq and Alami were added in 2004. The European Union has a similar list of 'persons, groups and entities involved in terrorist acts' whose assets are frozen, including Hamas.[18]

Yet Sinwar's appeal for international aid to help rebuild Gaza in 2021 highlighted the unavoidable reality that, after more than seventeen years of a sustained Israeli-led blockade, the population were left to pay a very heavy price. The majority of the Gaza Strip's more than 2.3 million population had been relentlessly pushed into poverty, and the economy to collapse. The Israeli-imposed strictures on the local population, and lengthy Egyptian closures after 2014, had left 80 per cent dependent on international humanitarian aid for simple basics such as food, shelter and water. Even before 7 October 2023, the UN, the World Bank and other institutions noted that rising unemployment and the death of agriculture and local industries was leaving Gazans without hope. 'Restrictions on the movement of people and goods, destruction of productive assets in frequent military operations and the ban on the importation of key technologies and inputs have hollowed out Gaza's economy,' concluded a 2022 report by the United Nations Conference on Trade and Development. 'Between 2006 and 2022, Gaza's real GDP per capita shrank by 37%.'[19]

Perhaps the most shocking statistic related to youth unemployment. 'Today marks 15 years of the blockade of the Gaza Strip,' said Stéphane Dujarric, spokesman for the UN Secretary-General, on 21 June 2022. 'More than half of Gaza's just over 2 million people live in poverty, and nearly 80 per cent of the youth are unemployed ... Only sustainable political solutions will relieve the pressures on the long-suffering people of Gaza.'[20]

The Agenda

One persistent criticism of Hamas is that its social programmes come with an expensive price label: social order, the Hamas way. Aside from the repeated and well-documented reports of enforcers bullying women into conforming to Islamic behaviour codes, Hamas has curbed other social activities of which it disapproves.

In 2005, soon after winning control of the West Bank town of Qalqilya in municipal elections, Hamas banned a decade-old dance and music festival – initially on the pretext that it wanted to protect the grass in the town's football stadium. The same year, Hamas gunmen also stopped a rap band performing in Gaza. Adding fuel to the critics' fire, after Hamas won the parliamentary elections in 2006 its Education Ministry ordered a 400-page anthology of forty-five Palestinian folk tales, including a tale called 'The little bird' about sexual awakening, to be pulled from school library shelves. The then education minister, Dr Nasser Eddin al-Shaer, confirmed that the title had been removed, saying that the book was 'full of clear sexual expressions'.[21] Following a public outcry, Hamas was forced to backtrack, and the book was quickly reinstated. Mr Shaer called the row a 'storm in a teacup'.[22]

Meanwhile, the anti-dancing edict was defended by Dr Mahmoud Zahar, Hamas's elder statesman. 'A man holds a woman by the hand and dances with her in front of everyone. Does that serve the national interest?' Zahar asked the Arabic website Elaph. 'If so, why have the phenomena of corruption and prostitution become pervasive in recent years?' Zahar also condemned gay marriage, saying: 'Are these the laws for which the Palestinian street is waiting? For us to give rights to homosexuals and to lesbians, a minority of perverts and the mentally and morally sick?'[23] Such intolerance instilled genuine fear. 'Hamas doesn't only impose its social agenda, it imposes a political, legal and social agenda,' said Naima al-Sheikh Ali, a Fatah activist in Gaza. 'Their attempt to impose their presence by force of weapons proves how strongly they are trying to impose their political and social agenda.'[24]

Certainly, in the Hamas summer camps for girls in Gaza the emphasis was on the role predestined for them, according to the movement's interpretation of Islam. 'Fatah used to run the camps only to indoctrinate for Fatah, but we are the opposite,' explained Riham al-Wakil, one of the camp instructors who had volunteered from the Hamas women's student association. 'Yes, we are Hamas,' she continued, 'but we teach the girls about the rules of our religion first. We show them how to be mothers and to respect the wishes of their father.'[25] The thirteen- to fifteen-year-old girls attending the camp were instructed in how to perform prayers, about relationships within the family, and about the *hadith* and *tafsir* (commentary) on the Koran. They also put on exhibitions, one about the Prophet Mohammed and another on the Hamas-supported boycott of Danish goods in the aftermath of the controversy about Danish cartoons of the Prophet. The girls sang songs about being a good daughter and then, amid paper flowers and crafts made from glitter and sequins, one young star was singled out to perform back-flips, cartwheels, and acrobatics for the women-only viewers.

By that era the good times were long gone for bar and nightclub owners in Gaza. Although restaurants serving alcohol are a feature of some West Bank towns such as Ramallah, there was no such freedom in Gaza. An empty, burned-out cinema stood in the centre of Gaza City for many years, even before Hamas became the government, as a daily reminder to everyone of what happens when social and entertainment institutions fall foul of its edicts. By December 2005 there was only one bar left selling alcohol in Gaza, and that was inside a United Nations beachside compound. Even this was bombed over the New Year's holiday, never to reopen.

Palestinian-run bars had long gone. Former club proprietor Nabil Kafarneh lamented that he lost $250,000 when his Gaza beachside clubs, the Sheherazade and the Appointment, were burned down in 2000, even though they had PA licences to operate legally. He said his nightclubs were torched after a Hamas rally in which the crowd was exhorted to 'burn casinos'. 'I had thirty dancers,' said a miserable Mr Kafarneh, as he sat in the gloomy, cold and damp lounge of his home, replaying on a large television monitor the only memory he has of the liberal 'old days' – a grainy video of Arab women dancers gyrating round a series of tables occupied by men eating meat and fruit and smoking nargilas. 'The dances we were offering were for art. I had a licence for alcohol and hundreds of people used to come and enjoy themselves here, and hundreds more were beneficiaries in terms of employment.' He complained that he could find no one brave enough to help him reopen the clubs under a Hamas regime. 'There were no previous warnings, it was a random attack,' he said.[26]

During the same period, as Hamas was consolidating its rule, a hitherto unknown Islamist organization calling itself the Swords of Islamic Righteousness began bombing internet cafés and chemists, accusing them of peddling pornography and illicit drugs. With Gaza's ineffective security agencies distracted by the civil war then raging between Hamas and Fatah gunmen, the group distributed communiqués in which they threatened to 'execute the laws of God' at cybercafés 'which are trying to make a whole generation preoccupied with matters other than jihad and worship.' The group also claimed attacks on unveiled women, threatened 'university girls putting on makeup and dressing in a satanic way', music shops, and motorists playing loud music.[27]

Fawzi Barhoum, a Hamas spokesman, denied that Hamas had anything to do with the attacks, protesting that it was 'among those most damaged by the lack of security'. He maintained that 'Our programme of change and reform regarding corruption and vice is not based on any sort of violence or fighting, but in an educated, civilized way that represents the culture of the Palestinian people and their faith. We adopt an Islamic approach to reach our targets.'[28]

Yet, once it had assumed total control of the Gaza Strip, Hamas instituted measures that would restrict people's freedoms according to its strict social agenda. It issued an edict imposing an internet filter which disrupted business and slowed down traffic so much, café owners complained, that it succeeded in closing down stores which had survived the earlier Islamist purges. 'I think it's because the government is trying to stop people from accessing porn,' said one internet café owner, who only agreed to speak on condition of anonymity, fearing reprisals. 'It is a useless decision because people always find a way around the controls. It is a form of trespass on individual rights, and I have lost customers because the filters slow considerably all the internet traffic in Gaza.'[29] Another internet café owner spoke of persistent harassment since Hamas had taken over. 'Their police have raided my premises many times looking for Fatah flags and pornography. They've arrested me more than once, and now people are afraid to spend time in the internet café.'[30]

Hamas was accused of imposing other social edicts, including the announcement by a senior judge of a dress code, under which female lawyers would have to wear conservative robes and headscarves in court, and a ban on women riding motorbikes. Rumours also spread that it had banned the sale of sexual performance-enhancing drugs such as Viagra. Hamas – according to the rumour – did not want the indolent and the unemployed engaged in prolonged carnal pleasures. Arson attacks and other violence continued against individuals, social clubs and cafés.

Human rights groups in Gaza and elsewhere say that, even if attacks are not being carried out by Hamas under the cover of anonymity – as many suspect – at the very least Hamas and its preachers, youth teachers, summer camps and public rallies are responsible for creating the atmosphere of intolerance and social oppression within which such attacks take place. Indeed, Hamas has produced a large cadre of social enforcers, and this network is a direct outcome of the decades invested by Hamas in running youth, social and charity programmes in the Gaza Strip in particular – creating a receptive audience for its message to ensure that today's audience are tomorrow's enforcers.

The Money Trail

To say that senior Hamas political leaders or Qassam Brigades commanders were coy about money, how much they raised, where it came from, and what it was used for, was something of an understatement. Money was the elephant in the room and not to be discussed with outsiders. Nor could Hamas be trapped into some embarrassing financially related disclosure. They weren't minor British royals or corrupt politician grifters or grafters. No fake sheikh was likely to trap them into revelations that could be sensationally headlined in the media. And it was true that, if they wanted, they could stand the price of a halal dinner of hummus and kofte or a round of drinks with a dizzying array of non-alcoholic choices for a guest.

As the organization grew, it was clear to analysts that Hamas's core activities – military expenditure to wage the 'jihad' against Israel and social 'hearts and minds' programmes to build and keep their supporter base – were by their nature long-term and vastly expensive.

For Israel, after first turning a blind eye to Hamas's social activities during its early years in order to create a domestic rival to Arafat, Hamas came to be seen as a serious threat in the mid-1990s when it jeopardized the Oslo peace process. In 1995 the White House designated it as a terrorist organization, along with eleven other groups, issuing an executive order 'prohibiting transactions with terrorists who threaten to disrupt the Middle East peace process.' The list included Hezbollah, the Popular Front for the Liberation of Palestine, the PFLP–General Command and two Israeli extremist organizations, Kach and Kahane Chai.[31]

Once the threat was recognized, Israel and its allies devoted significant intelligence efforts to combatting Hamas at source by identifying where the money came from and closing down the flow of funds into its coffers. By the early 2000s the Israelis were cautioning that the funds available to Hamas were contributing 'to the enhancement of its standing on the Palestinian street' and could 'eventually pose a threat' to the legitimacy of Arafat's Palestinian Authority. The group's leader, Sheikh Yassin, said in 2001 that Hamas was distributing $2–3 million in monthly stipends to support the relatives of Palestinians imprisoned by Israel and to the families of martyrs, including suicide bombers.[32]

In 2003, an Israeli intelligence assessment calculated that Hamas enjoyed access to extensive 'network[s] of financial sources' which gave it income to a 'total value of tens of millions of dollars a year.'[33] Even then Israel was highlighting the role of Hamas's political leadership outside Gaza in raising funds, saying the money was channelled into Hamas's coffers through 'bank transfers, moneychangers, private money services, unofficial networks for the transfer of funds' and other 'unsuspecting' agents, and then distributed for different purposes:

> All the monies flow into a common fund, and are then channelled to the relevant activities, in accordance with needs and in coordination with the functions of the organization in the territories and abroad. Thus, in view of the great difficulty in tracing the source of the money, its address, and the motives behind the transfer of funds, it is essential that a strict and vigilant approach be adopted towards the entire fundraising network, operating within the framework of *Da'wa* activity.[34]

Hamas tried to shrug off the intense scrutiny of its reliance on foreign money, pointing out that, under Fatah's control in previous years, Yasser Arafat's Palestinian Authority (PA) and Palestine Liberation Organization (PLO) had been almost entirely dependent on external assistance, with little by way of proper mechanisms of accountability. 'The West funded the PA and the PLO squandered it living the playboy lifestyle,' declared Ismail Haniyeh. 'We are accountable to the people and God above for every cent that is spent providing services to the people. We do not squander it but invest it in the welfare and safety of our steadfast nation.'[35] Hamas's victory in the 2006 Palestinian parliamentary elections triggered an immediate move by the international community to isolate the organization even further until it renounced violence and recognized Israel. Hamas's refusal to meet the conditions led to a direct aid embargo.

In those early months in power, Hamas made no attempt to hide the fact that it was receiving foreign donations; indeed, in months after the elections, Hamas leaders held press conferences in Gaza gleefully trumpeting promises of aid from Arab and Muslim countries. The aim appeared to be an attempt to switch from reliance on European and Western sources of funding to a 'Look East' policy championed by the newly appointed foreign minister, Mahmoud Zahar. The culmination of these defiant money-raising efforts came in the autumn of 2006, when Hamas ministers brought suitcases full of foreign cash across the border from Egypt to Gaza, declaring to the European Union Border Assistance Mission stationed at the Rafah crossing that they were funds for depleted PA coffers. One Hamas official confirmed that $2 million had been brought in to pay public servants such as police officers, doctors and teachers who hadn't received their salary in months.[36]

As Israel tightened its controls on Gaza, Hamas increasingly used tunnels from Egypt to bring in funds and trained their financial cadres to run digital finance tools to keep other flows of cash coming into their accounts. But, for all its efforts, Hamas could not replace the vast sums of foreign aid that had kept the Palestinian Authority and the entire Palestinian economy afloat in Gaza.

And, as Hamas resorted to tunnels and briefcases to bring cash into Gaza to keep paying for its operations – and government salaries – the United States was spearheading the international effort to cut off the money tap. Some US lawmakers made it clear that their intent was to crush the organization and its 'hearts and minds' activities. At a meeting of the House of Representatives Committee on International Relations in the aftermath of Hamas's victory, Democrat Representative Tom Lantos said the US had to do everything in its power to make sure that Hamas could not reap political benefits from American money entering the PA. 'Simply ending direct assistance to the PA does not cut it. There must be an end to all non-humanitarian assistance that could benefit Hamas,' he said. 'The last thing in the world we in Congress want to do is to let a Hamas government reap the credit for development projects that are funded by the American taxpayer.'[37]

When Hamas seized total control of Gaza in June 2007, Western aid into Gaza ceased almost at the same time that Israel imposed an air, land and sea blockade on the entire population of the densely populated enclave. Yet, as one money tap was closed, even Israelis knew funding would still come in. Yuval Diskin, the head of Shin Bet, said: 'Hamas doesn't need the PA's money, they smuggle money in. They have plenty of their own money.' He conceded that 'one of the bad fruits of the international siege on Hamas is that, once all the doors were closed, the only window open was to Iran.'[38]

Such views were affirmed by the leader of Gaza's civil police force. A year after Hamas's 2007 military takeover of Gaza, Tawfiq Jabr sat in the newly refurbished offices and premises of the Gaza police – which had been integrated with Hamas's newly created Executive Forces (*Tanfithiya*), a black-uniformed unit loyal to Hamas rather than to the Palestinian Authority leadership that Hamas had just ousted. Sitting at a huge executive desk with a 52-inch plasma TV behind him, the police chief said he wanted for nothing when asked if he needed money to rebuild the force. On the adjacent drill ground, hundreds of policemen were parading in fresh uniforms, and shining police cars were adorned with the force's new insignia. 'For the first time in the history of Gaza there has been a 95 per cent decline in criminality,' declared Jabr. 'The people feel safe, we meet our social responsibility and there is order.'[39] The money was coming despite the siege and was being spent by Hamas on restoring law and order. Six months later, after the first wave of Israel's aerial bombing offensive in December 2008, Jabr was lying dead on the very same parade ground, among dozens of police bodies and the rubble of the refurbished headquarters.

In 2007, the US Treasury disclosed that it had blocked $8,658,832 of Hamas's assets in the United States relating to anti-terrorist funding programmes. The Hamas total compared with $437,281 for Hezbollah, and a paltry $63,508 for Islamic Jihad. In the list of nine organizations, only al-Qaeda had more blocked funds, with $11,324,361.[40]

Gradually, the net tightened. Hamas itself was listed as a specially designated global terrorist organization (SDGT), and its leaders were targeted with measures that authorized the US government to block assets of individuals, entities, and their 'subsidiaries, front organizations, agents and associates'.[41] Individual Hamas leaders designated by the US over the years included the movement's founders Sheikh Ahmed Yassin and Abdel Aziz Rantissi, Ismail Haniyeh, former leaders Khaled Meshaal and Musa Abu Marzouq – who was accused of providing 'start-up funding and instructions' for one of the designated charities – and Lebanon-based Usama Hamdan. Of him, the Treasury said: 'funds transferred from charitable donations to Hamas for distribution to the families of Palestinian "martyrs" have been transferred to the bank account of Hamdan and used to support Hamas military operations in Israel.'

Gaza's Hamas leaders Yahya Sinwar, Mohammed Deif and Rawhi Mushtaha, along with Lebanon-based Saleh al-Arouri, were added in 2015, and others later, including Qassam Brigades deputy commander Marwan Issa in 2019.[42] Arouri was killed in an airstrike in Beirut in January 2024. In March, Israel claimed they had killed 'shadow man' Issa in an airstrike on Gaza's Nuseirat refugee camp; many others were also killed in the attack.

The money men were also targeted, accused of investing and transferring foreign funds to Gaza. In 2019, the US Treasury's Office of Foreign Assets Control (OFAC) identified what they called 'financial facilitators responsible for moving tens of millions of dollars' between Iran's Islamic Revolutionary Guard Corps-Qods Force and Hamas's Qassam Brigades in Gaza. They singled out Lebanon-based financial operative Muhammad Sarur as being 'in charge of all financial transfers' between the Qods Force and Qassam Brigades, the Treasury alleging that, 'overall, in the past four years, the IRGC-QF transferred over U.S. $200 million dollars to the Izz-Al-Din Al-Qassam Brigades.' It all pointed to an ever-tightening set of controls on the flow of money from Iran to Hamas.[43]

Speaking from his hideout in Beirut's Hezbollah-controlled areas in 2006, Hamdan told one of the authors of this book that one of the functions of the Hamas leadership outside Palestine was to raise money: 'This is one of the important roles ...' But he insisted that such funds did not go towards weapons. 'We don't use the money of the charities to finance Hamas,' he said. 'Those monies were sent to the people inside Palestine, and they helped the people inside Palestine.' Hamdan believed that one intended effect of the American and Israeli allegations that charity money goes towards weapons was 'putting pressure on the Palestinian people, turning them against Hamas. Everyone knows that, according to our beliefs or religion, we are not supposed to use the charities or their money to finance Hamas as a group, either a militant or a political group ... They want to turn the people against Hamas. They know well that Hamas is not taking any part of this money.'[44]

Women

> She is the maker of men. Her role in guiding and educating the new genera-
> tions is great.
>
> Hamas Covenant[1]

Ultimately it comes back to the name: the Muslim Brotherhood. Hamas's well-drilled and energetic women's movement has drawn a huge amount of domestic and international media attention since the election victory in 2006. Women do play a role, but by and large it is the men who monopolize control. The Brotherhood continues to take the decisions while the Sisterhood has, at best, a supporting role. Hamas remains patriarchal and conservative and defines the role for women in the movement.

After the victory, Jamila al-Shanti, the Gaza-based Islamist who headed Hamas's list of women candidates, was asked if there had ever been any women on the organization's main *shura* council, its supreme decision-making body. 'No, not until now,' conceded al-Shanti, the widow of Hamas's assassinated co-founder Abdel Aziz Rantissi. 'We have our own needs. Why should we be only a minority within a *shura* council in which the majority are men and their decisions have influence on us? No, we have two separate movements, the men and the women, and we work according to our needs. We have our own *shura*, our own movement.'[2] Things would change, albeit slowly. Al-Shanti would make her own piece of history in 2021 when she became the first woman 'elected' to the Hamas politburo. She did not get long in the position. On 19 October 2023, two weeks after Hamas's cross-border attack on Israeli kibbutzim, she was killed by an Israeli airstrike, meeting the same fate as her late husband. Her death was declared a martyrdom by Hamas spokesmen and the official Hamas media.

Despite Hamas's claim to involve women at all levels, its critics maintain that it is a rigidly conservative organization whose own founding manifesto defines women principally through a biological function as 'makers of men'. In the areas where it is strongest – most notably the Gaza Strip – Hamas has mounted a sustained campaign of Islamization, using preachers, social pressure and even intimidation to compel women to act and dress according to its own interpretation of Islam. Indeed, its attitude to a woman's place in society and politics became a key battlefield between Hamas and its secular opponents.

But, as the huge women's turnout for Hamas in the 2006 elections testified, Hamas had in recent years comprehensively outmanoeuvred its secular opponents in the battle for the hearts, souls and votes of Palestinian women. It mobilized them to help them win power and wage resistance against Israel. Why did Hamas single out women as a constituency likely to prove such willing recipients – and carriers – of its message? And how did it win them over in the face of competition from much larger and longer-established Palestinian women's organizations?

Covenant

When the Hamas movement was created during the First Intifada in 1987, it was exclusively male. The founding Covenant spelled out its view of how women could contribute to the cause. It depicts women as passive bearers of future generations of jihadists, and the Hamas ideal of Palestinian womanhood is evident from sections dedicated to their role in the home and society.

> The Muslim woman has a role no less important than that of the Muslim man in the battle of liberation. She is the maker of men. Her role in guiding and educating the new generations is great.
>
> Woman in the home of the fighting family, whether she is a mother or a sister, plays the most important role in looking after the family, rearing the children and imbuing them with moral values and thoughts derived from Islam.[3]

In Hamas's battle with Israel, women are confined to a support function on the home front, using their bodies and reproductive capacity to produce fighters. Hamas, like other actors in this conflict, understands the politics of demographics.

Historical Role

Palestinian women have always been active politically, especially compared with their sisters in other parts of the Arab world. During the first two decades of Israel's occupation of the West Bank, East Jerusalem and Gaza, from 1967 to 1987, Palestinian women participated in demonstrations, organized petitions and carried out other activities in support of the national struggle. Some were legends, lionized by the propaganda organs of the PLO. Among them was Laila Khaled, a member of the radical leftist PFLP, who in 1969 took part in the hijacking of a Trans World Airlines passenger jet and was arrested and jailed the following year after a failed attempt to hijack an El Al plane. Wearing a keffiyeh, carrying a gun, and sporting a home-made ring fashioned from the pin of a grenade and a bullet, she became an icon of the Palestinian movement, representing to her admirers a fusion of feminism, national struggle and guerrilla warfare. She was jailed for her part in the second hijack attempt but was released within weeks in a prisoner-exchange deal and was later elevated to the central committee of the PFLP.

Other female icons were the writer and women's emancipation activist Sahar Khalifa and the poet Fadwa Touqan, but there was barely a hijab between them.

In the early 1980s things began to change. Hamas's Islamist forerunners in Mujamma frowned upon the socially liberal outlook of Gaza's secularists towards the attire, behaviour and public role of women. They began harassing them and coercing them to wear clothes which conformed to their own interpretation of Islam. Women were pressured to abandon their short skirts, bare heads and even the traditional embroidered *thobe* worn by many Palestinian women in favour of what became known as shari'a dress – the hijabs and jilbabs which became ubiquitous on the campuses of educational institutions such as the Islamic University of Gaza (IUG) and Hebron Polytechnic in the West Bank.

At the IUG, gender segregation was enforced, and poorer female students received free clothing coupons donated by rich Gulf patrons which could only be redeemed for strict Islamic forms of dress purchased from local dress stores and boutiques. As Randa, a well-known Palestinian woman activist, remarked, 'They thought our hemlines were a threat to the national struggle and forgot that with our brains we could make all the difference to achieving our political goals as a nation. The problem was them, not us.'[4]

The outbreak of the First Intifada in December 1987 was to bring an escalation of the Islamization campaign amid the huge social and political changes that the uprising wrought across every sector of Palestinian society. During the Intifada, women were suddenly everywhere, experiencing a hitherto unprecedented level of visibility and public involvement in the political struggle. In every city, town and village, women threw aside their daily household chores to march, build barricades or join popular committees that were organizing everything from food distribution to medical supplies. As Umm (Mother of) Mohammed, from Bethlehem's Aida refugee camp, recalled: 'I knew that I had to do my duty and play my part ... our time had come and I was going to be part of it.'[5]

This new social-national empowerment of Palestinian women only increased when Israel began to arrest thousands of Palestinian men in an effort to break the Intifada. Women were left to support their families. When their men were killed, imprisoned or incapacitated by Israeli bullets, they became the head of their households. Wearing a full-face veil, known as a *niqb*, and gloves, and clothed in green with a cream hijab, Jamila al-Shanti recalled that this was the era in which she too became involved in the Islamic movement:

> For certain periods of time my husband was imprisoned or deported, and I shouldered the burden. I was the wife of one of the most well-known leaders. I stood by him and supported him in the way that he chose. It was a simple role as a woman. I often had to carry the burden of the whole family because he wasn't there – I had to raise the children.[6]

Hamas, determined to establish its credentials in a popular uprising, quickly seized upon the role of women. For Hamas, a woman's place was in the home and not out fighting the occupation in the street. This became apparent within a few months of the outbreak of the First Intifada, when it organized its supporters to mount a campaign centred on the most visible sign of women's status in society: whether they were bareheaded or wearing a hijab.

Even after years of creeping Islamization, there were at that time some public spaces in Gaza where women still enjoyed greater freedom. But social pressure increased until those spaces became squeezed and then non-existent. The ubiquity of the hijab was also achieved quickly, within a year or so of the creation of Hamas. Of course, some Palestinian women had always worn the hijab or other forms of head-covering. Their mothers and grandmothers had worn such scarves and they retained the custom, unquestioningly. But a large number of women had dispensed with the hijab altogether. It was against these women that Hamas directed its hijab campaign, sometimes even using violence and often intense social pressure to enforce its will, regardless of the fissures it created in Palestinian society at a time when there was otherwise great emphasis placed on the need for unity and solidarity within the community.

Acid and Stones

'Daughter of Islam, abide by shari'a dress!' ordered the graffiti on the walls of many a Gazan street. Gangs of Hamas 'enforcers' stormed into classrooms demanding that bareheaded girls put on the hijab. 'Before 1987 everything was normal; it was a personal freedom not to wear the *hijab*,' said Naima al-Sheikh Ali, the director of Fatah's women's section in Gaza. After that, she recalls, 'Hamas began imposing its agenda on the hijab in Gaza. Whenever they saw a woman without a veil they attacked her and sometimes threw acid in her face.'[7]

Before long, bareheaded women were being stoned and abused in the street; their moral and national commitment was openly questioned. Gangs of young men or boys with Hamas affiliations would roam Gaza's streets looking for bareheaded women whom they would target. Violence against women was never far from the equation. If males were accompanying bareheaded women, then they would be told to order 'their' women to cover up or share the shame of the bareheaded one. Such women were portrayed as symbols of corruption and national betrayal. Hamas communiqués, leaflets and articles warned that beauty salons, hairdressing salons and dress shops were dens of iniquity where Israeli intelligence operatives ensnared Palestinian women, then used their sexuality to lure Palestinian men into becoming collaborators.

As it grew stronger, Hamas began to denounce secular Palestinian women's organizations as being part of a plot to undermine the Muslim family. 'She is a woman, she is a Christian and she smokes,'[8] the Hamas hardliner Dr Mahmoud Zahar sneered of Dr Hanan Ashrawi, an erudite Palestinian national leader who rapidly ascended to international media stardom when she became the public face of the PLO and a negotiator during the peace talks of the early 1990s.

More than the Home

Hamas's agenda for women had other dimensions. During the First Intifada it was a powerful advocate of forcing women back into the homes (*beit al ta'a*) and marrying off girls as young as thirteen. The rationale for early marriage was twofold: to 'protect' the women and to accelerate the so-called biological reproduction of the 'living legacy' – a new generation of fighters. Hamas also believed that, if schools and universities were closed, girls and women should remain in the home and away from the streets, public squares, markets and other places in order to 'preserve' their honour.

Photo 10.1 A woman wearing a hijab in front of a graffiti-covered wall in Gaza

Hamas supporters consistently protest that it does not restrict women's rights and claim that the West unfairly views all Islamists through the distorting prism of perhaps the most notorious anti-women's movement of all: the Afghan Taliban. 'They know nothing about the Taliban,' responded an irritated Dr Mahmoud Zahar when confronted with the comparison in January 2006, shortly after Hamas's election victory.

> I will give you a personal example. My wife was a teacher, until the Israelis attacked my house and broke her back. My first daughter is an engineer .... The [second] is an English teacher. The third has graduated from accounting high school. The younger three boys are candidates for university. So I think this is a good answer to your question.[9]

His message is that hammered home from the senior leadership to the grassroots: that, because Hamas encourages women to be educated and to contribute to resistance against Israel, it cannot be accused of holding them back.

At the Islamic University of Gaza, where Dr Zahar once taught, Iman Abu Jazar, the leader of the Hamas women's student bloc, insists that Hamas 'is not what people think'. A veiled medical student, Iman was dressed in a full-length jilbab and blue cotton gloves and was chaperoned by Hamas minders throughout the interview in the offices of the university's segregated campus. 'In Hamas, women occupy every role, as doctors and engineers. They are on the councils and they are the mothers of many martyrs,' she says. 'Hamas gives woman her rights.'[10]

Women Suicide Bombers

One controversy surrounding women's participation in Hamas was that of military operations – chiefly, but not exclusively – suicide bombings. The vast majority of Palestinian suicide bombings and other attacks have been carried out by men. The first suicide bombing by a Palestinian woman was on 27 January 2002, by Fatah's Al Aqsa Martyrs' Brigades. Wafa Idris, a 28-year-old refugee from Ramallah's al-Amari refugee camp, killed an 81-year-old man and wounded more than 150 people when she blew herself up in Jerusalem's Jaffa Street.[11]

Usually determined to set the agenda on innovatory military tactics, Hamas found itself behind, for once, and confronted with a dilemma. On the one hand, women aroused less suspicion at checkpoints, were often searched less, and could conceal bombs beneath their robes. On the other, Sheikh Yassin was, according to some Hamas figures close to him, personally reluctant to deploy women as bombers. Faced with a wave of applications from women wanting to die for the cause, he delivered an ambivalent ruling – that Hamas would not permit women bombers for now but would leave the possibility open for later in the struggle. 'I'm saying that in this phase the participation of women is not needed in martyr operations, like men,' Yassin told the media at the time. 'We can't meet the growing demands of young men who wish to carry out martyr operations.' Yassin said that 'women form the second line of defence in the resistance to the occupation' but that, once the sixteen-month-old Intifada entered the 'decisive phase, everyone will participate without exception.' But he stipulated that, if a Hamas woman wanted to carry out an attack, she had to abide by the usual Islamic constraints and be 'accompanied by a man', such as a relative, 'if the operation requires an absence of more than a day and a night.'[12]

Reem

It started with Reem. On 14 January 2004, Reem al-Riyashi, a 22-year-old mother of two, became the first Hamas woman suicide bomber when she blew herself up at the Erez crossing in the Gaza Strip, killing four Israeli soldiers and guards. The Israelis said that, when she reached the zone where Palestinian workers are inspected, Riyashi told the guards that she had a metal plate in her leg which could set off an alarm, and a woman soldier was sent to inspect her. While she was waiting, Riyashi 'apparently succeeded in penetrating a meter or two into the inspection hall, and blew herself up.'[13] Mohammed, a veteran Hamas military wing member in Gaza, said that Riyashi was accepted because her attack came 'during a very tight security atmosphere which meant no man could get close to the Israelis at Erez.' He reported that it was Sheikh Yassin personally who took the decision to relax the ban. 'She put a lot of pressure on Sheikh Yassin, and she wasn't the only one … Many women were putting pressure on Yassin because they wanted to be operational.'[14]

Jamila al-Shanti confirmed the account, saying that many Palestinian women had 'grown accustomed over decades of conflict to living in houses where military equipment was stored, so many sought to be trained in weapons.' She stated that Riyashi decided to undertake the attack because 'she felt that the Israelis destroyed everything around her, killed everything. She took the decision that she was going to the resistance and she wanted to do something to express her anger.' Hamas's view, said Shanti, was that 'it is open for us to use any method to defend ourselves.'[15]

Riyashi's case was commemorated by Hamas. The movement made and screened a video on its own Al Aqsa television station which re-enacted the scene in her home the night before she blew herself up. It showed a four-year-old daughter watching her mother get dressed, and singing: 'Mummy, what are you carrying in your arms instead of me?' The next day she finds out it was a bomb. The two and a half minute video is dubbed with the haunting lament of the little girl. After the attack Hamas also broadcast interviews with Riyashi's two kindergarten-age children, asking them about their mother and the attack she perpetrated.

Duha, her daughter, is asked, 'Where is your Mama?' Her tiny voice piped up that her mother was in paradise as a martyr. Her young brother fidgets throughout the encounter as the bearded interviewer persists in asking the children questions, such as 'How many Jews did Mama kill?', 'Do you love Mama?', 'Do you miss her?'[16]

At the other end of the spectrum was Fatima Najjar, a seventy-year-old great-grandmother who blew herself up in northern Gaza during an Israeli raid in November 2006. Despite the fact that she injured two soldiers only slightly, she was awarded the posthumous *nom de guerre* Umm Fidayeeat – Mother of the Women Fighters. Hamas said that Najjar approached Hamas fighters who were unable to get near Israeli soldiers during the raid and told them, 'If you can't do something I can, because my house is close to the Israeli position.' Hamas's Jamila al-Shanti explained: 'Her land had been taken away from her. Who could prevent her? But it is not the policy of the movement. If someone volunteers, we will not stand against it, but it is not our policy to go and ask women.'[17]

Her family said that Najjar, who had nine children, forty-two grandchildren and two dozen great-grandchildren, had become radicalized after Israeli troops blew up her home in 1990 during the First Intifada. In the weeks before her death she had smuggled food, water and ammunition to Hamas fighters, and earlier in November she had also taken part in a women's march to break a siege on Palestinian fighters who were trapped by Israeli troops near a mosque in Beit Hanoun. Hoping to be 'martyred', she was bitterly disappointed when other women were killed but she survived. 'When she came back she was happy when she heard that everyone had got out of the mosque alive, but very sad when she heard some women had become martyrs and she hadn't, even though she was the first there,' said one of her sons, Saber.[18]

The women's march in which Najjar participated – and in which she had hoped to die – was unprecedented. On 3 November 2006, hundreds of women had walked and run through the streets of Beit Hanoun at first light, responding to all-night appeals over Hamas's Al Aqsa radio to come out onto the streets of the northern Gaza town after its fighters were trapped in a mosque there. Two women were killed and dozens injured when Israeli troops opened fire. Israeli commanders said that they shot at militants who were escaping disguised as women. A spokeswoman for the Israeli military condemned militants for acting 'with no shame' by using human shields, 'knowing the IDF would not shoot at women and children.'[19]

By noon on the day of the deaths, schoolchildren were handing out freshly printed leaflets bearing the Izz ad-Din al-Qassam Brigades logo and proclaiming: 'The women of north Gaza arose to help Beit Hanoun.' But, as the day wore on, Hamas appeared embarrassed by the deaths and the manner of their fighters' escape. Challenged by journalists about whether the gunmen had got the women killed by using them as cover, Abu Obaida, the Hamas military spokesman, would no longer confirm that smuggling the men out in dresses was part of the original plan, saying only that 'The women were coordinated to go in different directions so that the Israelis would be distracted.' When pressed, he mumbled testily about the movement's 'legitimate right to use popular resistance besides military resistance,' before trying to turn the accusation back on Israel: 'They are destroying civilian infrastructure and have been using Palestinians as human shields for years, which is well documented by Israeli and international human rights groups.'[20]

Hamas still seemed prepared to accept women into their military wing. In 2005, amid much publicity, it announced the formation of a women's own military wing with the declared aim of 'jihad and resistance'. The woman commander of the unit gave an interview, published in the Islamic press, which lauded the actions of suicide bombers. 'The martyr Reem Al-Riyashi is like a crown on our heads and a pioneer of the resistance. Nobody can fathom the magnitude of her sacrifice,' she said. The interviewer then asked the most mundane question of all: 'How do you manage to combine membership in a military unit, educating [your] children, and taking care of [your] husbands and your households?' The answer came: 'That's something completely normal. We manage our time and know our duties, like every working woman.'[21]

A Rose by Any Other Name

The first indication that Hamas could achieve its stated, but widely discounted, goal of attaining power democratically came in the municipal elections of 2005, a harbinger of the general election which it was to win a year later. In Gaza, Aziza Abu Ghabin was one of Hamas's successful women candidates, running her campaign from a basement office in the women's Islamic centre.

Other initiatives included preaching, youth education, women's literacy and charitable activities for the needy – orphans in particular. The women's campaigns were segregated: election rallies, canvassing, public meetings, and other events were women-only affairs except for the obligatory musclemen chaperones. By Hamas edict, Aziza's face – like those of other women candidates – did not appear on election posters next to the photographs of the men. Instead the spaces by their names were blanked out and replaced with a picture of a rose. A rose by any other name in these circumstances meant a Hamas woman electoral candidate.

Aziza won 5,000 votes and a seat on Beit Lahiya municipal council, insisting that she was not going to confine herself to women's issues: 'I am a Muslim and I want to play an active role in the municipality in all its affairs.' Women, she insisted, would help set the council's priorities and be decision-makers. 'This is our right preserved for hundreds of years. I know my rights in Islam.'[22]

However, these stated ambitions were dismissed by her secular rivals. 'They emphasize that the women's role is to stay in the house and bring up the children,' sniffed one PFLP rival. 'Even their women MPs were for show. Most of their doctors are doctors in shari'a law.'[23]

After its successes in the municipal elections, in which Hamas fielded female candidates for two quota seats per council, it put women up again for the January 2006 parliamentary general election, in which electoral legislation mandated a one-third quota of women.

Once it decided to drop its rejectionist stance to national elections, Hamas competed hard for women's votes. Thousands of women were repeatedly canvassed, and huge amounts were spent organizing women-only Hamas rallies and festivals. Its women candidates were a mixture of seasoned politicians, technocrats and cult figures. The most prominent of the six Hamas women MPs elected were Jamila al-Shanti and Maryam Farahat. Shanti was a well-known academic and administrator with years of experience working within Hamas. Farahat, known as Umm Nidal (Mother of the Struggle), was the complete opposite. She had no political experience but was a folk heroine to Hamas diehards after having given three of her sons as 'martyrs' to the cause. She was even filmed with her youngest son before the suicide mission in which he died, telling him not to come back to her unless he was a 'shaheed' (martyr). Then she said to the camera: 'I gave my sons to the jihad for Allah … it is our religious obligation.'[24]

After weeks of huge election rallies, where women such as Umm Nidal were billed as the 'star attraction', and a carefully orchestrated television and newspaper campaign, Hamas sprang one more surprise on its opponents on election day. When voters emerged from their homes to head to the polling booths, they were confronted by groups of Hamas women activists, all wearing green sashes and green and white headbands, chanting and carrying posters and leaflets.

Their presence had an electrifying effect on voters and rival parties because it was so unexpected, and it heightened the already existing sense that Fatah had yet again been taken by surprise at the end of a complacent, half-baked campaign rooted in the past. It was also a masterstroke of news management – capturing the news cycle on election day when the Palestinian and Western media were in full attendance. With television cameras and newspaper photographers giving the 'Sisterhood' saturation coverage, it helped transform the public image of Hamas.

Days later, Umm Nidal was back in front of the news media proclaiming her success at the polls. 'People see in me a symbol of sacrifice and struggle,' she declared, as she received plaudits from supporters at her house, and later from adoring women students during a victory rally at the Islamic University of Gaza. 'If I didn't give my sons to jihad, I would be a sinner.' But Umm Nidal provoked controversy after newspaper reports that she planned to introduce legislation forcing women to wear the hijab. She insisted that she was misquoted. 'I said I hoped all women would cover their heads, but I never said it should be compulsory.'[25]

Dr Hanan Ashrawi, who also won a parliamentary seat in the 2006 election, said that she had begun to notice the emergence of Hamas's black-veiled, green-sashed women's brigade during the municipal polls the year before. 'I saw some of it, but the extent, the pervasiveness, came out in the [2006] election,' she recalls.

That meant that they had been working for some time, because all of a sudden you saw these women come out. At every polling station the Hamas women were there, dressed almost in uniform. All of them! And not shy or demure – out there lobbying, asking you to vote, vote for Hamas, and so on. And they went from house to house to bring out the votes.[26]

Victory for Women Does Not Equal Liberation or Equality

Women activists and others have complained that, since it came to power, the Hamas government has failed to address the rising incidence of gender-based violence against women. 'The people who are most afraid of Hamas taking power are the women's movement because in oriental society the woman is always the weakest sector,' sighed Naima al-Sheikh Ali.[27] Indeed, upon acceding to power, the Hamas government made no statement on equality, and on International Women's Day in March 2007 the Hamas head of the PLC refused to meet the annual delegation of women handing in their petition for equal rights.

Within a year of its takeover, Hamas's image for cleanliness and incorruptibility was still a decisive factor in its favour on the streets of Gaza, despite the economic hardships caused by the international isolation and Israeli border closures imposed on the Hamas-led Palestinian Authority because of its refusal to renounce violence or recognize Israel. This played well with some women constituents: 'It is enough for us that our leadership and our government are standing with people,' said Umm Usama, a 45-year-old woman who attended a pro-Hamas rally in front of Gaza's parliament building in September 2006. 'Until now they haven't got their salaries either. They sold their women's gold to survive, like the rest of the population. That is good enough for us.'[28]

Her fellow demonstrator Zainab, forty, said that her only means of support came from the Islamists' food coupons, United Nations handouts and the income of her husband's one brother – out of eight – who still had a job. Her bitterness was not directed at Hamas but at its internal and external enemies. 'No matter how much they starve us we will continue to support this government. We will never stop,' she said. 'The world pushed for Hamas to participate in the elections, and, when the outcome wasn't the one they wanted, they retreated on democracy.'[29]

But other women were left deeply uneasy at Hamas's efforts to impose its social, political and religious agenda. Suha – she would identify herself only by her first name – was, in March 2007, the principal of an elementary school in the Gaza Strip where, she claims, three armed members of Hamas's paramilitary Executive Forces came into the school unannounced and demanded to see her. Angered that the rest of their paramilitary unit was standing in the school grounds, fully armed, she confronted them: I immediately said, 'What are you doing here? You know that it is forbidden to come to a school with weapons.' They told me that they had come to the school to 'suggest' a way to guide the girls of the school to go through the streets. They wanted us, as school principals and teachers, to say to the students that the girls should walk on, for example, the left side of the street to and from home, and the boys on the other side. I was astonished.

She continued nervously, asking once again for anonymity. 'I told them I rejected the idea, it was interfering in our personal freedoms. I told them, "I don't take orders from you." But they said, "It is the orders of our leadership."'[30] Hamas officials in Gaza City later said they had no knowledge of any such edict.

Why Women Voted for Hamas

There were many theories offered for Hamas's 2006 election victory and for its success in appealing to women. Hamas supporters attributed success to its grassroots network of food distribution centres, medical clinics and nurseries and its reputation for honesty. They also cited widespread disillusionment at the corruption and inefficiency of Fatah, together with its failure to secure peace or a viable Palestinian state after more than a decade of negotiations with Israel. There was also anger at the lawlessness and gang warfare between armed factions on the streets of the West Bank and, particularly, Gaza. But, as no further elections were held for many years, those factors were not put to the test again to see which proved the most decisive.

Giving a post-mortem on her own party's election defeat and the role played by women in that, the Fatah women's activist Naima al-Sheikh Ali believed Hamas's success lay in its skilful exploitation of women's fears – poverty, Israel, and corrupt Palestinian Authority officials looking after their own at the expense of the deserving poor. And also in Hamas's promotion of religious certainty as the balm for that fear.

> We are a conservative, poor society, and always where there is poverty the belief in religion and belief in abstract and unknown things plays an effective role in society. So the debate involved frightening women by saying: 'Those people are secular infidels, communists' and the like. In addition to that, Hamas had the capability to provide money and food. Bear in mind that it is part of an international organization, the Muslim Brotherhood, not like the other organizations, which only extend locally in Palestinian society.[31]

However, Mona Shawa, of the Palestinian Centre for Human Rights in Gaza City, believed that Hamas's rise had less to do with its provision of food coupons and more to do with its success in persuading women that, amid increasing instability, there was only one public refuge where they could feel secure. 'The place that they feel safest to go, and their husbands, brothers and fathers allow them to go, is the mosque,' she said.

The mosque is where women can go with no objections, and I have seen them. At prayer time they offer seminars. The ladies take lectures on religion there. In this way the mosque becomes the only space outside the home for every Palestinian girl and woman in the Gaza Strip, irrespective of their social status, level of education, whether they are single, married or widowed, literate or illiterate, refugee or city dweller. Many women go to the mosque, and Hamas is related more to religion than other movements, so they become closer to Hamas than other factions. This is very new.[32]

For the women of Hamas, electoral victory brought them – or so they hoped – closer to their ultimate goal of ending Israel's occupation and establishing a true Muslim society and state in an independent Palestine. Huda Naim, a Hamas woman MP, offers a vision of women participating in the struggle, and even expanding their role, but always within the context of Islam. 'It is time to change. Palestinian women should have all their rights, including in marriage, where our religion allows for a free choice,' she said. 'We must prepare for the jihad, and we women as mothers have a role in raising fighters ready for sacrifice for the homeland.'[33]

Other Hamas women activists insist that the West misrepresents its ethos.

In 2007, student activist Iman Abu Jazar said that she worked within a Hamas structure where the men had their decision-making councils and the women had theirs. 'When Hamas won the elections, all the Western media said Hamas would force everyone to be Islamic in everything. No. We are working with people to help give them the right way. We are working with the people politically. Islam is our reference.' Her enthusiasm growing, and barely confined by the small office she occupied in the segregated campus of the Islamic University of Gaza, she declared: 'Hamas shelters women in every place ... it gave women rights. Hamas is no Taliban. The women saw that Hamas is her ambition fulfilled.'[34]

In 2009, in the wake of Israel's Operation Cast Lead in the Gaza Strip, Hamas's women supporters tried to protect their families, pray to Allah to keep them safe, cook food when there was an opportunity, and fulfil the many other roles that they play. 'No doubt our work is totally supportive', said Jamila Al-Shanti, 'because we are part of that movement.'[35] Yet again, in 2012, 2014, 2018, 2021 and 2023, a heavy and lethal price was exacted by Israel on the women and their children in Gaza.

Israel's enduring blockade and 'protracted humanitarian crisis' in the Gaza Strip, according to UN reports, exacted a particularly heavy price on women, especially those with children. Their livelihoods were impacted, and the rising rates of gender-based violence (GBV) that were reported were identified as a 'key protection concern'. Indeed, GBV 'in all its forms, including sexual violence, domestic violence and child marriage', along with 'the negative impact of the blockade, electricity and fuel' crises, 'intensified' the suffering that women were experiencing in all aspects of their lives. This has left an enduring question – who was mandated to take responsibility for these key protection issues.[36]

In 2023, following the 7 October attack against Israel's southern communities, where civilians were attacked and killed and hostages dragged to captivity in Gaza, the Israeli response was described by a United Nations rapporteur as 'yet again indiscriminate' in targeting entire residential areas, schools, hospitals, mosques and churches, killing thousands.[37]

Gazan women and their children accounted for the majority of the killed, injured and displaced. Less than two weeks into the war, the UN was estimating that nearly half a million women and girls had been displaced from their homes, and, as the war dragged on, a growing number of women would have to assume new roles as widows and bereaved mothers heading families rather than households that were homeless, deprived, existing on emergency food and other aid, with little idea of what the future would hold. By March 2024, as a result of Israel's war on Gaza, more than 9,000 women had been killed, more than 19,000 of them had been injured, and thousands more widowed. More than thirty-five Gazan mothers were being killed daily.

Whatever way Palestinian women play their politics for Hamas – whether out of support for the resistance against Israel and affection for Hamas leaders, or because there is no credible alternative, Hamas leaders have long understood how important they were. On the segregated campus of the Islamic University, a young male student marvelled at the chants of female students attending an Islamist rally: 'In every family in Gaza you will now find these women,' said Abed Hamdan. 'In that family – the one of her father or the one of her husband – she will carry the torch.'[38]

Ballot

Israel and America say no to Hamas. What do you say?

Hamas election banner[1]

As the Islamist movement neared its twentieth anniversary, the grassroots and leadership believed the time was right to end its carefully cultivated outsider status and move into the political mainstream. The vehicle was the January 2006 elections for the so-called parliament of Gaza, East Jerusalem and the West Bank – the Palestinian Legislative Council (PLC).

Hamas had boycotted the first and only previous round of elections in 1996, scorning the PLC as little more than a rubber stamp for Yasser Arafat and the Oslo peace process. Hamas had debated whether it should participate, but the leadership decided against and set out throughout the rest of the 1990s to make sure that Oslo would fail. Publicly, Hamas insisted that it boycotted that poll out of principle – because it rejected any institution set up under the Oslo Peace Accords. But sceptics believe, and some Hamas officials concede, that the faction's motives were altogether more self-serving. Hamas was swimming against a tide of popular support for the peace process and faced certain electoral defeat.

One turning point was the July 2000 summit between Ehud Barak, Yasser Arafat and US President Bill Clinton at Camp David. It became an Israeli article of faith that Arafat turned down the best deal the Palestinians would ever be offered, while the Arafat camp protested that no Palestinian could have signed up to the concessions he was asked to make. Camp David convinced Israelis that Arafat was a man who was not serious about a deal. But Hamas's leadership came to exactly the opposite conclusion.

'People started thinking deeply, "Where are those brothers in Fatah heading?",' recalls Ahmad Yousef, a senior Hamas official. 'They felt our higher national interests were becoming threatened because there were people ready to compromise, or sell out. That "No" wasn't strong enough to convince people that they weren't saying "Yes, maybe".'[2]

Jamila al-Shanti, then Hamas's most prominent woman activist, said Hamas's strategy was the reverse of that in Northern Ireland, where the

Provisional IRA eventually agreed to decommission its weapons to allow its political wing to enter the government. 'The difference between us and Sinn Fein is that, when we entered the election, we entered it with the intention of sheltering the resistance,' she said. 'It wasn't a choice between resistance and politics, it was to protect the resistance.'[3] In other words, Hamas went into politics to keep its guns, not to lay them down.

After the failure of Camp David, and the eruption of the Second Intifada in September 2000, Palestinian politics entered a period of enforced paralysis. Arafat and the PA argued that it was impossible to hold elections of any kind while Israeli tanks sat on the streets of Ramallah, Nablus and Jenin and candidates and voters could not move through Israeli checkpoints. Throughout this period Fatah's aging clique of PLO veterans ignored repeated calls to restore their credibility by standing for long overdue internal Fatah and PLO elections. This created tensions with the ambitious younger Fatah generation – notably the West Bank political firebrand Marwan Barghouti and Gaza security chief and *bête noire* of Hamas Mohammed Dahlan – who were both keen to shove the old generation aside.

But, in the rush to prise power from Arafat's grip, few considered who might fill the vacuum. 'Everybody wanted to take powers from Arafat as quickly as possible and wanted to put that power in the hands of somebody else,' said the Palestinian analyst and pollster Dr Khalil Shikaki. 'The Americans and Israelis and old guard didn't care who would control the system once it was taken away from Arafat.'[4]

By May 2002, Arafat was forced to respond to the growing domestic and international calls for reform by promising new presidential and parliamentary elections and a 'comprehensive review' of the PA. In the event it proved academic – elections were not to be held until after his death. Fifty miles away from Ramallah, Dr Abdel Aziz Rantissi, Hamas's deputy leader, watched with barely concealed satisfaction from Gaza as '*al-Khetiyar*' (the Old Man) twisted in the political wind. Rantissi exuded confidence that a shift in public opinion insulated Hamas against a repeat of Arafat's 1990s crackdown on Islamist dissenters:

Today we have a different situation. Firstly, there is no political horizon. The Israelis are massacring our people, they have reoccupied the West Bank, and all the other factions are carrying out resistance, including Fatah – which means the Palestinian people would never accept the return to arrests of Hamas, or anyone else.[5]

While Hamas is always prone to maximizing its own importance and centrality to events, its analysis was nevertheless shared by other more neutral observers. 'Arafat is in control and not in control at the same time,' said former cabinet minister Ghassan Khatib. 'He has to have a peace process in his hands in order to use it as a tool. When the Israelis are killing civilians, it is difficult for him to swim against the stream.'[6]

But even Rantissi the hardliner was willing to entertain publicly the notion that Hamas could open a new front in its struggle. Assessing that the Islamic movement 'has strategic depth in all West Bank cities', he confirmed that it would certainly contest municipal elections 'if they happen, because this has nothing to do with politics.' In so doing, Rantissi was subtly shifting Hamas's position from one based on principled rejectionism to the altogether more pragmatic – and easily finessed – objection that the Palestinian parliament had little power because it was subordinate to Arafat. 'We will participate in any elections based on clear democratic principles,' he said.[7]

While Hamas repositioned itself, the Israelis appeared more focused on the political power struggle within Fatah. In March 2002, one senior Israeli military official in Tel Aviv said Fatah was undergoing an unseemly internal succession struggle even before Arafat's death, as the political wing – principally Marwan Barghouti – tried to wrest power from security chiefs Mohammed Dahlan and Jibril Rajoub. The analysis was astute. But, as so often, the Israelis seemed much less sure-footed about the Islamists. 'Although Hamas and Islamic Jihad are considered the opposition to Fatah, they are not really,' the official stated blithely. 'They are opposed to Oslo. But they don't have any ambition to become the next Palestinian regime.'[8]

Less than four years later, Hamas was the next Palestinian regime.

The Next Generation

From 2002 to 2005, the political and geographical landscape changed completely as a generation of leadership passed from the scene. The first to go was a phalanx of Hamas's senior figures – Salah Shehadeh, Ibrahim al-Maqadmeh, Ismail Abu Shanab, Sheikh Yassin and Dr Abdel Aziz Rantissi – all assassinated by Israel.

Israel's apparent aim was twofold: to punish those they considered directly responsible for organizing attacks against Israel and to weaken the movement to the point of collapse. It certainly brought about a changing of the guard and the first real chance for a new generation of Hamas leaders to emerge. But it did not break Hamas. Instead Ismail Haniyeh, widely seen as a pragmatist, became the face of the movement, first in Gaza and later of the Hamas movement worldwide.

Before Haniyeh became prime minister in 2006, his home was simply another nondescript refugee shelter in Gaza City's Shati refugee camp, one of the most crowded in Gaza.[9] He was born in the camp in 1961 to parents who were refugees of the war of 1948, having fled their home in al-Jura, the same coastal fishing village 6 miles north of Gaza that Sheikh Yassin was from. Of the camp and from the camp, he joined Hamas around the same time that he graduated from the Islamic University of Gaza with his degree in Arabic literature.

Visitors to the home were usually greeted by Haniyeh himself, dressed in a white *galabiya* and prayer cap. The dark serge suits, white shirt and tie would come only later. Haniyeh is always calmly spoken. In his sermons he never shouts and amid a crowd is never flurried or impolite. For years he headed Yassin's office and was a near permanent companion to the sheikh, a wheelchair user. For Israel, Haniyeh is a terrorist leader, arrested in the late 1980s, deported to Marj al-Zahour in 1992, and targeted for assassination on several occasions since.

Outside the Palestinian Territories, Khaled Meshaal was the exiled leader of Hamas's Damascus-based Political Bureau and assumed a greater role in the movement, particularly after Yassin and Rantissi's assassinations. Meshaal's public and international profile grew from his Syrian base. For the increasing number of foreign journalists and former diplomatic heavyweights and statesmen who wanted to visit him, securing an interview with the man at the top of Israel's 'most wanted list' required tenacity, patience and a willingness to accept strict security precautions. Meshaal would often 'gift' his guests with candied fruits or Palestinian handicrafts. But such simple gestures belied the serious political calculations behind his willingness to meet with each and every foreign visitor.

'There is no political horizon if Hamas is not included as a legitimate element of the Palestinian people,' he said during one interview, two months after Hamas had seized control of Gaza. Even at a time when Hamas had just made itself even more of a pariah to the international community, it was noticeable that a confident Meshaal used terminology akin to that of a national leader. Talking about Hamas's centrality to 'the national agenda' and 'the national objective', he reiterated the movement's position on eventual statehood: 'There can be no peace process without Hamas included in the equation.'[10]

Hamas has never been characterized by a theological hierarchy; therefore, even the loss of its founder Yassin did not fatally undermine the movement.

But unlike the founding generation, the younger leaders who were emerging and rising through the ranks in Gaza and the West Bank had often not worked or studied abroad. The world effectively began and ended at the Israeli checkpoints surrounding the Palestinian Territories. Instead, they had gained their experience in student council and professional elections and in Hamas's Islamic charities and associations. Through these they were familiar with the different Palestinian constituencies: the young, the old, women, men, the urban poor and the rural communities.

One such emerging leader was Mushir al-Masri. Born in the north Gazan town of Beit Lahiya in 1978, he wore a black leather bomber jacket over his brown thobe as he led hundreds in Friday prayers outside the ruins of a mosque bombed by Israel during Operation Cast Lead in January 2009. Three years earlier, he had been the youngest candidate elected to the PLC. Educated at the Islamic University in Gaza – first obtaining a degree in Islamic law (shari'a) and then a masters in *fiqh* (jurisprudence) – he was a product of generation Hamas. An activist on campus, he became a deputy leader on the student council and was involved as a board member of the Gaza-based charity al-Nour.

al-Khetiyar

But the leadership change that presented the biggest opportunity was outside Hamas. On 11 November 2004, Yasser Arafat died in a Paris hospital after a lengthy and mysterious illness. It followed an even lengthier period of marginalization and public decline during which he sat confined under virtual house arrest in his hilltop Muqata compound in Ramallah. He would greet visitors with a ceremonious kiss on the hand and the offer of tea served in mismatched crockery on a camping table set in a bare corridor. Arafat's view from the confines of the Muqata was framed by the Israeli destruction to his headquarters.

Although Arafat had become a shadow of the presence he once was, his death meant that Fatah had lost an iconic leader whose personal charisma and legacy of struggle was unique within his now squabbling and fractious movement. 'Until the death of Yasser Arafat everything was in his hands. Everyone worked for Arafat; they were puppets on his fingers. After Arafat, there was no one to work for and they didn't want to work for each other,' said Ambassador Dr Abdelrahman Bsaiso, then a senior Foreign Ministry official.[11]

Arafat's successor, Mahmoud Abbas, widely known as Abu Mazen, was never to emerge fully from Arafat's shadow and had little personal standing in opinion polls. Nevertheless, he easily won the presidential election in January 2005 – helped by Hamas's decision not to contest the ballot. Although Hamas was then actively considering engaging in politics, the election was deemed the wrong point of entry. Part of the president's role was to negotiate with Israel, so the position would have placed Hamas in an impossible position.

Abbas was far more willing than his predecessor to countenance new elections. Against the advice of many of his senior Fatah lieutenants, Abbas appeared to calculate that the only way to revitalize his sclerotic movement was to open it up to a challenge at the ballot box. Abbas also argued that, rather than risk military confrontation with Hamas, it would be better to wean it off violence by bringing it into the political process. 'This is the difference between the era of Arafat and Abu Mazen. Arafat was stalling the legislative and presidential elections, not because he wanted one-man power but because he was afraid that, if he allowed them, Hamas would win,' said Brigadier-General Nizar Ammar, a senior planner within the PA's General Security force in Gaza.[12]

The flaw in Abbas's plan – as it was in Hamas's own reasoning – was that it assumed that Hamas would participate and lose. Hamas leaders say that its decision to enter parliamentary polls was taken in early 2005 after extensive consultations of the grassroots and *shura* consultative councils, and that it had the blessing of the political leadership in Damascus led by Khaled Meshaal. The clearest indication that Hamas would run, and run hard, for political office came in April 2005 from the one-time sceptic Dr Mahmoud Zahar, by then the elder statesman of Hamas following the assassinations of Yassin and Rantissi. Zahar confirmed to one of the authors that it would run, and that, if it won seats in parliament or the government, it would fill them: 'We have three options: either to be the majority and to ask others to participate according to our programme; second, to be a minority and participate in government; or to be a strong political opponent in the parliament.'[13]

Election Preparations

Some things worked actively in Hamas's favour. In the summer of 2005, Israel's prime minister, Ariel Sharon, pulled all the Jewish state's settlers and soldiers out of the Gaza Strip, thirty-eight years after Israel seized it from Egypt in the Six Day War.

Sharon insisted on carrying out the evacuation unilaterally, presenting it to the Palestinians as a fait accompli rather than negotiating it with

Photo 11.1 Hamas Executive Forces training in the abandoned Israeli settlement of Neve Dekalim after Israel's pull-out from Gaza in 2005

Abbas. So Hamas lost no opportunity to proclaim the pull-out as a victory for Palestinian arms. It was an argument that gained widespread credence among Palestinians and helped propel Hamas to power, even if it deliberately glossed over the complex demographic, security and internal political considerations that prompted Sharon to order the withdrawal. No Gazan who watched the demolition of Israeli settlements felt anything but a sense of victory at the destruction of outposts whose watchtowers, snipers and Israeli-only highways had blighted their lives for decades. 'Hamas said that resistance is the solution, and events have proved it was correct. No one can claim the disengagement was a unilateral step and a gift from Sharon. It was a crushing defeat to the dignity of the Jewish State,' proclaimed Zahar.[14] To ram home the point within days of Israel's withdrawal, Hamas's propaganda unit erected green street banners in Gaza, proclaiming: 'Jerusalem and West Bank after Gaza – Hamas.'

Israel and secular Palestinians regarded Hamas's ambitions with deep suspicion, fearing its embrace of democracy to be a ploy to bring about theocracy and authoritarianism on a one-way ticket to 'Hamastan'.

With Israeli troops out of Gaza, Hamas felt increasingly secure on the streets as autumn gave way to winter and election day approached. On

Photo 11.2 A Hamas banner in Gaza in September 2005, shortly after the Israeli withdrawal from the Gaza Strip

election day itself, 25 January 2006, Hamas fighters quietly deployed near polling stations to ensure that the Fatah-dominated Palestinian security forces did not try to rig the ballots. They even had torches and battery-powered lamps ready to rush to polling stations if Fatah cut the lights to stuff ballots amid the confusion. Hamas was everywhere. According to Yehya Moussa Abbadsa:

> The withdrawal of Israel from Gaza created a new fact on the ground. We were stronger. Democracy could not be protected in 1996, but by 2006 Hamas was stronger on the ground than the PA. That is what created the balance. They couldn't tamper with the election because we could protect the process. Politics and democracy aren't protected purely by values. In Algeria, the Islamic Society won the elections but didn't have the power to save itself.[15]

Whatever its motivations for entering the elections, Hamas had long ago concluded that Fatah's corruption and bad management were not only electoral liabilities that Hamas could exploit but were now undermining Palestinian society to the point where its own armed activities were being jeopardized. 'It placed the internal front on very weak foundations with all the corruption and mismanagement, and when you have weak foundations you can't build a strong resistance,' said Ismail al-Ashqar, a senior Hamas strategist.

> We wished to obtain popular legitimacy for the resistance and legal legit-imacy. We knew we would be much stronger when we had legitimacy backing you up, because no one can accuse you of breaking the law ... In 2006 we had experienced the Second Intifada and the popularity of Hamas was very high, and the ability to capitalize on this politically was very obvious.[16]

For Israel, the European Union and the United States of America, the prospect of Hamas winning was alarming. Washington called – in vain – for Hamas to be excluded, and the Islamists were quick to point out the irony. 'The US and EU called for elections to get rid of Arafat and others – well, they got an election but they didn't get the result they wanted, because we in Hamas won. Now there is the demand by the US to exclude us from the political arena,'[17] said Mushir al-Masri.

Musa Abu Marzouq felt confident enough to boast about Hamas's prospects and unwittingly give a foretaste of events to come: 'When we win those elections it will be great problems for the Americans, I am sure. Is the international community prepared to ignore these elections and their results if they go in our favour?'[18]

But few seriously believed that Hamas would, or could, win. Its principal opponent – President Abbas – was by now a welcome guest in foreign capitals – most notably in Washington. Standing beside Abbas at the White House, President George W. Bush made clear his support by voicing a misplaced public confidence that secular Fatah would prevail over its Islamist opponents:

> Hamas is a terrorist group, it's on a terrorist list for a reason. President [Abbas] ran on a peace platform; you know, maybe somebody will run on a war platform – you know, vote for me, I promise violence. I don't think they're going to get elected, because I think Palestinian moms want their children to grow up in peace just like American moms want their children to grow up in peace. As a matter of fact, I think the people that campaign for peace will win.[19]

Campaigning

Once it had decided to run, Hamas united behind the new strategy. It deployed thousands of highly educated Islamist managers, media professionals, opinion-formers, teachers, engineers, doctors and political scientists – male and female – who gave it a sharpness and sophistication far superior to its more politically experienced, but fatally complacent, rivals. For its venture into the mainstream, Hamas deliberately and calculatedly toned down its rhetoric.

Even Hamas's opponents conceded that its choice of electoral label – 'Change and Reform' – was inspired, capturing the pent-up desire among Palestinians for a new broom. The election manifesto also downplayed Hamas's implacable external agenda, making no mention of its ultimate goal of eradicating Israel. Instead it spoke of 'resistance to the occupation' and 'balanced' relations with the West. Hamas's customary insistence on proclaiming its commitment to the armed struggle was sidelined behind management consultancy talk of priorities, competence, transparency and delivery of services.

'We have our electoral programme on politics, agriculture, health, education, and so on,' said Sheikh Mohammed Abu Teir, Hamas's Jerusalem figurehead, who had spent more than twenty-five years in Israeli jails. Just after being released from a night in the cells for defying an Israeli ban on campaigning in Jerusalem, the henna-bearded no. 2 on Hamas's electoral list took advantage of a brief gap between incarcerations to deliver the on-message Hamas electoral line: 'Even with modest means we have succeeded in gaining the trust of the people. We will fight the corrupt and serve the Palestinian people.'[20]

Compared with Hamas's energy and drive, the Fatah campaign seemed listless and complacent. Fatah's old guard – Arafat's generation – had spent three decades outside Palestine, from 1967 until 1994, and had lost touch with the Palestinian street, a criticism that was heard as often from their own ranks as from outsiders. Inside Fatah's pristine election headquarters near the counterfeit 'Stars and Bucks' coffee shop in the West Bank city of Ramallah, clean-shaven youths and affluent young women wearing fake designer labels handed out leaflets advertising the party's website: www.vote4fatah.plo.ps. But the election headquarters seemed stuck in another era. In the front lobby, the sound system played the 1960s Beatles song 'Revolution' – from a time long before many Palestinian voters were born – and the walls bore twenty-eight posters of the dead Yasser Arafat but just two of its current leader, President Mahmoud Abbas.

In a back room, elderly officials in tweed jackets and improbably black hair seemed bemused by questions about where Fatah was strong or weak in the West Bank. 'We don't have any indication of where Fatah or Hamas have strongholds or majorities,' said one, after going into a huddle for several minutes to confer with his colleagues.[21] Collectively, they assured journalists that voters would stick with the movement because of its self-proclaimed status as 'guardians of the national project' – an ancient PLO cliché devoid of specifics, inspiration or direction. Summarizing the mood of inevitability and entitlement, one elderly apparatchik pronounced, to general nods of assent: 'Fatah's history is evidence enough to testify that people will support it at the ballot box.'

Not all Fatah officials were so complacent. A younger generation had fought alongside Hamas, Islamic Jihad and the other factions during the

First and Second Intifada and appeared to recognize the threat from their religious contemporaries, whose rise they had seen up close from inside Israeli jails and on the barricades.

Mohammed Dahlan, by then a key aide to President Abbas, warned that those in Hamas were fanatics on their best behaviour for the elections. 'We pledge that the mistakes of the past will not be repeated,' Dahlan told one rally in Ramallah, apparently calculating that it was better to be frank and contrite about errors than to pretend they never happened. He urged Fatah's listless supporters against a protest vote mentality. 'Let us be clear: if anyone thinks that he can vent his anger upon Fatah by making them lose, he is making a mistake. You will not be able to practise what you are experiencing today. It will be the policy of mouth-shutting, those who take religion at the expense of freedom of speech.'[22]

Others were equally alarmed. Diana Buttu, a former communications director in President Abbas's office, said that, in the year leading up to the ballot, Abbas and his senior lieutenants on Fatah's principal decision-making committees were so focused on Israel's pull-out from Gaza that they paid no attention to much needed internal Fatah reforms. She said many party workers were dismayed by the lack of proper Fatah primary elections to decide candidates, an oversight which resulted in two competing lists being drawn up: one by the Fatah establishment and the other by the younger generation. A late compromise to merge the two lists left out many Fatah notables – prompting the rejects to stand as independent Fatah candidates, with electorally fatal results.

'Hamas had its election platform and a very clever name, Change and Reform. Fatah had nothing other than a slogan: "We have been with you forty-one years,"' Buttu said. Money was spent 'needlessly', she said. There was no week-by-week strategy about what Fatah's message should be or how they were going to get people out to vote. 'Hamas were arm-wrestling with a baby. It wasn't so much that Hamas were so superior; Fatah gave it to them.'[23]

Amani Abu Ramadan, who worked with the Fatah campaign dealing with the international media in Gaza, said she quit early because the campaign was so badly run. She recalls driving around Gaza four days before the election. 'We went from Erez to Rafah, one and a half hours in the car, talking about the elections. I remember counting the election posters, and there were one, two, three, four billboards for Hamas, maybe two for Fatah and then another for Hamas,' she said. 'It was complete chaos. The Third Way or Change and Reform had someone at reception giving you campaign materials. At Fatah there was basically a bunch of boys sitting at the desk pretending to be a campaign.'[24]

But the lack of preparation and wasted money could still have seen Fatah to victory had it not been a house divided against itself. Fatah's campaign chief, Nabil Shaath, brushed aside allegations of Fatah corruption, dismissing them as 'election rubbish'. The real cause of Palestinian hardship, he insisted, was 'the Israeli siege, the Israeli wall, the Israeli settlement policy, continued Israeli attacks and destruction ... It is the Israeli siege that has killed this economy and turned it into rubbish, and also caused the lawlessness.' About Hamas's role in that breakdown of law and order he was bitter, saying that it had in fact been a 'major factor' in the lawlessness by continuing to carry out rocket and mortar attacks against Israel in defiance of the PA, which left the Palestinian police looking impotent. But, while conceding that the PA was partly responsible for its plight, Shaath sought to put the Palestinian experience into wider perspective, pointing out that there were few examples of societies freeing themselves painlessly from external hegemony.

> Yes, part of this is our responsibility as a people, and not only as an authority. But look at it from a historical context of post-trauma societies such as Bosnia, Kosovo, Ireland, Lebanon, Somalia and Iraq. It took Lebanon twenty-five years, and they are not really out of the post-trauma period. Whenever you are in a conflict with a far superior occupation army, this immediately leads to the proliferation of small arms, which are used by guerrillas and other types of violent resistance to ambush and fight far superior forces. The problem is when that superior force either vanishes, withdraws or starts to reduce significantly its own campaign against the occupied territories, then those who fought with small arms look around and substitute the goals with other local, provincial, personal or sectarian objectives.[25]

Meanwhile Hamas's campaign was in full swing. It was a winter election, but only one party's posters were covered in plastic to protect them from the rain. Beneath the sheeting was the face of Hamas's founder Sheikh Yassin, invariably with a broad smile on his face. The Hamas art and design department clearly went into overdrive to produce variations of campaign posters, literature and propaganda for the Change and Reform candidates.

Dr Nashat Aqtash, a Nablus-born public relations expert, was among the professional image consultants hired to sharpen Hamas's image. They gave candidates training in public speaking, on how to appear on camera, and on how to address the national and international media. 'We organized rallies, meetings at clubs, in public places and individual meetings. Personal communication is number one in Palestine because there is historic mistrust of the media and because Fatah wasn't scheduling its candidates to meet

Photo 11.3 A Hamas election poster

people. Their candidates were ministers and public figures, so they had no time to go to the public. That was a plus for Hamas,' said Dr Aqtash. He said he adapted a three-week formula devised by the 1960s American advertising guru Rosser Reeves, which stipulated a different plan for each week of the campaign.

Ismail Haniyeh, who was a compelling public speaker, appeared in Hamas television advertisements. Candidates were advised not to campaign negatively against rival parties, not to use Mahmoud Abbas as a campaign issue, 'because he is the president and we have to respect that,' and to emphasize religion by suggesting that, if voters selected those who were weak in their practice of Islam, they would be punished by God. 'The failure of peace talks for the last ten years helped Hamas. People had started to believe the rhetoric that peace was a waste of time and that resistance was the answer. So the message was addressing internal Palestinian issues. It had nothing to do with the occupation, nothing to do with the Israelis. All internal issues.'[26]

Hamas had a far sharper grasp of the complex electoral system. The vote for the parliament's 132 seats was divided into two lists: half for a party and half for individual candidates in sixteen districts. While Fatah put its strongest people on the national list, Hamas did the opposite, because it calculated, correctly, that people would vote along party lines for the party list but would be swayed by personal considerations when choosing a local MP. Hamas's one major mistake, Aqtash said, was to try too hard, ignoring the international obstacles they would face if they won.

> They didn't listen to advice. I told them not to run more than 50 per cent of candidates in the election because, if they actually won, they would find themselves in an impossible position. They wouldn't be acceptable to the international community and they would be embarrassed in front of their people. But [Khaled] Meshaal insisted on running with a full list. I warned them they would fall into a Fatah trap, that the Fatah people and US wouldn't give them a chance to succeed. I told them, 'Assign a technocratic government, assign a Christian Prime Minister. You can embarrass the US and Israel with that.'[27]

Both Israel and the international community were increasingly alarmed by Hamas, which one poll showed at 31 per cent in Gaza, just four points behind Fatah. The European Union warned of a freeze in European aid to the PA if the Palestinians embraced a party which refused to abandon violence and continued to urge the destruction of Israel. This was a grave prospect for the Palestinians, as the EU was their single largest donor, contributing one-third of the PA's international funding in 2005, more than $340 million. Two days before the election, the British prime minister, Tony Blair, stepped up the pressure. 'It is very difficult for us to be in the position of negotiating or talking to Hamas unless there's a very clear renunciation of terrorism,' he said.[28]

The foreign interventions proved pointless, even counterproductive. To neutralize them, Hamas held back its closing message until the final days of the campaign – huge banners across the main streets of Palestinian cities which proclaimed: 'Israel and America say no to Hamas. What do you say?' It is not an original tactic, but a tried, trusted and highly effective one.

Two days before the election, the opinion pollsters, Fatah, and most voters were still expecting a slim majority. Only twelve months earlier the same corrupt, bickering Fatah had confounded widespread predictions of post-Arafat chaos by uniting behind his successor, Abbas. And most senior Hamas leaders later conceded that they did not expect outright victory either. Publicly, Dr Mahmoud Zahar was one of the few who continued to proclaim the possibility of a major upset. 'It may be 25 per cent, it may be 50 per cent, it may be more than that. Nobody can tell.'[29]

Victory

The outcome was emphatic. Hamas won seventy-four seats in the 132-seat parliament and Fatah won just forty-five. The turnout was high, around 77 per cent. But most startling was the disparity between the percentage of the vote and the seats won. Hamas won 56 per cent of the seats with just 44 per cent of the national vote, whereas Fatah had 41 per cent of the vote but gained only 36 per cent of the seats. The main factor was the Fatah independents, who took thousands of votes from their own party's official candidates and allowed Hamas to rout Fatah by forty-five seats to seventeen in the district lists. This was a wholly self-inflicted failure of party discipline, symptomatic of a movement grown complacent after years in power. Political analysts calculated that the unofficial candidates might have lost Fatah up to eighteen parliamentary seats.

A good indication of how Fatah fatally divided its vote was in Hebron, where Hamas gained 49.9 per cent (61,433 votes) and Fatah 35.98 per cent (44,668). But Hamas won all nine of the seats because it fielded only nine candidates, whereas Fatah split the field with nine official and other independent candidates. Fatah did better in areas where it put big-name candidates in their home towns, such as Mohammed Dahlan in Khan

Photo 11.4 A Hamas youth rally in Gaza in December 2006

Photo 11.5 An image of the newly elected Hamas leader, Ismail Haniyeh, next to a portrait of the jailed Palestinian leader Marwan Barghouti, beamed from Gaza to the Palestinian parliament building in Ramallah in the West Bank, March 2006

Younis and Saeb Erekat in Jericho. In the party list vote, the race was much closer: Hamas won twenty-nine seats with 44 per cent of the vote, and Fatah twenty-eight seats with 41 per cent. With an absolute majority in the parliament, Hamas had in a transparent democratic election won political power.

As dawn broke the day after the election, a chill wind scattered the last echoes of morning prayers down a deserted Izz ad-Din al-Qassam Street in Gaza City. For once, everything was quiet. In the skies above, Israeli spotter planes were buzzing overhead alongside huge white surveillance balloons. But that morning the electronic descendants of Gideon's spies had little to report to their commanders in Tel Aviv, 40 miles north. No one was being killed. No one was being wounded. Everything was normal – which is abnormal, for Gaza. Because Palestinians were in shock after waking to a new political power in the land – Hamas.

Pariahs

Either you want to remain a liberation movement struggling against occupation, or you want a quasi-state and accept the limitations that this will put on you, either by the international community or by your opponent, Israel.

Ali Jarbawi[1]

Power leaked rapidly from Fatah – cocky Palestinian Authority security forces who only a few hours earlier had hurtled through the streets in Western-funded armoured SUVs now sat back at headquarters, unsure of the chain of command which had sustained them in one form or another back through the PA, the PLO and Fatah since the late 1960s. The scale of Hamas's victory shocked even the majority of its leadership. Ismail Haniyeh, the new prime minister designate, was mobbed in Shati refugee camp as scores of journalists and well-wishers crammed into his home. But, outside, the stillness was funereal rather than celebratory. The leadership had banned celebratory gunfire or partying. Its message was clear: the new regime would be one of discipline, not chaos.

Publicly Hamas leaders tried to claim that they expected victory all along. But privately many conceded that they had wanted – and needed – a period in opposition. There was to be no long political transition. Hamas was propelled straight from political wilderness to political power in a development that was to be disastrous for the Palestinian people. 'The result was a shock for us ... we decided to go for elections, but we were not expecting that any great significance would come from it,' conceded Usama Hamdan in Lebanon.[2]

As Palestinians absorbed the shock, the question being shouted down the phone to every diplomat and foreign correspondent in Jerusalem was: 'What does this mean for the peace process?' Most outsiders could not understand how Palestinians would embrace a group so wedded to violence, having voted in President Mahmoud Abbas – a man openly critical of the path of the gun – just twelve months before.

Seeking some consolation, American diplomats highlighted the fact that Abbas was still in place as president and was committed to a negotiated two-state solution with Israel. David Welch, assistant secretary in the US State Department's Bureau of Near Eastern Affairs, told one congressional hearing that 'the Palestinian people's aspirations to live in peace remain strong' and that 'opinion polls and analysis of the balloting suggest the vote for Hamas was more a protest against Fatah's governance record than a vote of support for Hamas's political agenda.'[3]

But while this was partly true, one of the most insightful analyses came from Michael Tarazi, a former legal adviser to the PLO: 'This is part of the problem that Fatah faced. They had nothing to show for their many years of negotiation with Israel. They had nothing to show for their recognition of Israel.'[4]

Money, Money, Money

Money quickly emerged as the first tool of international pressure, but one that had to be used carefully. While no world leader wanted to fund Hamas's acquisition of arms, neither did they want the inevitable humanitarian and regional security consequences of pushing Palestinians into penury. James Wolfensohn, a former head of the World Bank who was Middle East envoy for the Quartet, warned that the PA could face a cash crisis if Israel and international donors withdrew funding.

Pointing out a direct linkage between international aid and regional security, Wolfensohn said that, without money, the PA could not pay its roughly 150,000 employees – 37 per cent of the Palestinian workforce in Gaza and 14 per cent in the West Bank. 'Non-payment of salaries to some 73,000 security staff risks rising criminality, kidnapping and protection rackets … the already highly charged environment needs no additional fuel for a spark to ignite.'[5]

Israel's acting prime minister, Ehud Olmert, immediately announced that his government 'will not negotiate with a Palestinian administration if its members include an armed terrorist organization that calls for the destruction of the State of Israel.'[6] He all but placed the blame at the door of the PA and the international community, accusing them of being gullible.

Establishing a bipartisan template for Republican and Democratic presidents alike over the coming years, George W. Bush came down unhesitatingly and unwaveringly on Israel's side when confronted with the first – but by no means the last – of Hamas's shocks to the international body politic. 'The United States does not support a political party that wants to destroy our ally Israel … it means you're not a partner in peace and we are interested in peace,'[7] he said.

Moving quickly, the United States, the United Nations, the European Union and Russia – the four international powers known as the Quartet – said they would refuse to deal with a Hamas-led government unless it accepted three conditions: renounce violence, recognize Israel and respect previous agreements signed by Hamas's predecessors. But Hamas knew that an armed movement which ran on the slogan 'Israel and America say no to Hamas. What do you say?' could not immediately capitulate at the first sign of resistance. Ismail Haniyeh made clear that Hamas would not soften its position: 'The Americans and the Europeans say to Hamas: either you have weapons or you enter the legislative council. We say weapons and the legislative council. There is no contradiction between the two.'[8]

Hamas found itself all but alone. Early talk of a national unity coalition foundered as defeated Fatah saw the scale of the international opposition to Hamas, and left it isolated. Hamas leaders tried to nuance its position, Dr Mahmoud Zahar first saying that it was ready to enter talks over the prospect of Israeli and Palestinian states coexisting, and then trying to remove itself from the equation by deferring major decisions on relationships with Israel to a referendum of the Palestinian people. 'We may need to ask the general attitudes of our people. This is the land of the people. It is not the land of the government. We are not the owners of Palestine.'[9]

Three months into its term, Hamas was performing even more verbal gymnastics. 'We accept a state on the 1967 borders without recognizing the legitimacy of occupation. They can have their state on the 1948 lands, but I don't recognize it,' said Usama al-Mazini, a member of Hamas's dialogue committee. 'That is not a recognition of Israel, and there is no acceptance of the two-state solution. We will not recognize its legitimacy. We will deal with them on daily matters, but not at a practical level.'[10]

Fatah's campaign chief, Nabil Shaath, proved remarkably prescient about the difficulties Hamas would face on the world stage. 'Hamas thought it could get away with muddied double-talk: "Yes, we will negotiate", "No, we will never negotiate", "Yes, we may negotiate", "No, we can't negotiate because it's useless", "Yes, we can negotiate only humanitarian matters." As if it is more important to negotiate a room in [Israel's] Hadassah Hospital for my sick grandmother than for a Palestinian state. Rubbish.' The best reason Israel could have for not returning to a peace process, he said, was 'if we have a government with Hamas eternally debating questions about violence, negotiation and dealing with Israel that Fatah settled under Arafat decades ago.'[11]

Certainly Hamas had little chance of finessing its way to legitimacy, especially as it only ever said 'No, no, no' to the three Quartet demands.

Summoned back to Washington to give their assessment of the new status quo, American envoys and security advisers quickly learned just how determined American lawmakers were to isolate Hamas. Calling its Covenant a 'hate-filled screed', California's ranking Democratic representative Tom Lantos told one Washington policy hearing:

> Hamas leaders have not changed their rhetoric one iota since winning the election, far from it. Hamas leaders are now holding out their hands and asking US taxpayers to continue the flow of dollars, but the blood of dozens of Americans and hundreds of Israeli men, women, and children is on those hands. It has long been US policy not to support terrorists in any way. We must make absolutely clear that we will not deal with the terrorist thugs who now lead the Palestinian Authority. Not a single penny of US taxpayer money should end up in Hamas coffers.

Establishing the tone which was to be the keynote of US policy over the coming years, he continued:

> I also want to make it clear that simply ending direct assistance to the Palestinian Authority does not cut it. There must be an end to all non-humanitarian assistance that could benefit Hamas. The last thing in the world we in Congress want to do is to let a Hamas government reap the credit for development projects that are funded by the American taxpayer. Of course, I support the continuation of humanitarian assistance to the Palestinians, but we must be clear about how we define such aid. The phrase 'humanitarian assistance' means just what it says, and it is clearly defined in our legislation: food, water, and medicine.[12]

There were other voices who – even years before the Arab Spring was to highlight deep and abiding frustrations at democratic deficits across the region – cautioned that obvious attempts to make Hamas fail could backfire, and only increase its domestic support. Robert Malley, then Middle East and North Africa program director for the International Crisis Group, acknowledged the 'temptation' to ensure Hamas's 'quick and painful failure' to teach the Palestinian electorate a lesson, but said:

> I think it's a very appealing logic. I also think it may be short-sighted and ultimately self-defeating. If the US and Israel and others are perceived as trying to engineer Hamas's downfall and quick disruption of the government, the Palestinian people are not going to take from that the lesson that Hamas

failed them, but that others failed them. And in that sense, Hamas's failure may not necessarily be America's success. It depends very much how it fails.

Malley also spelled out the distinction between Hamas, which was prepared to participate in elections, and more extreme jihadist organizations, which were not. 'There's a broader regional picture,' he told the policymakers.

> However, we may dislike it, the debate today in the Muslim world is not between secularists and Islamists … right now the real debate … is between political Islamists, who, however radical their views may be, are evolving toward greater acceptance of democracy, of elections, of the nation-state as a framework within which to wage their struggle, and the jihadi Islamists, al-Qaeda being the best example.[13]

Hamas leaders themselves also warned that, by failing to deal with them, the West would only have itself to blame if they were then pushed out of the way by radical jihadi organizations such as al-Qaeda. An irony, since this was precisely the argument that its Palestinian rival President Abbas had been making for years about the PLO – that the price of Israel and the West not doing business with it would be to strengthen Hamas.

While most observers judged that the election results were an aberration, one attributable largely to Fatah's underperformance, others gave a different assessment. Brigadier General Shalom Harari, a retired senior adviser on Palestinian affairs to Israel's Defense Ministry, said it bore out his long-held view that Hamas had a significantly larger underlying base of support than the 20 to 30 per cent usually cited by political analysts. 'For the last twenty years I have shouted that the Islamic bloc has for many years – not in the last year or two, not because of the Intifada, for the last twenty or thirty years – had 40 per cent support inside the Palestinian territories,' he said a year after Hamas's election. 'When the Islamic bloc was ready to go to elections they showed that they had 40 per cent. They don't have the 62 per cent that came out from the results of the parliamentary elections, but they no doubt have 40 per cent.'[14]

Other analysts were concerned that permitting Islamists to contest and win an election was damaging to America's standing in a region in which the US was already suffering huge self-inflicted human and financial losses after invading Iraq with no apparent end game in place. Jon B. Alterman, of the Center for Strategic and International Studies, told US lawmakers that, by allowing Hamas to compete in the election, the Bush White House had further demonstrated its poor judgement in the Middle East: 'Many have the sense that the United States is dangerously naive; they see US insistence pushing forward with Palestinian parliamentary elections in 2006 despite the disarray of Fatah and the gathering strength of Hamas as a prime example of that naivete.'[15]

Siege

Within two months of the election, the tighter border closures imposed by the Israelis were causing severe shortages across the whole of the Gaza Strip. Crops were spoiling because they could not be moved out through the Israeli-controlled Karni crossing into Israel and on to international markets. Gaza clothing factories – once a cheap source of labour for Israeli fashion stores in Tel Aviv – were shuttered, and Palestinian bakeries began rationing bread. Israel cited security concerns for its refusal to open Karni, saying Palestinian militant groups frequently tried to infiltrate and attack it. Israel was accused of collective punishment of an entire population, and international humanitarian agencies were forced to cancel food handouts to hundreds of thousands of needy people.

When Hamas did announce its cabinet line-up on 20 March, it was headed by Ismail Haniyeh, with Dr Mahmoud Zahar as foreign minister, the hardliner Said Siam as interior minister, and the American-educated West Bank economist Dr Omar Abdel-Razeq as finance minister. The government was shunned by the West from its first day, particularly by an international financial system terrified of stringent US legislation banning dealings with terrorist organizations.

After his first look at the Palestinian Authority accounts, Dr Abdel-Razeq said it had inherited $1.2 billion (£687 million) in debts to banks and unpaid bills to suppliers, including Israeli utilities companies. It also found itself unable to pay the PA workforce of 160,000. 'The government ran out of money before the Hamas government. Now the problem is becoming larger and larger because of the action taken by the donors and the Israeli government,' he said.[16]

Look East

While the political and security chiefs dealt with domestic problems, Mahmoud Zahar, Hamas's new foreign minister, signalled a radical new approach for the new government's international strategy. Scathing about previous Palestinian Authority agreements with Israel, he indicated that Hamas governors of Gaza wanted little from Israel, America and the West.

'We have to open the door to the Arab and Muslim world. We have to separate our relationship on all levels with Israel for our national interest,' he said.

It was a common Hamas charge that PLO negotiators were consistently out-negotiated by the Israelis into accepting deals harmful to Palestinian interests. 'The people before us, the Palestinian Authority, negotiated with them for many, many years and reached, lastly, a deadlock. So why should we be a new copy like Fatah, wasting time and money of the people negotiating with Israel for nothing?' Zahar asked. 'No projects, no offers, no intention of giving the Palestinian people their legitimate demands.'[17]

Fatah would have replied that Hamas and Israeli far-right extremists had between them done more than anyone to wreck such initiatives. Nevertheless, there remained widespread pessimism among Palestinians about talks with Israel, and Hamas capitalized on this. Dr Zahar singled out the 1994 Paris Economic Agreement which governed trade and tax issues. 'We destroyed our economic status by the linkage of our economy with the Israelis,' he said. 'Israel takes from us seventeen taxes, and they are destroying our industry,'[18] he complained, saying that Palestinians should be released from restrictive agreements that limited them to Israeli suppliers. Furthermore, Zahar had a long list of examples to hand, suggesting that Hamas's research units had spent considerable time before the election preparing the ground for such a radical series of departures with previous Palestinian Authority policy.

As the scale of the international embargo became clearer, Hamas was inevitably forced to double down on its 'Look East' strategy. Hamas leaders in Damascus went on fund-raising tours of the Arab and Islamic world. Early post-election jokes that Hamas would soon be reduced to bringing millions of dollars back into Gaza in ministerial briefcases quickly became a reality, as Ismail Haniyeh and other government officials began doing exactly that.

It quickly became clear that, with Israel closed to Hamas, Gaza's Rafah border crossing into Egypt had become the single most important route for people, goods and humanitarian aid to cross into an increasingly besieged territory – and was to remain so for years to come. The political calculus was simple: Israel exercises complete military control along 90 per cent of Gaza's 70 mile perimeter – the coastal, northern and eastern sides – and the sky. So if the Egyptian frontier remains closed, Gaza is sealed off from the outside world. But if Hamas could keep the big black gates at the Rafah crossing open it had a lifeline to those in the outside world willing to help.

However, Israel found a way to keep Rafah shut. The agreement was that Palestinian and Egyptian officials would control their own sides of the crossing, but it would open only when there were international monitors present. Israeli officials would monitor the crossing remotely on cameras from the nearby Kerem Shalom observation tower but would not be physically present at Rafah. However, the monitors lived in Israel, so Israel could, citing 'security reasons', shut the crossing at any time simply by closing the narrow access road between Gaza and the Egyptian border along which the monitors drove to reach it. No monitors meant no crossing.

But, as the power plays went on, Egypt's then all-powerful intelligence chief, Omar Suleiman, cautioned that, if the West cut off Hamas from funds, 'Iran will give them the money.'[19] His concern reflected that of other Arab states – Egypt, Saudi Arabia, Jordan and the Gulf countries – none of which wanted to see their Iranian rivals turn Hamas into a proxy agent. Meanwhile Hamas issued not so veiled warnings that Israel and the rest of the Middle East would pay a price if Palestinians continued to suffer in the drive to isolate Hamas. A full seventeen years before the conflagration of 7 October 2023, Hamas's finance minister Abdel-Razeq warned that the Occupied Palestinian Territories could become 'another Somalia' if they were allowed to fester.

> If there is chaos in this area it is going to affect the whole security of the region. The relationship with Israel is not going to stay this calm, I'm sure of that. I'm not saying that we will, as a government, push things in that way, but starvation and economic problems and not paying salaries is going to result in probably more resistance acts and security problems.[20]

With political options all but exhausted, and facing increasing discontent among a Gaza population facing severe shortages, Hamas reverted to type. While steadily building up its security forces to combat the domestic threat that everyone could see coming, it also entered into confrontation with Israel, firing rockets across the border in volleys that drew thousands of Israeli artillery shells into Gaza in reply.

Tunnels and Kidnap: A Foreshadowing

Hamas rocket attacks and Israeli retaliation were by now a familiar pattern: disturbing for the residents of southern Israel, but rarely troubling the Israeli heartland in the Tel Aviv to Jerusalem corridor and farther north. But patterns create expectations and habits, which can be exploited. Fenced off from the outside world, Gaza had not posed a land threat for years and Israel's eyes were mostly on the sky, even though its Iron Dome missile interception system was not to begin tests for another couple of years and would only be deployed in 2011.

The sudden attack came from the other direction – from beneath ground. In June 2006, Hamas, the Popular Resistance Committees and the Army of Islam took part in a tunnel raid on Kerem Shalom military base. Burrowing through a neary 2,000 feet long tunnel, they launched a surprise bomb and grenade attack on the installation that was supposed to be monitoring southern Gaza for threats, killing two Israeli soldiers and capturing a third, 19-year-old Corporal Gilad Schalit.

Israel launched a furious series of attacks in a vain effort to recover Schalit. The Israeli airstrikes shattered bridges and threw much of Gaza into darkness as they destroyed transformers at the only power station. In Gaza there was little empathy among Palestinians, many of whom regarded the Hamas-led assault as a legitimate raid on a military target. They were also angered that the fate of one Israeli soldier drew far more international attention than that of thousands of Palestinians held in Israeli jails. In a telling insight into the different mindsets, one Rafah-based tunneller with the Popular Resistance Committees reacted with scorn when Israel sought to engage sympathy for Schalit by disclosing that he also held a French passport. 'He has dual citizenship? This guy has two choices, one to live in Israel and one to live in France. For us, we have no other place to go,' he sneered.[21]

The impact of the Gaza closures was already beginning to tell when a new front in the conflict opened up. Three weeks after Schalit's capture, the Lebanese militant group Hezbollah attacked Israel from southern Lebanon, launching a cross-border raid, capturing Israeli soldiers and firing scores of Katyusha rockets into northern Israel. Pictures of Hezbollah leader Sheikh Hassan Nasrallah sprang up all around a gleeful Gaza, and Hamas was visibly emboldened by the sight of thousands of Israelis fleeing Hezbollah's rockets. This played to Hamas's long-standing obsession with proclaiming its own strength and the weakness of its enemies – partly to raise morale and partly to encourage *samud* (steadfastness) among the Palestinian population. 'I regret to say that many of the Arab regimes and international leaders were living under the illusion that the Israeli army was unbeatable,' said Abu Bakr Nofal, a Hamas negotiator.[22]

Schalit and his fate became a national rallying point as 'Israel's Lost Son'. The government, PR experts and pro-Israel groups used traditional news media and the relatively new phenomenon of mass social media platforms to send images of the young soldier worldwide during the years of his captivity. Israel had a policy for such situations. The 'Rabin Doctrine' held that first Israel had to try and mount a rescue operation but that, if that failed, then it would be willing to negotiate with the captors. The negotiations for his release, after five years in Hamas custody, were complex, drawn out, and involved a variety of mediators. And there was eventually a high price exacted for his freedom – the release of 1,027 Palestinian prisoners from Israeli jails.

When the jubilation died down, a public debate ensued in Israel – whether the freedom of just one soldier in return for the release of Palestinians convicted of terrorist crimes could be warranted when many feared that they would organize, direct and conduct attacks against Israelis all over again. There was another consequence. Hamas captors now knew the value that Israel attached to their citizens and the high price that could be exacted for their release. And Israel, likewise, could trade Palestinians in jail – civilians as well as fighters – for the freedom of their people in captivity. Capturing combatants and civilians was to be weaponized by both.

Internal Criticism

Hamas was increasingly isolated as time went on. Educated Palestinians were hesitant to take any role in a regime so toxic to the West, while ordinary Palestinians began muttering that they simply wanted food and access to the outside world. In his weekly sermons, Ismail Haniyeh sought to reassure Hamas supporters by comparing them to the early followers of the Prophet Mohammed – reviled and outcast, yet ultimately victorious. 'When things became so hard for him in many of his battles he had with the infidels, all of the Arab tribes united against him. That was described in the Koran,' he told listeners at the Sheikh Ahmed Yassin Mosque in Gaza. He pointedly sought historical precedent for Hamas's refusal to comply with the West: 'And people asked why God did not help them. There were dialogues and negotiations at that time. All of the negotiations were to make the prophet fail.'[23]

But the size of the congregations dwindled from month to month, and there was also desperation on the streets, with Gaza referred to by its inhabitants as a *sijen kbiir* (large prison). In September 2006, nine months after the election, Welfare Ministry employee Amal Saleem said: 'This government was for Change and Reform. This is not Change and Reform. This government is not accepted internationally and nobody is dealing with them. We are not selling our land or rights or recognizing Israel. But we want a government that can govern.'[24]

As Hamas adjusted to being a government expected to deliver services to a whole population – not just its members – it also had to be mindful of its other constituency: the refugees in Palestinian camps in Lebanon and Jordan who wanted it to bring them back home after decades in enforced exile. Many of those continued to insist there should be no compromise on territory and on their 'Right to Return' to Palestine. In Ein Hilweh refugee camp in southern Lebanon, Maher Sukkar, twenty-seven, spoke Arabic with a Palestinian accent, even though he had never visited there, denoting how little the Palestinian refugee population has been absorbed into Lebanese society. He believed Hamas was the organization best suited to achieve his long-term goal of return, and that the Islamist group was under concerted attack for what it was trying to do. 'There is a project to disarm Hamas and all the Islamic resistance movements around the world, but Hamas especially,' he said. 'These are American aims: to proclaim control from the Gulf to the Sea.'[25]

Brief Thaw

Inside Palestine, however, Hamas was losing support as Western countries increasingly channelled aid directly through President Abbas's office to bolster support for him – the most visible sign being teams of road sweepers wearing caps and vests bearing presidential office and international aid agency logos. Hamas and Fatah were finally persuaded by Saudi Arabia on 8 February 2007 into a power-sharing agreement, in which Hamas held nine cabinet seats and Fatah six. Hamas said its priority was to alleviate the Israeli siege on Gaza. 'There are spoiler factors that we are aware of, but we will still sit with them … to save the situation for ordinary Palestinians,' said Usama Hamdan.[26]

But it was immediately apparent that there would be difficulties in an administration half-filled with international pariahs and internationally respected figures such as the new finance minister, Salam Fayyad, the former World Bank and IMF official. Even as he left the swearing-in ceremony in Ramallah, Mr Fayyad said that, although he hoped 'to put the finances of the PA on a more sustainable path', Palestinians were going to need financial assistance for development needs for a long time.[27]

Desperately hoping for a 'unity dividend' from Israel and the West, President Abbas immediately called for a resumption of Western aid and for hundreds of millions of dollars of PA revenues confiscated by Israel.

Israel remained firm, but the installation of Fayyad and others began an immediate thaw in relations with other countries. Some believed that Hamas's agreement to enter a national unity government meant that it 'wants international acceptance and legitimacy and recognition, wants to be part of the international community and wants to stay in power,' according to Dr Hanan Ashrawi. 'The only way it can stay in power is to be accepted internationally and, if the price is a political flexibility and a political platform, I think they will pay that. They have already started,' she said. 'To run for elections is the first dramatic expression of this transformation.'[28]

But Yuval Diskin, the head of Shin Bet, assessed that Hamas was playing a much longer, very ambitious game. Fatah appeared to have no 'clear policy or strategy for internal matters', while Hamas was clearly intent on eventually assuming leadership in the Palestinian diaspora as well as inside the Palestinian Territories. 'It thinks it can control the PLO. Hamas is not in a hurry.'[29]

The national unity government was a doomed attempt to graft two antagonistic heads onto one body, and it proved short-lived. Soon, the violence resumed. In mid-April an American international school in Gaza was attacked, and the different factions' armed wings were acquiring arms and ammunition at a rapid rate. An early sign of what was to come was the audacious attack on a Presidential Guard position at an Israeli border crossing in mid-May 2007, in which Hamas forces quickly overwhelmed a position guarded by the US-backed and trained Palestinian soldiers.

The fact that Hamas could so quickly take a well-armed and trained position so close to the border with Israel was a dangerous portent. Much worse was to come. There was also a growing sense among the hardline elements in Hamas that Fatah had become an irritant that needed to be dealt with decisively in order to make the fight against Israel easier. 'Sometimes we are fighting Israel with one hand tied behind our back,' said one Hamas military commander. 'It is Fatah that tied it for Israel, and now we have to undo these bindings even if it means taking the knife against Fatah itself.'[30]

Looking back on Hamas's early attempts to reinvent itself, Professor Ali Jarbawi of Birzeit University said that the Islamists made two major misjudgements. First that, because Israel had withdrawn its forces from inside Gaza in 2005, Hamas would have free rein to rule, not fully appreciating the limitations that would be imposed by the fact that Israel's military still ringed the narrow coastal strip:

I think Hamas got delusions that Gaza was liberated when Sharon left ... and that they could act as a fully-fledged 'state' or liberated territory ... And

I think that was a factor that played a key role in how they dealt with winning the election. If Gaza had still been under direct Israeli occupation, I think the response would have been different.

Jarbawi also contended that, for all its decades of sneering at Arafat, Hamas made exactly the same mistake as Arafat by thinking that it could get away with flip-flopping between being an armed group and a legitimate government, and failing to appreciate that this would simply not be tolerated by the international community. 'Either you want to remain a liberation movement struggling against occupation, or you want a quasi-state and accept the limitations that this will put on you, either by the international community or by your opponent, Israel.'[31]

Hamastan

The past era has ended and will not return. The era of justice and Islamic rule has arrived.

Islam Shahwan, Hamas[1]

From a distance it looked like a grey hill that materialized overnight in a southern corner of Gaza. It was not a hill, it was a settlement graveyard: a 30-foot high pile of rubble whose broken chunks of stone were once the walls, ceilings and garden patios of Israel's settlements in Gaza. Those settlements were the bulwarks of the phase of Israel's military occupation of Gaza from 1967 to 2005, by the end of which 9,000 Jewish settlers lived in twenty-one settlements protected by high walls, watchtowers, and Israeli tanks and troops from the more than a million Palestinians living around but not among them.

Those settlements, considered illegal under international law, were evacuated and mostly destroyed in 2005 under the Disengagement Plan of then Israeli Prime Minister Ariel Sharon. At a stroke, that pull-out transformed the internal dynamics of the Gaza Strip. With Israeli soldiers gone, Palestinian armed factions moved into the once hated outposts.

Hamas used one of the largest, Neve Dekalim, as a training ground. In the former settlement's industrial estate, Hamas's black-uniformed weapons experts in the Executive Forces trained new recruits in unarmed combat and on shooting ranges, operating in broad daylight. 'This is a beautiful irony,' said Islam Shahwan, a spokesman for the Executive Forces, as he poured sugary orange squash for visitors. 'We are proud to be able to use this. I spend more time here than I spend in my house. We were deprived of this land for thirty years.'[2] Such a training base was possible only in post-disengagement Gaza. In the West Bank, Fatah outnumbers Hamas, and, even if Hamas defied the Palestinian Authority's West Bank security forces, Israel's ever-present troops, tanks, helicopters and patrols would never tolerate an overt Hamas armed presence there.

The Hamas commanders in Neve Dekalim were initially less than forthcoming about the source of money to buy the AK47 semi-automatic weapons, bullets and hundreds of brand-new black boiler suits on show. However, they eventually admitted that Iran was supporting them. After returning from a fund-raising trip to Tehran, one commander even encouraged his guests to oversee the distribution of money to rank-and-file Hamas armed forces – sitting in a building whose wall bore the defiant settler graffiti 'We Will Be Back!'

Power Games

Hamas had set up the paramilitary Executive Force[3] because it suspected that the United States was helping President Abbas launch a 'coup' against the new Hamas-led government. Such a move would strike at a proxy that Washington saw as part of an axis of Iranian power across the Levant.

In 2006 reports had begun to leak out from meetings of the Quartet powers in London and Cairo that Washington was pushing to contain the Islamists by supplying more guns and soldiers to Fatah. Non-American members of the Quartet were uneasy as senior US officials appeared to push Fatah's leader, President Mahmoud Abbas, to confront Hamas militarily. 'As far as we are concerned, what the Americans are proposing to do is back one side in an emerging civil war,' said one Western diplomat at the time. 'A lot of what the Americans are saying is: "If this is going to be a fight, we might as well make sure that the right person wins."'

Some of those familiar with the talks believed that the Americans were divided about the plan – their security advisers apparently reluctant to pump more guns and support to Fatah troops in Gaza – while others were being encouraged by neighbouring Arab regimes. These regimes feared that a strong Hamas would strengthen its Muslim Brotherhood cousins in their own countries and wanted a Palestinian proxy to crush it. 'It is the Arabs who are giving the Americans the ideas,' said the Western diplomat.[4]

The disruptors found willing ears in Washington. Within weeks of its election victory, neoconservative advisers to the incoming administration of President George W. Bush were urging action against Hamas and turned to their proxies in Fatah to offer them assistance. The tool was close at hand. One by-product of the Oslo era in the late 1990s had been a variety of security arrangements and agreements. To keep the peace process on track, the CIA had moved into an oversight and training support role in the developing security relationship between the PA and Israel. The Tenet Plan, signed in 2001 (and named after the former CIA director George Tenet), pledged that Israeli and Palestinian security chiefs would engage in senior-level meetings once a week with US security officials in Jerusalem. One object of the plan was to tackle the 'terrorism' threat in the West Bank and Gaza Strip. Everyone knew that meant Hamas.

American support for Fatah was ill-disguised. It wasn't just the frequent presence of armoured black GM Suburbans outside the headquarters of the Preventive Security Organization (PSO) which signalled that the CIA was in town meeting Palestinian security chiefs; it was that everyone else was bumped down the line, even other intelligence agencies. For regular visitors to the heavily fortified compound in Gaza, the presence of the CIA was palpable. As America and Israel had begun to regard Arafat as someone who had outlived his usefulness, they appeared to have found an heir apparent in PSO intelligence chief Mohammed Dahlan.

Born in Khan Younis refugee camp in 1961, Mohammed Dahlan was a Fatah activist from an early age. A member of the Fatah Youth Organization from 1981, he was imprisoned for political activism by the Israelis in the 1980s and became active in the First Intifada as a student leader and street captain. In 1988 he was rounded up by the Israelis and deported to Jordan. When he then arrived at the headquarters of the exiled PLO in Tunis, he was promoted by Arafat, allegedly, over the objections of the latter's suspicious deputy, Abu Jihad. His coronation as a future leader seemed assured. The word on the street was that Dahlan was tough, smart and sophisticated. After the PLO returned from exile in 1994, he was appointed Gaza's head of the newly created Preventive Security Organization.

For years, Dahlan's enemies claimed the American CIA and British MI6 had been grooming the man who had become derided in Hamas circles as 'Prince Charles'. He was sent to Cambridge to improve his English, reading copies of *The Times*. One Western military official acknowledged that, with the help of the government of Israel, he was bringing in weapons, ammunition, vehicles, camp stores and other equipment through Israeli-controlled crossings into Gaza. Dahlan, it was alleged, was also encouraged to form his own Special Force, cherry-picking men from the existing Fatah security organizations and preparing them through intensive training for a showdown.

Many Hamas leaders had nothing but contempt for Dahlan, arguing that foreign help would do Fatah no good in the long run. 'Does it buy loyalty stronger than the loyalty to Allah?,' asked Hamas's Mushir al-Masri.[5]

Rumours about the role of Fatah security officials exploded into the open eighteen months after the takeover, in 2008, when the American magazine *Vanity Fair* claimed to have obtained confidential documents 'which lay bare a covert initiative, approved by Bush and implemented by Secretary of State Condoleezza Rice, to provoke a Palestinian civil war.' It said the plan 'was for forces led by Dahlan, and armed with new weapons supplied at America's behest, to give Fatah the muscle it needed to remove the democratically elected Hamas-led government from power.'[6] When the *Vanity Fair* article broke, Rice refused to comment directly but did not deny it. 'It is very clear that Hamas is being armed and it's very clear that they're being armed, in part, by the Iranians. So if the answer is that Hamas gets armed by the Iranians and nobody helps to improve the security capabilities of the legitimate Palestinian Authority security forces, that's not a very good situation,' she said, elliptically.[7]

It is said that the plan was rejected by President Abbas. And some Israeli officials had also expressed reservations about a plan predicated on seeing more weapons flooding into Gaza. They feared, with good reason, that the guns would end up in Hamas's hands. This was precisely what a confident Hamas was already predicting. 'Disregard the intention,' said Khaled Abu Hillal, a spokesman for Hamas's interior minister, Said Siam. Pointing out how many PLO fighters who returned with Yasser Arafat from exile in 1994 later fought against Israel, he said: 'The weapons they brought and the bullets, where are they now? They were used against the Israelis. Let them remember the lessons of history.' Abu Hillal was contemptuous of what he referred to as the 'American currents' within Fatah. 'Despite all the channels of financial and military support, this is a weak, isolated and outcast current,' he sneered. 'They are like balloons.'[8]

Build Up

The balloon burst in 2007. After one particularly bloody round of infighting, one veteran Qassam fighter gloated that a series of Hamas raids on Fatah headquarters in northern Gaza had taken their enemy by surprise. 'They underestimated us. They weren't prepared for this day: they didn't know that we were holding back from confrontation not because we were weak, but because we were preparing.'[9]

Many speculated that Hamas used the first eighteen months after its victory to bring in arms and money for a showdown with Fatah. Hamas, according to Israeli intelligence sources, used tunnels from Egypt in 2006 to smuggle in 28 tons of explosives, 14,000 guns and 5 million ammunition parts, 40 rockets, 150 rocket-propelled grenades, 65 launchers, 20 'improved' anti-tank missiles and 10 anti-aircraft missiles.[10]

Gaza's tunnel operators readily confirmed many of the Israelis' claims. They were happy to show off the smaller commercial tunnels – waist-high, 3 feet wide and fitted with winches to drag goods through from Egypt using hollowed-out petrol barrels as sleds. But the tunnels dug and guarded by Hamas were far larger, more sophisticated and less public. Big enough for a man and beast to walk through, they are often shored up with wood or concrete. One Rafah tunnel operator, Abu Qusay, said that each hole took three to six months to dig by hand and machine and stretched for half a mile. It was a profitable but risky enterprise, he said, with profits of up to $100,000 in a single day, divided sometimes ten ways, between the tunnel's owners, diggers, guards and the smugglers who delivered the goods through the Egyptian territory of the Sinai desert. Abu Qusay said that much of what the tunnellers brought in was weapons. The most profitable were bullets, bought for $1 each in Egypt and sold for $6.5 in Gaza, and Kalashnikovs, bought for $800 in Egypt and sold for twice that in Gaza.[11]

According to Brigadier General Yossi Kuperwasser, a retired director of intelligence analysis for the Israeli military, Hamas was also able to smuggle in larger and longer-range rockets from East Africa, shipped up the Red Sea and smuggled in from the Sinai by long-established trading and criminal networks. Bemoaning Egypt's apparent inability to stop the smugglers, he said: 'Rafah is not New York City. This is something I just cannot understand: why they don't close them down.'[12]

In light of Hamas's growing strength in Gaza, many observers questioned how committed Fatah's security forces were likely to prove, manned as they were by people generally more interested in salaries than jihad. 'I'm not optimistic about Fatah,' said a prescient Yuval Diskin, the director of Shin Bet, in March 2007. He assessed that Fatah had done little to rebuild itself politically or militarily since its 2006 election defeat. 'If you speak to Fatah, they tell you about all their plans. But when you check, there is not much happening.'[13] Despite the overwhelming numerical superiority of the estimated 70,000 pro-Fatah forces against Hamas's 6,000-plus Executive Force and more than 10,000 members of the Izz ad-Din al-Qassam Brigades, Hamas was preparing for a confrontation.

Takeover

That confrontation came on Monday 11 June 2007, when Hamas launched a five-day military operation in which it took over the Gaza Strip, forcing hundreds of Fatah members and Egyptian intelligence officials to flee for their lives. In a carefully coordinated plan, Hamas's forces swept through the streets from southern to northern Gaza, besieging, attacking and capturing one Fatah stronghold at a time. Among the first to die was Jamal Abu al-Jediyan, the most senior Fatah official in northern Gaza, killed when

Hamas gunmen attacked his house in Beit Lahiya. Fatah claimed he was executed at gunpoint. The ruthlessness appalled onlookers, and both sides blamed each other, with Hamas accusing Fatah of having killed one of its preachers, Mohammed Rifat.

There were claims from both sides of supporters being thrown to their deaths from high buildings, including Mohammed Sweirki of Fatah, hurled from the fifteenth floor of one tower block, followed by Abu Kainas of Hamas, from the twelfth floor of another. Firefights broke out on the streets, moving through the city as Hamas quickly pushed Fatah back into its most heavily secured headquarters. Snipers took up positions on high buildings to control the ground below. Gunmen commandeered vehicles, and impromptu checkpoints were set up. The vast majority of Gazans stayed in their homes, too afraid to go out onto the streets. Many of the Fatah-dominated PA forces fled the Gaza Strip or hid at home.

On Tuesday 12 June, Hamas forces captured the headquarters of the Fatah-led General Intelligence services in northern Gaza – known locally as The Ship – after a day-long battle between 500 Fatah activists inside the building and an estimated 200 Hamas attackers. By nightfall Fatah had surrendered The Ship, and Hamas's fighters were 'requisitioning' anything they could lay their hands on. Hamas's propaganda operation was in full swing, abuzz with 'reports' of wine bottles and pornography found in Palestinian Authority filing cabinets, alongside intelligence reports that – Hamas threatened – would later be used as evidence against Fatah officials accused of collaborating with Israel. President Abbas described the fighting as 'madness', even as he and his chief negotiators were making panicked calls to Washington, already admitting that they had 'lost Gaza'.

Fatah appeared to be in a state of paralysis. 'There was no overall PSF commander in Gaza for the fight,' observed Colonel Michael Pearson, a Canadian assigned to work with the US Security Coordinator in the Middle East, General Keith Dayton. 'They did not support each other. They gave all power of movement and manoeuvre to Hamas, and so comprehensively lost.'[14]

In the south, Ali Qaisi, a Presidential Guard spokesman, claimed that Hamas overran a Preventive Security compound in Khan Younis by burrowing a tunnel beneath the building and setting off an explosion beneath it, after broadcasting warnings over loudspeakers that they were about to blow it up. Two days later Khan Younis was fully under Hamas control.

Hamas's radio station, Al Aqsa, explicitly outlined the endgame. An announcer declared that Hamas's offensive would push north through the Gaza Strip to Mahmoud Abbas's presidential compound and security headquarters in Gaza City. As each security installation fell into Hamas hands, the organization broadcast accompanying photographs revealing barrels of drugs, requisitioned vehicles plastered with posters of Hamas martyrs, and hundreds of seized security files. Hamas gave Fatah holdouts until Friday 15 June to surrender. Farther south, in Gaza City, it seized the Awdah building, an apartment complex which was home to many senior Fatah leaders, killing at least eight Fatah men during the battle, according to witnesses.

Many Gazans were furious at both sides for allowing the descent into civil war, and protesters marched through Gaza City, chanting 'Stop the killing'. But the situation was out of control. Fatah security chiefs fled, and their luxurious Gaza City homes lay as abandoned, looted and graffiti-scrawled as the Israeli settlers' homes less than two years before.

By the time Friday prayers were over on 15 June, Hamas was in charge of the Gaza Strip. President Abbas accused it of a coup, as masked Hamas gunmen posed for victory pictures in his beachside presidential palace, the national security headquarters known as the Saraya, the Rafah crossing terminal and other headquarters. Triumphant masked men carrying their guns and wearing ammunition belts were photographed in a variety of poses in the president's office, amid his personal possessions and sitting at his desk with their feet up. The images were a searing humiliation for the Palestinian president and his armed forces.

Aftermath

The attack drew widespread international condemnation and served to isolate Hamas even further from the international community. But Hamas insisted its onslaught was a counter-coup against Fatah conspirators who were planning to implement Israeli and American plans to bring down the elected government. 'We are here to defend the legitimately elected government of Hamas and bring public order,' said one Hamas official.[15] However, the charge of serving Israel's interests was thrown back in Hamas's face by Maher Miqdad, a Fatah commander, who, after fleeing with his family, said the takeover would make it easier for Israel to divide and rule the Palestinians. 'This is an Israeli plan,' he said. 'They want to connect the West Bank to Jordan and make Gaza a separate jail. This will be the end of an independent Palestinian state.'[16]

Other Hamas leaders were more frank about the realpolitik which underpinned Hamas's offensive. Hamas MP Ismail al-Ashqar said the continued infighting after its election victory had made Hamas look weak: 'We didn't want it to end like this. There was no political agenda in Gaza for that to happen. But when your back is put to the wall you don't have any choice. When people are being killed and houses being burned you are afraid that your own grassroots will turn against you and call you soft.'[17]

One reason for the swiftness of Hamas's takeover was that it had thoroughly infiltrated Fatah's security forces. Captain Abu Yazi, the newly appointed head of a Hamas border police station at Rafah, confirmed that, until the takeover, he had served in nearby Khan Younis as a member of the coastal police. But he had effectively switched sides long before that, after being approached by Hamas activists who told him that – when the day came – he could either run away and live or fight and die. 'I used to work secretly with the Qassam. Nobody knew I was Qassam,' he said.[18] 'The Preventive Security were so thoroughly corrupt that they melted away and lost their heart,' said one Western official closely involved in events.[19]

One of the most damaging legacies of the takeover was that Hamas demonstrated, time and again, its willingness to kill in cold blood. There were numerous accounts during and after the fighting, from eyewitnesses, survivors and officials, testifying that Hamas not only killed its enemies during the fighting but also executed them afterwards.

The most notorious case was that of Samih Madhoun, an Al Aqsa Martyrs' Brigades leader in northern Gaza and a close ally of security chief Mohammed Dahlan. Madhoun had alienated the Islamists by boasting in a radio interview that he had executed some Hamas activists and threatened: 'I swear to God I will kill every last member of Hamas.'[20] On 14 June a prominent Hamas preacher issued a religious edict, or *fatwa*, saying Hamas was entitled to kill Madhoun.

One of Madhoun's brothers later recounted the events that followed: 'My brother Samih was stuck at home during that time for fear of being killed by Hamas.' But, while making his escape, Madhoun ran into trouble: 'Hamas spotted Samih approaching one of their checkpoints and opened fire on his car.' Samih retaliated, his brother said, and in the ensuing gunfight killed a Hamas operative, Jamal Abu Swaileh. Hamas promptly seized Madhoun and took him to the home of the dead Hamas man. 'They told his parents to kill Samih for killing their son, and, when they refused to do so, Hamas killed Samih [themselves] in front of the people and then they mutilated him.'[21] After the lynching, Hamas posted a photograph on its website showing a crowd standing over Madhoun's body as it lay face down on the ground. A video of Madhoun's death and mutilation appeared on the internet, including YouTube. The Qassam Brigades later released a statement confirming that it had 'executed the collaborator Samih al-Madhoun'.[22]

When challenged later about the ruthlessness of the takeover, some Hamas leaders sought to minimize the numbers killed. Not so some hardliners, who made no excuses. Abu Thaer, an implacable Qassam border commander in Rafah, irritatedly waved away any criticism. 'If it had been a score-settling day we would have killed all the Fatah people, because everyone here has debts,' said the heavily bearded Abu Thaer, whose name translates as 'Father of Wrath'.

> The decision was taken that, instead of losing people over a long period of time, we should go in and fight and suffer 200 people killed at once, but after that there would be no more deaths. The majority were killed in battle but, maybe, yes, there were some people who deserved to be killed. I'm not going to hide it. For instance, Samih al-Madhoun. He killed twenty-five Hamas people, so there was no way he would be caught and not killed. He killed a guy ten minutes before he was killed, so feelings were high.[23]

Everyone was dazed by the speed of events, including Arab leaders. Addressing an emergency meeting of the Arab League, the Saudi foreign minister, Saud al-Faisal, said: 'The Palestinians have come close to putting by themselves the last nail in the coffin of the Palestinian cause.'[24]

Consolidation in Gaza

In the wake of the takeover, Hamas – for the first time ever – had complete control of the entire Gaza Strip. It had seized all the guns, cars, motorcycles, communications equipment and infrastructure of the PA's foreign-funded security forces and was unchallenged in its stronghold. But, although it had achieved a tactical victory, the strategy remained in doubt. It was in charge of the castle, but the drawbridge and moat were controlled by Israel and Egypt.

Faced with a stronger Hamas, Israel implemented an even tighter blockade on Gaza, including ordinary and everyday foodstuffs and school-books for children. The international reaction was as swift after Hamas's military victory as it had been after its political victory eighteen months earlier. Egypt closed down its Palestinian mission in Gaza and opened a new one in the Abbas-controlled West Bank. Gaza became more and more isolated. Hamas gambled, as it has done consistently before and since, that Palestinians would blame the country besieging them – Israel – not the government under siege – Hamas. Their propaganda machine went into overtime, running countless stories to hype the movement's victory.

As the Israeli siege tightened, basic supplies – such as construction materials – soon ran out in Gaza, and increasing numbers of Gazans became dependent on United Nations handouts. Israel repeatedly insisted that reports of a humanitarian crisis in Gaza were exaggerated. But United Nations officials cautioned that a collapsed economy and further privations would only fuel anger and instability. John Ging, the Gaza director of the UN refugee agency, said: 'If present closures continue, we anticipate that Gaza will become nearly a totally aid-dependent society, a society robbed of the possibility of self-sufficiency and the dignity of work.'[25]

Meanwhile, Hamas moved to consolidate its hold over Gaza. It fired long-standing Fatah loyalists from senior positions, including the head of Shifa hospital, and opened corruption investigations against some of them. It also closed Fatah's radio station, prompting Fatah to make similar moves against Hamas-backed newspapers in the West Bank. It raided weddings where Fatah partygoers sang songs in praise of Yasser Arafat. Public protests were subject to a Hamas permit. At a Fatah rally to commemorate the death of Arafat in November 2007, Hamas forces killed six people and wounded 100.

There was also a 'morality' crackdown. One Hamas leaflet circulated in Gaza read: 'Those who disseminate filth and vices such as licentiousness, drug and alcohol trafficking, lustful parties and outings, it is our religious duty to uproot. They poison the soul of society.'[26]

The Other Enemy

Hamas also continued to strike at Israel. Throughout 2007, according to Israel's domestic security agency, Shin Bet, Hamas fired or allowed others to fire more than 1,200 rockets from Gaza, of which more than 800 landed in Israel. Two Israelis were killed.[27] Shin Bet warned that one consequence of the Gaza takeover was that Hamas could now increase the number and range of the rockets it was firing into Israel. But the development that really appeared to concern the Israelis was what officials described as a 'leap forward' in Hamas to the stage of being 'an organized military apparatus'. They claimed that Hamas was receiving training in Iran and transmitting the skills back to the Izz ad-Din al-Qassam Brigades in Gaza. The Iranian link was also seized upon by Fatah, which increasingly taunted its fellow Sunni Muslims in Hamas for being Shi'a puppets of Tehran. The insult was calculated to capitalize on growing anti-Shi'a sentiment across the Sunni world in the aftermath of the post-2003 sectarian conflict between Shi'a and Sunni Muslims in Iraq.

Gaza continued to decline. At one point, when Israeli commercial banks stopped all transactions with Palestinian banks in Gaza, its banks even ran out of money. Once again, the only lifeline to the outside world was the Rafah border crossing into Egypt. But Hamas insisted that there must be no Israeli eyes or ears at the terminal, as there had been before its takeover. 'If we accept that mechanism, then Israel still has the veto,' said Mushir al-Masri. 'And if we accept the old mechanism, the border is effectively closed too.'[28]

Israel has always understood how important Gaza's crossings were to Hamas, and they became a crucial instrument of leverage. Israel's policy was to impose a siege to make clear to Palestinians the consequences of supporting Hamas. Meanwhile Hamas bypassed the closures through tunnels and – in January 2008 – went even further by bulldozing the old wall which ran along the border, opening up the Egyptian Sinai to tens of thousands of Palestinians, who streamed through the gap until it was once again sealed.

To Cease Fire Mutually

Throughout 2008, Hamas's continuing rocket fire increasingly dominated Israel's domestic news agenda. Hamas hoped that this would compel Israel to lift its siege on Gaza. There was a glimmer of mutual concession when, on 19 June 2008, an Egyptian brokered ceasefire between the two parties came into force – the first such reciprocal agreement. Israeli sceptics believed Hamas would use the cessation to rearm and prepare for the next round of the war against Israel, and Hamas's military commanders conceded the point. 'Listen, our men have been fighting daily for the last years now,' said one Hamas commander. 'Of course we will use the calm to benefit from it and do training ... it's a ceasefire, not the end of the war.'[29] Events six months later would prove that Israel would use the pause in hostilities in the same way.

As the ceasefire dragged on and the siege of Gaza continued, Hamas's strategy appeared to be failing. Within Gaza, Hamas spent the summer and autumn of 2008 extending its total control, including a crackdown on powerful clans such as the Hilles and Dogmush families, both linked to Fatah. Radical Islamist elements, such as *salafi* organizations, were also targeted, as Hamas sought to exert authority in an environment that was an increasingly fertile recruiting ground for discontented, radical youths frustrated by a lack of political progress, Hamas's failure to secure the opening of border crossings, and zero prospects of national unity with Fatah. 'Frankly speaking, since Hamas took over in Gaza, nothing got better in terms of achieving our goal of liberation from this illegal occupation,' lamented one armed fighter. 'Today I am hunted by Hamas and Israel. We are the Palestinian resistance between a hammer and an anvil.'[30]

In Gaza, the situation was desperate. Fuel shortages had compelled Gazans either to drive cars on cooking oil, ruining the engines and poisoning the atmosphere in the streets, or to travel on foot or by donkey cart. Shortages of food, building materials, manufacturing parts, school books and paper, as a direct result of the Israeli-led siege, were creating desperation.

Although unprecedented at the time, such scenes were to pale in comparison with the utter devastation of the post-2023 siege and bombardment by Israel of Gaza, reducing much of the population to homelessness, poverty, scavenging, and sending their children to line up with pots for food as the whole population faced the very real prospect of famine. Even a donkey cart ride was beyond the means of Gazans – the smallest trip would come to cost nearly US$140.

From 2008 onwards, Hamas increasingly resorted to maintaining order through fear. Towards the end of that year, Hamas had slumped in the polls. Just 19.5 per cent of Palestinians said they would vote for it, as against 36.8 per cent for Fatah, according to a survey by the Jerusalem Media & Communications Centre.[31]

Operation Cast Lead

Six months to the day after it began its ceasefire, Hamas ended it. It had become frustrated, repeating what it had long preached was the experience of Yasser Arafat and Fatah before it: to sign up to a deal with Israel and get nothing out of it. So, on 19 December 2008, rockets began flying across the border fence into Israeli towns, sixty in one day alone. The Hamas leadership went into hiding, apparently expecting a stern but limited Israeli response, swiftly followed by renegotiation of the ceasefire on more favourable terms.

But Israel had used the six-month lull in fighting to prepare a detailed plan, including extensive intelligence inputs, for a comprehensive military retaliation. On the evening of 19 December, Prime Minister Ehud Olmert and his defense minister, Ehud Barak, held a five-hour long cabinet meeting to green-light the plan, which involved hitting back far harder than Hamas had expected.

On 27 December 2008, Israel launched airstrikes the length and breadth of the Gaza Strip, destroying or damaging nearly every Hamas-controlled security installation. Palestinian medical officials said that at least 155 people were killed and 200 wounded in the first strikes, which began without warning shortly before noon as the opening wave of the offensive named 'Operation Cast Lead, the IDF's Fight against Terror in Gaza'. The airstrikes targeted Hamas security headquarters, training compounds and weapons storage facilities, the Israeli military and witnesses said.[32] At least fifteen traffic police were killed in one courtyard, where they were attending a graduation ceremony. Satellite television news channels showed non-stop footage of piles of Palestinian policemen's charred bodies lying on the parade ground.

At Shifa hospital in Gaza City, scores of dead bodies were laid out in front of the morgue waiting for family members to identify them. Many were dismembered. The Palestinian newspaper *al-Hayat al-Jadida* printed a black front page with white letters spelling out the headline: '1,000 Martyrs and Wounded in Saturday Slaughter'.[33]

In Israel, there was near universal support for the war. Israel launched an intensive and sustained *hasbara* (public advocacy) effort driving home its key talking points: that Hamas was 'hiding' behind civilians and that no country would accept rockets being fired into its territory. Prime Minister Ehud Olmert's spokesman, Mark Regev, accused Hamas of holding hostage a quarter of a million Israelis and the entire civilian population of Gaza. Israel, he said, had no choice but to strike hard to halt the rocket fire which was terrorizing border towns and increasingly cities as far north as Ashkelon and east to Beersheba – foreshadowing precisely the same arguments that he was to use more than a decade later in 2023. 'Our aim is to create a new reality, a new security environment in which no longer will hundreds of thousands of Israelis have to live in fear.'[34]

Israel's domestic audience was supportive. Standing in the road where a Hamas Grad rocket landed in Beersheba, narrowly missing his nine-year-old daughter and his wife and son, Yona Pavtulov said his army should press home the assault. The Ukrainian-born Mr Pavtulov's argument fused two common Israeli themes: that Israel is the world's front line against Hamas and other Islamist militants, and that Western countries unfairly judge it by different standards from those they apply to their own armies in conflicts such as in Iraq and Afghanistan. 'I hope the same thing that happened in Iraq will happen here. They should just change the [Palestinian] leadership. We will have quiet for a few years and, after that, well, God is big. He will solve the problem. In a country like ours we do

Photo 13.1 Israeli damage to the Palestinian neighbourhood of Izbit Abed Rabbo in Gaza, January 2009, after Operation Cast Lead

not know what will happen in a year, or two or five years. We don't plan for the long run.'[35]

Some Palestinians were furious at Hamas for bringing down such weight of Israeli fire upon their own people. But this was counterbalanced by growing anger at what was perceived to be the tepid response of President Mahmoud Abbas. At the time two commonly expressed sentiments in the West Bank, from Hamas and Fatah supporters alike, were that Abbas should be pressing Israel harder to stop the assault, and that 'at least Hamas are doing something,' This was borne out on the street and by opinion polls. 'I am originally Fatah and my voice will always be Fatah,' said Mustafa Saleh, a 37-year-old clothing store worker, as he hurried his two young daughters past a protest demonstration in the West Bank city of Ramallah. 'But Hamas is resisting and we are a nation under occupation. I support the resistance, even here in the West Bank.'[36]

Robert H. Serry, the UN envoy for the Middle East peace process, lamented the behaviour of both sides, saying: 'The protection of civilians, the fabric of Gaza, the future of the peace process and regional stability – they all are trapped between the irresponsibility of Hamas rocket attacks and the excessiveness of Israel's response.'[37]

During the campaign, Israel inflicted two major blows on the Hamas leadership: on 1 January 2009, the military commander Sheikh Nizar Rayan was killed, along with his four wives and nine of his children, when his five-storey home was bombed by Israeli jets. Then, in the closing days of the war, Israel bombed the hideout of Said Siam, killing him. Operation Cast Lead killed more than 1,300 Palestinians, among them more than 900 civilians, and destroyed thousands of homes, commercial buildings and government institutions, according to Palestinian human rights groups. But, despite short-term anger against Hamas, it was by no means clear that the offensive immediately succeeded in turning Palestinians away from the Islamists in significant numbers.

Once again, Hamas was playing to the core conviction among many Palestinians that they can achieve more through arms and negotiations than through negotiations alone – a phenomenon explained by critics as an addiction to violence and by supporters as the only realistic way of squeezing concessions from a more powerful enemy. Questioned about the possibility of embracing less violent means of dealing with Israel, Ismail Ashqar, a Hamas MP, replied scornfully: 'If we threw roses at Israeli tanks and slept under them, would we have the sympathy of the world? Would they give us our rights back?'[38] Following the war, one Palestinian poll found that Palestinians gave Hamas the highest positive rating for its performance at that time, at 51 per cent, followed by Haniyeh's government at 46 per cent; Iran, 41 per cent; Syria, 34 per cent; Fatah, 34 per cent; President Abbas, 25 per cent; and Salam Fayyad's government, 23 per cent.[39]

Was it Worth It?

Gaza's civilian infrastructure had been destroyed or damaged by Israel to such an extent that United Nations human rights investigators considered it a deliberate use of disproportionate force intended to punish the entire population of Gaza,[40] an accusation denied by Israel. Hamas's military infrastructure was also significantly reduced. It had promised that it would fight Israel face to face once a ground incursion commenced, but afterwards it claimed to have lost only forty-eight Qassam fighters. Numerous Gaza residents in the worst-affected areas said that they had heard little evidence of Qassam Brigades fighters taking the battle to the Israeli forces.

When the war ended, entire districts had been razed by Israel, and post-war estimates indicated that it would take more than $2 billion to reconstruct Gaza. Much of the economic infrastructure, including electricity supplies, water, sewerage, roads, factories and warehouse facilities, was also damaged in the Israeli assault. There was widespread criticism of Hamas for bringing down such destruction on their heads. As Gazans began to internalize the scale of the wreckage the mood was of anger, sometimes open, sometimes coded. In a score of interviews, from the southern tip to the northernmost towns in the Gaza Strip, fear and anger rose to the surface, and not all directed at Israel. 'I want to change the situation,' said Hazem Abu Shaaban. 'I will vote for those who deserve it, and I will vote in order to change the situation in Gaza.' He voted for Hamas in 2006, but barely three years after the slogan 'Change and Reform' propelled Hamas into power, the word 'change' had become a code word for a desire to end the Hamas experiment.[41]

Across Gaza, Hamas still had a large reservoir of loyal support. Some accepted its argument that Israel was simply using Hamas as a pretext to destroy Palestinian life and society, as it had with Yasser Arafat and the PLO before.

Amid mutterings of discontent there were signs that Hamas was clamping down on dissent and enforcing its Islamist edicts more tightly. One Rafah tunneller who dared to criticize Hamas was dragged away by bearded enforcers even as he was being interviewed by one of the authors. 'Under Hamas the border crossings are closed and everything is damaged,' he began to say. His colleagues grew visibly uneasy at his words, and one tried to silence him, but he continued, saying: 'They say that Fatah were corrupt and thieves, and they were, but the border crossings were open ...'[42] He got no further. As one of the listeners muttered, 'Stop him speaking,' a car filled with burly, bearded men drove up behind him – having evidently received a signal from one of the group – and one of those inside jumped out and grabbed the dissenter around the throat, dragging him away in mid-sentence. When the dissenter reappeared and tried to talk once more, he was again stopped by those around him. 'He is a big liar, a big liar,' the burly man interjected, and dragged him away. When he was approached for a third time a few minutes later, this time away from the sight of the crowd, the man refused to talk, saying: 'I don't want to get into any fights. I don't want to get shot.'[43]

It was no idle fear. Even amid the mayhem of the Israeli offensive there had been reports – confirmed even by Hamas sympathizers – of Hamas's opponents being executed or wounded in summary 'punishment' shootings of Gazans deemed to be collaborators. In the Sheikh Radwan district of northern Gaza, A'ed Sa'ado Abed, a Fatah loyalist, showed the blood-stained bandages on his left leg where, he said, Hamas had shot him twice on 26 January, 'only because I am a Fatah activist, to scare me and the Palestinian people.'[44]

Enemies Foreign and Domestic

Whether intentionally or otherwise, Hamas had succeeded in shifting Israeli public opinion to the right. Although the centre-right Kadima Party inherited by Tzipi Livni from the comatose Ariel Sharon and scandal-plagued Ehud Olmert won marginally more seats than Binyamin Netanyahu's right-wing Likud, Livni was unable to put together a coalition. So, a decade after he first held the position, Netanyahu once again became Israel's prime minister.

Both Hamas and Fatah were eager to be seen taking the lead in rebuilding Gaza, and the stakes for doing so increased dramatically in March 2009, when, at an Egyptian conference, international donors pledged $4.5 billion – much of it for reconstruction – to President Abbas's Palestinian Authority. As both sides manoeuvred to control the levers of money and patronage, they also continued to hold rounds of unity talks in Cairo. But these became bogged down in arguments over security and political issues.

President Abbas announced presidential and legislative elections for early 2010, but Hamas announced that it would not allow such elections to take place in Gaza and threatened dire punishments if anyone defied them. All the steam appeared to run out of the Obama administration's attempts at peace-making when Netanyahu's government resisted American pressure for a halt to settlement-building. Stasis, stalemate, intransigence and enmity clouded the political landscape.

Certainly it appeared that, as it emerged from the rubble, Hamas had survived yet again in what had become known as Hamastan. 'This is the Hamas era,' conceded depressed Fatah leader Husam Khader from his home in a refugee camp in the same city. 'Even if Gaza is destroyed, Hamas still wins. Yes, Hamas will win the battle, but the people of Gaza will lose the war.'[45]

'A General Rehearsal'

You opened the Gates of Hell Yourself.

Qassam Brigades[1]

For the first half-decade after its election victory, Hamas enjoyed the status of being the first Islamist power voted into government in the Arab world. But there was no groundswell, no Islamist ripple swelling into a wave across the Middle East. Hamas remained a pariah to the United States, Europe, and much of the international community. It was unable to operate openly in the West Bank, between Israel's checkpoints and military bases and the Fatah-dominated Palestinian Authority. It exercised power only in Gaza, where 37 miles of its land borders were blockaded by Israel and 8 by Egypt to the south.

Israel had destroyed the only airport in Gaza and its gunboats made sure no boat could leave or enter by sea to the west – a closure that was tested when an aid flotilla carrying hundreds of pro-Palestinian activists tried to break the blockade in May 2010, but were stopped in the Mediterranean by Israeli commandos who stormed one of the six vessels, the MV *Mavi Marmara*, and killed nine people.

However, Gaza's isolation began to recede as the phenomenon known as the Arab Spring emerged in Tunisia and in January 2011 spread across the region, toppling autocratic regimes. The tide of the Arab uprisings across the Middle East from late 2010 onwards never hit Gaza's shores. Tunisia, Yemen and Libya fell in quick succession, with Islamists prominent in the newly elected government in Tunis and among the Libyan rebels who toppled Colonel Muammar Qaddafi. But it was events in neighbouring Egypt – the mass uprising against President Hosni Mubarak's regime and the elections that put the Muslim Brotherhood in power – that impacted Gaza the most.

Even before Mubarak was toppled in February 2011, it was clear on the streets around Tahrir Square that those best poised to take electoral advantage of his political demise were not the Twitter-mobilized secular youth movements who had given the revolution its online buzz but had no coherent plan for the day after beyond wishful thinking. 'It's victory over Mubarak, and it's round one when it comes to democracy,' said Omar el-Shamy, a university student in the laptop-packed balcony apartment overlooking Tahrir Square that had become known as the Facebook Flat. 'We can start dreaming now,' he continued, idealistically. 'At least now no one's going to stand in our way because we are going to do good, and everyone wants us to do good. There's going to be a collective, like, everyone working together.'[2]

The people accustomed to working together were the Muslim Brotherhood – Hamas's parent organization – and, by the summer of 2012, Brotherhood leader Mohammed Morsi was elected president of Egypt. In Gaza, Hamas was especially pleased, sensing a shift in the regional power balance now that an ally held the keys to Gaza's only gateway to the outside world not directly controlled by Israel: the Rafah border crossing. After years of closures, poverty, unemployment and rates of dependency on outside aid had all risen steeply in Gaza. Hamas had increasingly relied on the clandestine network of cross-border smuggling tunnels into the Egyptian Sinai to bring in money, goods and fuel to supplement the meagre humanitarian rations on which many Gazans subsisted.

On the day Morsi's victory was announced, thousands in Gaza joined the celebrations. In Rafah itself – where the crossing had been closed for the two weeks leading up to the election – celebratory gunfire killed one person and wounded six.[3]

Hamas co-founder Dr Mahmoud Zahar – who had been educated in Egypt and joined the Muslim Brotherhood there – told Western diplomats he was certain that, with the Brotherhood in power, Gaza's lifeline into the Egyptian Sinai would let Gaza thrive and bring economic and development opportunities for all. This was Hamas setting its stall out early for domestic and regional audiences and maintaining its 'brotherly' alliance with the parent organization of the Brotherhood. Indeed, Morsi's victory emboldened Hamas to press for more support from its Egyptian counterparts. Having a patron such as Egypt under Morsi was perceived by Hamas as another advantage over Fatah. Reminded of the international response to Hamas's democratic victory at the polls in 2006, Zahar also said, 'We hope the world will give the Islamists the chance to rule, and not punish their victory like what happened to Hamas.'[4]

Hamas leader Ismail Haniyeh telephoned Morsi personally to congratulate him. 'We will look to Egypt to play a big, leading role, a historic role, regarding the Palestinian cause, in helping the Palestinian nation get freedom, return home, and totally end the Gaza siege,' Haniyeh said.[5]

In Israel, Prime Minister Netanyahu's government reacted with deep scepticism as it tried to gauge the implications of an Islamist government to its south, in a country Israel fought a war with in 1973 and signed a peace treaty with six years later – a treaty that was deeply unpopular among ordinary Egyptians. Netanyahu told his parliament that developments in the region were becoming an 'Islamic, anti-Western, anti-liberal, anti-Israel, undemocratic wave.'[6]

With Hamas's refusal in 2006 to commit to abiding by past agreements uppermost in everyone's minds, the prime minister's office statement emailed to journalists two and a half hours after the result did not bear Netanyahu's name and did not even mention Morsi or the Brotherhood, confining itself to respecting the outcome and, pointedly, including a link to the text of the peace treaty:

Israel appreciates the democratic process in Egypt and respects the results of the presidential elections. Israel looks forward to continuing cooperation with the Egyptian government on the basis of the peace treaty between the two countries, which is a joint interest of both peoples and contributes to regional stability.[7]

Hamas leaders such as Khaled Meshaal, Haniyeh and commanders of the Qassam Brigades flocked to Cairo and talked up their relationship with Morsi. But, in reality, Morsi's short-lived regime was presented with so many challenges that the fate of Gaza paled in comparison. Only the threat of al-Qaeda posed a big enough internal risk to Morsi to ensure cross-border cooperation against a common foe. Also a concern was the rise of a new regional Islamist phenomenon: the Islamic State in Iraq and Syria and its regional offshoots, including in the Sinai peninsula. Hamas itself soon faced internal challenges from radical factions in Gaza which publicly associated themselves with al-Qaeda and the new radical extremist and jihadist factions associated with Jaysh al Islam and Jund Ansar Allah. This was a green-on-green battle of an Islamist kind. Hamas won, ensuring that ISIS would not be able to gain a foothold or implant their vision for an Islamic State caliphate in Rafah, only in Raqqah.[8]

Meanwhile, the enemies of the Brotherhood, whether in Egypt or Gaza, were ready to scupper the bromance. Following an armed attack on Egyptian soldiers in August 2012 in which sixteen were killed, an accusatory finger was pointed at Hamas. Hamas denied it but said radical 'salafist' elements might have used parts of Gaza for a hit and run raid. Things got immeasurably worse in November 2012 when Israel assassinated Qassam

Brigades commander Ahmed Jaabari. Hamas retaliated, and an eight-day conflict ensued. President Morsi's decision to keep the gates of Rafah open during the conflict was welcomed but largely perceived in Gaza as less than adequate. A disgruntled Hamas was not mollified when Morsi then sent his prime minister to Gaza rather than coming himself. The Hamas leadership had far greater expectations than Morsi, now head of state as well as Brotherhood leader, was willing to deliver.

Resistance Credentials

Israel said the objective of the Jaabari assassination was 'reducing the number of rocket attacks at Israeli civilians'.[9] It had also accused Jaabari of overseeing Hamas's military wing and orchestrating the kidnapping of Schalit in 2006. The hostilities in November 2012 that followed his killing established a pattern that was to continue for a decade. Israel claimed military successes against Hamas during successive rounds of limited-duration strikes. Once again Israel deployed its 'mowing the grass' doctrine. In the 2012 round, it claimed to have killed around twenty Hamas and Islamic Jihad leaders, hit an estimated seventy-two command and control locations and destroyed nearly a thousand Hamas underground rocket-launchers and 140 tunnels.

'Hamas' strategy is simple: Use civilians as human shields. Fire rockets from residential areas. Store weapons in mosques. Hide in hospitals,' the Israeli military said, distilling into one tweet the substance of much of the rationale for its attacks that it was to rely on for the coming decade.[10] Hamas, in turn, told its domestic audience that its 'resistance' credentials were unimpaired, having managed to keep much of its tunnel network intact and to get past Israel's Iron Dome missile defences to land longer-range rockets in Tel Aviv and Jerusalem for the first time – Iranian-made Fajr-5s, according to the Israeli military.[11]

But, to the increasing frustration of many – especially in Israel's vulnerable Gaza border communities – dealing with eruptions of cross-border violence seemed to have become more about containment than meaningful attempts to find long-term solutions. International mediators would periodically shuttle between the two sides brokering Hamas's demands for open border crossings and Israeli demands that Hamas end rocket fire and police its own territory to stop wreckers from disrupting the peace. Israel also wanted much firmer measures put in place to halt Hamas's ability to smuggle arms and ammunition into Gaza from Egypt.

In essence, the requirements from Hamas and Israel were pragmatic rather than maximalist. There was no public clamour on either side for comprehensive negotiations to end Israel's occupation and grant Palestinians their legitimate rights to statehood. Hamas even stopped calling them ceasefires, preferring the Arabic term *tahdiyah* (calm) or the formal *hudna* (quiet). And, certainly, there was no sign of the Western powers relenting and accepting Hamas into the fold. The mediators, particularly the United States, were still principally looking beyond and around Hamas to find any other Palestinian political leadership that it could deal with. For President Barack Obama's administration, that meant focusing on the West Bank, trying to reform President Mahmoud Abbas's weakened Palestinian Authority security forces so that they would at least keep Hamas under control there and protect Israel's eastern flank.

In the West Bank, Hamas was firmly on the back foot. Fatah in its backyard had no intention of forgiving it for routing Fatah's forces in Gaza in 2007, and even less desire to engage with Hamas politically and thereby risk international isolation by association. Negotiations brokered by Egypt, the Saudis, Qatar and the Algerians consistently failed to achieve national unity. Indeed, Fatah continued rounding up Hamas leaders in the West Bank and criminalized its political and civil activities there. Israeli arrest raids and PA/Fatah crackdowns on political organizing kept Hamas's activities to a minimum. It could survive in the West Bank only in cooperation with other armed factions. With the Israeli occupation as a common foe, these Hamas–Fatah alliances led to the creation of urban myths about their heroic gun fights against Israeli forces in the Nablus casbah or Balata and Jenin refugee camps.

Confined to Gaza, Hamas had kept the economy going in 2011 through the upheaval of the post-Mubarak era through a greatly expanded ecosystem of tunnels used to bring commercial goods, cars, livestock and weapons in from Egypt. That had become much easier when the Muslim Brotherhood opened the Rafah crossing in 2012. But the Brotherhood's time in Egypt was nearing an end. In July 2013 Morsi was pushed from power by the Egyptian military, and its political rank and file was either imprisoned, driven into exile, forced underground or murdered. The new military-backed government then declared the Brotherhood a terrorist organization. The army-backed leader Abdel Fattah al-Sisi became president in 2014. Suspicious of Hamas as an offshoot of the Muslim Brotherhood, and wary of the risk that it might support Islamist insurgents in the Sinai, Sisi closed the border with Gaza. Gaza was once again isolated, and its economy went into reverse. But by now it was under new leadership, thanks to a calculated gamble years earlier that had paid off almost literally a thousandfold.

Release

Midweek evening in a diner in Gaza City, and not much is going on. Youths are chatting about the Arab Spring waves breaking at the feet of rulers far beyond Gaza. Some are watching football. Others are killing time as they finish off meals. Suddenly there is an eruption of noise from the street outside: cars honking, men yelling at the tops of their voices. Pandemonium – rarely something to run towards in Gaza. Within a couple of minutes, the TV station in the café catches up with news from across the fortified border: Israeli Prime Minister Netanyahu's government has agreed an exchange deal to free 1,027 Palestinian prisoners for one Israeli soldier, Gilad Schalit, captured in a Hamas cross-border tunnel raid in 2006.

Within minutes, the streets are a parade of cars cruising in a convoy along the street, passengers hanging out of windows shouting delightedly at passers-by. The political factions have switched into gear to capitalize on the moment – flatbed trucks appear with music blaring from huge loudspeakers in the rear, and Hamas and Palestinian flags start appearing everywhere. 'This is a victory for the steadfastness of the Islamic Resistance Movement, Hamas,' said Yousef al-Daloo, twenty-four, a taxi driver in one green-flagged procession. 'The martyrs of Palestine were patient, and our prisoners were patient.'[12] 'This will be a victory for Gaza,' shouted Osama Sarhan, thirty-four. 'Yes, Gaza has suffered, but it was worth it.'[13]

In the days leading up to the release, Gaza prepared itself to greet the returning prisoners, amid profoundly mixed feelings in Israel at the prospect of so many long-term inmates jailed for violent offences being released back into Gaza, the West Bank, and some into exile – around forty went to Turkey, Syria and Qatar. Families of Israelis killed by Hamas and other groups voiced criticism, and petitions to block or change the terms of the deal were presented to Israel's high court, but rejected.[14]

Welcome ceremonies were set up in the West Bank by President Mahmoud Abbas's Palestinian Authority, which was eager to take some share of the credit for the release. But it was Rafah in southern Gaza – right across from the Kerem Shalom military base where Hamas originally captured Schalit – that was the centre of attention. The first 477 prisoners were mobbed as they climbed one by one from buses at the gates of Rafah on 18 October 2011 and were led past a 'Welcome to Palestine' sign into the Gaza Strip. Among the most prominent were Yahya Sinwar and Rawhi Mushtaha, the original founders of the Qassam Brigades' precursor *al-Majd*, who had both spent a quarter of a century in jail since their arrests in the early days of the First Intifada.

Hamas, calculating that this was a rare day on which Israel would not launch airstrikes, put on perhaps the largest open-air display of Palestinian weaponry ever seen in Gaza. The convoy of buses carrying the newly freed prisoners from Rafah drove north along Gaza's main highway – Salah al-Din Street – which was lined with thousands of gunmen as an honour guard. Driving to Rafah ahead of the handover, one of the authors saw fighters posted on both sides of the street, each only a few metres apart. Many carried automatic weapons; some had rocket-propelled grenade launchers, their utility belts stuffed with wire-cutters and knives. All around them drove heavy pickup trucks and flatbed trucks with masked militants from all factions, some brandishing heavy machine guns.

As widely expected, senior Qassam Brigades commander Yahya Sinwar went straight back to a leadership role in Hamas. He was treated as a homecoming hero, and on the night of his release, alongside Haniyeh, he addressed a huge rally in Gaza City, where he told the crowd: 'I call on the resistance to pledge to free the remaining prisoners. This must turn immediately to a practical plan with all facilities being given to it.'[15]

'I'm Still Twenty-Five'

At Sinwar's green welcoming tent near his home in Khan Younis the next morning, Hamas had put on a carefully coordinated display fusing family, religion and politics. As he sat in pressed pale blue shirt and chinos, accepting greetings from a long line of well-wishers, around him were banners of the 'Brigades of the Martyr Izz al-Din al-Qassam' with which he was so closely associated. One poster showed a kneeling militant firing a rocket; another displayed a stylized tableau of the abduction of Schalit from Kerem Shalom in 2006 – one burly, masked Hamas paramilitary fighter carrying an Israeli soldier away from a watchtower on his shoulders, with the bodies of other Israeli soldiers lying in a ditch in the sand.

Always alert, always 'on', Sinwar dutifully rose from his chair with each new arrival, accepting every congratulation with a brief smile, a handshake, a perfunctory one-armed hug and a pat on the back while his eyes were ever elsewhere, constantly scanning the horizon behind the visitor's back. Granting interviews between breaks in the meet-and-greet, his manner was akin to that of Rantissi, another hardliner a generation before him, who had been assassinated by Israel. Like Rantissi, every Sinwar utterance seemed tailored to bolstering the myth and the mission of Hamas. For him, everything that happened was part of a Hamas plan, everything and everyone was a cog in the system, and everything turned out just as Hamas had intended. Addressing the most frequent question – about his time in prison – Sinwar framed half a lifetime in jail as little more than a prolonged residential course of advanced studies in 'know your enemy'. 'Undoubtedly, dealing with them closely teaches you a lot of things. I learned a lot,' he told one of the authors.

> They wanted the prison to be a grave for us. A mill to grind our will, deter-
> mination and bodies. But, thank God, with our belief in our cause, we turned
> the prison into sanctuaries of worship and to academies for study. We studied
> about them a lot. I studied the history of the Jewish people, and you can say I
> am a specialist in the Jewish people's history, more than many of them. Many
> of us learned to read, to listen and to speak in the Hebrew language, especially
> those who were in for a long time. There is spare time in prison, you know,
> and we benefited. We spent it either in worshipping or studying.[16]

For Sinwar, no sign of weakness could be permitted, no hint of having been ground down. His only concession to being surprised by anything in the world outside prison was the thousands of armed and masked Hamas fighters lining the route the day before, on his first glimpse of Gaza since he was a young man. 'I was surprised by the volume of the situation that exists in the Gaza Strip,' he conceded. 'One tries to imagine, but you cannot when you are away from the picture. The picture is amazing and beautiful, and I hope that the resistance will be stronger to defend the Palestinian rights.'

About the future, he was less forthcoming. 'It's early. I was away for about a quarter of a century and came out with the world around me changed. I need to relax and take my breath and know the situation around me. And after that, I will decide.'

It later emerged from Israel media reports that, in 2004, a few years before Sinwar's release, Israeli medics had removed a life-threatening tumour from his brain, according to Yuval Bitton, the former head of the Israeli Prison Service's intelligence division.[17] Of this there was no mention by Sinwar, who was intent on projecting himself as being as healthy and vital as the day he went into prison. 'Physically and mentally, I'm still twenty-five,' he asserted.

Farther north in the Gaza Strip, Sinwar's *al-Majd* co-founder Rawhi Mushtaha was similarly prompt in his return to work. Just three days after he emerged from prison, he appeared at a rally in Gaza City wearing a 'Palestine' scarf around his neck, with an automatic rifle slung over his shoulder and escorted by dozens of heavily armed Hamas fighters, most of whom had not been born or were young children when he went to jail. The rally was at night and held at short notice – the Qassam Brigades perhaps calculating that the window of immunity from Israeli attack would not remain open for long. 'You are our support and help in our battle, the battle of the whole nation,' the now grey-bearded Mushtaha told the cheering crowd. 'Our nation and our resistance are the head of your spear in the face of the oppressive enemy.'[18]

International Law

Grudgingly or otherwise, there was near unanimity that Hamas had pulled off a coup by securing the mass release. Certainly, it had boosted its credentials as a resistance movement immeasurably among Palestinians, at least in the short term. In Israel, the political and military leadership also sought to reap the rewards of Schalit's homecoming. Netanyahu himself, Defense Minister Ehud Barak and Lieutenant General Benny Gantz, the military chief of staff, were all at Tel Nof military base for the celebratory welcome home moment when Schalit was flown from Egypt to be reunited with his family. Netanyahu had to face down some criticism of the deal, with so many Palestinians released for one Israeli. 'I understand the difficulty to countenance that the evil people who perpetrated the appalling crimes against your loved ones will not pay the full price that they deserve,' he wrote to the families, warning the freed Palestinian prisoners that anyone returning to violence would be 'taking his life into his hands'.[19]

But one Palestinian analyst pointed out that the timing of the deal in fact benefited both Netanyahu and Hamas politically by pushing into the background the global headlines that Palestinian President Mahmoud Abbas had secured weeks earlier with an initiative that wrong-footed both Israel and Hamas. Having for years committed himself to negotiations rather than violence, Abbas had long found himself caught between a right-wing Israeli government with no inclination to let a new Palestinian state be created and a Hamas with even less inclination to recognize the Israeli one that already existed.

But, with little sign of the bilateral peace process going anywhere, Abbas suddenly went multilateral. In September 2011, three weeks before the Schalit prisoner exchange, he bypassed Israel, the United States and Hamas by going to the United Nations General Assembly in New York and formally requested the UN to recognize a Palestinian state. It gave Abbas a rare shot of momentum, delivering him international headlines, large crowds in the West Bank and a standing ovation at the General Assembly.

Netanyahu and Hamas united in rejecting Abbas's move, the Israeli leader calling the UN a 'theatre of the absurd' and Hamas rejecting it as 'begging' for statehood. Hamas banned public demonstrations in Gaza in support of the Abbas initiative.[20] The opposition from both sides raised questions about the timing of the prisoner exchange, which had been years in negotiations. 'Why now?' asked Professor Mkhaimar Abusada, of Al-Azhar University's political science department in Gaza.

> It seems to me that Israel is trying to undermine Abu Mazen politically after his historic speech at the UN General Assembly twenty days ago, and, after this, Palestinian, Arab, and even international support for Abu Mazen. I also believe that Hamas is definitely unhappy with this political support Abu Mazen has been able to grab over the last month … and Hamas is trying to steal the lights. The deal will definitely boost Hamas's popularity in the Palestinian Territories and especially in the Gaza Strip after four years of deterioration in Hamas's popularity as a result of taking over the Gaza Strip, the siege and blockage of Gaza and the internal problems Hamas is facing in Gaza.[21]

Analyst Ibrahim Ibrach also pointed out that the prisoner deal was a short-term feel-good measure for Hamas, and that it did not solve any of the underlying problems facing the movement, which still found itself squeezed between Israel and a hostile international community. 'The happiness overwhelming the Palestinian street because of the swap is temporary,' said Ibrach. 'After weeks, people will go back to reality and remember that there are 5,000 prisoners left in Israel.'[22]

Abbas's United Nations gambit ultimately fell short – the United States blocked the bid for full member status, and Palestine had to settle for becoming a non-member observer state at the General Assembly, like the Holy See.[23] But Abbas had experienced a rare moment of relevance after years of languishing on the sidelines, and he persisted with his initiative to embed Palestine into international agencies and treaties, with potentially far-reaching implications for Hamas. In 2014, he signed on to the Rome Statute of the International Criminal Court (ICC), clearing the way for the court to open investigations into allegations, including war crimes and crimes against humanity in the Occupied Palestinian Territories – not just by the Israeli military, but also by armed Palestinian groups for offences such as firing rockets from Gaza into civilian areas in Israel.

The ICC's outgoing prosecutor, Fatou Bensouda, followed through, announcing years later in 2021 that she had launched an investigation into allegations of war crimes since 2014. Specifically, she said she had 'found that there is a reasonable basis to believe that, in the context of the 2014 hostilities in Gaza, members of the Israel Defense Forces ('IDF') committed the war crimes of intentionally launching 'disproportionate attacks', wilful killing and other offences. She said there was also 'reasonable basis' to believe that 'members of Hamas and Palestinian armed groups' had committed war crimes of 'intentionally directing attacks against civilians and civilian objects', of 'using protected persons as shields', depriving people of fair trial, wilful killing and 'torture or inhuman treatment'. Ominously for all those cited, Bensouda said the 2014 allegations were illustrative only and 'the situation in Palestine is one in which crimes allegedly continue to be committed' – meaning that Abbas's decision to sign up to international treaties had potentially far-reaching ramifications for outbreaks of hostilities extending far into the future.[24]

Israel and the United States immediately criticized the ICC's intervention, both claiming that the court had no jurisdiction. Netanyahu released a video statement calling it 'absurd' and 'undiluted anti-Semitism' and insisting that Israel's soldiers 'take every precaution to avoid civilian casualties'.[25] Hamas reacted carefully, one of its spokesmen, Hazem Qassem, welcoming the investigation into Israel, but maintaining the standard Hamas line that the movement was 'totally certain that its resistance of the occupation is legitimate.'[26]

The fact that the US and Israel immediately questioned the ICC's jurisdiction signalled how politicized any such investigation into hostilities in 2014 and all future rounds would inevitably become. Human rights groups all but dared Bensouda's successor not to let the investigation slide. 'All eyes will also be on the next prosecutor Karim Khan to pick up the baton and expeditiously move forward while demonstrating firm independence in seeking to hold even the most powerful to account,' said Balkees Jarrah, of Human Rights Watch.[27]

Washington

As Israel and Hamas settled into the new normal – rounds of hostilities separated by periods of quiet – Netanyahu's focus increasingly turned to the West Bank, where by now more than 500,000 Israelis were living in Jewish settlements, regarded by most countries as illegal under international law. Over the decades these settlements had evolved far beyond small clusters of hilltop huts. The largest – Maale Adumim, Modiin Illit, Beitar Illit and the rest of the sprawling Efrat settlement block on hilltops between

Bethlehem and Hebron – were by now home to tens of thousands of settlers, encroaching ever further onto lands owned by Palestinians for olive groves, raising livestock and building homes.

The settlements had become a major obstacle to peace talks – Abbas's Palestinian Authority refusing to deal with Israel unless building stopped, and Netanyahu defying international pressure to rein in construction, his eye on the growing demographic and political power of right-wing parties in the Knesset representing settlers.

The Israeli government's focus on announcing new settlements in East Jerusalem and the West Bank embarrassed even the country's closest allies. During a visit in 2010 by then Vice President Joe Biden, Netanyahu's government announced that 1,600 new housing units would be built in Ramat Shlomo, a huge and expanding settlement between Palestinian territory on the road to Ramallah. Biden was furious at the announcement, and the timing. 'I condemn the decision by the government of Israel to advance planning for new housing units in East Jerusalem,' he said. 'We must build an atmosphere to support negotiations, not complicate them.'[28]

Amid ill-disguised antipathy between Obama and Netanyahu, the increasingly confident Israeli PM delivered a humiliating public rebuff to Obama while sitting alongside him in the Oval Office. During a visit to Washington in May 2011 to rally support against Abbas's statehood plan, and to voice disagreements over Washington's handling of the Arab Spring and Iran's nuclear ambitions, Netanyahu made clear that Israel's security demands and the desire to preserve its settlements – in his view – ruled out any solution based on the Green Line between Israel proper and the West Bank and East Jerusalem that Israel had captured and occupied in the 1967 war. 'I think for there to be peace the Palestinians will have to accept some basic realities. The first is that, while Israel is prepared to make generous compromises for peace, it cannot go back to the 1967 lines, because these lines are indefensible, because they don't take into account certain changes that have taken place on the ground, demographic changes that have taken place over the last forty-four years,' he told a silent Obama in front of the news cameras.

> Remember that, before 1967, Israel was all of 9 miles wide, half the width of the Washington Beltway. And these were not the boundaries of peace, they were the boundaries of repeated wars ... so we can't go back to those indefensible lines and we are going to have to have a long-term military presence along the Jordan. I discussed this with the president and I think that

we understand that Israel has certain security requirements that will have to come into place in any deal that we make.[29]

Many settlers went further, openly voicing their view that the West Bank was the biblical heartland of the Jewish people, that there should be no Palestinian state there, and, indeed, that the end goal was annexation of the West Bank. 'For myself, I don't see in the future any good results coming from those two slogans, Land for Peace and Two-State Solution,' said the late Ron Nachman, the founder and later mayor of Ariel settlement.[30]

Daniella Weiss, a veteran settler leader in the northern West Bank, was candid about the placing of Ariel, which sits on a hilltop more than 10 miles inside the Green Line, dominating the surrounding Palestinian villages.

> The basic purpose of the basic plans of the settlement movement was the spread of the settlements in a way that will block the option for the establishment of any substantial Arab state. Naturally, Ariel was part of it. This is why Ariel is deep in the area and not closer to the Green Line. That means that the area of Nablus-Sichem and the area of Ramallah-El Bireh cannot be connected.[31]

With Washington's focus increasingly drifting from the Middle East towards China – the 'pivot to Asia' – and its lack of influence over Abbas and Netanyahu plain to see, the long-moribund 'peace process' dwindled away to nothingness. The last direct talks between Israel and the Palestinian Authority finally collapsed in 2014 amid Israeli anger over a short-lived Fatah–Hamas unity government and Palestinian frustration at seeing the chances of a future state in the West Bank shrinking year by year.

The Palestinian unity government of 2014 was a marriage that both sides needed, but to which neither was really committed. With the Muslim Brotherhood gone and the avowedly anti-Islamist President Sisi in Egypt, the blockade on Gaza was back on, the tunnels were closed, and Hamas's domestic popularity was falling as Gazans wearied of endless hardship and isolation instead of the 'Change and Reform' that the 2006 election had promised them.

A poll in 2014 of 1,000 Palestinians by the Washington-based Pew Research Center found a third (35 per cent) of people expressing positive views about the Islamists. Negative views about Hamas were higher in the Gaza Strip, where people lived under its rule (63 per cent negative), than in the West Bank (47 per cent negative). The poll found that opinion had almost reversed itself in the seven years it had controlled Gaza, from 2007

(62 per cent favourable to Hamas, 33 per cent unfavourable) to 2014 (35 per cent favourable, 53 per cent unfavourable).[32]

Abbas's own five-year presidential mandate had long expired, and he had no peace process to offer his people. This left many Palestinians, especially a disaffected younger generation, to complain that Abbas's Palestinian Authority security forces were little more than security subcontractors for an Israel that continued to occupy them but showed no signs of permitting Palestinian statehood. When Abbas swore in the unity government of little-known technocrats, Israel refused to deal with it and was upset that Europe and the United States appeared more favourably inclined toward the Fatah–Hamas rapprochement.

2014 War

But the unity bid was overshadowed within days when three Israeli teenagers were kidnapped and later found dead in the West Bank. Israel blamed Hamas. A Palestinian youth was then found burned alive by suspected Jewish extremists in what appeared to be a revenge attack. The losses inflamed public opinion on both sides. Tension escalated into hostilities: Hamas fired rockets from Gaza further than ever before into Israel, and Israel hit back with airstrikes, with artillery bombardment and its ground forces deployed into Gaza.

Israel codenamed the war 'Operation Protective Edge'. Increasingly the Israeli effort was not just to halt the rockets but also to destroy Hamas's military capability, including its ever-growing network of tunnels from which the rockets were launched, and which militants also used to cross the border and launch surprise raids on Israeli border villages. One attack party killed five Israeli soldiers at a watchtower near Nahal Oz, just across the border from Gaza City. Israel had to face a well-organized enemy. One Israeli overview of the lessons learned from the 2014 war delivered the assessment: '[t]ogether with the Palestinian Islamic Jihad, on the eve of Operation Protective Edge, Hamas' integrated fighting force in Gaza numbered some 32,000 highly-trained, well-equipped, totally dedicated troops, unlike the fleeing Egyptians or Syrians found chained to their positions in the Yom Kippur War.'[33]

In the seven weeks of fighting that followed, 2,139 Gazans were killed, including nearly 490 children; 500,000 Palestinians in Gaza had been internally displaced, 1.3 million remained in need of humanitarian assistance, 47 per cent of Gaza households were either moderately or severely food insecure, and only 5 per cent of water was potable.[34] Six Israeli civilians and sixty-seven soldiers were killed – a far higher rate of attrition compared with the six soldiers killed during twenty-two days of fighting in Operation Cast Lead, the ground incursion in 2008–9.

But as the fighting waned and a ceasefire came into effect, once again the goals of the Israeli operation appeared to be limited and contained rather than finding a long-term solution. Israeli military spokesman Lieutenant-Colonel Peter Lerner said of the ground invasion that removing Hamas was 'not the goal of this mission'.[35] That left many Israeli border residents fearful of future incursions, a feeling that had been growing over the years as they watched Hamas entrench itself on the other side of the border fence, sensing the growing threat around and beneath them. 'Even if eventually there will be a peace agreement, I want to know for the sake of the security of my people what country and what sovereignty will tell all the terrorists and the extremists not to fire on innocent people. That is what I want to know. Who will give this guarantee?' asked Haim Jelin, former head of the Eshkol Regional Council and a resident of Kibbutz Be'eri, in 2011.[36]

The same feeling was echoed by Raz Shmilovich, a resident of Netiv Haasara, in 2014. 'We went to war, our soldiers and civilians were killed, we sustained huge damage to our economy, to our image, we killed hundreds of Palestinians and where are we today? Same place we were at three months ago,' he said, from the farming moshav that is one of the closest to Gaza. 'I have my gun on me all the time,' he continued. 'At night we lock the door, the windows. Locking the door in our community was once unheard of.'[37]

Two years after the war, the scale of Israeli destruction in Gaza was still startlingly evident. Of 100,000 Palestinians who had had their homes destroyed or severely damaged, 65 per cent remained displaced. The UN stated that over 160,000 children still needed 'psychosocial' support. Tellingly, the UN reported that, of funding requested from the international community as part of the UN Humanitarian Response Plan for Gaza-specific projects, only 27 per cent of support had been received.[38]

When the worst-case predictions became reality a decade later, in 2023, one of the abiding indictments against the Israeli government was that it could say it was taken by surprise on a given day, but it could not say that it had not been warned in general terms, and by the very communities that were to bear the brunt.

Across that nearby border, the 2014 war appeared to have reversed Hamas's decline in popularity, despite the destruction. One Palestinian survey found that 79 per cent of Palestinians believed Hamas had 'won' the war; 94 per cent were supportive of Hamas's military performance fighting Israeli troops. And, significantly, 86 per cent supported the firing of rockets if Israel did not lift its blockade of Gaza. Politically, Hamas had once again benefited from war, gaining a much larger increase in support than at any time since its 2006 election victory. Around 61 per cent of Palestinians said they would vote for Haniyeh over Abbas (32 per cent) in a presidential election (up from 53 per cent for Abbas and 41 per cent for Haniyeh just before the war). Also, 46 per cent said they would vote for Hamas in parliamentary elections, against 31 per cent for Fatah.[39]

Changing of the Guard

With many of the first generation of Hamas leadership gone, a new cadre was emerging, centred around Yahya Sinwar and Mohammed Deif. Sinwar was elected to Hamas's political bureau in the Gaza Strip in 2013, shortly after his release from prison, and in 2015 he, Deif and Rawhi Mushtaha were named by the United States as Specially Designated Global Terrorists, reflecting their growing importance within Hamas.[40] Just two years later, Sinwar was elevated to become Hamas's overall chief in Gaza, as Ismail Haniyeh prepared to step up to take over from Khaled Meshaal as the movement's worldwide leader.

But the new echelon found itself with little room for manoeuvre between Israel, a hostile international community, the anti-Islamist Sisi in charge of Egypt, and a strained relationship with Iran after Hamas refused to back Tehran's Syrian ally President Bashar al-Assad in a civil war against his own people. The rift was such that some in the senior Hamas leadership, including Khaled Meshaal, left Damascus and based themselves elsewhere.

At home, successive rounds of Israeli military assaults had devastated Hamas's Gaza stronghold. Of more than 2 million residents, an increasing number were living lives described by UN organizations as a humanitarian crisis. Under Hamas's rule and Israel's blockade, the numbers living below the poverty line rose steadily, to 80 per cent. The majority of the population was becoming totally aid-dependent. There was little by way of hope, especially for Gaza's young. More than 68 per cent of those aged twenty to twenty-four were unemployed, stuck in 'waithood', unable to live independent lives, afford to have their own family space, marry, travel or enjoy pastimes, all of which cost money that they didn't have. Gaza was also facing regular electricity blackouts, with its only power plant unable to pay for fuel due to power struggles between Hamas and the Abbas-controlled Palestinian Authority in the West Bank.

This material and humanitarian descent was exacerbated by a huge societal cost on everyone. Living in what many called an open-air prison, people were also paying a high psychological price. War and blockade were traumatizing. Mental health rates, especially among the young, were worsening. A Save the Children report published in 2022 which looked at mental health in Gaza found that, after fifteen years of Israeli-imposed blockade, three-quarters of children were reporting depression, grief and fear, with 80 per cent of children and young people reporting emotional distress.[41]

In May 2017, Hamas did something unexpected. In the Qatari capital Doha, word quickly spread that the movement's leaders were going to hold a press conference to make an important announcement. Throughout the day, news reporters, group supporters and a detail of security personnel moved from one hotel to another seeking out the breaking story. Finally, speaking in a large banqueting room at the Sheraton Hotel to the assembled crowd, Khaled Meshaal and the rest of the Hamas leadership announced a new covenant. In one of his last acts as leader, Meshaal said the 1988 founding charter of the group had been updated and revised. The new document had Hamas dropping its call for Israel's destruction and agreeing to a transitional Palestinian state in the West Bank, Gaza and East Jerusalem. With Mousa Abu Marzouk among those present – and Sinwar and Haniyeh in Gaza dutifully listening in on a simultaneous broadcast – Meshaal still had much to say about the Zionists, maintaining that Hamas would continue to fight them, 'the occupiers of the land of Palestine', but that Hamas respected the people of the Jewish faith and had no issue with them or other religions. 'We don't want to dilute our principles, but we want to be open. We hope this will mark a change in the stance of European states towards us,' Meshaal announced to the assembled audience. Warming to his theme, Meshaal went on to say, 'Hamas calls for the liberation of all of Palestine but is ready to support the state on 1967 borders without recognizing Israel or ceding any rights.'[42]

At the end of the event, the leaders formed a receiving line to shake hands with greeters and members of the interested press corps. Some wondered why Hamas had made the announcement. It was seen as an attempt to pacify not only Sisi, but Saudi Arabia and other wealthy Gulf Arab states, all of whom saw the Brotherhood as a regional threat to stability. The Israeli government instantly rejected the overture, a spokesman for Netanyahu dismissing it as a transparent attempt to 'fool the world'.[43]

Others saw hints of compromise from Hamas. 'Aside from the benefits of currying favor with Cairo or shifting media focus away from Abbas, a major component of Hamas's rebranding is strategic,' wrote RAND Corporation political scientist Colin P. Clark.

It considers the conflict with Israel an existential struggle rather than a mere dispute over borders. In the original charter of 1987, Hamas makes clear that its purpose is to elevate the concept of 'jihad of the sword,' or offensive military actions, in its efforts to mobilize Palestinians. The language in the revised charter, importantly, does not renounce violence and still considers jihad a legitimate right of the Palestinian people. But even before the charter's revisions, Hamas's tactics had proved flexible over time. Despite its occasional inflammatory rhetoric, its ideology – much like Hezbollah's – is pragmatic, and the group has demonstrated flexibility before.[44]

Haniyeh took over from Meshaal five days later, moving out of Gaza to Turkey and then Qatar to take over leadership of the political bureau. By then Sinwar had already been installed as his replacement in Gaza, in what was widely seen as a shift towards the hardliners. But in one of Sinwar's first public pronouncements, he said that, while Hamas did not fear war and was ready, it was not in the movement's strategic interests to fight one at that time. 'We want to push it backward as much as we could', he said, 'so that our people will relax and take their breath and at the same time we are building our power.'[45]

Trumped

By then a new and wildly unpredictable factor had entered the game. In January 2017, President Donald Trump was inaugurated in Washington, DC, a radical departure from the 'no drama Obama' era that had preceded him. After a relatively quiet first year, Trump suddenly decided to make his mark on the Middle East – announcing on 6 December 2017 that, after some 'very fresh thinking', he had decided 'to officially recognize Jerusalem as the capital of Israel.'[46]

He also announced that he would move the US embassy to Jerusalem from Tel Aviv, where the vast majority of countries have their embassies. It was hugely controversial, both because the United Nations regards East Jerusalem as occupied and the city's status as disputed until resolved by negotiations between Israel and the Palestinians, and because in 1980 Israel unilaterally annexed East Jerusalem, a move that was not recognized internationally.[47]

If the Obama years had been disappointingly unproductive for Palestinians, this was incendiary. It was clear that Trump was far more in lockstep with the ambitions of Israel's extreme right-wing coalition governments than Obama had ever been. On the Palestinian side, Trump's radical move had a far greater political impact on President Abbas's Palestinian Authority – putting him out in the cold and without any leverage, a position Hamas was already well used to. In devastatingly quick succession, the Trump administration, with Trump's son-in-law Jared Kusher acting as the Middle East's most poorly read point man, suspended US humanitarian payments to the Palestinian Authority and UN agencies providing humanitarian help to the Palestinians. This plunged the economy into freefall, especially in Gaza.

In the West Bank, PLO Executive Committee member Hanan Ashrawi warned that, by undermining moderates and inflaming anger, it would benefit only extremists:

> President Trump seems to be hell-bent on annihilating the chances of peace and destroying the stability and security of the entire region and beyond, provoking violence and playing into the hands of extremists and terrorists around the world. He is wilfully committing an act of the utmost folly which is not only illegal but also designed to inflame religious and spiritual sentiments and raise the spectre of sectarianism and religious strife. It simultaneously emboldens the most aggressive, hard-line and warmongering elements in Israel to guarantee the destruction of the two-state solution.[48]

Trump left office, reluctantly, in January 2021. But the Trump era could not be erased completely, nor could the Palestinians' fears of what his pro-Israel stance – recognizing Israel's claim over the occupied Golan Heights, moving the US embassy from Tel Aviv to Jerusalem, and proposing recognition of Israel's sovereignty over its settlements – had done to embolden the settler movement. Netanyahu had begun openly talking about annexing the West Bank and was now reliant on far-right parties such as the ultranationalist Religious Zionism, led by Bezalel Smotrich, a settler opposed to Palestinian statehood.

Even though Netanyahu was briefly ousted as prime minister in 2021 – he was replaced by Naftali Bennett, a former head of the main West Bank settlers' council – one important Trump–Netanyahu legacy remained in place: the Abraham Accords. These were normalization deals spearheaded by Jared Kushner that Israel had signed with the United Arab Emirates, Bahrain, Morocco and Sudan. In signing these, the Arab states upended their past commitment to accept peace and recognition of Israel only as part of a two-state solution giving Palestinians statehood, ending occupation and having East Jerusalem as their sovereign capital. For once, Hamas, Fatah and the leadership of the PA were united in their critique of the 'Arab leadership', accusing them of abandoning the principles of the Palestinian cause and the legitimate rights of all the Palestinian people with deals that bore little to no fruit for Palestinians. Nevertheless, the normalization deals were embraced by the incoming Biden administration. But they continued to be regarded by Palestinians as an effort to marginalize their cause, while Israel sidelined its local conflict in pursuit of the larger prizes of regional acceptance and lucrative trade and transport deals with wealthy Gulf Arab states.

Great March of Return

Every year since 1976, on 30 March, Palestinians have commemorated Land Day – commemorating the deaths of six members of Israel's Palestinian Arab minority who were killed during protests against the Israel government's seizure of their lands in the Galilee in northern Israel. After the annual Land Day marches in 2018, groups in Gaza decided to form a broader coalition of civil activism and protest focused on the Israeli-imposed border fence.

In a new and unexpected development, civil society groups arranged weekly protest marches at the border fence that came to be known as the 'Great March of Return', building up to the May commemoration of the seventieth anniversary of the 1948 *Nakbah*, when around 750,000 Palestinians were displaced. Even seven decades later, in Gaza and in refugee camps in Lebanon, Syria, Jordan and the West Bank, the trauma of displacement remained palpable. This was not a party issue or a narrative owned by one political faction. It was deeply communal and held in the body politic of the Palestinian people. The original generation of refugees could still produce the land deeds to their homes or pull out faded black and white photographs and meagre keepsakes attesting to their heritage and their rights. Two-thirds of Gaza's population were now refugees who regarded their real homes as the Palestinian cities, towns and villages that their families had been driven from in 1948, many of which no longer existed. By bringing thousands of refugees to within almost touching distance of their ancestral lands on the other side of the Gaza border fence, the march organizers sought to highlight the presence of the Israeli border fence that was the physical obstacle to their return.

Most of Hamas's leadership were children of the *Nakbah*. Its leader and co-founder Sheikh Yassin was born in the small fishing village of al-Jura in pre-1948 British Mandate Palestine, near the modern Israeli city of Ashkelon. Haniyeh's family came from the same village. Sinwar was from nearby Al-Majdal Asqalan. Rantissi's family home was Yibne, close to Mohammed Deif's roots in Al-Qubayba. Usama Hamdan's family was from Al-Batani al-Sharqi, near Ashdod. Most had grown up in Gaza's refugee camps, knowing nothing other than occupation by Israel (with a brief interlude by Egypt in the 1950s). So it was easy for them to identify with and tap into the refugee experience that bonded together many of Gaza's 2.3 million population.

The civil organizers at first tried to keep the symbols and emblems of Hamas away from the weekly protests – seeking to be independent – and stressed their credentials as a broad non-political civil coalition. Hamas was initially ambivalent about the protests, which were not their project. But, as momentum for the grassroots campaign grew, some in the Hamas leadership began to argue that they should claim the weekly protests for their own. Sinwar himself was there on the opening day, 30 March, walking along the fence with a posse of bodyguards, waving a flag and proclaiming it a 'new phase'.[49]

Israel responded with lethal force against the protesters, shooting into the crowd that was throwing stones and rocks and rolling burning tyres at the border fence. Within two weeks Haniyeh himself had realized the motivational value of the demonstrations and decided that Hamas should become involved. In early April, he went to the border for a stage-managed spectacle of support. Without a hint of irony, he took to a large stage and gave a speech against a backdrop of photographs of Mahatma Gandhi, Martin Luther King and Nelson Mandela – two Nobel Peace Prize winners and perhaps the most notable historical omission from the list of Nobel laureates. The mood of the assembled crowd was somewhere between confused and unimpressed, but Haniyeh ploughed on, assuring the 'heroes' of the latest uprising that under his leadership they would return to Palestine, to Jerusalem, and to the homes that they had been forced to abandon in 1948.

Many Palestinians who had organized the protests were annoyed that Hamas was trying to jump on the bandwagon. A few even believed that the presence of Hamas, so close to the border, was further provocation to Israel to kill protesters. No one seriously believed that Hamas was signalling a new direction or that its participation in the marches meant armed attacks on Israel would cease. But, on the ground in Gaza, there was a sense that, after a decade of grindingly hard rule under Hamas, including three wars that had destroyed vast swathes of infrastructure, the organization's popular appeal was waning. Opinion polls later that year reflected high levels of dissatisfaction with Hamas and Haniyeh personally, only 34 per cent of Palestinians saying they would vote for Hamas and only 40 per cent for Haniyeh. By swinging behind the protests, Hamas seemed to be hedging its bets, taking a pragmatic gamble on a form of protest that, if not exactly peaceful, was not rockets and suicide bombs.[50]

The protests hurtled towards their inevitable apex – the split-screen television day on 14 May 2018, which was simultaneously the seventieth anniversary of Israel's birth, the day the border protesters had set aside to mark the *Nakbah*, and the date the new US embassy in Jerusalem was to be opened. That grand opening went ahead at a ceremony attended by Trump's daughter Ivanka, his son-in-law Kushner and Israeli VIPs, even as 50 miles (80km) away Israeli troops were shooting and killing fifty-eight Palestinian protesters at the Gaza border fence. The Israeli military said that Hamas militants had for weeks been using the protests as cover to carry out surveillance of Israeli border defences, to launch attacks on its troops and to infiltrate Israel. Amid global criticism of Israel's deadly response, the International Criminal Court's prosecutor later confirmed that the border protests were yet further grounds for investigation into 'crimes allegedly committed in relation to the use by members of the IDF of nonlethal and lethal means.'[51]

By now, having been in charge of Hamas in Gaza for a year, Sinwar was becoming more confident. He even sent a written message to Netanyahu urging him to take a 'calculated risk' and agree to a long-term truce, using the Hebrew he had learned in prison. The message was delivered to an Israeli delegation through mediators during ceasefire negotiations to further the new – and increasingly controversial – arrangement in which Israel was to permit humanitarian aid from Qatar to enter the Gaza Strip to be distributed to impoverished Palestinians in return for a cessation of rocket fire. The existence of Sinwar's letter was revealed in 2022 to the Israeli newspaper *Yedioth Ahronoth* by Netanyahu's former national security adviser Meir Ben-Shabbat, who regarded it as a positive sign that 'here is the adversary begging us to take a risk.' But the veteran Shin Bet intelligence official also recognized that Sinwar was 'very attentive to what is happening on the Israeli side' and 'analyses every word that comes out of the mouths of politicians, understands the dilemmas, and is offering his own input.'[52]

Al Aqsa

Symbols, and particularly religious symbols, matter to Hamas. None more so than the two Muslim shrines in Jerusalem – Al Aqsa Mosque and the golden-roofed Dome of the Rock. Hamas's logo even includes the dome. Yet its leaders in the Gaza Strip had never prayed there. As preparations began for Ramadan in the spring of 2021, April had begun well for Palestinians. The Muslim holy month could be celebrated openly now the worst of the COVID-19 pandemic was past. Trump was gone from the White House, and his successor, President Joe Biden, lifted Trump-era sanctions on the International Criminal Court prosecutor and restarted hundreds of millions of dollars of US humanitarian aid to Palestinians that had been frozen by Trump. Israeli Prime Minister Netanyahu also went on trial on corruption charges, which he denied and vowed to fight, but which was creating a rift inside Israel over the propriety of having a leader facing criminal charges continuing to run the country.

But Ramadan itself quickly became a focus of renewed tensions. Israeli police stopped Palestinians gathering at Damascus Gate, a traditional meeting place after the evening *ifthar* breaking of the fast. Tension turned to confrontation and nightly clashes, with police raids on Al Aqsa Mosque compound and furious stand-offs in the nearby East Jerusalem neighbourhood of Sheikh Jarrah between Palestinian residents facing forced eviction and Jewish settlers who had already moved into houses on the same street. Israeli ultranationalists weighed in, forcing police in riot gear to keep the two crowds apart – right-wing Israelis shouting 'Death to Arabs'.[53] 'Take a good look at our flag,' shouted one Israeli right-winger through a loudhailer at Palestinian shopkeepers on the other side of the Street of the Prophets in East Jerusalem during one Israeli flag-waving rally. 'Live and suffer all your life.'[54]

The heart of the conflict remained, as always, Jerusalem. One of the most damaging accusations put to Israel's leadership after the security debacle of October 2023 was that, by pandering to the country's increasingly influential ultranationalist and settler base, they became too focused on the issues that mattered most to that constituency – Jerusalem and the West Bank – and underestimated Hamas in Gaza. In one way or another, this is what successive Israeli governments had done from its earliest days.

That ultranationalist element was out in force on 10 May 2021 – Jerusalem Day – when a march was planned from West to East Jerusalem through Damascus Gate to celebrate Israel's capture and 'unification' of the city in the 1967 war – a victory for Israel and a humiliating defeat for the Jordanian forces and the Arab world in general. Had the march been allowed to go through Damascus Gate, already a flashpoint, it would have provoked certain confrontation with the hundreds of Palestinians already gathered at the city walls.

To avoid a clash, Israeli police diverted the Israeli marchers through Jaffa Gate facing West Jerusalem, a much quieter entrance to the Old City. Some Israeli marchers were content to have been diverted, not wanting to provoke the Palestinians. Not so Daniel Louria, sixty-one, who saw it as a sign of weakness by Netanyahu's government. 'I am in absolute shock: this is a disgraceful capitulation to Arab violence and pressure,' he said. 'It basically shows that their violence and hatred works ...'[55] he was saying as the rocket sirens went off.

Hamas had issued a 6 p.m. deadline for Israel to remove the police from Al Aqsa, and it enforced the ultimatum by firing around 150 rockets into Israel. Some landed on the outskirts of Jerusalem, setting off the sirens and forcing Louria and his fellow marchers to run for shelter. As he did so, Louria cited it as evidence of his contention that appeasement, as he saw it, achieved nothing. 'The Arabs, they are laughing at us. To them this is nothing but a huge victory,' he said.

Netanyahu called firing on Jerusalem a 'red line' and launched airstrikes on Gaza, setting off an eleven-day war in which Hamas and other armed groups fired thousands of rockets into Israel, and Israel hit back with an intensive series of airstrikes. The Hamas missiles reached deeper into Israeli territory than ever before. Israelis all over the country sought refuge in shelters and safe rooms. By the time a ceasefire was brokered, Palestinian health officials said 248 Gazans had been killed, and Israel said its fatalities were one Israeli soldier and twelve civilians.

Both sides claimed a victory, of sorts. Hamas had always been clear about the objectives of such actions. It wanted to claim that it was doing more to defend Palestinian rights, Jerusalem, and the sanctity of Al Aqsa than Abbas's PLO, Jordan and Egypt put together. It also wanted to make sure that Israel could not sideline the Palestinian issue while it pursued normalization talks with its Arab leaders of choice in Morocco and the United Arab Emirates. This was a message that somehow many in Israel's political leadership appeared to be in denial about, or did not want to hear.

Helping its case was the widespread perception among Palestinians, and especially the younger generation, that the octogenarian President Abbas and his pro-negotiations PLO camp had little or nothing to offer, having not sat at a negotiating table with Israeli political leaders for nearly a decade. There were no longer US-brokered summits in Camp David. No sign, as there had been in the 1990s, of promising back channels to offer a prospect of peace through dialogue and an acknowledgement of Palestinian rights. Abbas was increasingly becoming an irrelevance to his own people, while Hamas stole the spotlight. Opinion polls confirmed this. One survey in June 2021, shortly after the war, found that 61 per cent of Palestinians believed a two-state solution was no longer practical because of Israel's continued expansion of Jewish settlements, while 49 per cent believed armed struggle was the most effective means of ending Israel's occupation. Only 27 per cent believed in negotiations. Hamas received 75 per cent approval for its performance in the recent conflict, with two-thirds of Palestinians believing that it had achieved its war aims. A majority, 53 per cent, said Hamas, not Fatah under Abbas, should represent Palestinian people, with Fatah dragged down by Abbas's dismal 8 per cent performance approval ratings.[56]

Hamas's strategic calculations added to its sense of self-validation and began to inform its future calculations. Qassam Brigades commanders at that point believed that Israel had a strong aversion to ground-based combat, particularly in the Gaza Strip, where they feared Hamas would take soldiers captive. Hamas also felt that Israel had no political or strategic appetite to reoccupy Gaza – believing that Israel's political leadership preferred to deploy military resources to expansion in the West Bank. There was no ideological or religious imperative to restore settlements in Gaza when the momentum was all in the West Bank. Israel's settlements, and the infrastructure servicing them, demanded that regulars, reservists and conscripts be deployed to run checkpoints, protect settler roads, and help what many saw as a creeping annexation of the West Bank.

For Israel, Netanyahu said the operation was an 'exceptional success' that had destroyed Hamas tunnels and rocket factories and killed more than 200 militants, including twenty-five senior figures. 'Hamas can't hide anymore,' he said. 'We eliminated an important part of Hamas's and Islamic Jihad's command echelon. And whoever was not killed knows today that our long arm can reach him anywhere, above ground or underground.'[57]

Netanyahu's confidence was misplaced. The Hamas leadership remained intact. Yahya Sinwar's family home was bombed, but he reappeared in public after the war, alive and well. Giving a TV broadcast, he appeared in his signature pressed blue shirt and, while shouting, lauded the sacrifices of the people of Gaza, the rise of pro-Palestinian protests among Israel's 20 per cent Palestinian Arab minority in Israeli towns such as Ramla and Lod, and mocked Israel's claims about destroying Hamas missiles and tunnels. He also spoke about the 'red line' that Jerusalem and Al Aqsa symbolized for Hamas, delivering a threat of his own. 'If you want to stay in existence for a long time, you should stay away from Al Aqsa and Jerusalem,' he warned. 'The enemy and the world must know that this was just a general rehearsal – a small manoeuvre – which shows what could happen if Israel tries to harm Al Aqsa again,' he continued. 'We have at least 10,000 martyrs in Israel who will each take a knife to stab, or a vehicle to run over, or a Molotov cocktail or a gasoline tank to burn forests.'[58]

15

'We Are at War'

'There are currently twelve people running towards the fence. There are two motorcycles, roger. We need an answer.'
'Commander ... Commander ... We Are At War.'
Field Intelligence Corps, Gaza Division, 7 October 2023[1]

Friday 6 October 2023 had been mostly unremarkable. Unaware of what was about to happen, Israelis had gone to bed marking the fiftieth anniversary of the Yom Kippur War in October 1973. It was always a solemn time, recalling how intelligence failures left them unprepared for attacks that dented the country's reputation for invulnerability. Within months of that war in 1973, Prime Minister Golda Meir and Defense Minister Moshe Dayan were driven from office.[2]

The fall of Dayan was especially surprising. In 1948 he had commanded Jerusalem's front line during the first Arab–Israeli war, and in 1956 he had delivered a eulogy famed in the annals of Zionism about the dangers of Israelis dropping their guard. The oration was for Rot Rotberg, a kibbutz security guard killed by infiltrators from Gaza, half a mile away. The kibbutz he guarded was Nahal Oz, one of those that was about to be attacked by Hamas in 2023. Dayan said:

Eight years have they sat in the refugee camps of Gaza, and seen, with their own eyes, how we have made a homeland of the soil and the villages where they and their forebears once dwelt. Have we forgotten that this small band of youths, settled in Nahal Oz, carries on its shoulders the heavy gates of Gaza, beyond which hundreds of thousands of eyes and arms huddle together and pray for the onset of our weakness so that they may tear us to pieces – has this been forgotten? For we know that, if the hope of our destruction is to perish, we must be, morning and evening, armed and ready.[3]

Dayan's awareness of the dispossessed and stateless Palestinians forced to live their entire lives in Gaza's impoverished refugee camps was couched in the terminology of military threat assessment, not of empathy. But it was a shrewd analysis of the underlying dynamics. And the eight years of Palestinian refugeehood of which he spoke were now nearly eighty.

So deep is the refugees' desire to go back home that it has become integral to Palestinian national identity. The right of return is symbolized by giant keys that hang over entrances to Palestinian refugee camps, representing the keys of the homes they were forced from or evacuated in the 1948–9 war, never to return. And, along the Gaza beachfront, more than 100 brightly painted concrete benches carried the Arabic names of now lost towns and cities formerly the homes of refugees that now lie inside Israel. These included many that Hamas's founders and leaders came from: Yafa (Jaffa), Osdod (Ashdod), Al-Majdal (Ashkelon), Akka (Acre or Akko), and long-destroyed villages between Gaza and Bir as-Saba' (Beersheba).

But Dayan's analysis was only partly correct. Israel's twenty-first century opponents in Hamas certainly prayed, but they also prepared. They had come to believe that the Israeli military was over-reliant on technology and afraid to get itself embroiled on the ground. And, from inside Gaza, the most visible signs of that technology were the drones (*zanana*), cameras, electronic fences, antennae and watchtowers along the border. Israel's perimeter 'fence' was in reality several layers deep, both above and below ground, with reinforced steel and concrete walls, underground fencing studded with surveillance sensors, restricted and no-go zones that stretched hundreds of yards into the Gaza side and, along the exterior, a military patrol road, heavily fortified crossing points, army positions, remote-controlled weaponry sand berms and artillery platforms.

At the main checkpoint and crossing, Erez, a foot passenger leaving Gaza had to pass through a Hamas forces-run checkpoint *Khamsa-Khamsa* (5-5), then a stretch of wasteland and ripped up tarmac, to begin walking through a concrete blast-walled and fenced passageway to a massive steel gate. To then wait at the gate for it to be opened on the orders of an Israeli security operator obtaining permission via a tannoy. On the other side of that gate is a vast cavernous space where passports are inspected and reasons for leaving Gaza and entering Israel are ascertained. There is also the possibility of being singled out for a strip search. This involves being directed remotely from Israeli operators high above in a gantry command room to a bomb-blast-proof zone. From behind a shatterproof glass cubicle, an Israeli soldier will order you to undress, place your clothes in a washing-up bowl to go through an X-ray conveyor forward and back again. Strip search or not, the foot passenger has to pass through several other security checks before an Israeli border official will stamp a passport and say, 'Welcome to Israel.' Hamas bomb attacks at such crossings in the past had led to this level of physical defences. By 2023, therefore, Erez seemed impregnable.

Along the rest of the 37-mile border with Israel, Palestinians are not permitted into the exclusion zones. But they know the terrain intimately. For decades, whether as farmers, residents or militants, the chain-link barrier was constantly scouted and the daily activities of the neighbouring Israeli communities always observed. Groups such as Hamas, Palestinian Islamic Jihad (PIJ) and other factions used such intelligence to launch scores of attacks. Hamas had also been probing, assessing and testing the Israeli defences with cross-border tunnels and rocket launching sites. Preparation and planning were everything.

Planning and Misdirection

Hamas's Qassam Brigades had developed their tactics, training, recruitment and strategic planning in the four decades since they were founded. What had begun as a poorly equipped militant group had grown into a modern armed force commanding up to 35,000 troops. Equipment was smuggled in, manufactured locally or derived from the PA armouries that survived previous Israeli attempts to destroy them. Intelligence gathering was innate to the organization, and the funds for arms reportedly included profits from crypto-currency trading. Some Hamas commanders and cadres were also organized into elite commando and cyber-ops units, including the Nukhba Force.

Hamas had developed its force capacity to inflict violence on a technically and numerically superior enemy force. Hamas commanders were tacticians and students of modern warfare – particularly urban guerrilla and insurgent tactics. They prided themselves on their planning abilities. They learned from many military encounters with Israel and combined this experience with unrivalled knowledge of the terrain in which they operated, including their network of tunnels beneath Gaza. And where some perceive the conflict to be a complex contemporary affair encumbered with the paraphernalia of modern warfare, Hamas kept it simple.

The military wing's objectives, as set and defined by Hamas's political leadership, were an end to Israel's occupation of the Palestinian Territories, violations of Islam's holy places – especially Al Aqsa – and to the Gaza blockade, and to free all Palestinian prisoners held in Israeli jails. These were to be the primary stated motives for the attack on 7 October 2023. A secondary aim was to derail the process of normalization between Israel and Arab states – in particular a much rumoured deal between Israel and Saudi Arabia's Crown Prince Mohammed bin Salman. No matter how much lip service Arab leaders paid to Palestinian rights, Hamas wanted no more deals which sidelined the Palestinians while allowing their occupier and neighbours to grow closer.

At least two years before 7 October, the Qassam Brigades planners knew what they had to do: breach Israel's security, immobilize its military and take control. They trained their fighters. Practice drills were regularized, with Hamas troops ordered to run mock assaults on sites simulated to look like Israeli targets.[4]

Some in Israel's reconnaissance and intelligence units had picked up on the signs and passed warnings up the chain of command. A forty-page document, which Israeli intelligence codenamed 'Jericho Wall', outlined details of several versions of Hamas's plans for an assault on their military positions on the Gaza border. The document reportedly detailed a set of tactics to overwhelm Israel by simultaneously firing rockets, disabling security and surveillance cameras, and undertaking a multi-pronged breach of the border, Israeli military posts, bases and even a divisional headquarters.[5] Moreover, ten months earlier Sinwar had publicly warned Israel: 'We will come to you, God willing, in a roaring flood. We will come to you with endless rockets, we will come to you in a limitless flood of soldiers.'[6]

Israel's full internal accountability over the failure to recognize such threats as imminent would come only after the war was over. But an investigative exposé of the first hours of 7 October highlighted how the warnings did not appear to have been acted upon:

> In the early hours of 'October 7th ... senior figures in the Israel Security Agency (Shin Bet) and the IDF were having a few conference calls. The main reason for these calls was that a short time after midnight, the Israeli intelligence community started picking up some significant indications ... that had started blinking in the days and weeks beforehand ... But despite the concerns, a senior intelligence figure determined at 3:10 am that 'we still believe that Sinwar is not pivoting towards an escalation ...'[7]

None of the planning would have worked if Hamas had not also gone to extreme lengths to disguise its true intent. That is no easy task in Gaza, where every electronic communication can be monitored by a world leader in cyber-espionage and military surveillance. So, Hamas operationalized two counter-strategies. The first was to stop using digital technology, such as the latest mobile phones, and instead use more basic forms of communication, such as word of mouth messages or telephone landlines.

The second was deception: knowing their phone calls and signals were being intercepted, they consistently misdirected the Israeli listeners into believing that Hamas had no appetite for further conflict and was instead more focused on the mundane task of governing the local population and getting more work permits for Gazans to enter Israel. Deception was a strategy long used in Gaza. In the First World War the British military deployed the haversack ruse – sometimes known as 'Meinertzhagen's Haversack' – in which they 'dropped' a bloodstained bag filled with false intelligence and sent dummy messages that they knew were being monitored and decoded to mislead Turkish forces into thinking the British were to attack Gaza instead of Beersheba, their real target. In the modern era, before launching its war in Gaza in 2008–9, Israel too lulled Hamas into a false sense of security, according to Israeli news reports at the time.[8] Fifteen years later, in 2023, Hamas was doing the same.

They had no choice. Their enemy possessed a qualitative military edge. That had been publicly guaranteed by successive American governments for decades. Israeli military forces possessed sophisticated technology and weaponry that would significantly boost their troops when they eventually mounted their ground assault on Gaza. Ranged against that, Hamas had thousands of 'resistance' fighters who believed death in battle guaranteed them the glory of martyrdom, a place in paradise and a release from being a blockaded and occupied people.

'Running Towards the Fence'

Having lulled the Israelis into thinking Hamas's intentions lay elsewhere or that manoeuvres in Gaza were nothing more than training exercises, the attack itself came swift and early.[9] Piecing together what happened afterwards, Israeli officials briefed journalists that Hamas stayed off the electronic grid, passing by word of mouth the message that their people should attend dawn prayers that morning.[10] Meanwhile, at 06:06 hrs, the Qassam Brigades Telegram channel posted a 25-second video clip playing a *nasheed* (hymn) intoning the words 'O Prophet, exhort the believers to fight' over scenes from Al Aqsa and attacks by Israeli security on Palestinian worshippers.

Once Hamas, and the other factions, had gathered their people together, weapons were handed out and units dispatched to the border.[11] Among the ringleaders according to the Israelis was Ibrahim Biari, the Qassam Brigades' Jabalia battalion commander. Military spokesman Rear Admiral Daniel

Hagari said Biari was 'responsible for a significant area from which the terrorists left to the massacre of October 7th',[12] and was then the 'dominant leader of their military activity during this war in northern Gaza'.

That morning Israel's Gaza Division field observers were the first to see the infiltrators nearing the fence, firing at them using a long-distance sniper sighting system. Knowing that they would be seen, however, Hamas sent drones ahead to cripple the border communications towers, closing many of Israel's electronic eyes. The drones also blew up the remote-controlled weaponry. The expendable one-mission attack drones deployed were the same kind being used in other conflicts such as the Ukraine war – the global market had grown so much that not only state but non-state armed actors could gain access to them. It also meant Hamas could hit Israeli forces with drone strikes before engaging with them directly on the ground.

The scale of what happened during that day unfolded as Hamas fighters filmed themselves and the military wing's social media team live-streamed and posted online. Simultaneously, Israelis hiding in houses, shelters and fleeing from gunmen were also filming the attacks and sending clips with pleas for help and last messages to their families.

In Israel's military headquarters in Tel Aviv, Israel's senior military commanders were initially in the dark; they too were relying on mobile phones to try and find out what was going on in military command posts and divisional headquarters near Gaza. They appeared immobilized. As Bergman and Zitun reported, 'one question echoed everywhere: where is the IDF?'[13]

Israeli military installations were among the first to be targeted, including the headquarters of the Israeli army's Gaza Division at Re'im. Also quickly overrun was the Erez crossing – the literal gates of Gaza. Israeli-built, unlike the Philistine gates of antiquity referenced by Dayan, they were the pre-eminent symbol of Israeli military control over Gaza.

More than 300 Israeli soldiers were killed on 7 October and its immediate aftermath, from full colonels to rank and file. Others were taken captive into Gaza. At the same time, villages and towns near the border were being attacked, and the site of the Nova festival near Re'im. The attackers shot and stabbed festival-goers. It was reported that more than 360 people were killed at the festival.[14] Festival survivor Rada Rashed ran for his life and hid as the gunmen advanced through the trees. 'What I lived through on 7 October are unbelievable things. What I have seen I never imagined I would see … I moved towards a tank because of the heavy shooting. Bullets were hitting near my face,' he recounted.

The girls around were shot down, and I was waiting to get hit. Then I saw a hole, like it was dug by someone. We went into it. The people who we lost have gone for nothing. The girls who have gone – for nothing. They were begging Hamas members not to kill them, but they were having fun with them. They took them by their hair and shot them in the head. Why? I will never see a day more difficult than that day. It is the toughest day in the history of the country.[15]

A Nahal Oz resident, Lishay Lavi, who survived the attack on her community, described how, amid reports of Hamas field exercises in Gaza, there had been a feeling of unease in the border communities in previous weeks. 'We thought there was going to be something – but not what happened, of course,' she said. After hearing gunfire around 8 am she, her husband and their young children hid in their safe room until armed militants broke into the house and forced a local boy to shout to them in Hebrew, 'Please open the door, otherwise they'll shoot me, and they'll shoot you.' The boy was later killed, and her husband was dragged away to be a captive in Gaza as she shouted to him 'I love you. I'm waiting for you.'[16]

After their fighters were on the ground, Hamas leaders went public. Qassam Brigades commander in chief, Mohammed Deif, issued a statement saying the goal of the operation was to start a 'revolution that will end the last occupation and the last racist apartheid regime in the world.'[17] Hamas leaders in Qatar's capital, Doha, were filmed watching the live TV coverage. They were filmed as they knelt together to pray. Haniyeh took the lead, intoning, 'This is a prayer of gratitude for this victory. Allah, please bestow your support and glory on our people and nation.'[18]

It would be some days before Israel could secure the areas around Gaza, and even longer for the full extent of what had taken place to be fully assessed. In the meantime, the virtual world was aflame.

World Wide Web War

From the first minutes of the attack, the war moved onto the airwaves and social media battlegrounds, with news media fact-checkers working flat out in the informational fog of war that has swirled around conflicts throughout history; the unfolding war would be no exception.

As Hamas streamed footage and photos of the attacks across its social media, Israel also moved into communications overdrive. Israeli diplomats held up images from 7 October at the United Nations and handed out QR codes labelled 'Free Gaza from Hamas, scan to see Hamas atrocities',[19] while foreign ministry teams sought to win hearts and minds with pro-Israel social media messaging in English, Hebrew, Arabic and other languages. All as Israeli political leaders pressed their *hasbara* (public advocacy) case worldwide that Israel should be allowed to respond as it saw fit. Among the Israeli material was footage compiled by the military spokesperson's unit and shown around the globe at invitation-only screenings to which the IDF's Public Diplomacy Unit invited journalists, diplomats, commentators, and other opinion-formers.[20] One such screening was attended by one of the authors in London on 23 November 2023.

The setting could not have been further from the bloodstained chaos of Gaza – the Royal United Services Institute in London, opposite Downing Street. The audience included actor Stephen Fry, journalist Rachel Johnson,[21] other journalists from *The Times*[22] and *The Guardian* columnist Owen Jones.[23] With little chatter, the viewers filed in, handing over mobile phones and recording devices at the door. There was a brief, sombre introduction by Sir Mick Davis, a former Conservative Party treasurer and ex-chairman of the Jewish Leadership Council. He said that, while there were legitimate grievances on both sides, 'Palestinian rights weren't on the agenda on 7 October. Terror was.' He added: 'Israel's almost inevitable response is, I think, the same response that citizens of any country would demand.'[24]

The screening began in silence, but with groans from members of the audience almost from the outset. The video was presented as having been taken from Hamas militants' body cameras, kibbutz surveillance CCTV, car dashcams, road traffic cameras, Israeli emergency responders and other clips harvested from mobile phones, Hamas and other social media. The video was impossible to verify independently without being able to check the source of the footage and what was omitted. It also had on-screen captions using Israeli military terminology – such as 'Hamas terrorist body camera'. Nevertheless, some of the clips – and hours of similar footage – had already appeared on social media in the aftermath of the attack, corroborating the wider context. And the video package was compelling in the sheer amount of footage of the same scenes taken from different angles. In addition, Hamas had also claimed and publicized the attack and released numerous video clips itself.

One of the first scenes shown was from the dashcam of a car that tried to get past gunmen in the road. It showed gunfire at the windscreen from the driver's point of view, before cutting to a camera outside the car, which showed it being hit repeatedly by bullets before the driver lost control, veered off the road and crashed.

Other clips showed people being dragged from cars by gunmen, some of them in combat fatigues, while others cheered and took selfies. One lengthy clip showed a decapitation of what seemed to be an already dead Israeli soldier – showing the beheading from beginning to grisly end, when the knifeman ran off with the head still in its helmet. Another depicted what appeared to be an attempt to decapitate a foreign worker with a garden instrument.

One of the most harrowing scenes was of two young boys and an adult man running out of a home dressed in their underpants and into a shelter, where there was then an explosion. The two terrified and blood-soaked boys were later filmed cowering in a kitchen as one cried 'I think we're going to die.' The gunman stationed with them casually opened the fridge to drink from a bottle. The boys' fates were not revealed.

Other scenes depicted groups of gunmen opening fire on people trying to hide behind desks or floor cushions, leaving what appeared to be piles of motionless bodies in some rooms. Other groups of fighters were shown bundling men and women into cars or onto the back of pickup trucks, intercut with scenes from Gaza of some being paraded through the streets as scores of bystanders filmed with their mobile phones. Footage from the Nova festival showed gunmen walking along a line of portable toilets firing into each one. The video then cut to Israelis hiding inside the toilets using their mobile phones to record the gunfire outside.

Among the final scenes were rescue workers moving through a carpet of dead people at the Nova music festival shouting, 'Anyone alive … no signs of life.' It showed 139 bodies in 43 minutes before fading to black. The film ended with images of bloody corpses, dismembered and charred bodies, including women lying dead and covered in blood, shot in the head or chest.

The audience left in complete silence, some later saying they had to avert their eyes at the grisliest scenes. As testimony, it was emotionally powerful, and the scenes depicted and many like them were to be studied by police, criminal, terrorist, forensic and sexual violence investigation teams, human rights groups, and international prosecutors to determine the exact nature and scale of the violence meted out that day by Hamas, PIJ and other attackers on Israelis and others, including civilians.

What it did not depict was direct evidence of some of the most headline-grabbing claims that swirled around news media reports and social networks in the first hours and days after the attack, such as a spokes-woman for the Israeli Prime Minister's Office telling an international TV news network that babies and toddlers had been found with their 'heads decapitated'.[25] This claim was magnified in the international echo chamber by President Biden remarking, 'I never really thought that I would see and have confirmed pictures of terrorists beheading children.' The Israeli government later told news organizations it could not confirm the report, and the White House said Biden had not seen any such photos but was relying on media reports.[26]

Hamas denied the claim, issuing a statement on its Telegram channel followed by later denials in the Hamas Media Office's document *Our Narrative ... Operation Al-Aqsa Flood*: 'It has also been firmly refuted the lie of the "40 beheaded babies" by the Palestinian fighters, and even Israeli sources denied this lie. Many of the western media agencies unfortunately adopted this allegation and promoted it.'[27] Hamas made extensive use of its Telegram channel to get its narrative across to global audiences. On 7 October alone it published hundreds of messages announcing the call to arms and tracking the attacks.

The task of sorting truth from fiction and distinguishing reliable sources from trolling factories was made harder by the disinformation spread by supporters of both sides globally, often using old or fake videos and photographs to promote their chosen narrative and to discredit the other. Marc Owen Jones, a disinformation expert at Hamad bin Khalifa University in Qatar, said:

> Hamas have been sending conflicting signals on social media and their communication channels. They release overtly brutal attack videos, while also making some efforts to project an image of humaneness in their dealings with hostages. It seems they're targeting different audiences, leading to a blurring of the truth in the conflict. Meanwhile, Israel's narratives seem to be trying to undermine the credibility of all Palestinians, for example claiming they are fabricating deaths – using baby dolls to simulate corpses for example. Of course, the purpose of this is to cast Palestinians as deceptive, creating scepticism about the authenticity of the images depicting Palestinian suffering. In other words, they want people to feel Palestinian claims of Israeli wrongdoing lack credibility.[28]

As Israel mounted its largest-ever assault on Gaza, a BBC analysis of the messaging platform X, formerly known as Twitter, found the largest spike in ten years of mentions of the term 'Pallywood', a conflation of Palestinian and Hollywood that, the BBC Verify team said, was 'used to deny or minimize human suffering in Gaza'.

During previous flare-ups of the Israeli–Palestinian conflict in 2014, 2018 and 2021 the word 'Pallywood' consistently peaked at either 9,500 or 13,000 mentions in a single month on X. After the 7 October Hamas attack, the number of mentions peaked at 220,000 in November. BBC Verify found that among those sharing the term 'Pallywood' on social media in the past months, including X, Facebook and Instagram, were Israeli officials, celebrities and popular bloggers from Israel and the US.[29]

Perhaps unsurprisingly, neither Israelis nor Palestinians seemed overly swayed by pressure or criticism from outside. In January 2024, an opinion poll found a large majority of Israel's Jewish population (75 per cent) was against US proposals to shift 'to a different phase of the war in Gaza, with an emphasis on reducing the heavy bombing of densely populated areas.'[30]

Meanwhile on the Palestinian side, a poll in December 2023 found not only that most Palestinians supported Hamas's attack (72 per cent) and believed that 'Israel's war objective is to destroy the Gaza Strip and kill or expel its residents' (53 per cent), but only 7 per cent said Hamas had committed atrocities against Israeli civilians.[31] Never close, the two sides had perhaps never been further apart. Driving this ever-widening chasm was the Hamas attack and the Israeli response.

The social media war raged on. Users began documenting their experiences on both sides of the Gaza border; rates of disinformation and online hatred grew, while conspiracy theories and false claims flourished. Users on platforms such as TikTok, Facebook, Instagram and X were banned, and shadow-banned. Hamas, in all its manifestations, continued, like Israel, to employ online and social media as part of the battle plan.

Gaza

In the last one hundred years Gaza has been accustomed to invasion and destruction. During the First World War the British invaded and occupied until 1948, and as the first Arab–Israeli war raged tens of thousands fled their homes, becoming refugees in Gaza. The succeeding decades have given rise to military rule, invasion, occupation and Intifada. And, in the twenty-first century, the Palestinian population of Gaza has had to live through another Intifada, the internal breakdown of law and order, a withdrawal of Israeli settlers and troops, a coup, a Great March of Return and five Israeli wars – 2008–9 Operation Cast Lead, 2012 Operation Pillar of Defense, 2014

Operation Protective Edge, 2021 Operation Guardian of the Walls, and May 2023 Operation Shield and Arrow.

But the Israeli land, sea and air siege and bombardment that began in October 2023 was unprecedented – certainly like nothing in living memory. Israel's political leadership would eventually have to deal with the anger of a nation against those who left it vulnerable, but in the immediate aftermath Israel was a nation in grief and supported 'shoulder-to-shoulder' by the leader of its biggest ally,[32] as well as by many European states. Israel's captives were in Gaza. Hamas was in Gaza. So, Israel would be too.

Still reeling from the body blow Hamas inflicted on his forces on 7 October, Israel's defense minister, Yoav Gallant, announced action not just at Hamas but the entire population of Gaza, imposing an intense siege on its 2.3 million Palestinian inhabitants. 'I have ordered a complete siege on the Gaza Strip. There will be no electricity, no food, no fuel, everything is closed,' he said.[33] The following day, 9 October, as he addressed Israeli troops on the border of Gaza, he declared:

I have released all restraints … You saw what we are fighting against. We are fighting human animals. This is the ISIS of Gaza. This is what we are fighting against … Gaza won't return to what it was before. There will be no Hamas. We will eliminate everything. If it doesn't take one day, it will take a week, it will take weeks or even months, we will reach all places.[34]

Expecting the playbook of previous encounters Hamas believed they were ready for the retaliation. They were wrong, and once again it was the whole of the population of Gaza that would experience the full brunt of Israel's retribution. The Israeli bombardment soon started in northern Gaza, targeting the Palestinian towns, villages and lands around Beit Lahiya and Beit Hanoun, down Salah al-Din Street, through Al Falouja to Jabalia and its massive refugee camp. Israel's airstrikes were augmented by naval and tank fire, day and night.

In Gaza, Hamas's attack had been as much of a surprise to most Palestinians as to the Israelis. Azmi Keshawi, a long-time colleague of the authors and a researcher for the International Crisis Group (ICG), described the moment he realized something was happening. 'We woke up on the morning of the 7th, a burst of rockets going toward Israel, and it was surprising to us because we thought the situation had de-escalated and we were going to be witnessing more of a calmer area because there was a lot of mediation between the Palestinians and the Israelis,' he told the ICG.

And then the news started coming about Hamas attacking Israel from Gaza, and then all the pictures started coming out. It was unbelievable, unimaginable. We never thought things would escalate up to this kind, the first time in my life I have witnessed such a huge escalation. This wasn't easy on anyone, including the Israelis. And the Israelis started retaliation for 7 October by the most severe air bombardment I have ever witnessed.

He said the Israeli air attacks destroyed entire city blocks, including the government and municipality buildings from which Hamas ran the affairs of the territory, as well as high-rise buildings, schools, hospitals and homes. 'All of this is gone now. If you open any window on your side, you will see destruction everywhere.'[35]

UN organizations for emergency assistance and humanitarian relief rapidly began compiling bulletins reporting the growing number of Palestinian civilians killed, injured and displaced. The vast majority were Palestinian children and women. Less than three weeks after the war had started, the UN child agency UNICEF issued a bulletin stating, 'Over the past 18 days, the Gaza Strip has borne witness to a devastating toll on its children.'[36] It also started tallying the physical destruction to homes, buildings, and public infrastructure such as schools, clinics and hospitals, and the impact on vital civilian infrastructure such as telecommunications shutdowns, internet closures, bakeries, obstetric and paediatric facilities, kindergartens, fuel reserves for electricity generators, and medical laboratories.

True to Gallant's command, electricity to Gaza was subject to a complete blackout after 11 October 2023, lasting well into 2024 and prompting the UN assessment on 31 January that 'the communications and industrial fuel shutdown continue to significantly hinder the aid community's efforts to assess and to adequately respond to the deepening humanitarian crisis.'[37] Water became increasingly scarce. Municipal well capacity dropped drastically, and Israel would permit only one of its water lines to Gaza to remain open. Most of the population was left homeless, as Israel warned 1.1 million residents of northern Gaza, then Gaza City, and then Khan Younis to move south to avoid what Israel commanders said was a mission to destroy Hamas tunnels, rocket-launching sites and other military infrastructure.

In northern Gaza, Ashraf Masri, a father to nine children, whose family home had previously been destroyed in the war of 2014, bemoaned their fate when they were forced to leave their partially rebuilt house. Fleeing Beit Hanoun, they sheltered in a camp for the displaced further south. 'It's hard to believe,' he said. 'War is always on our doorstep and we are the first to suffer and lose, and there is no end to the fear for our children.'[38]

Haya Abu Nasser, a young poet and NGO fund-raiser, who was displaced, first from her home in Gaza City to Khan Younis, spent weeks sheltering in a flimsy tent in the grounds of the local university with almost 30,000 other frightened Gazans. In January 2024, however, the Israeli military began attacking the campus, so she fled again, heading, like so many others, to Rafah. For days on end she lost contact with her nieces and nephews, fearing she wouldn't see them ever again. Writing of her ordeal, 'It is painful to remember the life that I had lost – my home, my job and the chance to study for a master's degree. In the face of this dismal war, I give up those grand aspirations and long only for fruit, warm baths, clean water and a bed sheltered by walls.'[39]

Displacement south to Khan Younis and Rafah placed impossible pressures on Gaza's southern region. An area of Al-Mawasi was where many Palestinians were ordered to move by Israel, the tiny coastal sand berm having to suffice as shelter for growing numbers of internally displaced people (IDPs) as a huge tent encampment sprang up, reminiscent of the 1948 refugee camps. But the safety of such areas was questioned by the UN, who said continued Israeli shelling was seriously endangering civilians, including those sheltering in health facilities. 'The IDF continues to shell areas that it has unilaterally designated as "safe" for evacuation, reinforcing that nowhere in Gaza is safe (for example, the Al Mawasi area in western Khan Younis),' it said.[40]

The United Nations humanitarian coordinator Lynn Hastings told the Security Council in late October that around 42 per cent of housing units in the Gaza Strip had been damaged or destroyed since 7 October. 'There is nowhere to seek refuge in Gaza. When it comes to decisions on whether and where to flee, civilians are damned if they do and damned if they don't,' she said.[41] By February 2024, UN agencies were reporting that more than 1.9 million Gazans had been internally displaced, frequently several times over as the population were forced by Israeli orders and continuous fighting to evacuate from one area to another, again and again. There were constant fears, fuelled by statements from top-level Israeli officials, that one of Israel's war aims was the forced displacement of the Palestinians not only within Gaza but out of it, forever.

War among the Rubble

As Israeli soldiers moved through the rubble of Gaza, they came under fire from the Qassam Brigades and other fighters, who disappeared in and out of the maze of alleyways and streets and the vast tunnel complex that

Hamas had spent years building. The issue of disproportionality came up time and again. One Israeli airstrike in Jabalia refugee camp on 31 October razed buildings and left huge craters in a camp whose narrow alleyways were home to 116,000 registered refugees. The Israeli military said the strike killed Ibrahim Biari, the Jabalia commander it accused of sending militants across the border, and the strike collapsed Hamas tunnels and military infrastructure beneath the camp, which in turn brought down other buildings.[42] The Gaza Health Ministry reported that at least 195 people were killed, with 120 missing and more than 700 wounded in that strike and in another the following day. Abdel Kareem Rayan said he lost fifteen family members. 'They were innocent, just staying (in the camp). What wrong did they do?' he asked.[43] The Jabalia strike prompted the office of the UN Human Rights commissioner Volker Turk to say: 'Given the high number of civilian casualties & the scale of destruction following Israeli airstrikes on Jabalia refugee camp, we have serious concerns that these are disproportionate attacks that could amount to war crimes.'[44]

In response, Israel's military leadership reverted to accusing Hamas leaders of using civilians as human shields. They also targeted Yahya Sinwar in particular, repeatedly calling him a 'dead man walking'. Yoav Gallant even called on Gaza's civilian population to hand Sinwar over. 'The Hamas leadership is responsible,' he said a month into the war. 'We will get to Yahya Sinwar and we will assassinate him. I say here to the people of Gaza, if you get there first, it will shorten this war.'[45]

But, increasingly, Palestinians, human rights groups and some of Israel's closest international allies accused it of using disproportionate force in killing thousands of civilians, including women, children, aid workers and journalists.[46] Visiting Gaza in December 2023, Mirjana Spoljaric Egger, president of the International Committee of the Red Cross, said: 'The level of human suffering is intolerable. It is unacceptable that civilians have no safe place to go in Gaza, and with a military siege in place there is also no adequate humanitarian response currently possible.' Egger added: 'An unimpeded and regular flow of aid must be allowed to enter Gaza. All those deprived of liberty must be treated humanely. The hostages must be released, and the ICRC must be allowed to safely visit them.'[47]

Many Palestinians feared that being pushed by the Israeli military to the south of Gaza could lead to a mass exodus from Gaza altogether, with fears of a looming 'second *Nakbah*'. This fear was heightened in November 2023, when Israeli security cabinet member Avi Dichter was asked about pictures of Gazans fleeing and said, 'We are now rolling out the Gaza Nakba. From an operational point of view, there is no way to wage a war – as the IDF seeks to do in Gaza – with masses between the tanks and the soldiers.'[48] Some went even further. In December 2023, one of Netanyahu's coalition partners, Finance Minister Bezalel Smotrich of the far-right Religious Zionism party, urged that Palestinians leave Gaza and be replaced by Israelis. 'What needs to be done in the Gaza Strip is to encourage emigration,' Smotrich told Israel Army Radio. 'If there are 100,000 or 200,000 Arabs in Gaza and not 2 million Arabs, the entire discussion on the day after will be totally different.' He added: 'Most of Israeli society will say "why not, it's a nice place, let's make the desert bloom, it doesn't come at anyone's expense."' Such talk led the Biden administration to say it had been assured 'repeatedly and consistently' by Netanyahu that it was not official government policy.[49] The fate of the Israelis held captive in Gaza, however, did form part of official government policy, but, as the war worsened, how that policy was being prioritized was called into question.

The Captive Equation

The business of armed groups taking captives or hostages is part of the decades-long dynamic between Israel and the Palestinians. In the 1970s, the PLO and its factions were infamous captive-takers and hijackers. In the 1980s and 1990s, Hezbollah and Israel developed a workable formula which involved negotiations to secure mutual prisoner releases. It was an equation that Hamas learned to understand. Hamas and other armed groups knew that Israel placed a huge premium on the life of its soldier combatants. '"Redeeming a captive" or *pidyon shvuyim*, as it is called in Hebrew, is considered a core Jewish value. It is one that resonates deeply in a country with compulsory military service, where the nation's youth are likely to be sent to battlefields from which they may not return,' wrote analyst Carmiel Arbit in October 2023.[50]

It is estimated, from publicly available sources, that since 1983 Israel had released as many as 8,500 detainees in return for nineteen Israelis and the remains of eight others.[51] In 1983, Israel released 4,600 prisoners in return for six soldiers from Lebanon. In 1985, in a deal with the PFLP–GC to return three soldiers, Israel released 1,150 prisoners, including Sheikh Yassin, and, in 2011, 1,027 Palestinian prisoners in return for Gilad Schalit. Shortly before his assassination a year later, Qassam Brigades commander Ahmed Jabaari crowed that some of those freed had been responsible for the deaths of more than 500 Israelis.

While Hamas had captured Israelis before – mostly soldiers – the sheer number, ages and composition of the more than 250 taken on 7 October

2023 presented them with what they initially considered to be a huge strategic opportunity. But, as with so much about the unfolding events, the past was no predictor of the present. Israel saw the captive issue from an entirely different perspective and, in the first 100 days of the war, strategically incorporated the narrative of the hostages' release into the continuation of its assault on Gaza, saying it would not stop until their people were free. The Biden administration supported Israel's stance, wanting the release of their own nationals and dual nationals. But that meant Netanyahu's war cabinet would have to engage with Hamas, albeit indirectly, and vice versa. Hamas, like other Palestinian factions, always called for the release of the tens of thousands of prisoners and detainees – men, women and children locked in Israel's jails and desert detention camps. Four in ten Palestinian men are imprisoned at one point or another in their lives by Israel. Hostages and prisoners mattered to both sides, but who could help with the necessary negotiations?

In Jerusalem and Washington there was one regional actor they knew they could rely on to mediate: Qatar. In the past, both Israel and the US had counted on Qatar to facilitate complex negotiations with Hamas. As a State Department spokesman put it: 'Qatar has been an integral, irreplaceable, key regional partner, not just as it relates to this current ongoing conflict, but other priorities that the United States has had in the region.'[52] Over a period of about twelve years, a modus vivendi had emerged by which successive Israeli governments, including those of Netanyahu, had endorsed Qatar's mediation both to achieve ceasefires and to deliver humanitarian aid into Gaza that ensured periods of calm for both sides. A decade earlier, Qatar had permitted some of Hamas's political leadership to reside in Doha. Qatar's rulers had been encouraged by the US to keep the door open to Hamas as a conduit when it was most needed, much as it had done with the Taliban. Within a relatively short time, contacts between Doha, Washington and Jerusalem were up and running. Everything had to be secret. So much so that US diplomats, according to a leaked State Department memo, forbade diplomats to use the words 'ceasefire/de-escalation', 'end to violence/bloodshed' and 'restoring calm' in public.[53] At the level of intelligence communications, it was soon established that the quid pro quo for any release of Israeli captives would be Palestinian prisoners freed from Israeli jails and a ceasefire.

When the death toll spiralled, the pressure on Qatar's mediators and the two conflicting parties grew. Among Doha's elite circles it was soon an open secret that Israeli mediators, chiefly Mossad, were in town. Mossad was also on an intelligence-gathering exercise; any information it could glean would be useful either in the present or when the final reckoning came against Hamas's leadership. In this climate, informal gatherings between Qataris and the visitors took on an unusual energy of simmering suspicion about the other party's true intentions. Some in Doha suspected that Israel had carried out a lot of intelligence groundwork on Hamas more than a year earlier during Qatar's hosting of the FIFA World Cup, when fans, including those working for a variety of foreign intelligence services, used it as an opportunity for espionage and recruitment. It soon became clear to Qatari mediators that the best chance of agreement to get urgent humanitarian aid into Gaza was for a ceasefire or truce deal that included the release of Israeli women, children and the elderly in exchange for Palestinian women and children prisoners.

Indeed, the most poignant voices were always those involving children. There followed a complex diplomatic dance to optimize hope, yet manage expectations. It was the middlemen that caused the most concern. Individuals with political agendas who were prepared to weaponize the distress of parents whose children had been taken, or who were tone deaf to the growing death toll visited on Palestinian children in Gaza.

There was a desire to demonstrate support but a political need to avoid exploitation by those with ill intent against the Qatari mediators. From the many phone calls, late-night advisory sessions and non-stop mediation, expectations were raised, dashed and raised again. On one occasion, three dual-national Israeli mothers who believed their children were being held in Gaza's increasingly war-ravaged territory met with senior Qatari diplomatic officials. They claimed their government was not helping or prioritizing their children.[54] For mothers such as B'atSheva Yahalomi, Hadas Kalderon and Renana Jacob, Qatar's embassy in London turned out to be the key address. They said they did not just want their children home but demanded Palestinian children be given safety too,[55] referring to Palestinian children who were incarcerated, often after being tried in Israel's military courts without proper due process. The negotiations were for those children to be released – in the Israelis' case after weeks, in some Palestinian cases after years.

The effort was relentless. Doha's capacity for mediation had never been tested so extensively. At the offices of the prime minister and minister of foreign affairs, Sheikh Mohammed bin Abdulrahman al Thani, near the Amiri Diwan in Doha's downtown Msheireb area, the contact group remained enduringly convened to try and facilitate, sequence, and arrange a halt to Israel's bombardment of Gaza. Clothed in traditional thobes, ghutra and agal, the Qatari diplomats conferred with their strategic partners from

Washington, including CIA chief William Burns, who became a frequent visitor to Doha. The arrival of Israeli Mossad chief David Barnea meant the Qataris could intercede between the two men and the Hamas political leadership more directly.

A few miles away, in the Ministry of Foreign Affairs building on Ambassador Street, the effort was also being augmented by senior ministry officials, diplomats, aides and advisers addressing the humanitarian task ahead. This included the diplomatic sequencing needed to coordinate with other countries, blocs and alliances. Everyone was focused on one task, a ceasefire. Among employees riding in the elevators between the twenty-three storeys of the ministry building, even casual conversation was about 'Gaza', '*tahdiyah*' (calm) or '*hudna*' (ceasefire). The sense of urgency was everywhere. The risks were high, but a ceasefire would let vital aid reach besieged Gazans and freedom for Israeli captives and Palestinian prisoners. Many plans were frustrated during the weeks of talks, but the parties remained committed to wrangling a deal. Even the semantics came down to the wire: would it be called a pause or a ceasefire?

Pause and Release

Finally, a 'humanitarian pause' was announced. At 07:00 hrs Gaza time on 24 November 2023 the guns on both sides fell silent. Captives were released. In exchange, Israel agreed to free Palestinian children (aged fourteen to seventeen) and women prisoners. Israel would allow some humanitarian aid to enter Gaza from Egypt. The initial four-day pause was extended to five, six, and a stuttering seventh day.

Adult Gazans were initially wary – their eyes lifted skywards to see if Israel's drones and planes had really fallen silent. But as the hours wore on more people emerged from their broken homes and shelters. Thousands of children came out to play. Running, racing, playing tag, lifting broken toys from the rubble of their homes, they, far more than their adult keepers, felt the freedom. But many of Gaza's surviving adult population were struggling to come to terms with the price Israel levied on them of living with Hamas. As aid began to trickle in, it became clear that it was nowhere near enough for the population. And much of the flour, oil and other foodstuffs that did arrive was soon being sold instead of donated. Gazans complained that black market activities were rife: 'Yes, they acknowledged that it was driven by desperation, but where were the Hamas police, the Hamas enforcement of law and order to halt such activities?' wrote one resident in a WhatsApp message to one of the authors.[56]

Back in Doha, Qatari officials had established a command-and-control room to work every side of the deal by every medium of secure communication possible. There was a sense of realism. The complex choreography, the risk calculus, they had to plan for setbacks or spoiler actions from either side – and from other parties. Every dimension of an agreement would be monitored to ensure that terms agreed between distrustful enemies would hold up.

But on day one the truce held. Trucks of aid carrying food, medical supplies and water came through to Gaza; the step-by-step orchestration then led to the release of the first captives that evening. Thirteen Israelis, ten Thai citizens and one Filipino were handed over by masked Hamas fighters into the hands of ICRC staff at Rafah and taken away to be reunited with their delighted families. It was clear that Hamas fighters, dressed in their combat fatigues and green bandanas, wanted to be part of the photo opportunity. The militants would descend upon the handover spot of their choice. Crowds of well-wishers, supporters and onlookers were orchestrated to fanboy them while cameras followed their every move.

Elderly, frail captives and bewildered Israeli youngsters were handed over by militants and female Hamas 'carers' in pink and white uniforms, to the bemused looks of Red Cross officials. The crowd roared its approval. Older captives, adolescents in sweatpants and one clutching a miniature dog were high-fived, shoulder-patted and seemingly buddied in strung out goodbyes. The Hamas propaganda machine went into overdrive. Hamas issued a series of statements, photos and videos declaring that its 'victorious resistance' had forced Israel into a deal.

In the West Bank, Palestinian families also welcomed their daughters and teenaged sons home from Israeli prisons. Days two and three of the ceasefire saw more humanitarian aid go into Gaza through Rafah and the release by Hamas of twenty-seven Israeli and seven Thai captives. In the West Bank, a further seventy-eight Palestinian women and teens were freed from Israeli jails and detention centres. The fourth day of the truce brought the news that B'atSheva Yahalomi, Hadas Kalderon and Renana Jacob had got back their children: Eitan (12), Sahar (16) and Erez (12) as well as Or (16) and Yagil (12). The remaining three days saw Hamas release more Israelis and Thais. Israel released a further ninety Palestinian prisoners.

By mutual agreement the truce was temporarily extended. But the mood soon soured, and on 1 December trust seemed lost and the war resumed. Delighted though the families on both sides were to get their relatives back, the brief pause did little to truly relieve the devastating pressure on all of Gaza's war-shattered population.

Back to War

Hamas tacticians always argued that they fought Israel best on home ground in Gaza. There was a long-held belief that Gaza was the Achilles heel of the Israeli army. On 7 October, Saleh Arouri had declared, 'For us, the possibility of a ground invasion into Gaza by the enemy is the best scenario to end this conflict and defeat the enemy.'[57] The reliability of such assessments was truly tested in the first sixty days. In the two months of fighting before the November ceasefire, Israel's military machine certainly degraded Hamas but did not defeat it. Hamas could demonstrate that it still possessed enough firepower to launch missiles against targets in Israel.

Disabling Hamas's tunnel network became a major military objective, even if it risked the lives of captives being held there. Israeli military spokesmen showed off tunnel entrances and networks they said they had discovered. But they also had to acknowledge that much of the vast subterranean network remained intact.

With the end of the humanitarian pause and an Israeli decision to prosecute the war into Gaza's southern region, the 'Palestinian resistance', as Hamas referred to itself, evidenced new military approaches that gave Israeli tacticians and their allies pause for thought. The Qassam Brigades deployed advanced weaponry that included highly effective anti-tank ammunition and drones carrying explosives.

As Israel deployed its $4 million, 70-ton Mark IV Merkava tanks into Gaza, Hamas was ready. The tanks had assumed a kind of military totemism for Hamas, featuring prominently in its propaganda videos. And Hamas was now also equipped with armour-piercing explosives known as 'Shawaz' that proved effective.[58] What caused Israel greatest concern was that Hamas had somehow acquired the requisite information to figure out the ways to identify their weaknesses and develop ways to attack. Hamas claimed it was also hitting Israeli military targets with anti-personnel mines and tandem charges.[59]

The International Court of Justice

As the war went on and the Palestinian death toll mounted, Israel repeatedly insisted that it was operating according to international law. Yet the rhetoric of its leaders was to be used against it. On 12 October 2023, President Isaac Herzog had said of Gaza:

> We are working, operating militarily according to rules of international law. Unequivocally. It is an entire nation out there that is responsible. It is not true

this rhetoric about civilians not aware, not involved. It is absolutely not true. They could have risen up. They could have fought against that evil regime which took over Gaza in a coup d'état. But we are at war. We are at war. We are at war. We are defending our homes. We are protecting our homes. That's the truth. And when a nation protects its home, it fights. And we will fight until we'll break their backbone.[60]

The Biden administration remained a staunch supporter of Israel and kept supplying it with weapons, greatly to the dismay of Palestinians. The human rights criticism of Israel came especially from the Global South, which called out the West for what it saw as double standards between its treatment of Palestine and Ukraine. That criticism was suddenly given sharp legal focus in December 2023, when South Africa brought a genocide case against Israel to the International Court of Justice (ICJ) in The Hague. South Africa's lawyers argued that, since 8 October 2023: 'Israel, its officials and/or agents, have acted with the intent to destroy Palestinians in Gaza, part of a protected group under the Genocide Convention.' Specifically, it accused Israel of incitement to genocide and 'killing Palestinians in Gaza, causing them serious bodily and mental harm, inflicting on them conditions of life calculated to bring about their physical destruction, and the forcible displacement of people in Gaza.'

In a preliminary ruling in January 2024, the court ruled that South Africa had presented a plausible set of legal arguments with respect to a number of violations of the articles of the Genocide Convention. The ICJ also ruled that Israel 'must take all measures within its power to prevent and punish the direct and public incitement to commit genocide in relation to members of the Palestinian group in the Gaza Strip'; and 'must take immediate and effective measures to enable the provision of urgently needed basic services and humanitarian assistance to address the adverse conditions of life faced by Palestinians in the Gaza Strip'.[61]

Delivering the ruling, the president of the ICJ, Judge Joan E. Donoghue, said the court had 'taken note of a number of statements made by senior Israeli officials' – including those by Gallant and Herzog. But the court stopped short of ordering a ceasefire, which drew a mixed reaction from Palestinians. 'The ICJ that encompasses all countries and all those who defend human rights, aren't we human beings? Don't we have rights? Where are our children?' one woman told BBC Arabic.[62] However, Palestinian Foreign Minister Riyadh Maliki said it showed no state was above international law. 'The ICJ judges saw through Israel's politicisation, deflection, and outright lies. They assessed the facts and the law and ordered provisional measures that recognised the gravity of the situation on the ground,' he said.[63]

Israel rejected any suggestion of genocide. Netanyahu called the accusation 'outrageous' and said his country was committed to international law and had an inherent right to defend itself against Hamas, calling it a 'genocidal terror organization' that had just 'perpetrated the most horrific atrocities against the Jewish people since the Holocaust, and it vows to repeat these atrocities again and again and again.' He added: 'The vile attempt to deny Israel this fundamental right is blatant discrimination against the Jewish state, and it was justly rejected.'[64]

South Gaza

With most of north Gaza destroyed, it was clear that the Israeli military and intelligence were looking next at the southern Gazan city of Khan Younis, calling it 'the Hamas capital in the southern strip'.[65] That included the city's vast refugee camp as its target of choice. The refugee camp had been established after the 1948 *Nakbah*. Its residents had fled from Palestinian towns and villages, including Jaffa and Majdal. These *Nakbah* survivors and their families and descendants lived an impoverished existence.

Even before 7 October, the camp's registered population was an estimated 90,000 people, most of whom subsisted on food and aid from the UN. And the influx of people fleeing Israel's war on northern Gaza had massively swelled the numbers of people in the city. By early December 2023, the UN estimated that 1 million had tried to seek shelter in Khan Younis. UN-run relief and humanitarian services were overwhelmed. In the camp and city, the displaced were sheltered in tents and cars or squeezed into the homes of friends and relatives.

As the battles raged on in Gaza throughout December and January, Israel's number one target was Sinwar. Israel was convinced that Khan Younis refugee camp, where he was born and raised, was where he was hiding. The town was also where Israel believed that at least four battalions of the Qassam Brigades were headquartered. Going after Sinwar and Hamas in Khan Younis would offer a tangible reward for the efforts of Israel's battered military and intelligence services. Likewise, with Mohammed Deif. In the first week of the war Israel destroyed his family home in the Qizan an-Najjar neighbourhood, killing his brother but failing to get the man himself. By December 2023, Israeli journalists were reporting that Shin Bet had received new video footage of Deif not only alive but well – and seemingly recovered from injuries inflicted on him in earlier airstrikes.[66] But Sinwar – the number one target – was nowhere to be found. In early February 2024 it was clear that Israel still had him in its sights. Gallant, appearing at a press conference, warned Sinwar again, 'Surrender or death; there is no third choice.'[67]

The second wave of the war was more ferocious than ever. Gaza's health authorities were announcing daily death tolls that grew ever higher, and again mostly children and women were being killed. But although Israel said 136 Israelis and foreign nationals were still being held captive in Gaza, mediation efforts were stymied by increasing political intransigence from both sides. Hamas's political leadership in Doha were reported to be holed up in what was locally known as the Red House, finding it harder to achieve their primary demands – release all prisoners and get Netanyahu's government to agree a long-term ceasefire immediately. Israel said it would not stop the war until all its captives were released. Yet by the spring of 2024 there was tumult within Israel over how the war should be waged, with a schism between the government and a section of the public over the release of the captives.[68]

There was also public anger when it was revealed that, in mid-December, Israeli troops in Gaza shot and killed three of their own hostages as they were trying to give themselves up, while stripped to the waist and holding a makeshift white flag. Palestinians seized upon the incident to support their claims that Israeli troops were firing even on those who posed no threat. In propaganda videos the Qassam Brigades taunted the Israelis, saying, 'The Zionist enemy is gambling with the lives of its soldiers held captive by the Palestinian resistance and thus doesn't care about the feelings of their families. Yesterday, the Zionist army intentionally executed three of them and preferred to kill them rather than liberate them ...'[69] Israel's military conceded that the hostage killings were 'against the rules of engagement' but said they happened during heavy fighting while troops were in combat and 'under pressure'.[70]

In late January 2024, the Israeli military suffered its deadliest single attack of the war when twenty-one reservist troops were killed. They were using explosives to demolish two buildings east of Al-Maghazi refugee camp near the border when they were hit by an RPG, which set off the explosives and brought down the buildings. Hamas claimed the attack.[71] The loss, combined with the increasing frustrations of the families of hostages, raised questions about the balance between the burden of loss and the government's political calculations and war strategy. Disagreements within Israel's war cabinet were also aired in public. 'Netanyahu's steadfast vow to eliminate ... Hamas

… is increasingly seen within the Cabinet as incompatible with returning hostages held in Gaza,' reported one news agency.[72]

Under strain, Netanyahu and his coalition allies started to turn even on the mediators, Netanyahu calling Qatar 'problematic' and complaining: 'Qatar hosts the leaders of Hamas. It also funds Hamas. It has leverage over Hamas. So they should be so good as to apply their pressure. They positioned themselves as mediators – so please go right ahead, let them be so good as to bring back our hostages.'[73] Qatari officials, speaking both publicly and in private, said they were 'appalled' by the remarks and considered them deeply unhelpful in progressing talks between all sides to release hostages and expedite urgent assistance to Gazans and release hostages.[74]

As each day of the war passed, defence and military experts were surprised that not only were the Qassam Brigades still standing in Gaza, but they were still launching attacks. But there was a toll. Israeli sources estimated that as many as 10,000 Hamas fighters had been killed, though no evidence was provided.[75] Israel also said it had killed some Qassam Brigades commanders.

On 2 January 2024, Saleh al-Arouri, the founder of the Qassam Brigades in the West Bank in the early 1990s, was killed by a drone in Beirut, along with Qassam Brigades commanders Samir Findi Abu Amer and Azzam Al-Aqraa Abu Ammar. One of Hamas's most senior officials in Lebanon, Arouri was a key conduit between Hamas, Hezbollah and Iran. Hamas immediately blamed Israel, Haniyeh calling it a 'cowardly assassination' and a 'terrorist act'.[76] Israel did not admit responsibility, but Arouri was a prized scalp. By that stage – three months into the war – Israel had failed to kill or capture Yahya Sinwar or Mohammed Deif in Gaza, despite calling them 'dead men walking' since the start of the war.

Even within Israel's intelligence community there was an understanding that, if Sinwar and others were assassinated, it was no assurance that Hamas would collapse. Hamas had the territorial advantage, and behind such leaders were the next in line of command ready and waiting. Israel was far less informed – its boots had left the ground in Gaza in 2005. In conventional military wisdom, both sides are assumed to battle until one achieves victory and the other suffers defeat. It still seemed too early to say when and how the war between Hamas and Israel would end, but the route would surely be through the framework of phased ceasefires if it were.

Conclusion: Fatal Embrace

One thing that emerged from the 2023–4 war was that Hamas, whether its enemies liked it or not, continued to be defiant. Its ability to regroup, rearm and keep resources coming in narrowed the asymmetric gap on Israel as it acquired the same kinds of sophisticated weapons, equipment and training as Israel's army. Being confronted with the uncomfortable reality that their military was routed at the Gaza border on 7 October, Israelis were left scarcely knowing where to begin working out what went wrong. One immediate focus was outrage at the slew of early reports that Hamas had been at best tolerated and at worst propped up in Gaza by Netanyahu and his right-wing coalition allies, who saw them as a useful Palestinian bogeyman to ward off any international pressure to create a Palestinian state.

After 7 October, the Israeli news media resurfaced remarks made by Netanyahu in March 2019 to his fellow Likud MPs in which he reportedly said that 'whoever is against a Palestinian state' should support transferring the funds to Gaza, 'because maintaining a separation between the PA in the West Bank and Hamas in Gaza helps prevent the establishment of a Palestinian state.' He reportedly added: 'Now that we are supervising, we know it's going to humanitarian causes.'[1] His ultra-right ally Bezalel Smotrich had gone even further in 2015 before becoming Netanyahu's finance minister. 'The Palestinian Authority is a burden, and Hamas is an asset,' Smotrich told an Israeli TV station. 'It's a terrorist organisation, no one will recognise it, no one will give it status at the [International Criminal Court], no one will let it put forth a resolution at the U.N. Security Council.'[2]

All of this was seized upon by Israelis as evidence of a failure across all branches of government, starting at the top. 'This was an epic debacle, and there's no way around it,' wrote former diplomat and commentator Alon Pinkas. 'The idea that Israel could effectively strengthen Hamas in order to weaken the Palestinian Authority and make any political solution unviable collapsed in the most conspicuous, shattering and bloody way,' he wrote.[3] Realizing the damage of headlines such as 'Mr Security: Hamas war tarnishes Netanyahu's image as Israel's Defender',[4] Israel's longest-serving prime minister went public with vehement denials. 'It's a big lie that I wanted to build [up] Hamas. Ridiculous,' he said. 'You don't go to war three times with Hamas or do major military operations if you want to build up Hamas.'[5]

Indirectly, but causally, Hamas's attack brought to the surface once again the fault lines that had divided Israeli society in the months before 7 October: polarizing judicial reforms and the rightwards shift of Netanyahu's coalition government, which included extremist religious nationalists prioritizing settler expansionism and annexation in the Occupied Palestinian Territories.

It is impossible to predict how Israel will be changed in the long run after its self-esteem and security were shattered by an enemy it had long underestimated. With the Israeli electorate not often being tolerant of weakness, Israel's leadership could be sure of only one thing: their involvement in the events of 2023 would be heavily scrutinized and would likely be the first line of their career obituaries. Another unforeseeable but unquestionable outcome of the Hamas attack was that what was once unsayable in Israel became publicly sayable. With the international community once again focused on the Israeli–Palestinian issue and starting to bring pressure to bear for a political, not just a security, solution, Netanyahu said publicly what many Palestinians had long suspected, that the pre-eminent Israeli politician of his generation who had opposed the 1990s Oslo agreements had little inclination to permit statehood for Palestine. 'I thought it [Oslo] was a terrible mistake and I still do,' he said in December 2023.

I'm proud that I prevented the establishment of a Palestinian state because today everybody understands what that Palestine state could have been now that we've seen the little Palestinian state in Gaza. Everyone understands what would have happened if we had capitulated to international pressures and enabled a state like that in Judea and Samaria [West Bank], surrounding Jerusalem and on the outskirts of Tel Aviv.[6]

Increasingly, though, Israeli analysts questioned the likelihood of Israel achieving its objective and eradicating Hamas forever. 'There aren't any absolute victories in the Palestinian arena. That's a shame. Israel and the region would benefit if the jihadist terrorist organization, Hamas, were to be destroyed down to the very last Hamasnik,' Israeli analyst Nahum Barnea wrote in January 2024. 'Netanyahu has been promising on a daily basis that the war will continue until total victory is achieved over Hamas. He hasn't clarified the nature of that victory and the reality that it will usher in. The political leadership's job is to turn the military achievement into an agreement, into a future in which we can live.'[7]

Israel's far-right settlers saw a chance to return to the Gaza from which they were removed, against their will, by the Israeli government in 2005. By early 2024, Israeli settlers were already gathering near the Gaza border. Daniella Weiss, who told one of the authors a decade earlier that West Bank settlements were built in strategic locations to block any chance of a Palestinian state, said her group Nahala planned to settle Gaza again after the war. 'The Nahala movement is organizing groups of families to settle the entire area of Gaza, and people registered, hundreds of families. The Arabs of Gaza will not stay in Gaza, period,' she said.[8]

International Ramifications

Hamas's attack had ramifications far beyond Israel and Palestine – as intended. Hamas certainly raised its profile, viralizing its level of fame, or notoriety. It forced global policymakers into hurried action. Escalation on other fronts, including from Hezbollah in Lebanon, Israeli attacks on Syria, the Houthis in the Red Sea, Islamic Resistance in Iraq on American targets in Jordan – and America striking back – had created the potential for the war in Gaza to undermine security in the Middle East and Western interests in it even further.

The attacks by Yemen's Iranian-backed Houthi rebels on Red Sea shipping lanes, as well as Israel itself, in retaliation for the latter's strikes on Gaza did indeed quickly become a new destabilizing factor in the region. One whose long-term cost to the global economy – and to famine-hit Yemen – rapidly mounted. Shipping and oil companies were forced to halt or divert ships, disrupting global distribution chains. And the US and Britain, among others, deployed warships to the Red Sea and carried out airstrikes against Houthi targets inside Yemen itself. Aboard the USS *Dwight D. Eisenhower*, the commander of a destroyer squadron said that the Houthi threat was the largest it had experienced since the Second World War. Then further US retaliatory strikes were ordered on Syria and Iraq. On the global high street, there were other reverberations. Fast food chains were soon counting the cost of their partisan positions as customers boycotted their stores.

Talks to further normalize Israel–Arab relations absent the Palestinians, such as occurred with the Abraham Accords a few years earlier, went into abeyance. The Israel–Gaza war had certainly derailed earlier talk in the summer and autumn of 2023 of a peace between Israel and Saudi Arabia brokered by the Biden administration. Indeed, in February 2024, following 'shuttle-diplomacy' to Riyadh by Secretary of State Blinken, American talk of hope for revived normalization received a further setback when the Foreign Ministry in Saudi Arabia publicly countered that there would be no peace with Israel without the Palestinians enjoying the right to a state in the West Bank and Gaza with East Jerusalem as their capital.

For eight years American governments had been attempting to pivot foreign policy towards the Indo-Pacific, counter China's ambitions in Asia and begin a process of decoupling from a bitter history of strategic loss and failure in terms of US objectives in the Middle East. Geopolitics, especially following Russia's invasion of Ukraine in February 2022, had also seemed to further reinforce the view that it was time for America to protect its interests elsewhere in the globe. Now, perhaps more than ever since the Eisenhower Doctrine had been published in 1957, the US was committing itself to the military doctrine of an ally – Israel – that would go into unchartered waters in testing the rules-based international system, the laws of war and crimes against humanity, as well as US deterrence doctrine and force posture. As the war dragged on, there was also concern that it was becoming increasingly difficult for US leaders to influence Israel on how things should end – such as a ceasefire and a political horizon that included a two-state solution.

There were also significant questions regarding the domestic impact on national politics in the US of American policy in unequivocally supporting and arming Israel's assault on Gaza. With 2024 being a presidential election year, pundits and policymakers began to work on a variety of risk analysis reports and scenarios with variables including who would be the next US president – Biden or Trump; the calculus of political leaders in Israel, Saudi Arabia and Tehran, and US domestic polling that demonstrated splits not only between Democrats and Republicans but between different classes, generations and other groupings. There was a generally accepted view that Netanyahu would try to stay in charge in hopes that a Trump presidency 2.0 might in turn prolong his position in power.

As for the world's other great power actors – Russia and China – both stood back, but with indications that in private, at least, Beijing was acting as a restraint in counselling Iran to stay as uninvolved in the unfolding regional conflict as possible. Israel and its allies had led the charge in holding Iran and its so-called proxies responsible for seeking to stir up the region even further into confrontation. These 'proxies' or allies – including the Houthis in Yemen, pro-Iranian militias in Iraq and Hezbollah in Lebanon – were all part of the wider 'Axis of Resistance' according to the Iranian narrative. For power-holders in Iran there was an unbidden irony that the Hamas attack on 7 October 2023 threatened to escalate in ways that would negatively impact the carefully crafted mutual deterrence mechanism that had developed between Tehran and some of its Arab Gulf neighbours, as well as Washington.

There was a perception that Iran could exercise leverage over the Houthis that, in reality, proved limited. Despite the Axis of Resistance narrative, Iran's leaders knew that they had to try and avoid direct confrontation with either the US or Israel. Support Palestine, contain Israel: that was the true limit of the axis, and all talk of revolutionary fervour in the Middle East was just that – talk. Domestic opinion across Iran had hardened in the face of what was also considered to be the run of resources abroad to groups such as Hamas, Hezbollah and the Houthis when at home the economy was struggling under sanctions and internal oppression made everyone's lives difficult and hard.

Where Iran had 'gained' was its position of championing the Palestinian issue at a time when other regional actors were drifting in their support, and that was playing well to external audiences that were now galvanized by what was happening in Gaza and Israel. Nevertheless, even the most hardline leaders in Tehran, the Iranian Revolutionary Guard and the religious leadership, understood that Israel would – sooner or later – exact a heavy price on Iran for its support of Hamas. And the day of reckoning was a prospect not to be underestimated.

It was also a form of conflict contagion that no state actor in the region really wanted. All-out war on many fronts was not in the strategic interests of Israel, Egypt, Lebanon, Syria, Iran, Saudi Arabia, Qatar or the UAE. Acts of strategic deterrence were, however, part of the calculation. Each state wanted to deter the others, defining its qualitative military edge so that the region would not explode any further. Such a strategy, though, particularly in the absence of a parallel track of diplomacy, ran the risk of someone making a mistake that could turn into a tipping point it would be difficult to walk back from.

Polycrisis has become distinct and impactful. Some regional diplomats suggested that, while armed strikes against militants in the Bab el Mandab waterway or Syria might have their own logic for politicians in Washington and London, it would only be by addressing the roots of the conflict in Gaza that the kinds of security, peace and prosperity that everyone wanted in the Middle East would truly be realized.

And in those capital cities, and others across the globe, the Hamas attacks and the war in Gaza have manifested a new dimension of the global concerns that grip the current age; culture wars, right-wing extremism, populism, protest, freedom of speech, ethics, rising hate crimes, competing narratives, distortion and debates about modern genocide, massacres, sex crimes in war, apartheid, human rights and the complicity of other states and actors.

A principal fear articulated in Western circles was that the sheer effrontery of a group such as Hamas taking on a far larger enemy would embolden others to take more risks. 'We assess that the actions of Hamas and its allies will serve as an inspiration the likes of which we haven't seen since ISIS launched its so-called caliphate years ago,' FBI Director Christopher Wray told the Senate Committee on Homeland Security and Government Affairs on 31 October 2023.

> Here in the United States, our most immediate concern is that violent extremists – individuals or small groups – will draw inspiration from the events in the Middle East to carry out attacks against Americans going about their daily lives. That includes not just homegrown violent extremists inspired by a foreign terrorist organization but also domestic violent extremists targeting Jewish or Muslim communities.[9]

Indeed, in the first months after the attack and the start of the war, incidents of anti-Semitism and Islamophobia increased at alarming rates within Europe, Canada and the United States. In the US, anti-Semitic incidents were reported to have risen in the four weeks after the 7 October attack by 388 per cent, and the number of Islamophobic incidents rose by 216 per cent.[10]

In an 'alternative' Christmas Day speech, the British celebrity Stephen Fry, one of the people who attended the Israeli military screening of the Hamas attack, delivered a sombre television address about the rise of anti-Semitism in Britain being experienced by his fellow Jews. During it, he said that the 'horrendous events of 7 October and the Israeli response seemed to have stirred up this ancient hatred.'[11] Yet it also became clear that Western media, social media and online platforms, political parties and groups, as well as some government-led narratives – particularly in Europe – were contributing directly to a hostile environment and climate of fear within their own societies.

Anti-Palestinianism and anti-Muslim racism were evident in an exponentially rising number of incidents, including, in the US, the murder of a six-year-old Palestinian-American child, Wadea Al-Fayoume, and the shooting of three college students in Vermont because they were wearing keffiyehs and speaking Arabic, and, in the UK, death threats to worshippers at a mosque. The Institute of Race Relations tackled the issue of anti-Palestinianism and its rise since October 2023 in the following way:

What we have witnessed here since 7 October is a transformation of a knee-jerk anti-Palestinianism into a fully-fledged anti-Palestinian racism permeating politics and British culture on a scale never witnessed before. For now the frameworks of the war on terror are superimposed on anti-Palestinianism, leading to the criminalisation of national symbols and cultural expressions in the diaspora such as the Palestinian flag or the keffiyeh …'[12]

Across the world, legislatures and parliaments held debates and electors asked questions of their politicians. Others mobilized en masse to organize rallies, vigils and marches, as well as huge print and online campaigns. By far the largest coalition was the one calling for an immediate ceasefire in Gaza. Millions from a wide array of societal viewpoints called on their governments to step up and not stymie diplomatic momentum. The call for an immediate ceasefire at the UN was consistently blocked by a veto-wielding US throughout early 2024. But domestic and international pressure mounted on the Biden administration to stop the escalating humanitarian crisis, as a UN-backed report in March – nearly six months after the war started – warned of imminent famine and 'catastrophic' food insecurity in Gaza.

On 25 March the US dropped its veto and abstained during a vote in the Security Council on a resolution that demanded an immediate ceasefire and the immediate and unconditional release of all hostages held in Gaza. This abstention drew instant criticism from Israel, but it did not stop the war or deflect the criticism. In the US, pro-ceasefire students mounted daily protests on college campuses. And in early May UN Secretary-General António Guterres appealed for the international community 'to do everything in their power to prevent an Israeli assault on Rafah at the southernmost edge of Gaza, where more than a million Palestinians were taking refuge'. 'We must do everything possible to avert an entirely preventable, human-made famine in Gaza,' he said.

Back in November 2023, marching in London under banners reading 'Free Palestine' and 'Gaza, Stop the Massacre', one of the marchers, Usman from Dagenham, said he and his friends attended the rally in person because they were more confident of being able to make their opinions felt that way rather than on the internet. 'I know people who have been posting, and some of the stories have been taken down. It's as clear as day that they are being taken down,' said the eighteen-year-old, who declined to give his full name, fearing he might be targeted online.[13]

The international furore and the unprecedented death toll – more than 35,000 Palestinians killed in Gaza, and 1,200 killed in Israel on 7 October and more than 250 soldiers killed later during the Gaza offensive – led many to question whether 'more of the same' policies that had repeatedly led to warfare over seven decades of the Israeli–Palestinian conflict should continue to be pursued. 'The big question I have is what does the day after tomorrow look like? Really, what this has, unfortunately, very sadly proven is the international community's attitude towards this conflict, which for twenty years has been: look the other way, in a moment of crisis try and dampen the flames and then go back to the status quo,' said Hannah Weisfeld of Yachad UK, a British Jewish organization which supports a political resolution to the conflict. 'What's very clear is that we cannot go back to October 6th, that what has happened now is so catastrophic that the idea that we will go back to managing this conflict is, I think, an idea that has now most definitely passed.'[14]

Inferno

When the first edition of this book was published in 2010, it concluded with a final chapter entitled 'Inferno'. Looking back, the title 'Inferno' and the analysis in that concluding chapter seems even more relevant in 2024. In the first three decades of its existence, Hamas's distinctive brand of religion and Palestinian nationalism had delivered the newcomer to power. The message that Hamas has communicated to the world since then is: we are here to stay.

The inferno ignited after 7 October 2023 leaves the future unclear. Israel's political and military leadership certainly vowed to destroy Hamas. However, few seasoned observers of the conflict credit the notion of eradicating an integrated religious, political, social and military movement that has become deeply embedded in Palestinian society and has widespread support far beyond Gaza. No doubt Hamas's military has been degraded by attrition after fighting against a far larger Israeli military backed by American firepower.

But a new energy and dynamic appeared within the wider Palestinian body politic. Addressing the issue of Hamas in the aftermath of the war in Gaza realized a deepening discussion across Palestinian political factions. Past foes from Hamas and Fatah in Gaza now sat together at meetings and conferences to address the Palestinians' political future. Fatah apparatchiks, some with an eye on a post-Abbas future, publicly acknowledged that Hamas could not be uprooted, no matter how hard Israel tried. They also recognized the extent to which the Hamas attack of 7 October 2023 had smashed the myths that had scaffolded their political existence since 1993 and the Oslo Accords.[15] There was a consensus that, with leaders like Netanyahu in power, it was a fiction to believe that there was a partner to work with in Israel and that the cause of the Palestinian people and the self-autonomy of the Palestinian Authority project had only made matters worse. The PA, they claimed, had been 'silent and uninterested in Gaza' and the top leadership of the PLO had strategically neglected the issue as an international lobbying effort.[16]

Such influencers and leaders spoke of new mechanisms for national unity. Some were based on the framework of the PLO and a route to include Hamas. Other options addressed a leadership renewal process that was generally more inclusive and presented a united front on Gaza, on Palestinian governance, and on the realization of their rights as a national movement for self-determination.[17] They argued that, whatever came in the aftermath of the war on Gaza, it had to have as its ultimate goal a final end to Israel's subjugation, self-determination and statehood. Such movement would rely on the leadership of Hamas being willing to work in alliance with leading national figures such as the popular Fatah leader Marwan Barghouti, seen as a unifying figure by Palestinians, jailed for life by Israel on terrorism charges. Indeed, it surprised no one familiar with the internal politics of the Palestinian camp that Hamas negotiators had repeatedly put his name on release lists for prisoner exchanges. Barghouti, seen by many in his community as the 'Mandela of Palestine', was consistently one of the most popular national leaders. Hamas had reached previous unity agreements with him in the past, including deals negotiated while leaders from both sides were in Israeli prisons. His release had been sought by Hamas in 2011 during the Schalit deal, and his name went on the list again in the 2023–4 captive and prisoner negotiations for exchange. There were other hints that the political future of Hamas in the aftermath of the war lay in unity with other Palestinian factions. Before his assassination in January 2024, Hamas Qassam Brigades founder Saleh Arouri had been having meetings with a senior Fatah leader and former security head of the West Bank, Jibril Rajoub.[18]

Even close associates of Mohammed Dahlan, Hamas's former Fatah foe and security chief in Gaza, were pictured in close consultation with Ismail Haniyeh just weeks after the Gaza war had started. At conferences abroad, Hamas leaders sat alongside Fatah figures and former security chiefs, while at public podiums speakers opined on what lay ahead in the aftermath of the war in Gaza. Did this mean that Hamas would be there to continue to govern Gaza alone in the future or lead on reconstruction efforts? This was very unlikely, but what had not been predicated was the inescapable fact that the Hamas attack had been a wake-up call of another kind for Palestinian factions in the Occupied Territories and abroad. This did not mean that all would be plain sailing.

One of the principal political objectives of Hamas when it had been created in 1987 was to challenge and rival the PLO. Yet it would be foolish to gaze into the crystal ball to try and predict how the Palestinians who survive the war on Gaza will feel about Hamas in the years and decades to come.

Palestinians also argued that the attack had revealed something important about Israel – a power that they experienced as an all-encompassing mechanism of occupation over their lives. Israel, they said, had proved not only to be weak on the day of the Hamas attack but strategically weak in its response.[19] Hamas had shaken the balance of power, the balance of deterrence and the balance of terror assumptions that had traditionally given complete dominance to Israel. There was also a certain confidence among its supporters, no matter how misplaced, that the Qassam Brigades could rebuild and threaten Israel again.

'You can't get rid of Hamas, period,' said Professor Ali Jarbawi, professor of political science at Birzeit University in the West Bank.[20] He cautioned that it was too early to say how the war would affect Hamas's level of support in the long run. 'We have to wait and see. Now they have popularity, but after the war and the destruction we have to see how the people of Gaza feel when things clear up. Would they continue to support Hamas after what has happened to their houses, to their families?'

Jarbawi, echoing the sentiments of many, did not believe Hamas would be able to rule Gaza by itself in the face of worldwide opposition. But he said it could not be excluded from any post-war scenario.

I don't think Hamas will be able to rule Gaza as it used to, alone. I don't think that will be acceptable to the world, acceptable to Israel, and it won't be beneficial to the Palestinians because aid to reconstruct Gaza is not going to flow if Hamas is in sole control of Gaza. And I think that Hamas understands that. Militarily it has been weakened, but I think that it will retain a power, a military capability, in Gaza after the war to block any other government from working if it chooses to. They would retain a disruptive power that you cannot do much in Gaza without their blessing.[21]

In the wake of the war in Gaza, Netanyahu and, inevitably, his successors will also have to restore the confidence of all its citizens in Israel's institutions. This may mean that Israel has to rethink the nature and mechanisms of how it secures itself and what that looks like in relation to its Palestinian neighbours. This means tackling the security equation by factoring in the consequences of continuing to pursue a prolonged military occupation of the Palestinian Territories. International justice will also feature in this future equation. Not only does Israel face years of inquiry from the ICC and ICJ regarding its investigations into its practices against the Palestinians, including the genocide allegations during the war in Gaza, but the ICJ has also been deliberating on significant questions relating to the legal consequences of Israel's 'prolonged occupation, settlement and annexation of the Palestinian territory occupied since 1967.'[22]

Hamas, like Israel, also faces questions of criminality as the ICC examines allegations of the perpetration of war crimes and crimes against humanity that arise from the attacks of 7 October and its aftermath – including the issue of captives held in Gaza. 'If there is evidence that Palestinians, whether they're Hamas or Al Quds Brigades or the armed wing of Hamas or any other person or any other national of any other state party, has committed crimes. Yes, we have jurisdiction wherever they're committed, including on the territory of Israel,' ICC prosecutor Karim Khan has stated.[23]

While there were disagreements within the Palestinian national movement over tactics, Hamas's calls – stop occupation, protect holy places, end Israel's occupation – resonated deeply and widely as articles of faith in the Palestinian nation. Even if the Qassam Brigades could be beaten, the fundamental causes that Hamas championed still had the power to draw support and galvanize the Palestinian people, as well as an increasing number of the disenfranchised in the Global South and the marginalized in the West. Decade after decade, Hamas has served as the unbidden reminder to Israel that, in the words of von Clausewitz, 'war is the continuation of politics by other means.' If neither Israel nor Hamas can win the war, then politics may be the only means forward.

Chronology

1516–1917	Palestine ruled by the Turks as one of the Arab territories of the Ottoman Empire.
1896–7	Publication of Theodor Herzl's *Der Judenstaat* [The Jewish State]. First Zionist Congress convenes in Basel, Switzerland.
1914–18	First World War: Turkey allies with Germany.
1916	Sykes–Picot agreement by Britain, France and Russia to divide the crumbling Ottoman Empire between them, including Palestine.
1917, November 2	The Balfour Declaration declares British government support for 'the establishment in Palestine of a national home for the Jewish people'.
1917, December 9	General Sir Edmund [later Viscount] Allenby captures Jerusalem from Turkish forces.
1920	At San Remo the victorious Allies divide the former Ottoman Empire; Britain is awarded the mandate for Palestine. Later approved by the League of Nations.
1921	Syrian-born Sheikh Izz ad-Din al-Qassam arrives in Haifa and begins work as a preacher. The British appoint Hajj Amin al-Husseini the mufti of Jerusalem.
1929	'Western Wall riots' in Jerusalem; Palestinian Arabs kill dozens of Jews in Hebron.
1935	Qassam's 'Black Hand gang' attacks British and Zionist targets.
1935, November 19	Qassam killed in a shoot-out with British police near Jenin.
1936–9	Palestinian Arabs stage a general strike and revolt; 'Qassamite' rebels involved.
1945–6	The Muslim Brotherhood, founded in Egypt in 1928 by Hassan al-Banna, opens its first branches in Palestine.
1947, November	United Nations Partition Plan: the General Assembly of the UN adopts UN Resolution 181 proposing the division of post-mandate Palestine into two separate Jewish and Arab states, with Jerusalem internationalized.

1948, May 14	Israel declares independence.
1948, May 15	The date set by Britain for ending the mandate.
1948, May 15	The first Arab–Israeli war begins.
1949, May 11	Israel becomes a member state of the United Nations.
February to July	Armistice agreements signed between Israel and neighbouring Arab states.
1954	President Gamal Abdel Nasser of Egypt cracks down on the activities of the Muslim Brotherhood in the Gaza Strip.
1964–6	Nasser orders another crackdown on leftists and the Muslim Brotherhood in Egypt and Gaza, leading to the imprisonment of activists.
1967, June	The Six Day War: Israel is victorious, capturing and occupying the West Bank, the Gaza Strip and East Jerusalem, including Al Aqsa Mosque and Dome of the Rock.
1973, October	Yom Kippur War between Israel, Egypt and Syria. Sheikh Ahmed Yassin forms the Mujamma in the Gaza Strip.
1978	Israeli civil authorities in Gaza register the Mujamma as a charity.
1980	Violent clashes in Gaza between Islamist supporters of the Mujamma and secular PLO loyalists.
1981	First cells of Palestinian Islamic Jihad established in the Gaza Strip.
1984	Israeli authorities arrest Yassin and his colleagues and imprison them for membership of an illegal organization, weapons possession and receiving funds.
1985	Yassin released from jail in Israel/PFLP–GC prisoner exchange.
1987, December	First Intifada breaks out. Hamas, the Islamic Resistance Movement, is formed.
1988, August	Hamas publishes its covenant.
1989	Hamas's first attacks against Israeli military targets, including the kidnap and murder of two Israeli soldiers. Israeli authorities outlaw Hamas and imprison Yassin.
1990–1	Gulf War: the PLO alienates its wealthy Gulf backers by siding with Saddam Hussein after his invasion of Kuwait. Hamas refuses to align itself with Hussein.
1991	Madrid Peace Conference between Israel, Syria and Jordan with a Palestinian delegation. Hamas denounces the peace initiative. Hamas announces its new armed wing: the Izz ad-Din al-Qassam Brigades.
1992	Israeli prime minister, Yitzhak Rabin, orders the

273

	deportation of more than 400 Islamists, including Hamas leaders, to south Lebanon after an Israeli police officer is kidnapped and murdered.
1993, September 13	After secret peace talks in Norway, Israel and the PLO sign the Oslo Accords. Hamas rejects the accords and escalates attacks on Israel.
1994, February 25	Baruch Goldstein, a far-right Jewish settler, kills twenty-nine Muslims at prayer in Hebron's Ibrahimi mosque during Ramadan.
1994, April 4	First Israeli troop redeployments from Jericho and Gaza.
1994, April 6	Hamas revenge for Hebron massacre, killing eight Israelis with a suicide bomb in Afula.
1994, April 13	Hamas suicide bomb in Hadera kills five Israelis.
1994, May 4	Israel and the PLO sign the Gaza–Jericho Agreement.
1994, July 1	Yasser Arafat returns to Gaza after three decades in exile.
1994, October 14	Israeli soldier Nachshon Waxman abducted and killed by Hamas.
1994, October 19	Twenty-two people killed in Hamas suicide bomb on a bus in Dizengoff Street, Tel Aviv.
1994, December 10	Yasser Arafat, Yitzhak Rabin and Shimon Peres awarded the Nobel Peace Prize in Oslo.
1995	Israeli authorities conduct arrest campaigns against Hamas in the West Bank. The Palestinian Authority conducts an arrest campaign against Hamas in the Gaza Strip and Jericho. Israeli troops redeploy from most major Palestinian towns in the West Bank.
1995, November 4	Yitzhak Rabin assassinated by an Israeli extremist. Shimon Peres takes over.
1996, January	Yahya Ayyash, the Hamas bomb-maker known as 'the Engineer', assassinated by Israel.
1996, January 20	First Palestinian parliamentary and presidential elections are held. They are boycotted by Hamas.
1996, February 25	Hamas suicide bombing kills twenty-six on a bus in Jerusalem.
1996, May	Binyamin Netanyahu elected prime minister of Israel. Hamas and Islamic Jihad engage in further suicide bombing attacks to derail the peace process.
1997, September 25	Mossad agents try to assassinate Khaled Meshaal in Amman but fail and are captured. Israel releases Sheikh Yassin to secure their return from Jordan.
1998, October 23	Wye River Agreement between Israel and the PA.
1999, May 4	Expiry of five-year deadline for final status negotiations.
2000, May	Israel withdraws from south Lebanon.

2000, July 11–25	Israeli Prime Minister Ehud Barak, Palestinian President Yasser Arafat and US President Bill Clinton fail to reach agreement at Camp David summit.
2000, September 28	Israeli opposition leader Ariel Sharon tours Temple Mount, prompting Palestinian riots which escalate into the Second Intifada.
2000, September 30	Mohammed al-Dura, aged twelve, killed during cross-fire between Israeli soldiers and Palestinian militants at Netzarim in the Gaza Strip.
2000, October 12	Two Israeli reservists, Yosef Avrahami and Vadim Norzhich, lynched in Ramallah.
2001, February 6	Ariel Sharon wins Israeli general election, becomes prime minister.
2001, April 16	First Palestinian rocket into Israel from the Gaza Strip.
2001, June 1	Hamas suicide bomber kills twenty-one Israelis, mainly teenagers, outside a Tel Aviv disco.
2001, August 9	Sbarro Pizzeria bombing in Jerusalem kills fifteen. Hamas and Islamic Jihad claim responsibility.
2001, December 1	Hamas double suicide bombing kills eleven people on Jerusalem's Ben Yehuda pedestrian mall.
2001, December 2	Hamas kills fifteen Israelis in a bus bomb in Haifa.
2001, December 16	Yasser Arafat orders a cessation of attacks on Israel.
2001, December 28	European Union adds Izz ad-Din al-Qassam Brigades to its list of terrorist organizations.
2002, January 3	Israeli commandos seize *Karine A* vessel, loaded with 50 tons of weapons believed to be for the Palestinian Territories.
2002, January 14	Israelis assassinate Fatah Al Aqsa Martyrs' Brigades militant Raed al-Karmi in Tulkarem.
2002, January 27	Wafa Idris, the first ever Palestinian woman suicide bomber, kills one Israeli and wounds 150 in Jaffa Street, Jerusalem. Al Aqsa Martyrs' Brigades claim responsibility.
2002, March 2	Eleven people killed in Al Aqsa Martyrs' Brigades suicide bombing in ultra-orthodox Jerusalem neighbourhood Beit Yisrael.
2002, March 27	Hamas suicide bomber kills thirty Jewish celebrants at a Passover seder dinner at the Park Hotel in Netanya.
2002, March 29	Israel launches Operation Defensive Shield military reoccupation of the West Bank and besieges Arafat's HQ in Ramallah.
2002, July 7	The Palestinian Basic Law comes into force, intended to form the basis for a constitution.
2002, July 22	Salah Shehadeh, Hamas's military leader, is among more

	than a dozen people killed when Israel drops a 1 ton bomb on the building where he is staying in Gaza.
2003, March 5	Seventeen people killed in suicide bombing of an Egged bus in Haifa. Hamas claims responsibility for the attack.
2003, May 19	Suicide bombing at a shopping mall in Afula kills three people.
2003, June 11	Seventeen people killed in a Hamas suicide bombing on a bus in Jerusalem's Jaffa Road.
2003, June 23	Hamas declares a ceasefire.
2003, August 19	Twenty-three people killed in a suicide bus bomb in Jerusalem. Hamas claims responsibility.
2003, August 21	Ismail Abu Shanab, one of Hamas's chief negotiators, killed in an Israeli missile attack on Gaza. Israel also tries to assassinate Yassin.
2003, September 10	Hamas leader Dr Mahmoud Zahar survives an Israeli missile attack on his house in Gaza City. His wife's back is broken and his son is killed.
2003, October 4	Suicide bombing at Maxim's restaurant in Haifa, in which twenty-one Israelis are killed.
2003, October 15	A bomb is detonated against a US embassy convoy in the Gaza Strip; three American security guards are killed.
2004, March 22	Hamas's leader and founder, Sheikh Yassin, is assassinated in an Israeli airstrike. Dr Abdel Aziz Rantissi is declared his successor.
2004, April 17	Less than a month after taking over in Gaza, Rantissi is also assassinated in an Israeli airstrike. The Hamas leadership goes into hiding and the identity of Rantissi's successor is kept secret. Khaled Meshaal, based in Damascus, is widely believed to be the new leader.
2004, August 31	Sixteen people killed in two suicide bombings on buses in Beersheba. Hamas claims responsibility.
2004, November 11	The Palestinian president, Fatah founder and PLO leader, Yasser Arafat, dies in a Paris hospital.
2004, November 12	Arafat buried in Ramallah.
2005, January 9	Mahmoud Abbas elected president of the Palestinian Authority to succeed Arafat. Hamas does not contest the election.
2005, January 15	Abbas sworn in to office.
2005, April	Cairo declaration: Hamas and Fatah agree to reform of the PLO. Hamas announces that it will contest forthcoming legislative elections for the first time.
2005, May	Hamas contests local municipal elections and wins the majority of seats in many constituencies.

2005, August	Israel evacuates all its settlers and soldiers from the Gaza Strip. Hamas declares the Israeli withdrawal its 'victory'.
2006, January 25	Hamas wins overall majority in the first parliamentary elections since 1996. The Quartet says 'all members of a future Palestinian government must be committed to non-violence, recognition of Israel, and acceptance of previous agreements and obligations.'
2006, March 17	Said Siam, Hamas's minister of the interior, announces the founding of a new Hamas police force in the Gaza Strip, the Executive Forces.
2006, March 29	The newly appointed, Hamas-nominated, twenty-four-member cabinet of the Palestinian National Authority sworn in, led by Prime Minister Ismail Haniyeh.
2006, May 15	Hamas deploys first Executive Forces to restore law and order in the Gaza Strip, creating tension with civil police still loyal to Fatah.
2006, June 25	Hamas, the Popular Resistance Committees and the Army of Islam carry out a tunnel raid near Kerem Shalom military base on Israel's side of the Gaza border, killing two Israeli soldiers and abducting Corporal Gilad Schalit. Israel arrests and imprisons Hamas legislators and leaders.
2006, July 12	Hezbollah kills eight Israeli soldiers and kidnaps two in a cross-border attack from southern Lebanon. It fires nearly 4,000 Katyusha rockets into Israel, which retaliates with airstrikes, artillery shelling and a ground invasion.
2006, August 14	Ceasefire. On the Israeli side, forty-four civilians and 121 soldiers killed (including the two kidnapped soldiers, whose bodies were returned on 16 July 2008). More than 1,000 Lebanese killed, mostly civilians.
2006, September– December	Fighting between Hamas and Fatah breaks out in Gaza and the West Bank, leaving many dead, including three children murdered on their way to school.
2007, January	Fighting between Hamas and Fatah paralyses the streets of Gaza. Women and children are among the dead.
2007, February 8	Hamas joins Fatah in signing up to the Mecca Agreement on power-sharing and the formation of a National Unity Government.
2007, March 17	The new government is sworn in.
2007, June 10	New outbreaks of violence in Gaza.
2007, June 15	Hamas seizes control of Gaza after five days of fighting. Hundreds of Fatah security personnel flee the Gaza Strip. President Abbas declares a state of emergency and dismisses the Hamas-led government.

2007, June 17	Abbas announces an emergency Palestinian government based in Ramallah in the West Bank, headed by Salam Fayyad. The government is made up of independent and Fatah ministers.
2007, June 27	The former British prime minister Tony Blair appointed the Quartet's special envoy to the Middle East.
2007, July 4	The kidnapped BBC journalist Alan Johnston released in Gaza and handed to Hamas officials.
2007, September 2	Abbas changes the electoral law to eliminate district voting in place of a party list system. All presidential and parliamentary candidates are required to recognize the PLO as the sole legitimate representative of the Palestinian people.
2007, September 19	The Israeli security cabinet votes to declare Gaza an 'enemy entity'.
2007, November 2	President Abbas meets Hamas officials for the first time since the June takeover of Gaza.
2007, November 12	Hamas police kill at least six people at a Fatah rally in Gaza to mark the anniversary of Arafat's death.
2007, November 27	US-sponsored peace conference at Annapolis involving Israel and President Abbas.
2008, January 23	Hamas encourages thousands of Palestinians to break the siege of Gaza by smashing the border with Egypt at Rafah.
2008, February 4	Suicide bomb attack in Dimona, Israel.
2008, March 7	Hamas and Israel enter into an informal ceasefire.
2008, April	Former US president Jimmy Carter meets with exiled Hamas leader Khaled Meshaal in Damascus.
2008, June 18	Hamas and Israel enter into first mutual six-month ceasefire agreement.
2008, July 25	A bomb at a Gaza City beachside café kills five Hamas militants and a little girl. Hamas blames Fatah and shuts down its remaining offices. Abbas responds with a similar crackdown on Hamas in the West Bank.
2008, December 19	Hamas and Israel ceasefire ends without renewal.
2008, December 24	Palestinian militants in Gaza fire more than sixty rockets into Israel.
2008, December 27	Israel launches Operation Cast Lead in Gaza. In the first week 400 Palestinians are killed. Palestinian rockets kill four Israelis.
2009, January 1	Sheikh Nizar Rayan, a senior Hamas leader, killed in his home in Jabalia by an Israeli airstrike.
2009, January 3	Israel launches a three-pronged ground offensive into Gaza.

2009, January 15	Said Siam, Hamas's interior minister, killed by Israel.
2009, January 18	Israel declares a unilateral ceasefire in Gaza. More than 1,300 Gazans and thirteen Israelis killed. Hamas announces a unilateral one-week ceasefire, calling for a complete Israeli withdrawal. Israeli troops commence withdrawal.
2009, February 10	Israeli general elections held. Likud's Binyamin Netanyahu becomes prime minister.
2009, February	Hamas and Fatah enter national unity talks hosted in Cairo.
2009, March	Hamas and Israel engage in Egyptian-mediated indirect negotiations on the release of prisoners, including Israeli soldier Gilad Schalit.
2009, May	Six killed in clashes between Hamas and Palestinian security forces during a raid in the West Bank town of Qalqilya.
2009, June 1	UN Human Rights Council investigative panel led by Judge Richard Goldstone enters the Gaza Strip to investigate alleged war crimes during Operation Cast Lead. Israel refuses to cooperate with the investigation.
2009, July	Hamas and Fatah both complain of tit-for-tat arrest campaigns organized in Hamas-controlled Gaza Strip and Fatah-controlled West Bank.
2009, August	Fatah holds sixth congress in Bethlehem, its first for twenty years, to elect new leaders and debate reform. Israel permits activists from Lebanon and Syria to attend. Hamas stops Fatah delegates leaving the Gaza Strip.
2009, September 15	UN Human Rights Council report into Israel's Operation Cast Lead is released. It concludes that there is evidence indicating serious violations of international human rights and humanitarian law, actions amounting to war crimes, and possibly crimes against humanity committed by Israel during the Gaza conflict. The report also finds evidence that Palestinian armed groups – principally Hamas – committed war crimes, as well as possibly crimes against humanity, in their repeated launching of rockets and mortars into southern Israel.
2009, October	Abbas calls for presidential and parliamentary elections in January 2010. Hamas announces a boycott in the Gaza Strip.
2010, September	Israel and the PLO/PA leadership hold direct negotiations, but they result in collapse.
2011, May	A unity agreement between Hamas and Fatah is signed.

	Hamas leader Khaled Meshaal joins President Abbas in Cairo to ink the deal.
2011, October 18	The first of 1,027 Palestinian prisoners, including Yahya Sinwar, are released from Israeli prisons in exchange for Israeli soldier Gilad Schalit, who was captured in a Hamas tunnel raid in 2006.
2012, November 14	Israel assassinates Hamas military commander Ahmad Jaabari. Eight days of Palestinian and Israeli violence ensue.
2014, July–August	The kidnap and killing of three Israeli teenagers by Hamas leads to a seven-week war in which it is reported that Israel kills more than 2,100 Palestinians in Gaza; seventy-three Israelis are reported dead, sixty-seven of them military.
2015, May	In a report from human rights group Amnesty International, Hamas is accused of a 'brutal campaign of abductions, torture and unlawful killings against Palestinians accused of "collaborating" with Israel and others.'
2015, October 1	Hamas militants kill two settlers from the West Bank.
2015, October 20	Israeli soldiers arrest Hassan Yousef, the senior Hamas leader in the West Bank.
2015, October 9	Hamas leader Ismail Haniyeh declares a 'new' 'Third' Intifada.
2016, April	Hamas surges its troops to the border with Egypt to prevent an ISIS infiltration.
2017, February	Yahya Sinwar elected Hamas chief in Gaza.
2017, May	In the Qatari capital Doha, the Hamas leadership present their new and revised charter-covenant. As Hamas leaders now set about revising the charter, they appeared to set aside the exhortation to jihad against Israel. Instead, for example, it offers the possibility of Hamas accepting political solutions to achieving Palestinian statehood in the territory of the West Bank, the Gaza Strip, and East Jerusalem.
2018, March	The Palestinian civil protest the 'Great March of Return' begins at Gaza's fenced border with Israel. Israeli troops open fire to keep protesters back. Israel kills more than 170 Palestinians. Fighting also flares between Hamas and Israeli forces.
2021, March	Yahya Sinwar re-elected Hamas chief in Gaza.
2021, May	After weeks of Israeli provocation during Ramadan, hundreds of Palestinians are wounded when Israeli armed

forces open fire at Al Aqsa compound in Jerusalem, Islam's third holiest site.

2021, May 10 After demanding Israel withdraw security forces from Al Aqsa compound, Hamas sends barrages of rockets from Gaza into Israel. Israeli airstrikes on Gaza result in the deaths of an estimated 250 Palestinians and thirteen in Israel. Qatar, Egypt, and the UN mediate a ceasefire.

2022, August In Israeli airstrikes, a senior Palestinian Islamic Jihad leader is assassinated; at least forty-four people, including fifteen children, are also killed. Palestinian Islamic Jihad fires a reported 1,000 rockets towards Israel.

2023, January After Israeli troops raid a refugee camp and kill nine people, Palestinian Islamic Jihad fires two rockets from Gaza towards Israel. Israel responds with airstrikes on Gaza.

2023, September Rumours of a normalization deal between Saudi Arabia and Israel, brokered by the US, circulate at the same time that extremist right-wing Israelis are allowed onto the Temple Mount/Al Aqsa compound in Jerusalem.

2023, October 7 Hamas launches the biggest attack on Israel in years from the Gaza Strip. Hamas code-names the attack 'Operation Al Aqsa Flood'. Israel estimates that more than 1,200 are killed, thousands are injured and an estimated 240 are taken hostage. Palestinian Islamic Jihad says its fighters have joined the attack.
Israel declares war and vows to eliminate Hamas and end its rule over Gaza. US President Joe Biden calls PM Netanyahu and declares unwavering support for Israel.

2023, October 8 300,000 Israeli military reservists are called up to aid the war effort. The West Bank and its Palestinian population are placed under total Israeli lockdown.

2023, October 9 Defense Minister Gallant announces a 'total' siege on Gaza's 2.3 million Palestinian residents, cutting electricity, food, water and fuel supplies.

2023, October 10 Israeli warplanes target more than seventy sites in north Gaza. Weapons shipments from the US arrive. Houthi leaders in Yemen announce that US support to Israel would lead to their own involvement on behalf of the Palestinians.

2023, October 11 As Israeli bomb attacks on Gaza increase, power outages are reported, and Hezbollah steps up attacks from Israel's northern border. Pope Francis calls for the release of all hostages held in Gaza and expresses concerns at Israel's 'total siege'.

2023, October 12	More than 200 sites in Gaza are targeted by Israel, which warns that water, fuel and electricity supplies will only resume if the hostages are released. Israel bombs Syrian airports in Damascus and Aleppo.
2023, October 13	Israeli military issue orders to some 1.1 million Gazans living in the north to evacuate within 24 hours. The UN warns such a move would prompt a humanitarian catastrophe. Human rights organization Amnesty International calls on Israel to rescind the evacuation orders.
2023, October 14	Hamas commander Murad Abu Murad killed in an Israeli raid. Israel warns that its war on Gaza could take months. Martin Griffiths, the UN humanitarian aid chief, states that 'the noose around the civilian population in Gaza is tightening.'
2023, October 15	President Biden, appearing in a TV interview, called the Hamas attack in Israel as consequential as the Holocaust.
2023, October 16	Hamas releases the first video of some of the Israelis it is holding hostage in Gaza.
2023, October 18	In an act of solidarity, President Biden arrives in Israel but does not call for an immediate ceasefire.
2023, October 21	Following mediation by Qatar, Hamas releases two American-Israeli hostages.
2023, October 22	In Gaza, UNRWA announces it will run out of fuel within three days, resulting in 'no water, no functioning hospitals and bakeries'.
2023, October 23	Following Qatari mediation, two more Israeli hostages are released by Hamas.
2023, October 24	At a press conference, a released Israeli hostage states that she 'went through hell', but that she was treated well in captivity.
2023, October 25	Turkish President Erdogan states that 'Hamas is not a terrorist organization, but a "mujahideen" liberation group struggling to protect its people and lands.'
2023, October 26	Israeli PM Netanyahu asserts that Israeli forces have 'eliminated thousands of terrorists – and this is only the beginning.'
2023, October 27	Israel imposes communications blackout on the whole of the Gaza Strip.
2023, October 28	Israel begins its ground invasion of Gaza.
2023, October 31	Yemen's Houthis launch missiles and drones targeting Israel. They warn that more strikes will come.
2023, November 1	Israeli airstrikes hit Jabalia refugee camp.
2023, November 3	Qassam Brigades and Israeli forces clash in northern Gaza.

	The entrance to Shifa hospital, a bakery, and a school are hit by Israel.
2023, November 4	Hamas Qassam Brigades fire rockets at Israel. Israel responds with airstrikes on Gaza schools and al-Mughazi refugee camp. Calls for negotiations for an immediate ceasefire, hostage releases, prisoner exchanges and urgent humanitarian aid deliveries.
2023, November 9	Qatar mediates talks involving Hamas, the CIA and Israel's Mossad chief.
2023, November 13	Senior Hamas intelligence official Mohammed Dababish killed by Israel.
2023, November 18	Israeli forces drop leaflets over southern Gaza ordering evacuation.
2023, November 19	In the Red Sea, the Yemen-based Houthis hijack the partly Israeli owned tanker *Galaxy Leader*.
2023, November 24	A ceasefire mediated by Qatar (the US and Egypt), otherwise known as a 'humanitarian pause' between Israel and Hamas, comes into force. The deal allows for the release of Israeli hostages (and those of other nationalities) – primarily children and women. In return, Israel agrees to the exchange of Palestinian children and women detained or imprisoned by them. Israel also agrees to allow some humanitarian aid into Gaza.
2023, November 25	Hamas releases thirteen Israeli and four Thai hostages. In exchange Israel releases thirty-nine Palestinian women and youths.
	Hamas's Qassam Brigades use the first day of the ceasefire to flood its social media sites with posts, communiqués, and videos.
2023, November 27	Qatari officials announce that Israel and Hamas have agreed to extend the truce by two further days. Hamas releases eleven Israeli hostages; Israel sets free thirty-three Palestinian prisoners.
2023, November 29	More hostages and prisoners released from both sides.
2023, December 1	The truce breaks down and war resumes. During the truce a total of 102 hostages were released from Gaza, while 210 Palestinian detainees and prisoners were freed by Israel. Israel drops leaflets into areas of Gaza ordering more evacuations to so-called safe zones. Hamas claims rockets launched and targeting Tel Aviv.
2023, December 2	Israel claims it killed Hamas battalion commander Wissam Farhat. The Qassam Brigades claim targeting an Israeli command and control position in Gaza.

2023, December 7	Two months on from the 7 October attacks, and Israeli PM Netanyahu warns Hezbollah not to join the fray. A senior Israeli military official claims that Israel has killed over 5,000 'enemy combatants' in Gaza.
2023, December 8	The US vetoes a UN Security Council resolution calling for an immediate ceasefire in Gaza.
2023, December 10	Hamas leaders warn Israel that none of their hostages will leave Gaza alive unless they are part of a negotiated exchange.
2023, December 12	US President Biden calls out Israel for 'indiscriminate bombing' of Gaza.
2023, December 15	Israeli authorities admit they killed three of their own hostages in Gaza by mistake. The hostages were waving a white flag when they were shot.
2023, December 17	The Israeli military claim they have found one of the largest Hamas tunnels to date.
2023, December 18	Hamas's Qassam Brigades release a video showing Israeli Defense Minister Gallant in a captured 'Hamas tunnel' and then splice it to footage of their attack on the Erez crossing on 7 October.
2023, December 19	Israel claims to have killed senior Hamas financier Subhi Farwana in Gaza. Israeli commander of the 162nd Division claims they have broken Hamas operational capacity in northern Gaza.
2023, December 21	Israeli military spokesman claims it has killed more than 2,000 Hamas fighters since the end of the ceasefire. A UN report states that over 500,000 people, a quarter of Gaza's population, are starving.
2023, December 24	In an act of solidarity with Gaza, Palestinians announce Christmas is cancelled in Bethlehem.
2023, December 26	The Gaza Health Ministry states that, in a 24-hour period of Israeli attacks on Gaza, 241 Palestinians had been killed.
2023, December 28	The Euro-Mediterranean Human Rights Monitor releases a report stating that, since 7 October, 29,124 Palestinians (including 11,422 children and 5,822 women) had been killed by Israeli attacks on the Gaza Strip since 7 October. They additionally reported that 56,122 Palestinians had been injured.
2024, January 2	Hamas deputy leader Saleh al-Arouri and military wing commanders killed by a drone strike in Beirut. Israel does not admit responsibility.
2024, January 7	According to the UN, an estimated 1.7 million of Gaza's 2.3 million population have been internally displaced.

2024, January 20   The UN Secretary-General stated: 'People are dying not only from bombs and bullets but from lack of food and clean water, hospitals without power and medicine and gruelling journeys to ever-smaller slivers of land to escape the fighting. This must stop. I will not relent in my call for an immediate humanitarian ceasefire and the immediate and unconditional release of all hostages.' The Israeli military reports that, since the start of its ground operations in Gaza, more than 250 soldiers have been killed.

Notes

Chapter 1 What is Hamas?

1 Yahya Sinwar, Gaza City, 14 December 2022. Stephen Farrell and Samia Nakhoul, 'Hamas leader Sinwar plotted Israel's most deadly day in plain sight', *Reuters*, 6 December 2023; www.reuters.com/world/middle-east/hiding-plain -sight-hamas-leader-sinwar-plotted-destruction-2023-12-01/.

2 Avi Dabush, 'I too am a survivor of a massacre: this is what needs to be done now', *Haaretz*, 31 October 2023; www.haaretz.com/opinion/2023-10-31 /ty-article-opinion/.premium/i-too-am-a-survivor-of-a-massacre-this-is-what -needs-to-be-done-now/0000018b-8538-d055-afbf-b7bba2180000.

3 Israel Defense Forces, 'Hamas–Israel War: real time updates', 7 October 2023, www.idf.il/en/mini-sites/hamas-israel-war-23/real-time-updates/#october.

4 Amnesty International, 'Israel: Palestinian armed groups must be held accountable for deliberate civilian killings, abductions and indiscriminate attacks', 12 October 2023.

5 Gilad Erdan, Israel's ambassador to the United Nations, 'This is Israel's 9/11', New York, 8 October 2023, www.youtube.com/watch?v=pPnC8ie4_yE.

6 Usama Hamdan, author interview, Beirut, 30 January 2024.

7 Catherine Russell, UNICEF, 'Two thirds of Gaza war dead are women and children, briefers say, as Security Council debates their plight', 22 November 2023, https://press.un.org/en/2023/sc15503.doc.htm.

8 Yoav Gallant, Israeli Defense Minister, in Emanuel Fabian, 'Defense minister announces "complete siege" of Gaza: no power, food or fuel', *Times of Israel*, 9 October 2023; www.timesofisrael.com/liveblog_entry/defense-minister -announces-complete-siege-of-gaza-no-power-food-or-fuel.

9 International Rescue Committee, 'Aid is not enough: civilians in Gaza need protection', press release, 20 November 2023; www.rescue.org/uk/press-release /aid-not-enough-civilians-gaza-need-protection.

10 Office of the High Commissioner for Human Rights, 'UN report: Türk warns of rapidly deteriorating human rights situation in the West Bank, calls for end to violence', press release, 28 December 2023; www.ohchr.org/en/press-releases /2023/12/un-report-turk-warns-rapidly-deteriorating-human-rights-situation -west-bank.

11 Yahya Sinwar, Gaza City, 14 December 2022; www.reuters.com/world/middle -east/hiding-plain-sight-hamas-leader-sinwar-plotted-destruction-2023-12-01/.

12 Yahya Sinwar, author interview, Khan Younis, Gaza, 19 October 2011.

13 Lieutenant General Herzi Halevi, 'Address from the IDF chief of the general staff', Southern Israel, 12 October 2023; www.idf.il/en/mini-sites/idf-recaps -daily-summaries-of-the-hamas-israel-war/hamas-war-daily-recaps/daily-recap -october-13th-2023-17-00/.

14 Ismail Haniyeh, 'Haniyeh: we shook Israel's balance and our aim is liber- ating our land and prisoners', *Al Jazeera*, 7 October 2023 [in Arabic]; www.aljazeera.net/news/2023/10/7/%d9%87%d9%86%d9%8a%d8%a9 -%d8%a3%d9%81%d9%82%d8%af%d9%86%d8%a7-%d8%a5%d8%b3%d8 %b1%d8%a7%d8%a6%d9%8a%d9%84-%d8%aa%d9%88%d8%a7%d8%b2 %d8%aa%d9%87%d8%a7-%d9%88%d9%87%d8%af%d9%81%d9%86%d8 %a7. Transcribed into English in Middle East Monitor, 'Haniyeh outlines context and objectives of Hamas Operation Al-Aqsa Flood', 7 October 2023; www.middleeastmonitor.com/20231009-haniyeh-outlines-context-and- objectives-of-hamas-operation-al-aqsa-flood/.

15 Ibid.

16 Mark Regev, *CNN*, 1 November 2023, www.youtube.com/watch?v= JOINc6J8sno.

17 Bilal Y. Saab, 'The Israel–Hamas War: what escalation looks like', Chatham House webinar, 23 October 2023, https://twitter.com/i/broadcasts/1DXxyjwLBabKM.

18 Ayman Safadi, Jordan's deputy prime minister, 18 November 2023, International Institute for Strategic Studies Manama Dialogue, www.iiss.org/events/manama -dialogue/manama-dialogue-2023/.

19 António Guterres, 'Secretary-General's remarks to the Security Council – on the Middle East', 24 October 2023; www.un.org/sg/en/content/sg/speeches /2023-10-24/secretary-generals-remarks-the-security-council-the-middle-east %C2%A0.

20 Gilad Erdan, Israel's ambassador to the United Nations, New York, 24 October 2023; https://twitter.com/giladerdan1/status/1716831294536261905 and https:// twitter.com/giladerdan1/status/1716837646813614354.

21 The Covenant of the Islamic Resistance Movement, 18 August 1988, Article 11, the Avalon Project, Documents in Law, History and Diplomacy, Lillian Goldman Law Library, Yale Law School, https://avalon.law.yale.edu/20th _century/hamas.asp.

22 Dr Abdel Aziz Rantissi, author interview, Gaza City, 8 July 2002.

23 Dr Ibrahim Ibrach, author interview, Gaza City, 20 December 2006.

24 Sheikh Saleh al-Arouri, author interview, Aroura, West Bank, 25–6 March 2007.

25 Israeli Ministry of Foreign Affairs, *Victims of Palestinian Violence and Terrorism since September 2000*, www.gov.il/en/departments/general/victims-of-palestinian -violence-and-terrorism.

26 Ismail Haniyeh, author interview, Gaza City, 26 January 2006.

27 Michael Tarazi, *Associated Press* report, 27 January 2006.

28 Professor Ali Jarbawi, author interview, Ramallah, 18 May 2009.
29 Binyamin Netanyahu, 'Remarks at the memorial ceremony for victims of terror attacks at Mount Herzl', 18 April 2009, Israel Prime Minister's Office, www.gov.il/en/departments/news/event_hate_har180418.
30 'PM Netanyahu's statement at the press conference with Defense Minister Yoav Gallant and Minister Benny Gantz', Prime Minister's Office, 11 November 2023, www.gov.il/en/departments/news/spoke-statement111123.
31 Mushir al-Masri, author interview, Beit Lahiya, 13 March 2008.
32 Christine Abizaid, 'Annual threat assessment to the homeland', testimony to Senate Committee on Homeland Security and Government Affairs, 31 October 2023; www.dni.gov/index.php/newsroom/congressional-testimonies/congressional-testimonies-2023/3735-nctc-director-christine-abizaid-statement-for-the-record-senate-committee-on-homeland-security-and-government-affairs.
33 Sheikh Saleh al-Arouri, author interview, Aroura, West Bank, 25–6 March 2007.
34 Hamas Covenant, August 1988, Article 20, the Avalon Project, Yale Law School; https://avalon.law.yale.edu/20th_century/hamas.asp.
35 Ibid., Article 22.
36 Member States of the United Nations, www.un.org/en/about-us/member-states.
37 United Nations Non-Member States, www.un.org/en/about-us/non-member-states.
38 Likud Party, original party platform, 1977, Jewish Virtual Library; www.jewishvirtuallibrary.org/original-party-platform-of-the-likud-party.
39 'Netanyahu says he told the US that he opposes a Palestinian state in any postwar scenario', *Associated Press,* 19 January 2024; https://apnews.com/article/israel-hamas-war-news-01-18-2024-73d552c6e73e0dc3783a0a11b2b5f67d.
40 Dr Eyad Sarraj, author interview, Gaza City, 13 March 2007.
41 Dr Abdel Aziz Rantissi, author interview, Gaza City, 22 June 2002.
42 Abu Bakr Nofal, author interview, Gaza City, 6 September 2006.
43 Avi Dichter, speech at Jerusalem Centre for Public Affairs, 12 March 2007.

Chapter 2 *In the Path of al-Qassam*
1 *Al-Jamia'a al-Islamiyya,* editorial, 25 November 1935.
2 Anonymous, author interview, Galilee, northern Israel, 11 June 2008.
3 Hamas Covenant, August 1988, Article 7: 'The universality of Hamas'; https://avalon.law.yale.edu/20th_century/hamas.asp.
4 The Balfour Declaration, 2 November 1917; https://avalon.law.yale.edu/20th_century/balfour.asp.
5 PRO, file CO733/257/12, 'Situation in Palestine', 1935.
6 Middle East Centre, St Antony's College, Oxford, Tegart Papers, Box 1, File 3C, from 'Report on terrorism 1936–37', p. 7.

7 'Alleged terrorists' case continued', *Palestine Post*, 2 March 1936, p. 1.

8 Ibid.

9 Ibid.

10 Anonymous, author interview, Galilee, northern Israel, 11 June 2008.

11 'First sentence of death passed by military court', *Palestine Post*, 25 November 1937, p. 1.

12 'Between the lines', *Palestine Post*, 22 November 1935, p. 8.

13 *Al-Jami'a al-Islamiyya*, editorial, 25 November 1935.

14 'Large crowds at burial of three Arab terrorists – police on guard at funeral procession', *Palestine Post*, 22 November 1935, p. 1.

15 Rawiya Shawwa, author interview, Gaza City, 14 March 2007.

16 'Arab leaders admit losing influence', *Palestine Post*, 27 November 1935.

17 'Arabs decry council', *Palestine Post*, 6 January 1936, p. 5.

Chapter 3 Sowing

1 Dr Haider Abdel Shafi, author interview, Gaza City, 14 November 1989.

2 Subhi Anabtawi, author interview, Nablus, 12 August 1989.

3 Ilan Pappe, *The Ethnic Cleansing of Palestine*. New York: Simon & Schuster, 2006.

4 Michael Bachner, 'Israel should "wipe out" Palestinian town of Huwara, says senior minister Smotrich', *Times of Israel*, 1 March 2023.

5 Human Rights Council, Report of Special Rapporteur Michael Lynk on the situation of human rights in the Palestinian territories occupied since 1967, UN Doc. A/HRC/49/87, 12 August 2022, para. 46; https://documents.un.org/doc/undoc/gen/g22/448/72/pdf/g2244872.pdf?token=5zQvFUKLIm6KSPT30s&fe=true.

6 Amnesty International, *Israel's Apartheid against Palestinians: Cruel System of Domination and a Crime against Humanity*, 1 February 2022, p. 67.

7 Beverley Milton-Edwards, *The Israeli–Palestinian Conflict: A People's War*. Abingdon: Routledge, 2008.

8 Mohammed Habash, author interview, Nusseirat refugee camp, Gaza Strip, 6 September 1993.

9 Sheikh Ahmed Yassin, author interview, Gaza City, 11 July 2002.

10 Dr Atef Adwan, author interview, Gaza City, 8 September 2002.

11 Abu Mohammed, author interview, Nusseirat refugee camp, Gaza Strip, 5 September 1993.

12 Sheikh Ahmed Yassin, author interview, Gaza City, 11 July 2002.

13 Abu Zaki Mohammed al-Radwan, author interview, Gaza City, 17 November 1989.

14 Dr Mahmoud Zahar, author interview, Gaza City, 27 November 1989.

15 Rawiya Shawwa, author interview, Gaza City, 13 March 2007.

16 Dr Mariam Abu Dagga, author interview, Gaza City, 14 March 2007.

17 Adnan Pachachi, author interview, Baghdad, 25 April 2008.

18 A. Azzam, *Hamas: al-judhour al-tarikhiyya wal-mithaq* [Hamas: history and charter] Peshawar, 1989.

19 Dr Mahmoud Zahar, author interview, Gaza City, 27 November 1989.

20 Sheikh Ahmed Yassin, author interview, Gaza City, 11 July 2002.

21 Dr Atef Adwan, author interview, Gaza City, 8 September 2002.

22 Dr Mahmoud Zahar, author interview, Gaza City, 29 May 1995.

23 A. Idwan, *Shaykh Ahmad Yassin: hayatah wa jihad* [Sheikh Ahmad Yassin: his life and jihad]. Gaza, n.d., p. 40.

24 This also happened at Birzeit University in the West Bank. See W. Claiborne, 'Brotherhood blooms on the West Bank', *Washington Post*, 15 March 1982.

25 Dr Riad al-Agha, author interview, Gaza City, 28 November 1989.

26 Professor Ali Jarbawi, author interview, Ramallah, 5 May 2009.

27 Brigadier General Yossi Kuperwasser, author note, Israel Newsmakers Forum, Mishkenot Shananim, Jerusalem, 11 November 2007.

28 Brigadier General Itshak Segev (retired), author interview, Ramat Gan, 18 May 2009.

29 Dr Haider Abdel Shafi, author interview, Gaza City, 14 November 1989.

30 Dr Riad al-Agha, author interview, Gaza City, 28 November 1989.

31 Dr Haider Abdel Shafi, author interview, Gaza City, 14 November 1989.

32 Danny Rubinstein, 'Rising Hamas is undaunted by loss of leader Yassin', *Independent on Sunday*, 28 March 2004, p. 10.

33 Dr Eyad Sarraj, author interview, Gaza City, 13 March 2007.

34 Dr Rabbah Muhanna, author interview, Gaza City, 28 November 1989.

35 Basim, author interview, Khan Yunis, Gaza, 19 October 1989.

36 'Islamic bloc enlist thugs to break employee strike at Islamic University', *Al-Fajr*, 3 June 1983, p. 3; and 'Muslim fanatics attack Bir Zeit and Gaza University', *Al-Fajr*, 10 June 1983.

Chapter 4 *The First Intifada*

1 Sheikh Ahmed Yassin, author interview, Gaza City, 11 July 2002.

2 John Kifner, 'Kill us or get out!' Arabs taunt as rocks and bullets fly in Gaza', *New York Times*, 16 December 1987.

3 Statement in the Knesset by Defense Minister Rabin, 23 December 1987, Israel Foreign Ministry, historical documents 1984–1988, no. 312.

4 Interview with Vice Premier and Foreign Minister Peres on Israel Radio, 23 December 1987, Israel Foreign Ministry, historical documents 1984–1988, no. 313.

5 Interview with Defense Minister Rabin on Israel Television, 14 January 1988, Israel Foreign Ministry, historical documents 1984–1988, no. 322.

6 Yitzhak Rabin, 'Israel's new violent tactic takes toll on both sides', *New York Times*, 22 January 1988.

7 Statement in the Knesset by Defense Minister Rabin, 23 December 1987.

8 *New York Times*, also quoting *Haaretz*, 22 and 25 January 1988.

9   Statement in the Knesset by Defense Minister Rabin, 23 December 1987.
10 Avner Cohen, author interview, Moshav Tekuma, 7 May 2009.
11 Hamas communiqué no. 3, February 1988.
12 Musa Abu Marzouq, author interview, Beirut, 22 March 2005.
13 Hamas communiqué, 'In memory of the massacres of Qibyah and Kufr Qassam', 5 October 1988.
14 Mahmoud Musleh, author interview, Ramallah, 12 January 2009.
15 Hamas communiqué, 'In memory of the massacres of Qibyah and Kufr Qassam', 5 October 1988.
16 Bashir Barghouti, author interview, Ramallah, 26 March 1990.
17 Marwan Gheneim, author interview, Ramallah, 27 March 1990.
18 'News reports', *Crescent International*, September 1988, pp. 5–6.
19 'Grassroots forcing change in Hamas?', *Muslimedia*, 16–31 December 1989.
20 Dr Mahmoud Zahar, author interview, Islamic University of Gaza, 12 February 1990.
21 Interview with Defense Minister Rabin on Israel Television (Arabic Service), 27 July 1989, Israel Foreign Ministry, historical documents 1988–1992, no. 85.
22 Dr Raanan Gissin, author interview, Jerusalem, 7 March 2007.
23 Avner Cohen, author interview, Moshav Tekuma, 7 May 2009.
24 Brigadier General Shalom Harari, author note, Institute for Contemporary Affairs lecture, Jerusalem, 9 January 2007.
25 'Sheikh tried for army deaths', *The Times*, 4 January 1990.
26 Abu Zaki Mohammed al-Radwan, author interview, Gaza City, 11 March 1990.
27 Dr Mahmoud Zahar, author interview, Gaza City, 1 September 1992.
28 Dr Atef Adwan, author interview, Gaza City, 11 September 2002.
29 Yitzhak Rabin, speech to the Israeli Knesset, Israel Government Press Office, 21 December 1992.
30 Dr Abdel Aziz Rantissi, author interview, Gaza City, 10 September 2002.
31 See A. Gowers and T. Walker, *Arafat: The Biography*. London: Virgin Books, 1994, p. 162.
32 Dr Mahmoud Zahar, author interview, Gaza City, 29 May 1995.

Chapter 5 Oslo and Collapse

1   H. Salman, 'Interview with Musa Abu Marzouq', *al-Safir*, 25 August 1994, p. 1.
2   'Mideast accord: statements by leaders at the signing of the Middle East pact', *New York Times*, 14 September 1993.
3   Hamas communiqué, issued 30 August 1993.
4   Dr Mahmoud Zahar, author interview, Gaza City, 29 May 1995.
5   Hamas communiqué, issued 7 September 1993.
6   F. Al-Shubayl, 'Hamas spokesman on strategy', *al-Wasat*, 25 October 1993, p. 5.
7   Hamas communiqué, issued 8 October 1993.
8   H. Salman, 'Interview with Musa Abu Marzouq', *al-Safir*, 25 August 1994, p. 1.
9   Anonymous, author interview, Beirut, 22 March 2005.

---

10 Mousa Abu Marzook, 'Hamas is ready to talk', *The Guardian*, 16 August 2007.

11 Hamas communiqué, 'The Gaza–Jericho Accord', issued 29 August 1993.

12 Mohammad Issa, author interview, Aida refugee camp, West Bank, 30 June 1994.

13 President Yasser Arafat, author interview, Muqata, Ramallah, 12 July 2004.

14 Dr Mahmoud Zahar, author interview, Gaza City, 29 May 1995.

15 Dr Abdelrahman Bsaiso, author interview, Gaza City, 14 March 2007.

16 Ismail Abu Shanab, author interview, Gaza City, 13 September 2002.

17 Abu Islam, Izz ad-Din al-Qassam Brigades, author interview, Gaza City, 18 March 1995.

18 'Rabin's speech extracts', *New York Times*, 1 March 1994.

19 Josh Breiner, 'Video shows Ben-Gvir giving speech with words praising extremist Meir Kahane in background', *Haaretz*, 2 May 2023; www.haaretz.com/israel-news/2023-05-02/ty-article/.premium/video-shows-ben-gvir-giving-speech-with-words-praising-extremist-meir-kahane-in-background/00000187-dd31-dea8-af97-dfb1cbaf0000.

20 Hamas communiqué, 'The settlers will pay for the massacre with the blood of their hearts', February 1994.

21 Yitzhak Rabin, *Daily Mail*, 14 April 1994.

22 Musa Abu Marzouq, author interview, Beirut, 22 March 2005.

23 Dr Abdel Aziz Rantissi, author interview, Gaza City, 14 September 2002.

24 Usama Hamdan, author interview, Beirut, 22 March 2005.

25 Hamas communiqué, 'Rabin's attempt to cover up his failing criminal policies', 16 April 1994.

26 *Palestine Report*, 23 October 1994, p. 1.

27 Colonel Nasr Yusuf, author interview, Gaza City, 14 July 1995.

28 Jibril Rajoub, author interview, Jericho, 20 October 1999.

29 Hamas statement, issued 1 July 1994.

30 Ibrahim Ghosheh, *Al-Sharq al-Awsat*, 16 August 1994, p. 18.

31 Mohammed Abu Warda, in Serge Schmemann, 'Target was Israeli government, says Arab linked to 3 bombings', *New York Times*, 7 March 1996.

32 Youssef M. Ibrahim, 'Hamas political chief says group can't curb terrorists', *New York Times*, 9 March 1996.

33 Bassam Jarrar, author interview, El-Bireh, 22 May 1995.

34 Bassam Attiyah, author interview, Ramallah, 13 March 1996.

35 Sheikh Ahmed Yassin, press conference, Gaza City, 6 October 1997.

Chapter 6 The Second Intifada

1 Jamila al-Shanti, Hamas MP, author interview, Gaza City, 19 March 2008.

2 Senior Israeli intelligence official, author interview, Jerusalem, 3 November 2002.

3 Israeli Prime Minister's Office, author interview, Jerusalem, 13 September 2001.

4   'Terrorist attack on bus at Immanuel, 12 December 2001', Israeli Ministry of Foreign Affairs; www.gov.il/en/departments/news/terrorist-attack-on-bus-at-emmanuel-12-dec-2001.

5   Prime Minister Ariel Sharon, author interview, Jerusalem, 3 November 2002.

6   Senior Israeli intelligence official, author interview, Ashkelon, 3 November 2002.

7   Abu Ahmed, author interview, Gaza City, 26 July 2003.

8   Abu Yousef, NSF commander, author interview, Gaza City, 29 July 2003.

9   Dr Mahmoud Zahar, author interview, Gaza City, 19 June 2002.

10 Senior Israeli military official, author interview, 5 March 2002.

11 Hussein Abu Kweik, author interview, Ramallah, 4 March 2002.

12 Dr Abdel Aziz Rantissi, *New York Times*, 9 February 2002.

13 Sheikh Hassan Yousef, author interview, El Bireh, 4 March 2002.

14 Senior Israeli military official, author interview, Tel Aviv, 5 March 2002.

15 Al Aqsa Martyrs' Brigades leader, author interview, Ramallah, 22 March 2002.

16 Hussein ash-Sheikh, author interview, Ramallah, 22 June 2002.

17 Senior Israeli military official, author interview, Jerusalem, 5 March 2002.

18 Efrat, author interview, Jerusalem, 9 March 2002.

19 Hamas communiqué, issued 27 March 2002.

20 Paulette Cohen, author interview, Netanya, 17 April 2002.

21 Arye Mekel, author interview, Jerusalem, 28 March 2002.

22 Amram Mitzna, in Ross Dunn and Stephen Farrell, 'Sharon orders assault on Palestinian terrorism as bomber kills 14 Israelis', *The Times*, 1 April 2002.

23 Meir Sheetrit, Reuters, 1 April 2002.

24 Mustafa, author interview, Nablus, 10 April 2002.

25 Jamila al-Shanti, author interview, Gaza City, 19 March 2008.

26 Jerusalem Issue Brief, 'What really happened in Jenin?', 2 May 2002; www.jcpa.org/art/brief1-22.htm.

27 'Anti-Israeli terrorism, 2006: data, analysis and trends', Intelligence and Terrorism Information Center at the Center for Special Studies, March 2007; www.terrorism-info.org.il/Data/pdf/PDF_07_010_2.pdf.

28 Ministry of Foreign Affairs, 'Summary of terrorist activity 2004'; www.gov.il/en/Departments/General/summary-of-terrorist-activity-2004.

29 B'Tselem, '2004 summary statistics', https://www.btselem.org/statistics/20043112_2004_statistics.

30 'Suicide bombing terrorism during the current Israeli–Palestinian confrontation (September 2000 – December 2005)', 1 January 2006, Intelligence and Terrorism Information Center; www.terrorism-info.org.il/Data/pdf/PDF_19279_2.pdf.

31 United Nations, 'Israeli-Palestinian fatalities since 2000 – key trends', August 2007; www.un.org/unispal/document/auto-insert-208380/.

32 Ismail Abu Shanab, author interview, Gaza City, 15 September 2002.

33 Josef Federman, 'Israel prepared to "liquidate" Hamas militants', *Mail &*

Guardian, 29 January 2006, https://mg.co.za/article/2006-01-29-israel-prepared-to-liquidate-hamas-militants/.

Chapter 7 Qassam Brigades

1 Abu Mohammed, author interview, Gaza City, 16 July 2008.
2 President Isaac Herzog's statement to the international community, Israel Ministry of Foreign Affairs, 9 October 2023; www.gov.il/en/departments/news/president-herzog-s-statement-to-the-international-community-9-oct-2023.
3 Maher Shaban, author interview, Shati refugee camp, Gaza Strip, 9 March 2006.
4 Abu Khalil, author interview, Gaza Strip, 15 March 2007.
5 Mohammed, author interview, Gaza Strip, 15 March 2007.
6 Sheikh Saleh al-Arouri, author interview, Aroura, West Bank, 25–26 March 2007.
7 Abu Khalil, author interview, Gaza Strip, 15 March 2007.
8 Ministry of Foreign Affairs, 'Ahmed Yassin, leader of Hamas terrorist organization', 22 March 2004.
9 Sheikh Saleh al-Arouri, author interview, Aroura, West Bank, 25–26 March 2007.
10 Amnesty International, *Israel and the Occupied Palestinian Territories: Briefing to the Committee against Torture*, 2021, p. 5; www.amnesty.org/en/wp-content/uploads/2021/07/mde150402008en.pdf.
11 Sheikh Saleh al-Arouri, author interview, Aroura, West Bank, 25–26 March 2007.
12 'Hamas official: we were behind the kidnapping of three Israeli teenagers', *The Guardian*, 21 August 2014; www.theguardian.com/world/2014/aug/21/hamas-kidnapping-three-israeli-teenagers-saleh-al-arouri-qassam-brigades.
13 US Department of State, 'Rewards for Justice – Reward Offer for Information on Hamas and Hizballah Key Leaders, 13 November 2018, https://2017-2021.state.gov/rewards-for-justice-reward-offer-for-information-on-hamas-and-hizballah-key-leaders.
14 Hamas communiqué, 'Rabin's attempt to cover up his failing criminal policies', 16 April 1994.
15 Mushir al-Masri, author interview, Beit Hanoun, 19 March 2008.
16 Abu Mohammed, author interview, Gaza City, 16 July 2008.
17 *Human Rights in Palestine and Other Occupied Arab Territories: Report of the United Nations Fact Finding Mission on the Gaza Conflict*, 15 September 2009, p. 21; https://image.guardian.co.uk/sys-files/Guardian/documents/2009/09/15/UNFFMGCReport.pdf.
18 Knel Deeb, author interview, Gaza City, 23 July 2002.
19 Gideon Meir, author interview, Jerusalem, 21 July 2002.
20 'Salah Shehadeh – Special Investigatory Commission', Israel Prime Minister's Office, 27 February 2011; www.gov.il/en/Departments/news/spokeshchade270211.

21 Dr Abdel Aziz Rantissi, author interview, Gaza City, 9 July 2002.

22 'Suicide bombings and underground attack tunnels: who is Mohammed Deif?', Israel Defense Forces website, 15 October 2023; www.idf.il/en/mini-sites/hamas -israel-war-24/all-articles/suicide-bombings-and-underground-attack-tunnels -who-is-mohammed-deif/.

23 'The hospitality of the gun', Al Jazeera documentary, July 2006.

24 International Court of Justice, 'Legal consequences of the construction of a wall in the Occupied Palestinian Territory', 9 July 2004; www.icj-cij.org/case/131.

25 Bilal Y. Saab, Chatham House webinar 'The Israel–Hamas War: what escalation looks like', 23 October 2023; https://twitter.com/i/broadcasts /1DXxyjwLBabKM.

26 Abu Bakr Nofal, author interview, Gaza City, 6 September 2006.

27 Yuval Diskin, press briefing, Tel Aviv, 5 March 2007.

28 Abu Khaled, author interview, Gaza Strip, 20 March 2008.

29 US Department of State transcript, Jerusalem, 5 March 2008.

30 Abu Khaled, author interview, Gaza Strip, 20 March 2008.

31 Abu Mohammed, author interview, Gaza City, 16 July 2008.

32 'Hamas military chief killed in Israeli attack', Al Jazeera, 14 November 2012; www.aljazeera.com/news/2012/11/14/hamas-military-chief-killed-in-israeli -attack.

33 Anshel Pfeffer, 'Screening Hamas atrocities: why hasbara is another Israeli concept that's failed', Haaretz, 26 October 2023; www.haaretz.com/israel -news/2023-10-26/ty-article-opinion/.premium/screening-hamas-atrocities -why-hasbara-is-another-israeli-concept-thats-failed/0000018b-6ce7-db57-a7cb -ecff6ae90000.

34 'Fighters attempt raid on Israel army base', Al Jazeera, 9 July 2014; www .aljazeera.com/news/2014/7/9/fighters-attempt-raid-on-israel-army-base.

35 'Palestinian Hamas official defects from Gaza to Israel: reports', Al-Arabiya, 12 July 2020; https://english.alarabiya.net/News/middle-east/2020/07/12 /Palestinian-Hamas-official-defects-from-Gaza-to-Israel-Reports.

36 'The Hamas terrorist organization', Israel Defense Forces website, 2023, www .idf.il/en/mini-sites/the-hamas-terrorist-organization/#full.

37 'Israel finds Gaza–Egypt Palestinian tunnel', Reuters, 3 November 1992; 'Egypt finds Palestinian tunnels in Rafah', Reuters, 12 July 1994.

38 'Hamas leader Yahya Sinwar threatens: this was just a dress rehearsal', Israel National News, 26 May 2021; www.israelnationalnews.com/news/306946. 'Hamas leader Yahya Sinwar, live broadcast', Al Jazeera Arabic, Sinwar: we warn the occupation that the decision to end it depends on harming Jerusalem and Al-Aqsa, news politics, 26 May 2021; aljazeera.net.

39 'Israel completes "iron wall" underground Gaza barrier', Al Jazeera, 7 December 2021; www.aljazeera.com/news/2021/12/7/israel-announces-completion-of -underground-gaza-border-barrier.

40 Jonathan Saul and Stephen Farrell, 'The Hamas tunnel city beneath Gaza – a

hidden frontline for Israel', *Reuters*, 27 October 2023; www.reuters.com/world
/middle-east/hamas-tunnel-city-beneath-gaza-hidden-frontline-israel-2023-10
-26/.

41 Peter Beaumont, 'Yocheved Lifshitz, Israeli hostage, 85, told Hamas chief he
should be "ashamed of himself"', *The Guardian*, 29 November 2023; www
.theguardian.com/world/2023/nov/29/israeli-peace-activist-85-yocheved-lifshitz
-told-yahya-sinwar-hamas-chief-he-should-be-ashamed-of-himself.

42 Adolfo Arranz, Jonathan Saul, Stephen Farrell, Simon Scarr and Clare Trainor,
'Inside the tunnels of Gaza', *Reuters*, 31 December 2023; www.reuters.com
/graphics/ISRAEL-PALESTINIANS/GAZA-TUNNELS/gkvldmzorvb/.

43 Mark Regev, 'CNN anchor presses Netanyahu adviser on civilian deaths at
Jabalya camp', *CNN*, 1 November 2023; https://www.youtube.com/watch?v=
JOINc6J8sno.

44 Darren Major and Rosemary Barton, 'Trudeau says allies "increasingly
concerned" about Israel's tactics eroding its international support', *CBC*, 21
December 2023; www.cbc.ca/news/politics/trudeau-israel-hamas-war-two-state
-solution-1.7065535.

45 John Kirby, US National Security Council spokesman, *CNN*, 1 November
2023; https://www.youtube.com/watch?v=JOINc6J8sno.

46 Awad al-Rujoub, 'Palestine urges UN to add Israel to "list of shame"
for violating children's rights', *Anadolu News Agency*, 6 November 2023;
www.aa.com.tr/en/middle-east/palestine-urges-un-to-add-israel-to-list-of-
shame-for-violating-childrens-rights/2281157.

47 Emanuel Fabian, 'IDF uncovers largest-ever Hamas attack tunnel, near northern
Gaza border crossing', *Times of Israel*, 17 December 2023; www.timesofisrael
.com/idf-uncovers-largest-ever-hamas-attack-tunnel-near-northern-gaza
-border-crossing/.

48 Izz ad-Din al-Qassam Brigades website, 18 December 2023, https://alqassam.ps
/arabic/videos/index/2982.

Chapter 8 Martyrs

1 Khaled Meshaal, Hamas leader, statement on Gaza crisis, 28 December 2008.
2 Mohammed, author interview, Gaza Strip, 15 March 2007.
3 Anonymous, author interview, Jenin refugee camp, 11 September 2001.
4 Ibid.
5 Hamas Covenant, August 1988, Article 8, https://avalon.law.yale.edu/20th
_century/hamas.asp.
6 Sheikh Ahmed Yassin, author interview, Gaza City, 13 June 2003.
7 Dr Eyad Sarraj, author interview, Gaza City, 13 March 2007.
8 Hamas Covenant, Article 35.
9 Dr Atef Adwan, author interview, Islamic University of Gaza, Gaza City,
8 September 2002.
10 IDF Editorial Team, 'Final conclusions of Shireen Abu Akleh investigation',

5 September 2022; www.idf.il/en/articles/2022/final-conclusions-of-shireen-abu-akleh-investigation/.

11 'Mural of killed journalist Shireen Abu Akleh inaugurated in Bethlehem', *Al Jazeera*, 30 August 2023; www.aljazeera.com/news/2023/8/30/mural-in-memorial-of-shireen-abu-akleh-inaugurated-in-bethlehem.

12 Efraim Benmelech and Claude Berrebi, 'Human capital and the productivity of suicide bombers', *Journal of Economic Perspectives*, 21/3 (2007): 223–38; https://pubs.aeaweb.org/doi/pdfplus/10.1257/jep.21.3.223.

13 Golden Globes, 2006, Best Motion Picture – Non-English Language, *Paradise Now*, Palestine, Dir: Hany Abu-Assad; https://goldenglobes.com/film/paradise-now/.

14 Mohammed Odeh, author interview, Tulkarem, 25 March 2007.

15 Mohammed and Ala'a Zakout, author interview, Gaza City, 3 November 2006.

16 Mohammed Abu al-Jidyan, author interview, Gaza City, 3 November 2006.

17 Husam Khader, author interview, Nablus, 2 October 2002.

18 Letter, *Al Quds*, 19 June 2002.

19 Jerusalem Media and Communication Centre, Poll no. 45, 29 May–2 June 2002, 'On the Palestinian attitudes towards the Palestinian situation in general', www.jmcc.org/polls.aspx.

20 Anonymous, senior Israeli military official, press briefing, Tel Aviv, 9 October 2002.

21 Abu Ashraf, author interview, Beit Lahiya, Gaza, 21 July 2003.

22 Sheikh Ahmed Yassin, author interview, Gaza City, 20 July 2003.

23 Chris McGreal, 'Bomber's family hits out at Islamic Jihad', *The Guardian*, 16 January 2004.

24 Joel Greenberg, 'Hamas signals suspension of suicide bombings', quoting Khalil Shikaki, *New York Times*, 24 September 2001.

25 Usama Hamdan, author interview, Beirut, 22 March 2005.

26 Mohammed, author interview, Gaza, 15 March 2007.

27 C. Price Jones, 'Speaker says terrorists are normal people', *Michigan Daily*, 12 February 2002.

28 Human Rights Watch, 'Israel: Collective punishment against Palestinians', 2 February 2023; www.hrw.org/news/2023/02/02/israel-collective-punishment-against-palestinians.

29 Colonel Noam, Israel Defense Forces, author interview, Nablus, 2 October 2002.

30 Ghassan Shakah, author interview, Nablus, 2 October 2002.

31 International Court of Justice, 'Legal consequences of the construction of a wall in the Occupied Palestinian Territory', 9 July 2004; www.icj-cij.org/case/131.

32 'Israeli military says Hamas hiding tunnels, operations centres in Gaza hospital', *Reuters*, 27 October 2023; www.reuters.com/world/middle-east/israeli-military-says-hamas-hiding-tunnels-operations-centres-gaza-hospital-2023-10-27.

33 Major Rafi Laderman, author interview, Jerusalem, 19 April 2002.

34 Umm Subhi, interviewed by Hassan Jabr, Gaza City, 11 January 2009.

35 Isaac Herzog, Israeli minister of social welfare, Radio Netherlands, 8 January 2009.

36 'Israeli President Herzog on Israel–Hamas War', 19 December 2023, www
.c-span.org/video/?532500-1/israeli-president-herzog-israel-hamas-war.

37 Malcolm Smart, Amnesty International statement, 'Gaza civilians endan-
gered by the military tactics of both sides', 8 January 2009; www.amnesty.org
/en/latest/news/2009/01/gaza-civilians-endangered-military-tactics-both-sides
-20090108/.

38 Amnesty International, 'Israel: Palestinian armed groups must be held
accountable', 12 October 2023; www.amnesty.org/en/latest/news/2023/10/israel
-palestinian-armed-groups-must-be-held-accountable-for-deliberate-civilian
-killings-abductions-and-indiscriminate-attacks/.

39 Amnesty International, 'Damning evidence of war crimes as Israeli attacks wipe
out entire families in Gaza', 20 October 2023; www.amnesty.org/en/latest/news
/2023/10/damning-evidence-of-war-crimes-as-israeli-attacks-wipe-out-entire
-families-in-gaza/.

Chapter 9 Harvesting

1 Mushir al-Masri, author interview, Gaza City, 6 September 2006.

2 Abdullah, author interview, Gaza City, 15 July 2008.

3 Statement by PM Netanyahu, Israeli Ministry of Foreign Affairs, 19 November
2023;   www.gov.il/en/departments/news/statement-by-pm-netanyahu-19-nov
-2023.

4 Riham al-Wakil, author interview, Gaza City, 15 July 2008.

5 Anonymous, author interview, Gaza City, 15 July 2008.

6 United Nations Conference on Trade and Development (UNCTAD) report,
'Intensified aid and urgent action needed to avert Palestinian economic
collapse', 12 September 2006.

7 Saher Jarbouah, author interview, Rafah, 15 September 2006.

8 Nasser Barhoum, author interview, Rafah, 15 September 2006.

9 Mushir al-Masri, author interview, Gaza City, 6 September 2006.

10 Israel Defense Forces, 'Pulling the strings: senior Hamas leaders who direct
terrorism in Gaza without living in it', 7 November 2023; www.idf.il/en/mini
-sites/hamas-israel-war-24/all-articles/pulling-the-strings-senior-hamas-leaders
-who-direct-terrorism-in-gaza-without-living-in-it/.

11 Israel Defense Forces, 'Hamas' exploitation of humanitarian aid', 25 January
2018;   www.idf.il/en/mini-sites/the-hamas-terrorist-organization/hamas
-exploitation-of-humanitarian-aid/.

12 Nidal Al-Mughrabi and Aidan Lewis, 'U.S., Egypt working closely to reinforce
Gaza ceasefire, Blinken says', *Reuters*, 26 May 2021; www.reuters.com/world
/middle-east/blinken-visits-cairo-us-seeks-secure-gaza-ceasefire-2021-05-26/.

13 US Department of the Treasury, 'Treasury targets covert Hamas investment

network and finance official', 24 May 2022; https://home.treasury.gov/news /press-releases/jy0798.

14 US Department of the Treasury, 'Following terrorist attack on Israel, Treasury sanctions Hamas operatives and financial facilitators', 18 October 2023; https:// home.treasury.gov/news/press-releases/jy1816.

15 Allyson Versprille, 'Binance was used to funnel money to Hamas, other militant groups', *Bloomberg*, 21 November 2023; www.bloomberg.com/news/articles/2023 -11-21/hamas-use-of-binance-cited-in-4-3-billion-settlement-with-us.

16 US Department of the Treasury, 'Following terrorist attack on Israel, Treasury sanctions Hamas operatives and financial facilitators'.

17 HM Treasury, 'Consolidated list of financial sanctions targets in the UK', 1 March 2024; https://ofsistorage.blob.core.windows.net/publishlive/2022format /ConList.html.

18 Summaries of EU legislation, 'Freezing funds: list of terrorists and terrorist groups', https://eur-lex.europa.eu/legal-content/EN/TXT/HTML/?uri=OJ:L: 2022:025:FULL.

19 United Nations Conference on Trade and Development (UNCTAD), 'Prior to current crisis, decades-long blockade hollowed Gaza's economy, leaving 80% of population dependent on international aid', 25 October 2023, https://unctad .org/press-material/prior-current-crisis-decades-long-blockade-hollowed-gazas -economy-leaving-80.

20 Stéphane Dujarric, 'Fifteen years of the blockade of the Gaza Strip', 3 July 2022; www.unicef.org/mena/press-releases/fifteen-years-blockade-gaza-strip.

21 Mohammed Daraghmeh and Dalia Nammari, 'Hamas orders book of Palestinian folk tales pulled from schools', *The Independent*, 6 March 2007.

22 Dr Naser Eddin al-Shaer, author interview, Nablus, 12 January 2009.

23 Dr Mahmoud Zahar, in Stephen Farrell, 'No dancing and no gays if Hamas gets its way', *The Times*, 7 October 2005.

24 Naima al-Sheikh Ali, author interview, Gaza City, 13 March 2007.

25 Riham al-Wakil, author interview, Gaza City, 15 July 2008.

26 Nabil Kafarneh, author interview, Beit Hanoun, 14 March 2007.

27 Swords of Islamic Righteousness communiqué, Gaza City, 20 December 2006.

28 Fawzi Barhoum, author interview, Gaza City, 21 December 2006.

29 Anonymous internet café owner #1, author interview, Gaza Strip, 16 July 2008.

30 Anonymous internet café owner #2, author interview, Gaza Strip, 16 July 2008.

31 White House Executive Order 12947, 'Prohibiting transitions with terrorists who threaten to disrupt the Middle East peace process', 23 January 1995; www .govinfo.gov/content/pkg/FR-1995-01-25/pdf/X95-110125.pdf.

32 Lee Hockstader, 'Palestinians find heroes in Hamas', *Washington Post*, 11 August 2001; www.washingtonpost.com/archive/politics/2001/08/11/palestinians-find -heroes-in-hamas/36d3d4d9-4282-4a44-96f8-89ba8fa202d8/.

33 Israeli Foreign Ministry, 'The financial sources of the Hamas terror organiz- ation', 30 July 2003.

34 Ibid.
35 Ismail Haniyeh, author interview, Shati refugee camp, Gaza City, 22 July 2002.
36 Abu George, author interview, Gaza City, 12 November 2006.
37 Tom Lantos, Committee on International Relations, US House of Representatives, 2 March 2006; https://commdocs.house.gov/committees /intlrel/hfa26332.000/hfa26332_of.htm.
38 Yuval Diskin, Shin Bet director, briefing to foreign journalists, Tel Aviv, 5 March 2007.
39 Brigadier Tawfiq Jabr, chief of police, author interview, Gaza City, 15 July 2008.
40 *Calendar Year 2007: Sixteenth Annual Report to Congress on Assets in the United States of Terrorist Countries and International Terrorism Program Designees*, https://ofac.treasury.gov/media/8461/download?inline.
41 US Department of the Treasury, Office of Terrorism and Financial Intelligence, additional background information on charities designated under executive order 13224, www.state.gov/executive-order-13224/.
42 US State Department, 'Individuals and entities designated by the State Department under E.O. 13224', www.state.gov/executive-order-13224/.
43 US Department of the Treasury, 'Treasury targets facilitators moving millions to HAMAS in Gaza', 29 August 2019; https://home.treasury.gov/news/press -releases/sm761.
44 Usama Hamdan, author interview, Beirut, Lebanon, 6 October 2006.

Chapter 10 Women

 1 Hamas Covenant, 1988, Articles 17 and 18: 'The role of the Moslem woman', http://avalon.law.yale.edu/20th_century/hamas.asp.
 2 Jamila al-Shanti, author interview, Beit Hanoun, Gaza, 4 November 2006.
 3 Hamas Covenant, Articles 17 and 18.
 4 Randa, author interview, Gaza City, 12 March 2007.
 5 Umm Mohammed, author interview, Aida refugee camp, West Bank, 12 February 1989.
 6 Umm Mohammed Rantissi, author interview, Beit Hanoun, 13 July 2005.
 7 Naima al-Sheikh Ali, author interview, Gaza City, 14 March 2007.
 8 Dr Mahmoud Zahar, author interview, 29 May 1995.
 9 Dr Mahmoud Zahar, author interview, Gaza City, 23 January 2006.
10 Iman Abu Jazar, author interview, Islamic University of Gaza, 13 March 2007.
11 'Suicide bombing terrorism during the current Israeli–Palestinian confrontation (September 2000 – December 2005)', 1 January 2006, Intelligence and Terrorism Information Center; www.terrorism-info.org.il/Data/pdf/PDF_19279_2.pdf.
12 Israeli Ministry of Foreign Affairs, 'Victims of Palestinian violence and terrorism since September 2000', www.israel-mfa.gov.il.
13 'We don't need women suicide bombers: Hamas spiritual leader', Agence France Presse, 2 February 2002.

14 Israeli Ministry of Foreign Affairs, 'Terror victims 2004', www.mfa.gov.il.
15 Mohammed, author interview, Gaza City, 15 March 2007.
16 Jamila al-Shanti, author interview, Gaza City, 19 March 2008.
17 Al Aqsa television, 8 March 2007.
18 Jamila al-Shanti, author interview, Gaza City, 19 March 2008.
19 Saber al-Najjar, author interview, Beit Hanoun, 27 November 2006.
20 Israel Defense Forces spokeswoman, author interview by telephone, 3 November 2006.
21 Abu Obaida, author interview, Gaza Strip, 3 November 2006.
22 Interview with commander of Hamas women's armed wing, al-Risala, 18 August 2005.
23 Aziza Abu Ghabin, author interview, Beit Lahiya, 13 September 2005.
24 Anonymous, author interview, Gaza City, 14 March 2007.
25 Umm Nidal [Maryam Farahat], Hamas video, March 2002.
26 Umm Nidal [Maryam Farahat], author interview, Gaza City, 28 January 2006.
27 Dr Hanan Ashrawi, author interview, Ramallah, 20 March 2007.
28 Naima al-Sheikh Ali, author interview, Gaza City, 14 March 2007.
29 Umm Usama, author interview, Gaza City, 6 September 2006.
30 Zainab, author interview, Gaza City, 6 September 2006.
31 Suha, author interview, Gaza City, 14 March 2007.
32 Naima al-Sheikh Ali, author interview, Gaza City, 14 March 2007.
33 Mona Shawa, author interview, Gaza City, 14 March 2007.
34 Huda Naim, author interview, Gaza, 12 February 2006.
35 Iman Abu Jazar, author interview, Islamic University of Gaza, 13 March 2007.
36 Jamila al-Shanti, author interview, Beit Hanoun, 13 July 2005.
37 UNFPA, 'The humanitarian impact of Gaza's electricity and fuel crisis on gender-based violence and services', May 2017; https://palestine.unfpa.org/sites/default/files/pub-pdf/Humanitarian%20Impact%20of%20Gaza%27s%20Electricity%20and%20Fuel%20Crisis%20on%20Gender-based%20Violence%20and%20services%20-%2029%20May%202017.pdf.
38 As Civilian Casualties Reach Record Levels in Gaza, Third Committee Underscores Need to End War, Lift Blockade of Essential Needs, Hold Parties Accountable, 24 October 2023; https://press.un.org/en/2023/gashc4390.doc.htm.
39 Abed Hamdan, author interview, Islamic University of Gaza, 13 March 2007.

Chapter 11 Ballot

1 Hamas election banner, January 2006.
2 Dr Ahmad Yousef, author interview, Gaza City, 18 March 2008.
3 Jamila al-Shanti, author interview, Gaza City, 19 March 2008.
4 Dr Khalil Shikaki, author interview, Yale University, 25 October 2006.
5 Dr Abdel Aziz Rantissi, author interview, Gaza, 22 June 2002.
6 Dr Ghassan Khatib, author interview, Ramallah, 22 June 2002.

7 Dr Abdel Aziz Rantissi, author interview, Gaza, 22 June 2002.
8 Senior Israeli military official, author interview, Tel Aviv, 5 March 2002.
9 UNRWA (United Nations Relief and Works Agency for Palestine Refugees in the Near East), 'Beach Camp'; www.unrwa.org/where-we-work/gaza-strip /beach-camp.
10 Khaled Meshaal, author interview, Damascus, 2 August 2007.
11 Ambassador Dr Abdelrahman Bsaiso, author interview, Gaza City, 14 March 2007.
12 Brigadier General Nizar Ammar, author interview, Gaza, 19 January 2005.
13 Dr Mahmoud Zahar, author interview, Gaza City, 5 April 2005.
14 Dr Mahmoud Zahar, *Asharq al-Awsat*, 18 August 2005.
15 Yehya Moussa Abbadsa, author interview, Gaza, 19 March 2008.
16 Dr Ismail al-Ashqar, author interview, Gaza City, 19 March 2006.
17 Mushir al-Masri, author interview, Gaza Strip, 9 July 2005.
18 Musa Abu Marzouq, author interview, Beirut, 22 March 2005.
19 White House, Office of the Press Secretary, 26 May 2005.
20 Sheikh Mohammed Abu Teir, author interview, Jerusalem, 16 January 2006.
21 Fatah election headquarters, author interview, Ramallah, 15 January 2006.
22 Mohammed Dahlan, author notes, Ramallah, 15 January 2006.
23 Diana Buttu, author interview, Ramallah, 20 March 2007.
24 Amani Abu Ramadan, author interview, Gaza City, 14 March 2007.
25 Nabil Shaath, author interview, Gaza City, 13 January 2006.
26 Dr Nashat Aqtash, author interview, Ramallah, 14 November 2006.
27 Ibid.
28 Tony Blair, in Stephen Farrell, 'Hamas tries to exploit its pariah status at ballot box', *The Times*, 24 January 2006.
29 Dr Mahmoud Zahar, author interview, Gaza City, 23 January 2006.

Chapter 12 Pariahs

1 Professor Ali Jarbawi, author interview, Ramallah, 18 May 2009.
2 Usama Hamdan, author interview, Beirut, 6 February 2007.
3 Honorable C. David Welch, assistant secretary, Bureau of Near Eastern Affairs, Department of State, US House of Representatives, 2 March 2006, 'Hearing before the Committee on International Relations: United States policy toward the Palestinians in the aftermath of parliamentary elections'; https://commdocs .house.gov/committees/intlrel/hfa26332.000/hfa26332_0.htm.
4 Michael Tarazi, Associated Press Report, 27 January 2006.
5 Testimony of James D. Wolfensohn, Quartet special envoy for disengagement, to the Foreign Relations Committee, United States Senate, 15 March 2006.
6 Israel Prime Minister's Office, 'Acting PM Olmert held a security discussion in the wake of the results of the Palestinian Authority (PA) elections', 26 January 2006.
7 President George W. Bush, *The Times*, 27 January 2006.

8 Ismail Haniyeh, author interview, Shati refugee camp, 25 January 2006.

9 Dr Mahmoud Zahar, author interview, Gaza City, 6 April 2006.

10 Usama al-Mazini, author interview, Gaza City, 23 June 2006.

11 Nabil Shaath, author interview, Gaza City, 24 January 2006.

12 Tom Lantos, 'United States policy toward the Palestinians in the aftermath of Parliamentary elections', Committee on International Relations, US House of Representatives, 2 March 2006; https://commdocs.house.gov/committees /intlrel/hfa26332.000/hfa26332_0.htm.

13 Robert Malley, Senate Committee on Foreign Relations hearing on the Middle East after the Palestinian elections, 15 March 2006; www.govinfo.gov/content /pkg/CHRG-109shrg33728/pdf/CHRG-109shrg33728.pdf.

14 Brigadier General Shalom Harari, author note, Jerusalem Institute for Contemporary Affairs lecture, Jerusalem, 9 January 2007.

15 Jon B. Alterman, director and senior fellow, Middle East Program of the Center for Strategic and International Studies, statement to House of Representatives Committee on Foreign Affairs, subcommittee on the Middle East and South Asia, 5 June 2008.

16 Dr Omar Abdel-Razeq, author interview, Ramallah, 11 April 2006.

17 Dr Mahmoud Zahar, author interview, Gaza City, 23 January 2006.

18 Ibid.

19 Omar Suleiman, in Stephen Farrell, 'Hamas starts fundraising tour of the Arab world', The Times, 3 February 2006.

20 Dr Omar Abdel-Razeq, author interview, Ramallah, 11 April 2006.

21 Popular Resistance Committees tunneller, author interview, Rafah, 27 June 2006.

22 Abu Bakr Nofal, author interview, Gaza City, 6 September 2006.

23 Ismail Haniyeh, author note, Friday sermon at Sheikh Ahmed Yassin Mosque, 23 June 2006.

24 Amal Saleem, author interview, Gaza City, 6 September 2006.

25 Maher Sukkar, author interview, Ein Hilweh refugee camp, Lebanon, 8 October 2006.

26 Usama Hamdan, author interview, Beirut, 6 February 2007.

27 Dr Salam Fayyad, author interview, Ramallah, 17 March 2007.

28 Dr Hanan Ashrawi, author interview, Ramallah, 17 March 2007.

29 Yuval Diskin, Shin Bet director, briefing to journalists, Tel Aviv, 5 March 2007.

30 Izz ad-Din al-Qassam commander, author interview, Gaza Strip, 11 May 2007.

31 Professor Ali Jarbawi, author interview, Ramallah, 18 May 2009.

Chapter 13 Hamastan

1 Islam Shahwan, author interview, Gaza City, 19 June 2007.

2 Islam Shahwan, author interview, Neve Dekalim, Gaza Strip, 2 November 2006.

3 Beverley Milton-Edwards, 'Order without law? An anatomy of Hamas security:

the Executive Force' (*Tanfithya*), *International Peacekeeping*, 15/5 (2008): 663–76, DOI: 10.1080/13533310802396236.

4 Anonymous Western diplomat, author interview, 15 November 2006.
5 Mushir al-Masri, author interview, Beit Lahiya, Gaza Strip, 13 September 2005.
6 David Rose, 'Gaza bombshell', *Vanity Fair*, April 2008.
7 Condoleezza Rice, '"US plot against Hamas" revealed', *Al Jazeera*, 4 March 2008, www.aljazeera.com/news/2008/3/4/us-plot-against-hamas-revealed-2.
8 Khaled Abu Hillal, author interview, Neve Dekalim, Gaza Strip, 2 November 2006.
9 Mohammed, author interview, Gaza City, 15 March 2007.
10 Shin Bet, '2006 summary – Palestinian terror data and trends'; www.jewishvirtuallibrary.org/trends-in-palestinian-terrorism?utm_content=cmp-true.
11 Abu Qusay, author interview, Gaza City, 20 March 2008.
12 Brigadier General Yossi Kuperwasser (retired), author interview, 9 January 2009.
13 Yuval Diskin, Shin Bet director, briefing to journalists, Tel Aviv, 5 March 2007.
14 Colonel Michael Pearson, USSC, author interview, Jerusalem, 11 August 2008.
15 Islam Shahwan, author interview, Gaza City, 19 June 2007.
16 Maher Miqdad, *New York Times*, 14 June 2007.
17 Dr Ismail al-Ashqar, author interview, Gaza City, 19 March 2008.
18 Captain Abu Yazi, author interview, Rafah, 20 March 2008.
19 Anonymous Western security official, author interview, Jerusalem, 13 August 2008.
20 'Hamas hunts "collaborators" after Gaza rout', *Reuters*, 14 June 2007.
21 Ibrahim Madhoun, author interview, Ramallah, 20 May 2008.
22 'Hamas says "executed" top Fatah militant in Gaza', *Reuters*, 14 June 2007.
23 Abu Thaer, author interview, Rafah, 20 March 2008.
24 Saud al-Faisal, *New York Times*, 16 June 2007.
25 John Ging, *New York Times*, 19 July 2007.
26 Hamas leaflet, Gaza City, June 2008.
27 Shin Bet, 'Palestinian terrorism in 2007: statistics and trends'; www.jewishvirtuallibrary.org/trends-in-palestinian-terrorism?utm_content=cmp-true.
28 Mushir al-Masri, author interview, Beit Lahiya, 18 March 2008.
29 Mohammed, author interview, Gaza City, 16 July 2008.
30 Abu Ahmad, author interview, Shejaiyah, Gaza Strip, 14 July 2008.
31 JMCC (Jerusalem Media & Communications Centre), Poll no. 66 Part 1, November 2008: A public opinion poll on the 20th anniversary of the Independence Declaration; www.jmcc.org/Documentsandmaps.aspx?id=432.
32 *New York Times*, 27 December 2008.
33 *Al-Hayat al-Jadida*, 28 December 2008.
34 Mark Regev, author telephone note, 28 December 2008.

35 Yona Pavtulov, author interview, Beersheba, 4 January 2009.

36 Mustafa Saleh, author interview, Ramallah, 28 December 2008.

37 Robert H. Serry, author interview, Jerusalem, 2 January 2009.

38 Dr Ismail al-Ashqar, author interview, Gaza City, 19 March 2008.

39 Palestinian Center for Policy and Survey Research, Ramallah, 31 May 2009.

40 UN Human Rights Council, *Report of the United Nations Fact Finding Mission on the Gaza Conflict*, 29 September 2009; www.ohchr.org/en/hr-bodies/hrc /special-sessions/session9/fact-finding-mission.

41 Hazem Abu Shaaban, author interview, Gaza City, 28 January 2009.

42 Anonymous, author interview, Rafah, 28 January 2009.

43 Ibid.

44 A'ed Sa'ado Abed, author interview, Sheikh Radwan, 29 January 2009.

45 Husam Khader, author interview, Nablus, 13 January 2009.

Chapter 14 'A General Rehearsal'

1 @QassamBrigade, 19:04 14 November 2021.

2 Omar el-Shamy, author interview, Tahrir Square, Cairo, 11 February 2011.

3 'Gazans celebrate Brotherhood victory in Egypt', *Associated Press*, 24 June 2012.

4 Dr Mahmoud Zahar, author interview, Gaza City, 8 December 2011.

5 'Hamas hopes Morsi's Egypt will focus on Palestine', *Reuters*, 24 June 2012.

6 C. Jones and B. Milton-Edwards, 'Missing the "devils" we knew? Israel and political Islam amid the Arab awakening', *International Affairs*, 89/2 (2013): 400–1.

7 PMO statement on the Egyptian presidential elections, 24 June 2012, https:// embassies.gov.il/london/NewsAndEvents/press-release/Pages/PMO-Statement -on-the-Egyptian-Presidential-Elections.aspx.

8 B. Milton-Edwards, 'Islamist versus Islamist: rising challenge in Gaza', *Terrorism and Political Violence*, 26/2 (2014): 259–76.

9 Israel Defense Forces, 'Operation Pillar of Defense', 30 October 2017; www .idf.il/en/mini-sites/wars-and-operations/operation-pillar-of-defence/operation -pillar-of-defense.

10 Israel Defense Forces tweet, 18 November 2022; https://twitter.com/IDF/status /270106439199121409.

11 Israel Defense Forces, 'Operation Pillar of Defense'.

12 Yousef al-Daloo, author interview, 11 October 2011.

13 Osama Sarhan, author interview, 11 October 2011.

14 Ethan Bronner and Stephen Farrell, 'Israeli soldier swapped for hundreds of Palestinians', *New York Times*, 18 October 2011.

15 Yahya Sinwar, author notes, Gaza City, 18 October 2011.

16 Yahya Sinwar, author interview, Khan Younis, Gaza Strip, 19 October 2011.

17 Yuval Bitton, Israel's Channel 12, October 2023.

18 Rawhi Mushtaha, author notes, Gaza City, 21 October 2011.

19 Bronner and Farrell, 'Israeli soldier swapped for hundreds of Palestinians'.

20 'Abbas stakes Palestinian claim to state at UN', 23 September 2011, www .arabnews.com/node/392060.

21 Professor Mkhaimar Abusada, author interview, Al-Azhar University, Gaza City, 12 October 2011.

22 Fares Akram, interview with Ibrahim Ibrach, *New York Times*, 27 October 2011.

23 United Nations website, non-member states, www.un.org/en/about-us/non -member-states.

24 Office of the Prosecutor, International Criminal Court, 'Situation in Palestine: summary of preliminary examination findings', 3 March 2021; www.icc-cpi .int/news/statement-icc-prosecutor-fatou-bensouda-respecting-investigation -situation-palestine.

25 Israeli Prime Minister's Office YouTube channel, 'Remarks by Prime Minister Benjamin Netanyahu on the ICC decision', 3 March 2021; www.youtube.com /watch?v=1ayddGxVXgk.

26 'ICC launches war crimes probe into Israeli practices', *Associated Press*, 3 March 2021; https://apnews.com/article/israel-west-bank-palestinian-territories-courts -crime-19117d4265f5d564256ea7fe75854aa6.

27 Ibid.

28 Paul Richter, 'Biden's Israel visit takes a rocky turn', *Los Angeles Times*, 9 March 2010;   www.latimes.com/archives/la-xpm-2010-mar-09-la-fg-biden-israel10 -2010mar10-story.html.

29 Obama White House YouTube channel, 'President Obama meets with Prime Minister Netanyahu', Washington, 20 May 2011; www.youtube.com/watch?v= ShP8hQ431HU.

30 Ron Nachman, author interview, Ariel, occupied West Bank, September 2011.

31 Daniella Weiss, author interview, Ariel, occupied West Bank, September 2011.

32 Pew Research Center, 'Concerns about Islamic extremism on the rise in Middle East', 1 July 2014; www.pewresearch.org/global/2014/07/01/concerns -about-islamic-extremism-on-the-rise-in-middle-east/.

33 Hirsh Goodman and Dore Gold, eds, *The Gaza War 2014: The War Israel Did Not Want and the Disaster it Averted*. Jerusalem Center for Public Affairs, 2015, p. 25.

34 UNOCHA, 'Gaza: two years since the 2014 hostilities', fact sheet, August 2016; www.un.org/unispal/document/auto-insert-198812/.

35 Peter Lerner, IDF, 'Israel's Gaza invasion not meant to topple Hamas', *Reuters*, 17 July 2014; www.reuters.com/article/us-palestinians-israel-invasion-hamas -idUSKBN0FM2P220140717.

36 Haim Jelin, author interview, Jerusalem, 24 July 2011.

37 Raz Shmilovich, 'Gaza war leaves Israeli border villages seething with anger', *Reuters*, 14 September 2014; www.reuters.com/article/us-mideast-gaza-israel -border-idUSKBN0GZ1ZN20140904/.

38 UNOCHA, 'Gaza: two years since the 2014 hostilities'.

39 Palestinian Center for Policy and Survey Research (PSR), 'Special Gaza war poll', 26–30 August 2014; www.pcpsr.org/en/node/492.

40 US Department of State, Bureau of Counterterrorism, Executive Order 13224; www.state.gov/executive-order-13224/.

41 Save the Children, *Trapped: The Impact of 15 Years of Blockade on the Mental Health of Gaza's Children*, 2022; https://resourcecentre.savethechildren.net/pdf/gaza_blockade_mental_health_palestinian_children_2022.pdf/.

42 Author notes, Doha, Qatar, 1 May 2017.

43 'Hamas softens stance on Israel, drops Muslim Brotherhood link', *Reuters*, 1 May 2017; www.reuters.com/article/idUSKBN17X1N9/.

44 Colin P. Clarke, 'Hamas' strategic rebranding: what to make of its revised charter', *Foreign Affairs*, 17 May 2017; www.foreignaffairs.com/articles/middle-east/2017-05-17/hamas-strategic-rebranding.

45 Nidal Al-Mughrabi, 'After Syria fall-out, Hamas ties with Iran restored', *Reuters*, 28 August 2017.

46 'Statement by President Trump on Jerusalem', Washington, DC, 6 December 2017; https://trumpwhitehouse.archives.gov/briefings-statements/statement-president-trump-jerusalem/.

47 United Nations, UNISPAL, *The Status of Jerusalem*, New York, 1997; www.un.org/unispal/wp-content/uploads/2016/07/The-Status-of-Jerusalem-Engish-199708.pdf.

48 WAFA News Agency, 'Ashrawi: Trump's decision to move the US embassy to Jerusalem is a fatal blow to peace and security', 5 December 2017; https://english.wafa.ps/page.aspx?id=2gDQjWa95481764466a2gDQjW.

49 Yahya Sinwar, Gaza Strip, *Reuters TV*, 30 March 2018.

50 Palestinian Center for Policy and Survey Research, Public Opinion Poll no. 70, 27 December 2018; https://pcpsr.org/en/node/740.

51 Office of the Prosecutor, International Criminal Court, 'Situation in Palestine: summary of preliminary examination findings', 3 March 2021; www.icc-cpi.int/sites/default/files/items/Documents/210303-office-of-the-prosecutor-palestine-summary-findings-eng.pdf.

52 Shelly Yachimovich, 'Calculated risk: the note in Hebrew that Sinwar wrote to Netanyahu during negotiations for a deal', *Yedioth Ahronoth*, 14 April 2022.

53 Stephen Farrell and Rami Ayyub, 'Scores injured in Jerusalem clashes: Israeli nationalists shout "Death to Arabs"', *Reuters*, 23 April 2021; www.reuters.com/world/middle-east/police-arrest-dozens-jerusalem-clashes-israeli-nationalists-chant-death-arabs-2021-04-23/.

54 Anonymous, author note, East Jerusalem, 15 June 2021.

55 Daniel Louria, author interview, Jerusalem, 20 May 2021.

56 Palestinian Center for Policy and Survey Research, Public Opinion Poll no. 80, 4 July 2021; https://pcpsr.org/en/node/845.

57 Nidal al-Mughrabi, Jonathan Saul and Rami Ayyub, 'Israel and Hamas both claim victory as ceasefire holds', *Reuters*, 21 May 2021; www.reuters.com/world

/middle-east/gaza-truce-between-israel-hamas-begins-mediated-by-egypt-2021
-05-20/.

58 'Hamas leader Yahya Sinwar threatens: this was just a dress rehearsal', *Israel National News*, 26 May 2021; www.israelnationalnews.com/news/306946. 'Hamas leader Yahya Sinwar, live broadcast', *Al Jazeera Arabic*, Sinwar: we warn the occupation that the decision to end it depends on harming Jerusalem and Al-Aqsa, news politics, 26 May 2021; aljazeera.net.

Chapter 15 'We Are at War'

1 Israel Defense Forces, '"Commander, commander – we are at war!": first documentation of terrorist neutralizations from the Field Intelligence Corps', 16 October 2023; www.idf.il/en/mini-sites/hamas-israel-war-articles-videos -and-more/general-articles/commander-commander-we-are-at-war-first -documentation-of-terrorist-neutralizations-from-the-field-intelligence-corps/ and https://videoidf.azureedge.net/30b2365e-c599-47ec-b9a5-cceeee4da80a.

2 Avi Shlaim, 'Failures in national intelligence estimates: the case of the Yom Kippur War', *World Politics*, 28/3 (1976): 348–80.

3 Mitch Ginsburg, 'When Moshe Dayan delivered the defining speech of Zionism', *Times of Israel*, 28 April 2016; www.timesofisrael.com/when-moshe -dayan-delivered-the-defining-speech-of-zionism/ and www.youtube.com /watch?v=tZBjFqkT_aQ.

4 BBC News, 'Hamas training for raid on Israel revealed', 27 November 2023; www.youtube.com/watch?v=eVfMkKltBrk.

5 Ayala Hasson, 'The Hamas plan to conquer', *KAN News Hebrew*, 28 November 2023; ‫לאתר כאן הרשמי‬ • http://www.kan.org.il/.

6 Stephen Farrell and Samia Nakhoul, 'Hamas leader Sinwar plotted Israel's most deadly day in plain sight', *Reuters*, 6 December 2023; www.reuters.com/world /middle-east/hiding-plain-sight-hamas-leader-sinwar-plotted-destruction-2023 -12-01/.

7 Ronen Bergman and Yoav Zitun, 'The Black Time', *Yedioth Ahronoth*, 12 January 2024; http://www.envirosagainstwar.org/2024/01/22/the-black-time -7-days-time-of-darkness/.

8 U. Segal, 'Mitaḥat lepnai hashetaḥ: targil hahat'aya haYisraeli shekadam lamivtsa be'aza', [Beneath the surface: the Israeli misdirection ruse that preceded the operation in Gaza], Channel 12 News, 15 November 2012 [in Hebrew], www.mako.co.il/news-military/security/Article-812624f87c00b31004 .htm; B. Ravid, 'Oferet Yetsuka: ḥashayut honaah vehata'ya, kakh tatsa laderekh hamivtsa' [Cast Lead: secrecy, deception, and misdirection], *Haaretz*, 27 December 2008 [in Hebrew], www.haaretz.co.il/news/politics/1.1369969.

9 Samia Nakhoul and Jonathan Saul, 'How Hamas duped Israel as it planned devastating attack', *Reuters*, 10 October 2023, www.reuters.com/world/middle -east/how-israel-was-duped-hamas-planned-devastating-assault-2023-10-08/.

10 Jason Burke, 'A deadly cascade: how secret Hamas attack orders were passed

down at last minute', *The Guardian*, 7 November 2023; www.theguardian.com
/world/2023/nov/07/secret-hamas-attack-orders-israel-gaza-7-october.

11 Gabrielle Weiniger, '"We knew what would happen": how Hamas attacked on 7
October', *The Times*, 10 November 2023; www.thetimes.co.uk/article/we-knew
-what-would-happen-how-hamas-attacked-on-october-7-63dd3c8cx.

12 Israel Defense Forces, 'Press briefing by IDF spokesperson Rear Admiral
Daniel Hagari', 1 November 2023; www.idf.il/en/mini-sites/hamas-israel
-war-24/briefings-by-idf-spokesperson-rear-admiral-daniel-hagari/november
-press-briefings/press-briefing-by-idf-spokesperson-rear-admiral-daniel-hagari
-november-1st-10-10.

13 Bergman and Zitun, 'The Black Time'.

14 David Issacharoff, 'At the Nova rave massacre, selfies and reels were an act
of defiance', *Haaretz*, 1 January 2024; www.haaretz.com/israel-news/2024-01
-01/ty-article-magazine/.premium/at-the-nova-rave-massacre-selfies-and-reels
-were-an-act-of-defiance/0000018c-c092-d4e1-ad8f-fcb3d00d0000.

15 Mustafa Abu Ganeyeh and Leonardo Benassatto, '"I was reborn" on Oct. 7 says
survivor of Hamas attack on Israeli festival', *Reuters TV*, 31 October 2023; www
.reuters.com/world/middle-east/i-was-reborn-oct-7-says-survivor-hamas-attack
-israeli-festival-2023-10-31/.

16 Bryan Pietsch, 'An Oct. 7 survivor lives in fear for her husband, a hostage in
Gaza', *Washington Post*, 13 December 2023; www.washingtonpost.com/world
/2023/12/13/israeli-hostage-omri-miran-october-7/.

17 Statement from Mohammed Deif, commander in chief, Qassam Brigades,
broadcast, 7 October 2023; https://alqassam.ps/arabic/videos/index
/2796https://english.almayadeen.net/latestnews/2023/10/7/commander-in
-chief-of-al-qassam-brigades-mohammad-al-deif:-t.

18 'Hamas leader celebrates and prays for ongoing operation from likely location in
Qatar', video clip, 7 October 2023; www.youtube.com/watch?v=UgnkAbKxqvU.

19 'At UN podium, Israel's envoy plays gruesome Hamas attack video', *Reuters*, 26
October 2023; www.reuters.com/world/middle-east/un-podium-israels-envoy
-plays-gruesome-hamas-attack-video-2023-10-26/.

20 Israel Defense Forces video, 'Hamas massacre, collected raw footage, 7 October
2023'.

21 Rachel Johnson, 'Rape, murder and mutilation on an industrial scale – why
I had to watch the film of Hamas's atrocities', *The Standard*, 20 November
2023; www.standard.co.uk/comment/hamas-atrocities-rape-murder-film-rachel
-johnson-b1123922.html.

22 Robert Crampton, 'The 43-minute film of the Hamas massacre is the worst thing
I've seen', *The Times*, 24 November 2023; www.thetimes.co.uk/article/the-43
-minute-film-of-the-hamas-massacre-is-the-worst-thing-ive-seen-hf59h20v7.

23 Owen Jones, 'I watched the Hamas massacre film. Here are my thoughts',
https://twitter.com/OwenJones84/status/1729487180630786219?lang=en.

24 Sir Mick Davis, author notes, London, 23 November 2023.

25 NBC, 'White House clarifies Biden's claim he saw photos of terrorists beheading children in Israel–Hamas war', 11 October 2023; www.nbcnews.com /politics/white-house/biden-deliver-remarks-roundtable-jewish-community -leaders-rcna119865.

26 Glenn Kessler, 'Biden yet again says Hamas beheaded babies. Has new evidence emerged?', *Washington Post*, 22 November 2023; www.washingtonpost .com/politics/2023/11/22/biden-yet-again-says-hamas-beheaded-babies-has-new -evidence-emerged/.

27 *Our Narrative … Operation Al Aqsa Flood*, www.palestinechronicle.com/wp -content/uploads/2024/01/PDF.pdf.

28 Marc Owen Jones, author interview, Doha, 29 January 2024.

29 BBC News, 'False claims of staged deaths surge in Israel–Gaza war', 22 December 2023; www.bbc.co.uk/news/world-middle-east-67760523.

30 The Israel Democracy Institute, 'Most Israelis oppose meeting US demands to shift to new phase of war', 2 January 2024; https://en.idi.org.il/articles/52085.

31 Palestinian Center for Policy and Survey Research (PSR), Public Opinion Poll no. 90, 13 December 2023; https://pcpsr.org/en/node/963.

32 President Joe Biden, Twitter/X, 9 October 2023; https://twitter.com/POTUS /status/1711500536040620345?lang=en-GB.

33 Emanuel Fabian, 'Defense minister announces "complete siege" of Gaza: no power, food or fuel', *Times of Israel*, 9 October 2023; www.timesofisrael.com /liveblog_entry/defense-minister-announces-complete-siege-of-gaza-no-power -food-or-fuel.

34 Yoav Gallant, Israeli defense minister, 9 October 2023, order of 26 January 2024; https://www.icj-cij.org/node/203447.

35 International Crisis Group, 'Hold your fire!' podcast, Episode 1: 'No going back? Hamas's atrocities and another catastrophe in Gaza', 13 October 2023; www.crisisgroup.org/global/hold-your-fire.

36 UNICEF, 'Child casualties in Gaza "a growing stain on our collective conscience"', 24 October 2023; www.unicef.org/press-releases/child-casualties -gaza-growing-stain-our-collective-conscience.

37 UN OCHA, 'Hostilities in the Gaza Strip and Israel: flash update #107', 1 February 2024; https://reliefweb.int/report/occupied-palestinian-territory /hostilities-gaza-strip-and-israel-flash-update-107.

38 Ashraf Masri, author interview by WhatsApp, Gaza, 29 October 2023.

39 Haya Abu Nasser, 'Surviving beneath Gaza's tempest skies', 28 January 2024; https://wearenotnumbers.org/surviving-beneath-gazas-tempest-skies/.

40 UN OCHA, 'Hostilities in the Gaza Strip and Israel: flash update #101', 24 January 2024; www.unocha.org/publications/report/occupied-palestinian -territory/hostilities-gaza-strip-and-israel-flash-update-101-enarhe.

41 Lynn Hastings, 'Ongoing crisis in Gaza – SecCo open debate – press release', 24 October 2023; www.un.org/unispal/document/ongoing-crisis-in-gaza-secco -open-debate-press-release.

42 Israel Defense Forces, 'Press briefing by IDF spokesperson Rear Admiral Daniel Hagari', 1 November 2023.

43 Stephen Farrell, Aditi Bhandari, Prasanta Kumar Dutta and Clare Trainor, 'No place of refuge: Israeli strikes hit Gaza refugee camps', *Reuters*, 3 November 2023; www.reuters.com/graphics/ISRAEL-PALESTINIANS/GAZA-JABALIA /byprrdygjpe/.

44 UN Human Rights, 1 November 2023; https://twitter.com/UNHumanRights /status/1719783887633527153.

45 Yoav Gallant, 'Gallant vows Israel will kill Sinwar, says if Gazans reach him first "it will shorten the war"', *Times of Israel*, 4 November 2023; www.timesofisrael .com/liveblog_entry/gallant-vows-israel-will-kill-sinwar-says-if-gazans-reach -him-first-it-will-shorten-the-war/.

46 'Journalist casualties in the Israel–Gaza war', 31 January 2024; https://cpj.org /2024/01/journalist-casualties-in-the-israel-gaza-conflict/.

47 'President of the ICRC arrives in Gaza, calls for the protection of civilians', 4 December 2023; www.icrc.org/en/document/israel-and-occupied-territories -president-icrc-arrives-gaza.

48 Avi Dichter, '"We're rolling out Nakba 2023," Israeli minister says on northern Gaza Strip evacuation', *Haaretz*, 12 November 2023; www.haaretz.com/israel -news/2023-11-12/ty-article/israeli-security-cabinet-member-calls-north-gaza -evacuation-nakba-2023/0000018b-c2be-dea2-a9bf-d2be7b670000.

49 'Israeli minister repeats call for Palestinians to leave Gaza', *Reuters*, 31 December 2023; www.reuters.com/world/middle-east/israeli-minister-repeats -call-palestinians-leave-gaza-2023-12-31/.

50 Carmiel Arbit, 'The kidnapping of a peace activist by Hamas reveals the cruel irony of the situation Israel faces', 25 October 2023; www.atlanticcouncil.org /blogs/menasource/peace-activist-vivian-silver-hamas-hostage-israel/.

51 'Factbox: Israeli prisoner swaps', *Reuters*, 19 December 2011; www.reuters.com /article/idUSTRE7BH0TO/.

52 Vedant Patel, principal deputy spokesperson for the US Department of State, 25 January 2024; www.state.gov/briefings/department-press-briefing-january-25 -2024/.

53 Akbar Shahid Ahmed, 'Stunning State Department memo warns diplomats: no Gaza "de-escalation" talk', *Huffington Post*, 13 October 2023; www.huffpost.com/entry/state-department-internal-emails-gaza-israel _n_65296395e4b0a304ff6ff95d.

54 Author interview, anonymous, Doha, 6 November 2023.

55 Simon Hattenstone, 'The mothers whose children are held hostage by Hamas: "I heard him crying, begging them not to take him"', *The Guardian*, 9 November 2023; www.theguardian.com/world/2023/nov/09/mothers -children-held-hostage-hamas-all-we-want-is-them-home.

56 Anonymous Gaza resident, interview with author, Khan Younis, 25 November 2023.

57 Saleh Arouri, Al Jazeera Arabic, 7 October 2023.

58 Ali Halawi, 'Hamas unveils groundbreaking armor piercing EFP devices in Jenin', *Al Madayeen English*, 15 July 2023; https://english.almayadeen.net/news /politics/hamas-unveils-groundbreaking-armor-piercing-efp-devices-in-j.

59 Qassam Brigades Telegram channel, 1 December 2023.

60 President Isaac Herzog, 12 October 2023: International Court of Justice, Order of 26 January 2024; www.icj-cij.org/node/203447.

61 International Court of Justice, Order of 26 January 2024, Application of the Convention on the Prevention and Punishment of the Crime of Genocide in the Gaza Strip (South Africa v. Israel), articles 79 and 80; www.icj-cij.org/sites /default/files/case-related/192/192-20240126-ord-01-00-en.pdf.

62 BBC News, 'Gazans give their thoughts on the ICJ ruling', 26 January 2024; www.bbc.co.uk/news/live/world-68097640.

63 'World reacts to ICJ interim ruling in Gaza genocide case against Israel', *Al Jazeera*, 26 January 2024; www.aljazeera.com/news/2024/1/26/world-reacts-to -icj-ruling-on-south-africas-genocide-case-against-israel.

64 Prime Minister of Israel, https://twitter.com/IsraeliPM/status /1750872239954686271.

65 Briefing by IDF spokesperson, Rear Admiral Daniel Hagari, 29 January 2024; www.idf.il/en/mini-sites/hamas-israel-war-24/briefings-by-idf-spokesperson -rear-admiral-daniel-hagari/january-24-press-briefings/press-briefing-by-idf -spokesperson-rear-admiral-daniel-hagari-january-29th-2024/.

66 Channel N12, 23 23 מוחמד דף מתפקד טוב והולך על רגליו: "לא הופתענו" 23 December 2023; www.mako.co.il/news-military/6361323ddea5a810/Article -ef61c387de58c81026.htm.

67 Jewish News Syndicate, 'IDF forces progress towards Rafah as they continue to pursue Sinwar', 5 February 2024; www.jns.org/idf-forces-progress-towards -rafah-as-they-continue-to-pursue-sinwar/.

68 Noa Shpigal, 'What if it was your son?', *Haaretz*, 25 December 2023; www .haaretz.com/israel-news/2023-12-25/ty-article/.premium/hostages-families -disrupt-netanyahu-speech-calling-for-military-pressure-to-free-captives /0000018c-a1a9-df1f-a7bf-b7ed8cfa0000.

69 Abu Obaida, Qassam Brigades Telegram Channel, 16 December 2023.

70 Israel Defense Forces, 'Chief of the general staff's statement regarding the incident in which 3 hostages were mistakenly identified as a threat', 16 December 2023; www.idf.il/en/mini-sites/idf-press-releases-regarding-the-hamas-israel-war /december-pr/chief-of-the-general-staff-s-statement-regarding-the-incident-in -which-3-hostages-were-mistakenly-identified-as-a-threat/.

71 Josef Federman, Najib Jobain and Samy Magdy, '21 Israeli troops are killed in the deadliest attack on the military since the Gaza offensive began', *Associated Press*, 24 January 2024, https://apnews.com/article/israel-hamas-war-news-01 -23-2024-6f6e893b6dfa05ddf5a81ecb67b72d05; Jon Gambrell, 'Analysis shows destruction and possible buffer zone along Gaza Strip's border with Israel',

Associated Press, 2 February 2024, https://apnews.com/article/israel-palestinians
-war-gaza-strip-buffer-zone-72a782ddd532a4331b660a735e36acb0.

72 'Netanyahu under pressure over Israel troop losses, hostages', *Agence France-Presse*, 27 January 2024; www.voanews.com/a/netanyahu-under-pressure-over
-israel-troop-losses-hostages/7460331.html.

73 Dan Williams, 'Israel pressures Qatar over Gaza hostages ahead of spy chiefs'
meeting', *Reuters*, 27 January 2024; www.reuters.com/world/middle-east/israel
-qatar-hosts-funds-hamas-should-pressure-it-free-hostages-2024-01-27.

74 Anonymous Ministry of Foreign Affairs official, author interview, Doha, 28
January 2024.

75 'Israeli forces have killed 10,000 Gaza fighters, minister says', *Reuters*, 1
February 2024; www.reuters.com/world/middle-east/israeli-forces-have-killed
-10000-gaza-fighters-minister-says-2024-02-01.

76 Jonny Hallam, 'Hamas political leader calls "cowardly assassination" of Saleh
Al-Arouri a "terrorist act"', CNN, 2 January 2024; https://edition.cnn.com
/middleeast/live-news/israel-hamas-war-gaza-news-01-02-24/h_62646384e4b9
3f83d31ebe0a55b0f2a4.

Conclusion

1 Lahav Harkov, 'Netanyahu: money to Hamas part of strategy to keep
Palestinians divided', *Jerusalem Post*, 12 March 2019; www.jpost.com/arab-israeli
-conflict/netanyahu-money-to-hamas-part-of-strategy-to-keep-palestinians
-divided-583082.

2 Alice Speri, 'Before they vowed to annihilate Hamas, Israeli officials considered
it an asset', *The Intercept*, 14 October 2023; https://theintercept.com/2023/10/14
/hamas-israel-palestinian-authority/.

3 Alon Pinkas, 'October 7, 2023: a date that will live in infamy in Israel', *Haaretz*,
7 October 2023; www.haaretz.com/israel-news/2023-10-07/ty-article/.premium
/october-7-2023-a-date-that-will-live-in-infamy-in-israel/0000018b-0bbf-dc5d
-a39f-9fff47680000.

4 'Mr Security: Hamas war tarnishes Netanyahu's image as Israel's defender',
Financial Times, 15 October 2023; www.ft.com/content/2f826acb-c1d2-4144
-a9cc-73d008a727a3.

5 Paul Ronzheimer and Claudia Chiappa, 'Netanyahu: don't accuse me of
boosting Hamas with Qatari money', *Politico*, 28 November 2023; www.politico
.eu/article/benjamin-netanyahu-hamas-qatar-money-war-israel-gaza-palestine.

6 Binyamin Netanyahu, press conference, Tel Aviv, 16 December 2023; www
.timesofisrael.com/liveblog_entry/pm-im-proud-i-blocked-a-palestinian-state
-looking-at-gaza-everyone-sees-what-would-have-happened/.

7 Nahum Barnea, 'The day after the blow', *Yedioth Ahronoth*, 24 January 2024 [in
Hebrew].

8 Daniella Weiss, 'The Israelis who campaign to occupy Gaza', *DW News*, 22
January 2024; www.youtube.com/watch?v=pfeLzXqL-nI.

9   Christopher Wray, 'Director Wray's opening statement to the Senate Committee on Homeland Security and Governmental Affairs', 31 October 2023; www.fbi.gov/news/speeches/director-wrays-opening-statement-to-the-senate-committee-on-homeland-security-and-governmental-affairs#:~.

10 VOA, 'Antisemitism, Islamophobia surge in 2023, watchdogs say', 29 December 2023; www.voanews.com/a/antisemitism-islamophobia-surge-in-2023-watchdogs-say/7407451.html.

11 'Stephen Fry addresses the nation: Channel 4 alternative Christmas Message', 25 December 2023; www.youtube.com/watch?v=G7uUGJhiehM.

12 Institute of Race Relations 'Anti-Palestinianism, suspect communities, and the racist backlash – time to take a stand', 27 October 2023; https://irr.org.uk/article/anti-palestinianism-suspect-communities-and-the-racist-backlash-time-to-take-a-stand/.

13 Usman, author interview, London, 25 November 2023.

14 Hannah Weisfeld, Yachad UK, 'The Israel–Hamas war: what escalation looks like', Chatham House, 23 October 2023; www.chathamhouse.org/events/all/research-event/israel-hamas-war-what-escalation-looks.

15 Tarik Hammad, 'Hamas in the aftermath of the war in Gaza', Second Annual Palestine Forum, Doha, Qatar, 12 February 2024.

16 Mouin Rabbani, author interview, Doha, Qatar, 11 February 2024.

17 Leila Seurat, 'Hamas in the aftermath of the war in Gaza', Second Annual Palestine Forum, Doha, Qatar, 12 February 2024.

18 Anonymous former Fatah security chief, author interview, Doha, Qatar, 13 February 2024.

19 Hammad, 'Hamas in the aftermath of the war in Gaza'.

20 Professor Ali Jarbawi, author interview, 5 February 2024.

21 Ibid.

22 International Court of Justice, Press Release, 20 January 2023; www.icj-cij.org/sites/default/files/case-related/186/186-20230120-PRE-01-00-EN.pdf.

23 'Exclusive: Hamas attack, Israeli response fall under ICC jurisdiction, prosecutor says', *Reuters*, 13 October 2023; www.reuters.com/world/middle-east/hamas-attack-would-fall-under-jurisdiction-war-crimes-court-prosecutor-2023-10-12/.

Index

Page numbers in *italics* refers to an illustration

Haniyeh, Ismail 13–14, *39*, 74, 135, 142,
144, *178*, 180, 182, 185, 189, 226,
260, 269
and attack on Israel (2023) 242
background 165, 230
becomes the face of Hamas 164–5,
175
and Great March of Return 231
and Morsi's election to power in
Egypt 212
Harari, Brigadier General Shalom 55,
184
Hastings, Lyn 249
Hawatmeh, Nayef 37
Hebron massacre (1994) 69–70, 71, 100
Herzog, Isaac 95, 128, 256–7
Hezbollah ix, 13, 81, 142, 251
attack on Israel (2006) 189
blocked funds 144
war with Israel (2006) 106
hijab *151*
hijab campaign 149–50
hostage taking 251
and Gaza war (2023–4) 251–4, 259
Houthis 16, 264, 265
attacks on Red Sea shipping 263
Hussein, King of Jordan 62, 75
Hussein–McMahon correspondence 24
Al-Husseini, Hajj Amin 26, 28, 31

Ibrach, Ibrahim 11, 220
Ibrahimi Mosque massacre (Hebron)
(1994) 69–70, 71, 100
ICC (International Criminal Court)
232, 270, 271
Rome Statute 220
war crime investigations 220–1
Idris, Wafa 152
Ihbeishi, Muhammad Shaker 116
Institute of Race Relations 266–7
International Court of Justice (ICJ)
256–8, 270
International Criminal Court *see* ICC

International Rescue Committee 4
internet cafés, attacks on 140
internet filters
imposing of by Hamas in Gaza 140
IRA (Irish Republican Army) 13, 163
Iran ix, 81
and 'Axis of Resistance' narrative
264–5
and Gaza war (2023) 264–5
relations with Israel 81
support of Hamas xi, 81, 106–7, 145,
194, 196, 202
Iraq 81
donating money to families of
suicide bombers 123
sectarian conflict between Shi'a and
Sunni Muslims 203
Irgun 32
ISIS (Islamic State) 16, 213, 266
Islamic fundamentalism
spread of across region 41
Islamic Jihad 144, 164
Islamic Revolutionary Guard
Corps-Qods Force (IRGC-QF)
145
Islamic University of Gaza (IUG) 44–5,
55, 148
Islamophobia 266
Israel
Arab population 116
assassination of Hamas leaders 101–3,
117, 126, 164, 214, 314
attempt to destroy tunnels in Gaza
112, 113
blockade of and border closures with
Gaza xii, 6, 143, 160, 185, 186, 189,
201–2, 203–4, 211, 226
building new settlements in the West
Bank and East Jerusalem 221–2
collapse of peace talks with PA
(2014) 223
crackdown on Hamas by Rabin 71–2
creation of 4, 32

growth of 45–6
growth of influence in the Islamic
University of Gaza 44–5
relations with Israel 40–1, 42–3, 45,
52
mukhabarat (Jordanian secret service)
36
Mushtaha, Rawhi 96, 145, 216, 218
Musleh, Mahmoud 50
Muslim Brotherhood ix, xii, 9, 33, 146,
194
crackdown on by Nasser 35
elected to power in Egypt 211–12
ending of power in Egypt (2013) 215
erosion of support for 35
Hamas set up as a Palestinian wing
of 9–10
laying roots and establishing military
cells in Gaza 32, 34
puts jihad on hold 38
rise of 55
in the West Bank 36
Muslim Young Men's Association
(MYMA) 25, 29

Nablus 90, 163
Nachman, Ron 223
Nahal Oz kibbutz 236
Nahala movement 263
Nahariya (Israel)
suicide bombing (2001) 115–16
Naim, Huda 160
Najjar, Fatima 154–5
al-Najjar, Issa 39
Nakbah (1948) 4, 33, 230, 258
Nasrallah, Sheikh Hassan 189
Nasser, General Abdel 34–5, 36, 37
Netanya (Israel)
killing of Jews at Passover dinner by
Hamas 12, 88, 120
Netanyahu, Binyamin 15, 73, 132, 213,
235
allegations of early toleration of

Hamas in order to weaken the PA
261–2
and building of Jewish settlements in
the West Bank 221–2
corruption charges against 233
elected prime minister (1996) 74
elected prime minister (2009) 209
and Gaza war (2023–4) 3, 258,
259–60, 262–3
opposition to two-state solution
18–19, 262
ousted as prime minister (2011) 229
and release of Schalit in prisoner
exchange 219
Neve Dekalim (training ground)
(Gaza) 193
Nidal, Umm *see* Farahat, Maryam
9/11 (2001) 80, 115, 125
Nofal, Abu Bakr 19, 106, 189
North Korea 81
Nova music festival attack (2023)
241–2, 244
Nukhba Force 110–11, 238

Obama, Barack 215, 222, 228
Odeh, Abdel Basset 120–1
Office of Foreign Assets Control
(OFAC) (US Treasury) 136, 137
Olmert, Ehud 181, 204, 209
Operation Al Aqsa Flood (2023) 3, 5
Operation Cast Lead (2009) 166,
204–8, *206*, 225
Operation Defensive Shield (2002)
89–90
Operation Protective Edge (2014) 224
Operation Swords of Iron *see* Gaza war
(2023–4)
Oslo Accords (1993) 11, 62–6, 67, 71,
74, 80, 118, 162, 268
concerns and criticism of 63
growing disillusionment with 73
Hamas's opposition to 63–6, 75
Ottoman Empire 23